Cases & Readings in Strategic Cost Management

for use with

Cost Management
A Strategic Emphasis

Edward J. Blocher
University of North Carolina

Kung H. Chen
University of Nebraska

Thomas W. Lin
University of Southern California

Boston   Burr Ridge, IL   Dubuque, IA   Madison, WI   New York   San Francisco   St. Louis
Bangkok   Bogotá   Caracas   Lisbon   London   Madrid
Mexico City   Milan   New Delhi   Seoul   Singapore   Sydney   Taipei   Toronto

Irwin/McGraw-Hill

A Division of The McGraw·Hill Companies

234567890 CUS/CUS 932109

ISBN 0-07-366252-6

http://www.mhhe.com

Preface

To extend the teaching materials of *Cost Management: A Strategic Emphasis*, this book provides additional cases and articles for each chapter. The cases and articles are an important part of the text and have the same teaching objectives. The problem material in the text includes short cases and exercises, while this book provides longer cases and articles to facilitate more extensive discussion and analysis.

We feel that longer cases serve a very important role, and should be an integral part of each chapter of the text. We know of many faculty who use longer cases from a variety of sources to supplement the text they are using. We have provided these materials in this book for easier access, greater convenience, and lower overall cost to the instructor and student.

Using longer cases has two important benefits. First, the use of a longer case requires the student to develop analytical skills by organizing the unstructured information in the case, devising appropriate analyses, and drawing appropriate conclusions. Second, the longer cases permit a more thorough strategic analysis of a given firm than would be possible with a short case. With a richer amount of information about the case firm and its environment, the student can more effectively apply the concepts of strategy and competitive advantage explained in chapter 2: Strategic Analysis and Strategic Cost Management.

Each of the cases can be used as an exercise in competitive analysis to set the stage for the decision problem in the case, whatever that might be. A firm facing a lease-or-buy decision will want to asses the strategic, competitive situation of the firm before making the decision. Similarly, a firm considering the outsourcing of a department or activity will want to begin the analysis with an assessment of the strategic issues facing the firm, and then to make the outsourcing decision with these issues in mind. In this way, the longer cases can be used to effectively put each decision problem in a strategic context. Rather than to make a cost calculation and then "consider the qualitative factors," which can be done with short cases, the longer case more readily allows an approach in which the strategic issues are considered first and are an integral part of the solution of the case.

One or two articles are included for each chapter to provide an opportunity for more in-depth coverage. We have included discussion questions for each article. Some of the articles are examples of how actual firms have implemented the cost management methods explained in the chapter. These stories show some of the implementation issues that arise in practical situations. Other articles report the results of surveys, which provides a perspective for how the cost management methods are used in practice. Others have a technical focus, and provide an opportunity to look more closely at the methods explained in the chapter and on the effects of using the methods.

We hope you will find these cases and readings helpful. We welcome feedback from students and instructors.

Edward J. Blocher
Kung H. Chen
Thomas W. Lin

Acknowledgments

"The Practice Analysis of Management Accounting," "Look Out, Management Accountants," "How Nonfinancial Performance Measures are Used," "The Changing World of Management Accounting and Financial Management," "How ABC Changed the Post Office," "Target Costing at ITT Automotive," "How Xerox Solves Quality Problems," "How to Find the Right Bases and Rates," "Measuring Learning Costs," "How Challenging Should Profit Budget Targets Be?" "Accounting for Magic," "Perceptions of Earnings Quality: What Managers Need to Know," "Does ROI Apply to Robotic Factories?" "Setting the Right Transfer Price," and "Using Shareholder Value to Evaluate Strategic Choices" reprinted with permission from Management Accounting. Copyright by Institute of Management Accountants, Montvale, N.J.

Case 7-2 reprinted with permission from Volume 1 of Cases from Management Accounting Practice, from the IMA/AAA Management Accounting Symposium Series.

Cases 2-1 and 19-1 reprinted with permission from Volume 2 of Cases from Management Accounting Practice, from the IMA/AAA Management Accounting Symposium Series.

Case 18-2 reprinted with permission from Volume 4 of Cases from Management Accounting Practice, from the IMA/AAA Management Accounting Symposium Series.

Case 10-4 reprinted with permission from Volume 6 of Cases from Management Accounting Practice, from the IMA/AAA Management Accounting Symposium Series.

Case 14-1 reprinted with permission from Volume 7 of Cases from Management Accounting Practice, from the IMA/AAA Management Accounting Symposium Series.

Case 5-1 reprinted with permission from Volume 8 of Cases from Management Accounting Practice, from the IMA/AAA Management Accounting Symposium Series.

Cases 4-1, 20-1, and 20-3 reprinted with permission from Cases from Management Accounting Practice, from the IMA/AAA Management Accounting Symposium Series.

Case 14-2 reprinted with permission from AICPA Development Program Copyright © 1995 by the American Institute of Certified Public Accountants, Inc.

Table of Contents

Chapter 1
Cost Management: An Overview

Cases

Readings

Robin Cooper: **Look Out, Management Accountants**

Robin Cooper's article is representative of a number of articles and editorials which have made the point that the role of management accounting and management accountants have changed. The management accountant must become an effective part of the management team, with expertise beyond what has been considered the traditional role of the accountant. This includes nonfinancial information in operations, marketing, finance, and human resources. All of these functions are critical to the firm's success, but it is the effective integration of these functions that makes the firm succeed. The accountant is no longer a functional expert, but a business partner, as this article explains. A few examples, primarily from Japanese industry, are used -- target costing and Kaizen costing. These management techniques are introduced in chapter one, and will be covered more extensively in later chapters.

Discussion Questions:
1. Give some examples of how the role of the management accountant has changed in recent years.
2. Why is target costing a good example of the new role of the management accountant?
3. What does Cooper say about the right size of business units within firm?
4. Does the role of the management accountant of the future seem to be very exciting, demanding, or just "dead end?"

Gary Siegel and C.S. "Bud" Kulesza: **The Practice Analysis of Management Accounting**

This article reports the findings of an extensive survey of thousands of management accountants to elicit their perceptions of the critical factors in their work. Consistent with Cooper's ideas in the previous article, the survey shows a profession in transition. Strategic planning is listed as the most important work activity for the future. Also, performance evaluation, profitability assessment, and process improvement are noted as critical future activities.

Discussion Questions:
1. What type of education and training is necessary for the management accountant of the future?

2. Access the Institute of Management Accountants' Home Page (http://www.rutgers.edu/accounting/raw/ima), and explain what you found.
3. Why are management accountants more likely to refer to themselves as finance professionals than accountants?

Cost Management: An Overview

1-1. Critical Success Factors

Kirsten Malon has found a way to profitably exploit her computer know-how. She has started a firm that offers consulting services for computer and software repair and analysis. Most of her customers have purchased computers or software systems with little vendor support and need help in installing and using the systems effectively. Kirsten has expanded her business recently to include 25 technicians besides herself, and her client base has grown to over 1,900. Many of these clients are on a retainer arrangement (a fixed fee per month which guarantees access to a certain number of hours of technician time) to stabilize her cash flow. With the success of the business, Kirsten is now thinking about beginning a related business which would publish books and newsletters on computer and software issues.

REQUIRED:

What are the critical success factors likely to be for Kirsten's business, now and into the future? What cost management information is she likely to need: management planning and decision making, management and operational control, or product and service costing, and why?

1-2. Contemporary Management Techniques

DeLight Inc., is a large manufacturer of lighting fixtures for both wholesalers and electrical contractors. An important aspect of the business with electrical contractors is DeLight's ability to develop product leadership through innovation, quality, and service. In contrast, in the wholesale business, DeLight competes primarily on the basis of lowest price. De-Light has prospered in the recent five years because of its careful attention to developing and maintaining a sustainable competitive advantage in each of its markets.

REQUIRED:

Which of the ten types of contemporary management techniques does DeLight probably use? Explain your answer.

1-3. Ethics, Pricing

AeroSpace Inc is a manufacturer of airplane parts and engines for a variety of military as well as civilian aircraft. Though there are many commercial customers for most of the company's products, the U.S. government is the only buyer of the firm's rocket engines. Because AeroSpace is the sole provider of the engines, the government buys the engines at a price equal to cost plus a percent markup.

The cost system in place at AeroSpace is under review by top management, with the objective of developing a system which will provide more accurate and more timely cost management information.

At the current phase of the study of the cost system, it is now apparent that the new system, while more accurate and timely, will result in lower costs being assigned to the rocket engines and higher costs being assigned to the firm's other products. Apparently, the current (less accurate) cost system has over-costed the engines and under-costed the other products. On hearing of this, top management has decided to scrap the plans for the new cost system, because the rocket engine business with the government is a significant part of AeroSpace's business, and the reduced cost will reduce the price and thus the profits for this part of AeroSpace's business.

REQUIRED:

As a staff cost analyst on the cost review project, how do you see your responsibility when you hear of the decision of top management to cancel the plans for the new cost system?

1-4. Selected Ethics Cases

After his first two years at Bronson Beverages (BB), a publicly held wholesaler of beers and wines, Jim Best has advanced to a senior cost analyst position with a very good salary.

REQUIRED:

For each of the following situations Jim will face in the coming year, indicate how you see his responsibility, and how he should respond.

1. Jim learns that a significant portion of the firm's beer inventory has passed its shelf life and by local ordinance and company policy, should be destroyed. Because of concern about the effect on profits and his bonus, the chief operating officer decides that the beer should be sold anyway.

2. As part of his regular duties, Jim reviews BB's financial statements for inconsistencies and errors. While reviewing the recent report, Jim notices that non-trade accounts receivable (note: non-trade receivables arise from non-operating events, such as a loan to an employee, customer, etc; trade receivables arise from sales on credit) have increased sharply over the prior year. Upon inquiry, Jim finds out that the firm is lending money to one of its customers so that it can make purchases from BB. Jim knows that in his state, beer and wine purchases must be paid for in cash, by state law. Jim wonders if the treatment of the loan as a non-trade receivable is OK, or if it should be classified as a trade receivable?

3. Jim learns that BB has just been granted the franchise to sell a popular new line of custom-brewed beers. The franchise will improve BB's sales and profits substantially, and should mean a significant boost to BB's share price. Jim knows that, until the news of the franchise is made public, he is restricted by the SEC from using this insider information to trade in BB's shares and make unfair profits as a result. That evening, Jim and his wife have dinner with some friends, and one of them says she has heard there are some good things going on at BB, and asks Jim to comment. What should Jim say?

4. Jim is analyzing the sales and cost of sales in specialty wines when he discovers that one of the firm's customers has greatly increased purchases in this, the last month of the firm's fiscal year. Jim goes to talk to the salesperson for this customer to offer his congratulations. The salesperson says that he has simply shipped in advance the customer's order for the following month, so that it would appear on the current year's financial report. This tactic would help the salesperson meet his sales target and would also improve BB's sales and profits for the current year. The salesperson says there is a small chance that the customer will reject the shipment and send it back, but then says, "We will worry about that if it happens."

5. Working late one night, Jim notices that one of the top marketing executives has come into the office and is removing a box full of office supplies. He says in a joking manner to Jim as he leaves, "BB won't miss this stuff, and I really need it for my other business."

Look Out, Management Accountants

As companies move to cost management, they will need more management accounting information but fewer management **accountants**. And the remaining management accountants will play a supporting role, not a leadership role.

By Robin Cooper

With the emergence of the lean enterprise and increased global competition, companies must learn to be more proactive in the way they manage costs. For many, survival is dependent upon their abilities to develop sophisticated cost management systems that create intense pressure to reduce costs across the entire value chain. This increased importance of cost management is a central theme of *When Lean Enterprises Collide:*

> Firms that adopt a confrontation strategy (an intense form of competition) must become experts at developing low cost, high quality products that have the functionality customers demand....A firm that fails to reduce costs as rapidly as its competitors will find its profit margins squeezed and its existence threatened....Cost management, like quality, has to become a discipline practiced by virtually every person in the firm. Therefore, overlapping systems that create intense downward pressures on all elements of costs are required.[1]

As cost management becomes more critical to a company's survival, two trends emerge. First, new forms of cost management are required, and, second, more individuals in the firm become actively involved in the cost management process. Management accountants, observing the growth in importance of cost management, might feel tempted to assume that a similar increase in the importance of their role will follow. Recent articles that call for them to become more involved in the management process support this assumption. For example, Robert Kaplan argues that management accountants should:

- Become part of their organization's value-added team;
- Participate in the formulation and implementation of strategy;
- Translate strategic intent and capabilities into operational and managerial measures; and
- Move away from being scorekeepers of the past to become the designers of the organization's critical management information systems.[2]

Unfortunately, getting more involved in the management process is only part of the story. The rest deals with decentralizing the management accounting process and empowering the workforce. *The result is fewer management accountants in the company but a much wider use of management accounting information.* To understand why these changes are occurring, we must look at the evidence from practice.

Evidence from five cost management techniques used in highly competitive environments will show how the growing importance of cost management is changing the practice of management accounting. The evidence for the first two techniques—activity-based costing and treatment protocols—is drawn from Western practice. The evidence for the next three techniques—target costing kaizen costing, and harnessing the entrepreneurial spirit—is drawn from Japanese practice.

Activity-based costing illustrates that when a management accounting technique is used for cost management, the role of the management accountant is not as central as might be expected. Treatment protocols illustrate cost management practices in a non-manufacturing setting where, historically, cost management has not played a critical role. The partnership role of the management accountant, not the leadership role, will be described.

ACTIVITY-BASED COST MANAGEMENT (ABCM)

The development of practical ABCM systems in the late 1980s highlights the subtle but profound interplay between management accounting and cost management in intensely competitive environments. ABCM derives its power from the way its outputs can be used for cost management:

> ABC information, but itself, does not invoke actions and decisions leading to improved profits and operating performance. Management must institute a conscious process of organizational change and implementation if the organization is to receive benefits from the improved insights resulting from an ABC analysis.[3]

For ABCM systems to be effective, everyone in the company—from top management to operating personnel—must view them as cost management tools rather than as accounting tools. To achieve this objective, the accounting or finance department must relinquish ownership of these systems to the users. If accounting or finance fails to understand this key point, then ABCM is unlikely to succeed.

> (T)he finance sponsor is following what could be called a field of dreams strategy: "If I build it [the ABC model], the line managers will come [and take action]." Unfortunately, the field of dreams strategy usually proceeds with the project team being asked to refine the model, re-estimate it on new data (e.g., this year's actuals, next year's budget), and develop new models for different organizational sites. The danger of this pattern is that after several years of refinement, re-estimation, and extension, but no managerial decisions or actions, the ABC project becomes viewed as a concern of the finance group only. It is not thought of as an initiative that has to be addressed, accepted, internalized and acted upon by operating managers.[4]

One significant outcome of the decision to give up ownership of the cost system is that accountants must have only limited involvement in its design. While traditional systems are the property of accounting and are used to support the financial accounting process, successful ABCM systems are owned by the functions and are designed to support the needs of cost management, not financial accounting. The result is a reduction in the role of accounting in the management of costs:

> One of the primary objectives the plant controller had in implementing the new system was for it to be viewed as a management system instead of a financial system. The controller wanted production and engineering to "take ownership" of the system...To achieve this objective, the implementation team included members from several disciplines other than finance. This was done to foster commitment to the new system throughout the company.[5]

The importance of cost management to the success of ABCM has confused many observers. Some management accountants—in their roles as controllers and chief financial officers—argue that ABCM simply represents new accounting systems. Unfortunately, forcing ABCM systems to comply with financial accounting guidelines risks comprising the ability of those systems to support cost management. For example, a manager at Hewlett-Packard's Queensferry Telecommunications Division (QTD) said, "We implemented cost driver accounting primarily to influence the manufacturability of our products. We wanted our engineers to understand the economic consequences of their design choices. We wanted to ensure that our products were both competitively priced and profitable."[6]

But when production volume dropped and volume variances became significant, senior management adjusted the overhead driver rates for financial accounting purposes:

> When the production volumes dropped in the first half of the year, we began to encounter volume variances. These variances were not significant in the first quarter, but by the second quarter they were very high...To avoid reporting large variances in the second half of fiscal 1990, QTD management decided to compute the cost driver rates for the second half of fiscal 1990 using the lower production volumes.[7]

The outcome of this decision is that the cost driver rates no longer reflect the underlying economics of the activities. Product designers using the new rates are unlikely to design the most cost effective products. For example, they will shy away from designing products consuming activities that currently have high levels of over-capacity, which is exactly the opposite to what is required. Consequently, most companies that implement ABCM systems run them in parallel to their financial accounting systems. Parallel systems remove the risk of compromising the cost management capabilities of ABCM to accommodate financial accounting rules and regulations. This isolation, however, reduces the accounting knowledge required to design and implement such systems. The result is a reduction in the role of the management accountant. The users now take a more predominant role in the design of the system.

TREATMENT PROTOCOLS

The U.S. healthcare industry provides an important window into the future of management accounting because it is an environment in which cost management historically has not been practiced. Such environments allow the relationship between management accountants and functional specialists to reflect the demands of modern cost management and not the demands of yesterday.

Most management accountants practicing in the healthcare industry accept that they lack the clinical knowledge necessary to manage costs effectively without the help of functional specialists. The functional specialists accept that they lack the knowledge and skill to develop cost systems. Consequently, the relationship between the groups can evolve based upon mutual respect, with the two working together to create effective new cost management systems. Given this mutual respect, management accountants can help create a culture of change with regard to cost management. For example, at Brookwood Medical Center (BMC) cost accountants played a vital role in the restructuring process. They provided cost analysis data and evaluated the cost impact of proposed changes.

Treatment protocols, a cost management technique used in healthcare to reduce costs, show how management accountants and functional specialists can operate together to create effective cost management programs. Treatment protocols represent standardized ways to treat a particular medical condition, such as appendectomies, total hip replacements, or chemotherapy for leukemia. The objective behind treatment protocols is to give every physician a concrete idea of the minimum cost procedure the average patient should receive to obtain effective treatment. The actual treatment received depends on the severity of the condition, physical condition of the patient, and any other relevant factors that the physician must take into account..

Treatment protocols reduce costs by cutting back on unnecessary tests and inefficient delivery of treatment. For example:

Dissemination of data collected by the case management process resulted in significant reductions in length of stay and costs at BMC. Physicians were given resource utilization data (adjusted for severity) that compared their resource usage (variable cost per case) with that of other BMC physicians. Therefore physicians could share information about treatment protocols that resulted in favorable clinical outcomes and lower resource utilization.[8]

Cost information plays a critical role in the development of treatment protocols and similar techniques. But such information usually is not collected, so management accountants must develop the systems that create the cost information required to support cost management. For instance:

BMC installed a computerized information system known as Transition 1 (TSI) to assist with standard costing, financial modeling, forecasting, and product line management (such as open heart surgery or neonatal intensive care). TSI allowed the creation of a database with cost and demographic information that could be sorted by demographic elements. For example, information from the database was used in the Outcomes Management (OM) program to identify costs associated with each physician and DRG (diagnostic related group).[9]

Detailed information allowed BMC to obtain more accurate measurements of the costs to provide patient care and to monitor and improve the quality of that care. Example: The patient number, length of stay, total charges, direct costs, and indirect costs for all appendectomy patients treated during a specific time period were summarized by the TSI system.

Management accountants are responsible for developing these cost systems but not the treatment protocols, which usually are established by a committee of healthcare professionals. For example at BMC:

Critical paths (treatment protocols) were developed by interdisciplinary teams and focused on the expected sequencing and timing of patient treatment processes. The quantity and type of all procedures, tests, and lab work needed by patients in each DRG classification were specified by the critical path. Interdisciplinary team members established anticipated length of stay and average resource utilization by reviewing aggregate data provided by BMC's cost accounting department and by analyzing local, regional, and national benchmark data. Cost data were evaluated to choose DRGs that represented opportunities for cost and quality improvement and to evaluate the amount of variation from patient to patient.[10]

Individuals with clinical knowledge administer the protocols. At BMC, case managers, with either masters' or doctoral degrees in nursing, were responsible for aggregate financial and quality outcomes across specific patient populations. They collected and analyzed clinical and resource utilization data obtained from the specialty nurses and cost accountants and disseminated it to members of the healthcare team. As case managers had direct knowledge of physician-specific practice patterns, they were in a unique position to supplement cost accounting data with clinical information that physicians needed.[11]

Thus the growth in jobs does not occur primarily in the management accounting department but in the functional specialties where new positions are created for individuals with the responsibility to integrate the cost and functional information and disseminate it to the final users. Although considerable new management accounting information is generated to support the cost management programs, the management accounting department remains small and highly focused.

The role of the management accountant in such a setting is clear. It is one of partnership, not leadership. While the management accountant does become more important, his or her role is not one of senior manager with strategic responsibility but of key specialist providing strategically critical information to help manage costs. At BMC the director of cost accounting and administrative leader attributed BMC's improvements to the "marriage" between BMC cost accountants and clinicians who worked together to identify, measure, and control costs and revenues as well as to improve patient outcomes.

LESSONS FROM JAPAN

The next three techniques are drawn from Japanese practice. Target costing deals with cost management in the design stage of a product's life. It demonstrates the decentralization of the cost management process. Kaizen costing demonstrates that even when management accounting techniques are used to achieve cost management, management accountants play a small and decreasing role. Finally, harnessing the entrepreneurial spirit encompasses cost management techniques that do not involve any management accounting.

While generalizing across cultural boundaries is dangerous, the point of drawing on Japanese practice is to demonstrate what the future might look like. Japanese firms have been lean longer than their Western counterparts and have extensive experience with the cost management systems that support lean competition. As Western companies become lean,

they will be forced to adopt cost management techniques such as target and kaizen costing.

Structural differences between Japanese and Western practices come into play here. Most Japanese firms have rotation programs for engineers that are designed to expose them to accounting and other aspects of business. These programs play a critical role in enabling engineers and other managers to undertake the management accounting tasks associated with cost management. In Western companies, where such programs do not exist, management accountants perform many of these tasks. But if Western firms adopt a more Japanese approach to cost management, which they might be forced to do in order to remain competitive, the situation could change.

TARGET COSTING

Target costing[12] is a structured approach for determining the cost at which a proposed product with specified functionality and quality must be produced to generate the desired level of profitability at the product's anticipated selling price. Target costing starts with estimating the selling price at which the proposed product will sell. Marketing determines this target selling price through market survey, consumer analysis, and other market research techniques. The second step is the determination of the new product's target profit margin. Reviewing historical trends, estimating competitive offerings, and sometimes running computer simulations achieve this objective. The third step is to determine the product's target cost by subtracting the target profit from the target selling price.

The fourth step is to use value engineering to find ways to design a product so that it can be manufactured at its target cost. Value engineering assesses ways to increase the functionality of a product without incurring a cost penalty and to reduce costs without incurring a functionality penalty. The task of value engineering lies in the domain of product design, not management accounting. At Olympus Optical:

> Aggressive cost reduction was achieved by applying three rationalization objectives. First, the number of parts in each unit was targeted for reduction...Second, expensive, labor-intensive, and mechanical adjustment processes were eliminated wherever possible. Finally, metal and glass components were replaced with cheaper plastic ones.[13]

In target costing, the primary role of management accounting occurs when value engineering is being applied. Management accountants provide estimates of future manufacturing costs that product engineers can use in designing new products so the products can be manufactured at their target costs. This information is critical to helping the engineers design to target, but the role of the management accountant is one of support not leadership.

This support role is highlighted by the fact that, in many Japanese companies, the accounting function has virtually no involvement in the target costing process. Instead, accounting is the "gatekeeper of last resort." For example, at Nissan:

> Accounting was not involved in the value engineering process, which was the responsibility of the cost design and engineering department. The primary function of accounting was to set the final target cost for each model variant and ensure that the vehicles were manufactured for that amount. As the vehicle entered production, accounting would monitor all component and assembly costs, and, if these were not in line with the final target costs, accounting would notify cost design and engineering that the final target costs were not being met.[14]

Thus a powerful cost management technique is undertaken by product engineers and production personnel, not by management accountants. The critical knowledge required includes anticipated market conditions, long-term profit objectives, and product design. Other than providing some supporting information, accountants are relegated to the end of the process where the analysis shifts from ex-ante to ex-post.

KAIZEN COSTING

Kaizen costing[15] is the application of kaizen or continuous improvement specifically to reduce costs. It focuses on making production and service delivery processes more efficient. Unlike target costing, kaizen costing accepts the design of the product or service as given and focuses on finding ways to reduce the cost of the manufacturing and delivery processes. A cost reduction objective is set for each process, and then value analysis, a form of value engineering, is used to achieve these objectives. Little management accounting is required in the value analysis process, which, like value engineering, requires technical expertise.

When management accounting information is required to support a kaizen program, management accountants do not have to collect it. In fact, it is preferable for the users to collect the information. At Sumitomo the trend was to delegate cost reduction to the factory level...To transfer ownership of accounting information from the accounting department to the shop floor, factory personnel began to prepare shop floor cost management information, and subsequently some of it was used by the accounting department to produce financial reports.[16]

The shift of management accounting away from management accountants and into the hands of the manufacturing workforce helps empower the cost management process. This decentralization is different from simply assigning management accountants to the factories. The task of management accounting itself is decentralized, thus reducing the role of the management accountant.

Even when a management accounting technique such as variance analysis is used to monitor the progress of a kaizen program, the role of the management accountant is surprisingly small. Often the management accountant just installs the system. Once the system is installed, the management accountant plays virtually no role because the computer calculates the variances automatically. The workforce analyzes cause and effect and takes appropriate action. At Shionogi Pharmaceutical:

> The workforce reported to the technical development department after every lot was completed to discuss the effectiveness of their kaizen activities. The workers were expected to identify the portion of the variance that was due to kaizen. Once the standard setter and the workers responsible for that chemical process had agreed on the level of kaizen improvement, the updated, but not the budgetary, standards were adjusted accordingly.[17]

For the kaizen costing program to be effective, standards must be accurate and believable. Consequently, great care is taken to ensure that they are fair. At Shionogi, specially trained individuals with a significant background knowledge of production set the standards:

> Standard setters were selected from among the most highly knowledgeable, skilled, and reliable workers in the technical development staff. Many were holders of a master's degree in chemistry or pharmacy. There were usually assigned from the beginning to a technical development department. Sometimes, standard setters were temporarily assigned to the production floor to increase their in-depth understanding of the production process. This increased knowledge was considered valuable because it allowed them to set more accurate standards.[18]

The transfer of the standard setters to the production floor to increase their knowledge of the production process parallels the suggestion that management

11

accountants should become more knowledgeable about production. The obvious difference is that the standard setter already is a highly trained specialist, not a management accountant. One of the primary lessons is that it is easier to bring management accounting to the functional specialist than it is to bring functional knowledge to the management accountant.

HARNESSING THE ENTREPRENEURIAL SPIRIT

The desire to push the pressure to manage costs deep into production systems can lead to innovative forms of cost management that require almost no management accounting to support them. One such approach is called harnessing he entrepreneurial spirit of the workforce.[19] There are two ways to do this. The first technique creates pseudo microprofit centers from cost centers, and the second converts the company into numerous real microprofit centers or small firms. The two are highly interrelated because it is not possible to reduce company size without first creating more profit centers.

Three factors help a company determine whether to create pseudo or real profit centers and whether to create business managers or to also manage firm size. They are:

- The ability to identify someone with the capability to manage the profit centers,
- The existence of external customers that are willing to buy the intermediate outputs of the profit centers, and
- The willingness to sell the intermediate outputs of the profit centers to external customers.

When a group is treated as a profit center instead of a cost center, the leader's responsibility shifts from managing costs to managing profits. This change has two effects. First, it causes the group members to treat revenues as a part of their responsibility. Second, it causes the group to place increased pressure on members to reduce costs. This pressure to reduce costs is due to individuals taking an entrepreneurial stance with respect to their group's performance. To manage costs better, these individuals often require improved cost measurement systems. For example, at Kirin's Kyoto brewery:

> To measure costs so that profit center profits could be determined required locating more cost measurement points in the brewery. For example, to allow electricity usage to be monitored at the profit center level, additional meters were installed throughout the factory. Separate metering was considered important for two reasons. First, it allowed each center

to determine its actual electricity costs and hence profits; second, it allowed each center to monitor its electricity consumption, and, if it was too high, to introduce cost reductions designed to bring it back to planned levels.[20]

Such actions focus on ways to improve production yields and hence revenues and on ways to reduce costs. Management accounting plays only a minor support role in providing some of the information required. In fact, "fancy" accounting would have gotten in the way by confusing the workforce. For example, at Higashimaru Shoyu, where Okuno, the plant manager, introduced a micro-profit center system he called the price control system (PCS):

> The rationale behind keeping both raw material prices and budgeted profit margins constant was that it allowed the work groups to more easily understand the effect of their actions on group profitability. Okuno believed that if raw material and selling prices were allowed to vary, then it would be too difficult for the groups to observe the effects of their improvements. In addition, Okuno did not want the PCS to become an accounting system replete with variances and other forms of reconciliations. Instead, he wanted a very simple system that everyone could understand.[21]

Thus even where management accounting plays a role in a microprofit center cost management system, it is simplified to such an extent that accountants are not required. While the management accounting function could have prepared the books of the profit center, Okuno himself chose to do so. His preparing the books allowed him immediate in-depth access to group performance and helped create new communication pathways between him and the groups. If the books had been kept by a management accountant, this would not have been the case. The result is a decentralization of management accounting to the plant manager.

When companies are able to find internal and external customers for the outputs of their production groups, they can convert their production processes into real profit centers. This ability allows them to take advantage of the second technique of reducing effective firm size. In highly competitive environments, compactness can play a critical role in firm survival. According to Kuniyasu Sakai, the founder of the Taiyo Group, it also is a powerful cost management technique:

> It is the size of a company that matters. When a company gets too large it cannot respond in time. You need small, flexible firms to survive. Breaking large companies into smaller inde-

pendent units is a powerful form of cost management.[22]

By becoming many autonomous smaller entities, companies have harnessed the entrepreneurial spirit of their employees and used firm size as a mechanism to increase efficiency and cut bureaucracy. But these cost management techniques do not rely upon management accounting to any significant extent. Often, in fact, they reduce the need for formal management accounting systems. For example, at Kyocera, where the small firms are called amoebas:

> Amoebas were sufficiently small and simple so that they did not require sophisticated systems to either determine product costs or control overall expenditures. Instead, engineers in each amoeba had access to most cost data relating to raw material, equipment and other costs. Such access to cost data, combined with their up-to-date knowledge of changes in the production processes, allowed the engineers to calculate up-to-date costs for all of the products their amoeba produced. These cost estimates were used for pricing purposes. Thus, one of the advantages of the simplicity of the amoebas was that it allowed engineers to participate in the price-setting process.[23]

Under this cost management technique, history has been reversed. Management accounting emerged at the beginning of the century to enable managers to understand the complex organizations that were emerging. By converting itself into 800 small firms, Kyocera reduces that complexity to a point that sophisticated management accounting no longer is required. The result is to decentralize management accounting to the workforce.

End of part 1. In part 2, I will discuss the implications for management accountants and present some challenges for the profession.

---

[1] Robin Cooper, *When Lean Enterprises Collide*, Harvard Business School Press, Boston, Mass., 1995, p. 7. (For a review of this book, see "Library," MANAGEMENT ACCOUNTING®. April 1996, p. 53.)

[2] Robert S. Kaplan, "New Roles for Management Accountants," *Journal of Cost Management*, Fall 1995, p. 13.

[3] Robin Cooper, Robert S. Kaplan, Lawrence S. Maizel, Eileen Morrissey, Ronald M. Oehm, *Implementing Activity-Based Cost Management: Moving from Analysis to Action, Institute of Management Accountants*, Montvale, N.J., 1992, p. 308.

[4] Ibid., p. 8.

[5] Robin Cooper, "Implementing an Activity-Based Cost System," Journal of Cost Management, Spring 1980, p. 34.

[6] Robert Cooper and Kiran Verma, Hewlett-Packard: Queensferry Telecommunications Division, Harvard Business School Press, Case 9-191-067, Boston, Mass., copyright 1990, by the President and Fellows of Harvard College, p. 1.

[7] Ibid., p. 4.

[8] Tom Albright and Robin Cooper, Brookwood Medical Center (B), Harvard Business School, Boston, Mass., 1996 forthcoming.

[9] Tom Albright and Robin Cooper. Brookwood Medical Center (A), Harvard Business School, Boston, Mass., 1996 forthcoming.

[10] Albright and Cooper (B).

[11] Ibid.

[12] Much of the material for this section was taken from Chapter 7 of *When Lean Enterprises Collide*.

[13] Robin Cooper, Olympus Optical Company, Ltd. (A): Cost Management for Short Life Cycle Products, Harvard Business School, Case 9-195-072, Boston, Mass., copyright 1994 by the President and Fellows of Harvard College, p. 6.

[14] Robin Cooper, Nissan Motor Company, Ltd.: Target Costing System, Harvard Business School, Case 9-194-040, Boston Mass., copyright 1994 by the President and Fellows of Harvard College, p. 5.

[15] Much of the material for this section was taken from Chapter 11 of *When Lean Enterprises Collide*

[16] Robin Cooper, Sumitomo Electric Industries, Ltd.: The Kaizen Program, Harvard Business School, Case 9-195-078, Boston Mass., copyright 1994 by the President and Fellows of Harvard College, p. 6.

[17] Robin Cooper, Shionogi & Co., Ltd.: Profit Planning and Product Costing Systems, Harvard Business School, Boston, Mass., forthcoming, p. 13.

[18] Ibid., p. 11.

[19] Much of the material for this section was taken from Chapter 13 and 14 of *When Lean Enterprises Collide*

[20] Robin Cooper, Kirin Brewery Company, Ltd., Harvard Business School, Case 9-195-058, Boston Mass., copyright 1994 by the President and Fellows of Harvard College, p. 11.

[21] Robin Cooper, Higashimaru Shoyu Co., Ltd. (A): Price Control System, Harvard Business School, Case 9-195-050, Boston, Mass., copyright 1994 by the President and Fellows of Harvard College, p. 4.

[22] Robin Cooper, The Taiyo Group: The Bunsha Philosophy, Harvard Business School, Case 9-195-080, Boston Mass., copyright 1994 by the President and Fellows of Harvard College, p. 1.

[23] Robin Cooper, Kyocera Corporation: The Amoeba Management System, Harvard Business School,

The Practice Analysis of Management Accounting

By Gary Siegel, CPA, and C. S. "Bud" Kulesza, CMA

In the early 1990s, financial executives began voicing concern about the academic preparation of entry-level accountants. They told the IMA leadership that people were not coming to corporate jobs with the appropriate skill set and that their companies could not afford to wait 12 to 18 months for entry-level accountants to be productive. The initial action in addressing this concern was to determine what corporate executives expect in entry-level accountants. *What Corporate America Wants in Entry-level Accountants*[1], the IMA/FEI research published in 1994, revealed a sizable gap between expected and actual skills.

Following up on this initial research effort, IMA commissioned the *Practice Analysis of Management Accounting* in response to its members' needs for better-prepared entry-level accountants. The purpose of this article is to briefly describe what the Practice Analysis is, what it reveals, how it can be accessed and used, and what it means for Corporate and Academic America and the management accounting profession.

IMA realized that the solution to closing the skills gap was for Corporate America to work together with Academic America. Consequently, IMA initiated an ambitious, multiphase plan to bring the two groups together to promote discussion and cooperation. Because curriculum change is in the domain of accounting educators, the centerpiece of the plan—the Practice Analysis of Management Account—is intended to give Academic America the tool it needs for curriculum change.

The IMA Practice Analysis documents the work that management accountants currently do and anticipates the work they will do in three to five years. IMA believes that accounting educators, armed with this detailed factual information about current and future practice, will create more meaningful curriculum.

OVERVIEW OF RESULTS

The Practice Analysis includes comprehensive lists of work activities and KSAs (knowledge, skills, and abilities) that delineate the scope of management accounting and the competencies necessary to perform the work effectively. These lists did not exist in this usable format before the Practice Analysis.

Practicing management accountants, from entry-level to CFO, in "typical" as well as "leading edge" companies, reported their level of involvement with each work activity and the importance of each KSA to their work.

Mail questionnaires and in-depth, in-person interviews were used to collect information. The questionnaires were sent to 4,000 corporate accountants randomly selected from the membership rosters of IMA,

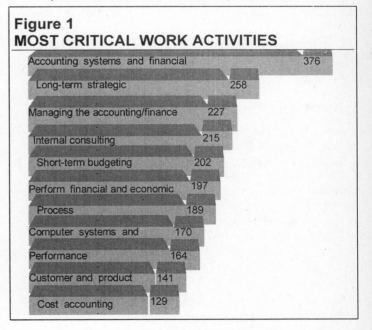

Figure 1
MOST CRITICAL WORK ACTIVITIES

Activity	Value
Accounting systems and financial	376
Long-term strategic	258
Managing the accounting/finance	227
Internal consulting	215
Short-term budgeting	202
Perform financial and economic	197
Process	189
Computer systems and	170
Performance	164
Customer and product	141
Cost accounting	129

Financial Executives Institute, American Institute of CPAs, and Institute of Internal Auditors, The interviews were conducted at nine U.S. corporations.

The Practice Analysis captures the essence of management accounting practice and provides a database that can be assessed easily and applied to a variety of business and educational objectives.

Management accountants engage in a wide variety of work activities. Not surprisingly, their work differs depending on a number of factors such as position in the firm, years of experience, and size of company. In some companies, management accountants engage in traditional accounting work (cost accounting systems, financial reporting, resource management, and so on), while in others they engage in activities that are relatively new to the profession (internal consulting, process improvement, customer and product profitability, and so on).

They consider the work activities in Fig. 1 to be most critical to company success. They consider the knowledge, skills, and abilities (KSAs) in T-1 to be most important for their work. Importance was measured on a five-point scale where 1 indicated "not important" and 5 indicated "very important." The mean importance score is shown in T-1.

In addition to the work ethic, the highest-rated KSAs have to do with communication and problem-solving skills, understanding the business, and the basics of accounting. The results clearly indicate that management accountants are expected to have a thorough knowledge of basic accounting. Beyond these basics, management accountants need excellent communication, interpersonal, analytical, and computer spreadsheet skills. This essential knowledge is part of the minimum requirement for work in management accounting.

A PROFESSION IN TRANSITION

The management accounting profession has been in transition for the past five to 10 years. Advances in information technology, competitive pressures, and corporate restructuring due to reengineering have resulted in the automation and centralization of many transactional aspects of accounting. Closing the books at year-end used to take weeks. Now many companies close in a few days. Software is being developed that will provide for virtual close of the books. Information is becoming much more accessible than it was in the past.

Consequently, management accountants in many companies have been liberated from the mechanical tasks of their work. Instead of collecting information, management accountants are expected to use that

TABLE 1
MOST IMPORTANT KNOWLEDGE, SKILLS, AND ABILITIES FOR WORK

KSA	Mean
Work ethic	4.67
Analytical/problem-solving skills	4.66
Interpersonal skills	4.64
Listening skills	4.58
Use of computerized spreadsheets	4.51
Understanding the business	4.48
Understanding bottom-line implications of day-to-day business and accounting decisions	4.44
Writing skills	4.32
Familiarity with business processes	4.32
Relationship between balance sheet, income statement, and cash flow statement	4.31
Leadership skills	4.30
Understanding/preparing financial statements	4.29
Accounting system: The "books," cost flows, double entry, etc.	4.25
Use of computerized accounting systems	4.22
Interpreting or analyzing financial statements	4.19
Measurement, valuation, and presentation of revenue and expenses	4.17
Accruals and deferrals, adjusting and closing entries	4.15
Speaking/presentation skills	4.11
Information needs of internal customers	4.03

freed-up time to analyze it. Instead of preparing financial statements, they interpret the financial information and explain the business implications to managers. They are doing more financial planning and more financial modeling. They work with managers to make informed business decisions. As some of the executives and managers interviewed for the practice analysis noted:

> I think the change is accelerating as we go. The change in the last five years is much more dramatic than say the previous five or 10. Now the accountants are not only the interpreters, but they help drive management toward the proper response to what the numbers are telling us and toward helping them tie together the financial results with the business strategies. In a nutshell, going from a numbers-crunching type mode to a business partnership, more strategic approach. (ITT Automotive)

> You notice none of my people are called clerical this or that; they are all analysts. That is

deliberate. I expect them to think, to, I hope, know what the end point is, what the requirements are, what the timetable is, and what our expectations are. That is a huge change. (Takata)

The major changes...I'd say the team involvement. When I came into this organization the thrust was to be more traditional accounting-like. Now the thrust is to be customer driven, to be much more business oriented rather than accounting oriented, if you understand my differentiation there. All that financial stuff that you learned in college is good because you need a strong understanding of how the financials work in an organization. But, really, where you are going to be successful in an industrial setting like this is to understand the business and to have an interest in marketing and to have an interest in processing and operations, to have an interest in design work. It doesn't mean that that is your career path, but what it means is that you become a better manager. (Caterpillar)

A Hewlett-Packard finance manager summed up the change: "We are not accountants; we are analysts and business partners."

The work environment. Management accountants do not work in isolation. Nearly half (48%) of the respondents—in both large and small companies—report that they are members of cross-functional teams, bringing the financial perspective to bear on corporate decisions. This role requires excellent communication and interpersonal skills, an understanding of all phases of business, and an appreciation for the inter-

---

WHAT IS A PRACTICE ANALYSIS?

A practice analysis is the study of work. Typically conducted by professional associations or human resource firms, practice analyses collect information about the tasks or activities that people perform on their jobs, the competencies or skills necessary to do their work, or critical incidents that a job incumbent might encounter at work.

This information can be used for a variety of purposes including developing or verifying professional and licensing examinations, writing job descriptions, designing education and training materials, and developing performance evaluation standards. A practice analysis usually is a massive research project. An enormous amount of data has to be collected, organized, sifted, reorganized, analyzed, summarized, and reported.

---

relatedness of the financial function with marketing, engineering, production, and other functional areas.

The "finance function." The management accountants interviewed for the Practice Analysis refer to themselves not as accountants, but as members of the finance function. In fact, in many companies you seldom hear the word "accounting." When asked why they use the word finance instead of accounting, most interviewees (who tend to hold degrees in accounting) said that finance has a broader connotation than accounting. Another explanation is that accounting reports on what happened in the past, while finance focuses on the future. In two companies we visited, the management accountants shun the word finance and call themselves decision-support specialists; their reasoning is that it is a much better description of what they do.

Regardless of how they refer to themselves, they see their role as distilling diverse information, putting it into a useful format, and facilitating management decision making.

FUTURE PRACTICE

We looked into the future, and this is what we found. Everyone we interviewed expects management accountants to do less data collection and statement preparation and more financial analysis and business partnering in the future.

Those interviewed offered their views about the future of management accounting:

We will get more and more to the point where accountants won't spend a lot of time doing accounting, but they will be more analytical and more planning oriented and more of a partner with the operational side of the business. (ITT Automotive)

I think you will find finance people with their teams. All the financial information that we give today, purely financial, will be accessible to managers online. They won't need finance people to give them the numbers. They will have them there as their business managers. We will have very centralized transaction processing areas—have a lot of specialists centralized. The generalists will be out in the functional areas and part of the team. (Hewlett-Packard)

The world that we're describing isn't specialized like we were trained to be, either an accountant or a business analyst or whatever you want to call it. It's going to be more a generalist. A generalist has to be able to take the detail data, which will be managed by a computer system supposedly with some smarts to it, and interpret it for use by the management team. So we're going to have to be more of a generalist because we're going to take not just the financial data that we're talking about here, but maybe the human resources data and the scheduling data and the other metrics that the business manager needs, and we're going to have to report out to the guy. So we're going to have much more general knowledge of how the business works. (Boeing)

THE PRACTICE ANALYSIS REVEALS WHAT TOP FINANCE EXECUTIVES DO IN COMPANIES WITH $50 MILLION OR MORE IN SALES

MOST FREQUENTLY PERFORMED WORK ACTIVITIES
10% or more of the executives perform this work at least daily

	Daily	Weekly	Monthly	Quarterly	Annually	Never Perform
Managing the accounting/finance function	64%	14%	11%	3%	2%	7%
Internal consulting	36	32	19	6	1	7
Accounting systems and financial reporting	18	28	36	6	3	8
Human resources and personnel	11	23	25	14	8	19
Perform financial and economic analysis	10	15	39	21	3	11
Investment of funds	10%	13%	19%	8%	3%	47%

LEVEL OF INVOLVEMENT IN THE WORK ACTIVITIES
Rank ordered by work finance executives perform themselves

	Perform work	Review others' work	Perform work and review others' work
Professional and civic activities	74%	5%	21%
Educating the organization	55	11	34
External financing	44	14	41
Human resources and personnel	38	21	41
Internal consulting	37	8	55
Managing the accounting/finance function	36	18	46
Mergers, acquisitions, and divestments	32%	10%	59%

Rank-ordered by work of others finance executives review

	Review others work	Perform work	Perform work and review others' work
Tax compliance	72%	9%	19%
Consolidations	70	11	19
Credit and collection	67	10	24
Accounting systems and financial reporting	61	6	33
Customer and product profitability	59	7	34
Computer systems and operations	59	7	34
Resource management	59	6	34
Compliance reporting	58	9	32
Cost accounting systems	58	4	38
Project reporting	57%	7%	36%

Rank-ordered by work finance executives perform and review

	Perform work and review others' work	Perform work	Review others' work
Long-term strategic planning	65%	24%	11%
Short-term budgeting process	61	11	29
Process improvement	61	15	24
Mergers, acquisitions, and divestments	59	32	10
Internal consulting	55	37	8
Performance evaluation	54	11	35
Perform financial and economic analysis	53	20	27
Quality systems and control	52	6	42
Capital budgeting	46	12	41
Managing the accounting/finance function	46%	36%	18%

EXECUTIVES WHO THINK THAT THESE WORK ACTIVITIES WILL BECOME MORE IMPORTANT

Long-term strategic planning	61%
Performance evaluation	60
Customer and product profitability	57
Process improvement	55
Cost accounting systems	52
Computer systems and operations	50
Internal consulting	48
Short-term budgeting process	43
Mergers, acquisitions, and divestments	43
Quality systems and control	43
Project reporting	41
Educating the organization	41
Perform financial and economic analysis	40%

20 MOST IMPORTANT KNOWLEDGE, SKILLS, AND ABILITIES FOR THEIR WORK

The number shown is the mean importance score on a 1-5 scale

Interpersonal skills	4.72
Work ethic	4.71
Understanding bottom-line implications	4.64
Analytical/problem-solving skills	4.61
Understanding the business	4.59
Leadership skills	4.53
Listening skills	4.52
Use of computerized spreadsheets	4.46
Familiarity with business processes	4.4
Relationship between balance sheet, income statement, and cash flow statement	4.4
Interpreting or analyzing financial statements	4.4
Understanding/preparing financial statements	4.38
Writing skills	4.35
The major responsibilities of the financial executive	4.28
Information needs of internal customers	4.25
Purpose and use of management information system in business	4.25
Relevant costs for decision making	4.23
Long-range planning/budgeting	4.23
Speaking/presentation skills	4.22
Measurement, valuation, and presentation of revenues and expenses	4.22

ACCESS TO THE PRACTICE ANALYSIS DATABASE

IMA's Practice Analysis of Management Accounting has been completed and will be available on the Internet to accounting educators, employers of management accountants, CPE course designers, human resource professionals, and other interested users.

The complete Practice Analysis report and the Practice Analysis database will he made available on the IMA home page on the Rutgers Accounting Web on the Internet. The database is in the form of an SPSS system file and raw data file. Information on the format and structure of the data are in Appendix F of the Practice Analysis report. Permission is granted to use the Practice Analysis database for educational purposes. Any publications based on practice Analysis data should contain the appropriate citations.

The IMA Home Page can be found at http://www.rutgers.edu/accounting/raw/ima.

Instructions on how to download the data are available on IMA's Home Page. Or call Shahe Sanentz, manager of IMA's Information Center, at 800-638-4427, ext. 235.

...what we think we should become in the future is a business partner who helps people understand what the financials are saying, helps them design their businesses, showing them what financial expectations can be, not-beating them up with the numbers but showing them trends and helping them understand how they can measure themselves. Basically the term is used over and over again, I guess: partnering. (US West)

...within the five years we are going to be seeing a marked change, an emphasis on general knowledge versus specialized knowledge. You are going to be expected to have the knowledge in a specified area, but you are also going to be expected to be able to look at the whole and see how the whole fits. [Cost accounting will be] much more of a consulting type field than it is today. (Boeing)

In my mind, cost accountants are going to be business analysts. (Boeing)

Some anticipate that finance will go beyond business partnering and broaden its role to strategic partner. Rather than support only what happens in the division, management accountants will look at the marketplace and at what the competition is doing. They will need to be more strategic, be better visionaries, and be more proactive:

In five years [we will become] even more strategic. Instead of business partners you might need strategic partners. Really understanding the ins and outs of all the organizations, and what are their buttons and really trying to be visionary—understanding what is happening to our business. So you have to have somebody who understand the business (who really wants to work and really has a commitment and interest to that. So not accountants anymore, not even analysts. (Hewlett Packard)

We've got to be an integrated, expert business adviser to whoever the equivalent of the CEO is. (Boeing)

The consistency with which the future is described is remarkable. You could pass the microphone from Boeing to HP to ITT Automotive to Caterpillar and not miss a beat. People convey the same message and paint the same picture. The work will be different, and it will be exciting.

THE "NEW ACCOUNTING"

In the new milieu, the role of the management accountant has undergone a striking metamorphosis: from numbers-crunching preparer of financial statements to high-level decision support specialist. Management accountants are business partners with their customers (managers in operating or service units), internal consultants, and organizational educators.

This is not to say that management accountants do no transactional work. As reported above, management accountants are engaged in a wide variety of accounting tasks. But given the pace of technological change and the competitive advantage that accrues to companies that can use their accountants in ways that add value, the future of the profession appears to be one in which management accountants put their skills to new uses.

When asked which work activities would become more important to the company over the next two to three years, respondents cited those associated with the new role of management accounting. Fig. 2 shows the work activities that more than 40% of the respondents say will increase in importance to their company.

USES OF THE PRACTICE ANALYSIS DATABASE

Information in the Practice Analysis database can be sorted by company size (sales or number of employees), zip code, respondents' hierarchical level in the organization, age, years of management accounting experience, years of public accounting experience, industrial category, and extent of international business activity.

The Practice Analysis results can be used in a variety of ways by accounting educators, human resource professionals, corporate training directors, and CPE providers. Here are some possibilities.

For accounting educators:

- To evaluate the curriculum. How well does the curriculum cover the most important work activities and KSAs?
- To improve the curriculum. The Practice Analysis database can inform and guide the process of course modification and curriculum design.
- To plan for the future. Assess the extent to which the current curriculum will meet anticipated future needs.

For human resource professionals:

- To write job descriptions.

- To develop job families.
- To develop skills-based guidelines for recruitment.
- To develop skills-based performance evaluation standards.

For corporate training personnel:

- To develop skills-based training modules.
- To develop just-in-time training modules.

For CPE developers:

- To design courses and curricula for management accountants at different stages of their careers.
- To expand the range of courses to include nonaccounting KSAs.

FROM NUMBERS CRUNCHER TO DECISION-SUPPORT SPECIALIST

The IMA Practice Analysis of Management Accounting reflects the shift from numbers cruncher and corporate cop to decision-support specialist and reflects what it takes to complete in today's lean, global, technologically driven environment. The Practice Analysis is a powerful tool that will help individuals and organizations, whether corporate or academic, to analyze and develop programs that meet their needs. It is not intended to be used in isolation. The usefulness of its comprehensive database will be enhanced significantly if supplemented with other information.

For instance, curriculum designers are certain to want to obtain the perspectives of their constituents as part of the planning and development phases of their work. The power and relevance of the Practice Analysis are limited only by the user's ability to tailor the data to meet their university or corporate needs.

Both Corporate and Academic America are urged to use the Practice Analysis within their own environments and as partners to close the preparation gap between what is taught and what is practiced. We encourage you to experiment with the database in developing innovative applications. As you travel down the Information Highway, please let IMA know how you are using the Practice Analysis data so that we can share your experience with others.

[1] Gary Siegel and James E. Sorensen, *What Corporate America Wants in Entry-Level Accountants*, Institute of Management Accountants, Montvale J.J. 1994. The research results were summarized in the September 1994 issue of MANAGEMENT ACCOUNTING, pp. 26-31.

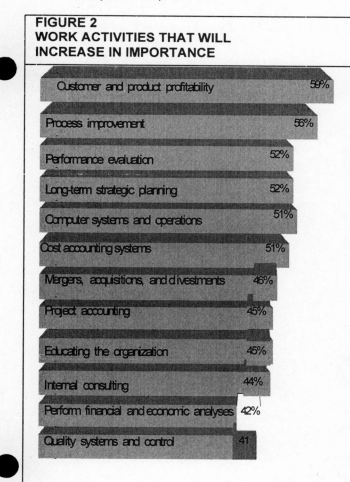

FIGURE 2
WORK ACTIVITIES THAT WILL INCREASE IN IMPORTANCE

Work Activity	Percent
Customer and product profitability	59%
Process improvement	56%
Performance evaluation	52%
Long-term strategic planning	52%
Computer systems and operations	51%
Cost accounting systems	51%
Mergers, acquisitions, and divestments	46%
Project accounting	45%
Educating the organization	45%
Internal consulting	44%
Perform financial and economic analyses	42%
Quality systems and control	41

Chapter 2
Strategic Analysis and Strategic Cost Management

Cases

Readings

Bonnie P. Stivers, Teresa Joyce Covin, Nancy Green Hall, and Steven W. Samit: How Nonfinancial Performance Measures are Used

This article presents the findings of a survey of top executives regarding the use of nonfinancial information in evaluating the performance of managers and the firms they work for. The results are given for both United States and Canadian respondents, to provide an opportunity to compare the two. The discussion is particularly relevant for firms using the balanced scorecard, because of its focus on nonfinancial as well as financial information.

Discussion Questions:

1. Do the results of the survey support the use of the balanced scorecard as described in the chapter?
2. How would you tie together the five categories of nonfinancial information mentioned in the article with the four groups of critical success factors in the balanced scorecard?
3. Identify the differences in response between the United States and Canadian respondents, and explain the significance of these differences.

Cases

12-1. Atlantic City Casino

Several years ago the management of a large hotel chain, Hotel Corporation of America (HCA) purchased a casino in Las Vegas. Pleased with the results HCA constructed another casino in Atlantic City shortly after casino gaming was legalized in that city. At the time the proposal in this case arose (see below) there were 9 other casinos operating and 2 additional casinos under construction.

The casino is an independent operating unit within the hotel chain. For example, all financial and accounting services are provided in-house. The casino has been profitable since the day it opened. However, the level of profits has not been satisfactory. Corporate management is well aware that HCA would have been better off if the huge sums involved in the construction of the casino had been invested in certificates of deposit.

The Proposal

Management of the Atlantic City Casino has employed several consulting services to study the market and the casino's position in the market. Consumer surveys have shown that the casino is viewed as an average casino, with no distinguishing characteristics. Coupled with its location (several blocks from where most of the casinos are located) this perception of blandness seems to explain the casino's relatively small walk-in trade (most visitors to Atlantic City visit more than one casino; people staying at one casino who visit a second are considered walk-ins at the second casino).

A proposal has been made to expand the casino and hotel (state law prescribes a fixed number of hotel rooms per square feet of casino space). As part of this expansion, the proposal includes the construction of a theme entertainment center. The center would be separate from, but attached to, the casino. The showpiece of the center would be a large Ferris wheel designed to look like a giant wheel of fortune. It would be visible from a large portion of the boardwalk. Additionally, the area would include a unique water slide, bumper cars, a space capsule ride and a fun house. Throughout the area would be a number of small souvenir and snack shops, push carts, tent shows and midway-type games to provide an old-fashioned style carnival atmosphere. An admission fee would be charged to enter the theme center and most of the rides and entertainment would be included in the admission fee. Management expects to be able to use free admission tickets to the center as a promotional item. There would be easy access from the center to the casino floor. It is anticipated that a large number of the visitors to the center would also visit the casino.

Although management is impressed by the plan and has already had detailed architectural plans prepared for the expansion, they are cautious. When the casino was first built, everyone was enthusiastic about the casino's potential, but the results have been disappointing. Management wants a thorough study made of the financial prospects for this expansion before committing funds to it.

Detailed financial data for every casino in Atlantic City are public information and are routinely exchanged. Thus, data such as that given in Tables A, B, and C are readily available.

Required:

1. Complete a value chain analysis. Describe your understanding of the competitive position of the Atlantic City Casino. Identify areas for potential cost reduction and/or value added for customers.

2. Should HCA make the investment in the theme entertainment center? Why?

3. HCA is considering a balanced scorecard for the Atlantic City Casino. For each of the four areas within the balanced scorecard, list two or three examples of measurable critical success factors which should be included.

(IMA adapted)

TABLE A
Selected Annual Financial Data 19x4
(000s omitted)

Property	Revenues			Net Income
	Casino	Rooms	Food and Beverage	
Atlantic City Casino	$220,183	$14,862	$36,833	$23,921
Competitors				
1	254,753	17,604	36,457	40,979
2	224,077	14,836	34,493	18,834
3	237,700	15,787	35,168	47,146
4	158,602	9,897	18,788	1,574
5	210,848	13,870	35,265	64,765
6	251,675	17,665	33,867	17,904
7	147,037	10,191	35,020	(9,075)
8	121,581	13,469	21,863	2,246
9*	123,947	12,157	22,643	(1,176)

* In operation in 19X4 for only 6.5 months

TABLE B
Selected Statistics for 19X5

Property	Casino Space (square feet)	Number of Rooms	Number of Restaurants
Atlantic City	50,850	521	7
Casino			
Competitors			
1	59,857	727	9
2	59,296	645	9
3	59,439	512	9
4	49,639	501	14
5	52,083	750	7
6	40,814	504	8
7	50,516	500	5
8	34,408	504	6
9	60,000	612	8

TABLE C
Operating Results for Selected Casinos
Month Ending 5/31/X4

Game	Atlantic City Casino	Competitor			
		1	2	3	4
Slots					
$.05 win	$274,600	$206,763	$353,340	$115,335	$202,869
Units	76	62	99	56	61
win %	15.5%	14.4%	14.7%	10.3%	12.2%
$.25 win	$6,054,677	$4,759,519	$6,916,104	$3,492,458	$4,955,619
units	1,028	688	1,147	596	788
win %	14.0%	14.5%	14.6%	13.3%	12.6%
$1.00 win	$2,195,362	$2,521,683	$3,010,912	$984,133	$4,673,435
units	271	259	244	146	284
win %	10.6%	12.9%	14.0%	11.2%	12.1%
Blackjack	$4,612,343	$4,316,849	$4,212,851	$3,121,488	$3,500,286
units	76	53	76	45	57
win %	16.3%	18.0%	17.3%	17.4%	16.4%
Craps win	$3,596,646	$4,176,917	$2,735,108	$3,385,787	$3,554,037
units	24	24	22	16	20
win %	16.6%	16.4%	13.1%	19.6%	$11.2%
Roulette	$839,442	$710,619	$876,411	$613,066	$947,679
units	11	7	12	11	10
win %	26.9%	29.3%	25.6%	26.8%	29.9%
Big Six win	$242,085	$221,610	$264,405	$143,966	$365,856
units	3	3	4	2	4
win %	49.0%	46.6%	47.4%	44.8%	51.5%
Baccarat	$761,302	$719,868	$484,919	$51,788	$826,101
units	3	4	3	2	2
win %	22.1%	9.9%	14.9%	1.5%	22.2%

12-2. Strategic Analysis

Sovera Enterprises, an expanding conglomerate, was founded 35 years ago by Emil Sovera. The company's policy has been to acquire businesses that show significant profit potential; if a business fails to attain projected profits, it is usually sold. Currently, the company consists of eight businesses acquired throughout the years; three of those businesses are described here.

LaBue Videodiscs produces a line of videodisc players. The sale of videodisc players has not met expectations, but LaBue's management believes that the company will succeed in being the first to develop a moderately priced videodisc recorder/player. Market research predicts that the first company to develop this product will be a star.

Ulysses Travel Agencies also showed potential, and the travel industry is growing. However, Ulysses' market share has declined for the last two years even though Sovera has contributed a lot of money to Ulysses' operations. The travel agencies located in the Midwestern and eastern sections of the country have been the biggest drain on resources.

Reddy Self-Storage was one of the first self-storage companies to open. For the last three years, Reddy has maintained a large market share while growth in the self-storage market has slowed considerably.

Ron Ebert, chairman of Sovera, prepared the agenda for the company's annual planning meeting where the present businesses were evaluated and strategies for future acquisitions were formulated. The following statements of strategy for each of the subsidiary companies discussed were formulated on the basis of the master plan:

LaBue Videodiscs. Sovera's discretionary resources are to be employed to support the growth of this business. The future officers of Sovera are to be developed here.

Ulysses Travel Agencies. An orderly disposal of the least profitable locations is the initial objective. Once the disposals are complete, an acceptable profit and growth strategy for the remaining locations will be formulated.

Reddy Self-Storage. The strategy for this company is to maintain efficient operations and maximize the generation of cash for use in the further development of Sovera's other businesses.

These strategy statements were part of the strategic plan presented to Sovera's board of directors. The directors' only debate was whether Sovera should sell the entire Ulysses organization rather than parts of it. However, the board approved all three statements as presented and circulated them to managers throughout the three units as the corporation's "new marching orders."

Required:

1. Identify at least four general characteristics that differentiate the three businesses described above, and explain how these characteristics influenced the formulation of a different strategy for each business.
2. Discuss the likely effects of the three strategy statements on the behavior of top management and middle management of each of the three businesses.
    (CMA adapted)

12-3. Business Strategy

FASTSOFT is a small software developer that markets a software system (FAST-PAK) which provides a very fast back-up of computer disk drives. The firm has also begun to develop and will soon test market some software utilities that improve the performance of other software systems on personal computers. FAST-PAK has been the principal source of cash flow for the firm since its outset, but now the product is beginning to mature, and competitive products are beginning to erode the market share of FAST-PAK. FASTSOFT is hoping that the new utility products will replace these declining cash flows.

Required:

1. How would you describe FASTSOFT's competitive strategy?
2. What strategies would you consider to slow the decline of sales of FAST-PAK?

12-4. Strategy, International

Barry McDonald, CFO for Recreational Products, Inc (RPI), is convinced it would be profitable for his firm to invest in a manufacturing operation in Singapore. RPI makes a variety of recreational products, including sporting goods, sportware, and camping equipment. RPI is known as a very high quality producer, with features and prices greater than most in the industry. One of the largest divisions in RPI is the boating division, which makes a variety of sailboats and fishing boats from 16 feet up to large sailboats of 40+ feet in length. These boats are now manufactured in two US plants. Barry's idea is to utilize the available low cost labor, materials resources and the favorable business climate in Singapore to build a manufacturing plant there for producing the larger sailboats. The finished boats would be sold to existing customers (boat dealers) in the United States and Canada, and a new effort would be made to sell some of the product in Asia and Australia. Barry forecasts sales of $50US million, cost of sales (manufacturing in the Singapore plant) of $34 million, and other expenses of approximately $10 million. The government of Singapore would provide a tax holiday for the project, but the return of profits to the United States would be taxed in the US at the US rate of 34%.

Barry's research showed that the cost of the plant in Singapore would be $20 million. Funds for the investment could come from the firm's own resources at a cost of approximately 12%, or through a subsidized loan from the government of Singapore at a 5% rate. With these figures and other estimates, Barry figured the after-tax cash flow of the plant would be a positive $4 million per year for the next 15 years, the expected life of the plant.

Required:

1. What does RPI's competitive position appear to be for the entire firm, and for the boating division? What are some of the likely critical success factors for the boating division?
2. Does Barry's plan for the Singapore plant fit the strategic competitive position you developed in (1) above?
3. What do you think are some of the key international issues that are relevant for Barry's proposal?

How Non-financial Performance Measures are Used

By Bonnie P. Stivers, CPA; Teresa Joyce Covin;
Nancy Green Hall, and Steven W. Samlt, CPA

Certificate of Merit. Most executives agree that there is no magic formula—or one right measure—for evaluating business performance. Therefore, in an effort to capture the essence of business performance, many companies are creating new performance measurement systems that include a broad range of financial and non-financial measures.

Although we know much about the use of financial measures in companies, our knowledge of these new, non-financial performance measures is limited. To determine the scope of current practice, we surveyed top executives in U. S. Fortune 500 firms and in Canadian Post 300 companies. The study was sponsored by the Michael J. Coles College of Business at Kennesaw State University and funded by the Canadian Institute of Chartered Accountants. Study results indicate that top executives in both countries believe that non-financial measures are important. But the study also identifies two serious drawbacks: (1) Although non-financial factors are viewed as important, they may not be measured, and (2) Even when non-financial factors are measured, they may not be used. (For a description of the study design and survey sample, see sidebar.)

THE STUDY OF NON-FINANCIAL PERFORMANCE MEASURES

Although much is being written about non-financial performance measures, very little is known about actual current practices. The objective of this study was to provide a comprehensive picture of the process of non-financial measurement. Specifically, the study examined the degree to which top executives in Fortune 500 and Post 300 firms identify particular non-financial performances factors as important, whether firms are measuring important non-financial factors, and whether or not companies actually are using non-financial performance factor information in their planning processes.

The questionnaire asked study participants to indicate, using a five-point scale, the importance of each of 21 non-financial performance factors in setting company goals. For discussion purposes, we have grouped the factors into five general categories: customer service, market performance, innovation, goal achievement, and employee involvement.

The five categories of non-financial performance measures are illustrated in Fig. 1. For each individual performance measure, the figure shows of the 253 firms in the total sample: (1) number of firms identifying the factor as important, (2) number of firms actually measuring the factor, and (3) number of firms actually using the factor in the planning process.

An individual factor was identified as highly important if it received a rating of four or greater on the five-point scale of importance. Results of the study indicate that customer service factors are perceived to be the most important measures. Of the 253 responding firms, 235 (92.9%) rated "customer satisfaction" and "delivery performance/customer service" as highly important. "Product/process quality" was rated as highly important by 206 (81.4%) of the responding firms and "service quality" by 205 (81.0%) of the 253 firms (Fig. 1).

Market performance and goal achievement also are perceived to be highly important categories. "Market share" in the market performance category was rated highly important by 200 (70.1%) of the responding firms, and "productivity" in the goal achievement category was rated highly important by 211 (83.4%) of the firms (Fig. 1).

FIGURE 1
NONFINANCIAL PERFORMANCE MEASURES

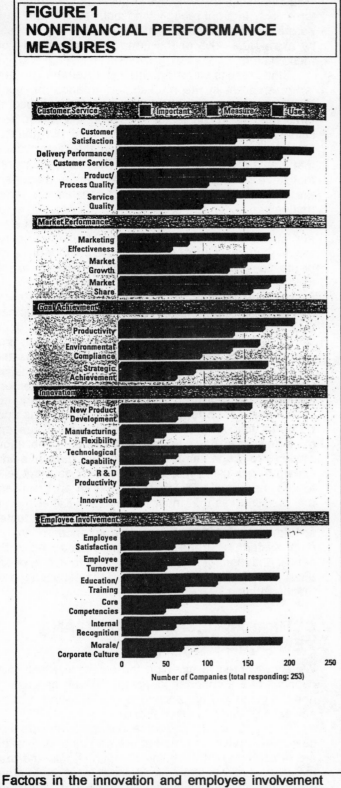

Number of Companies (total responding: 253)

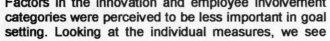

Factors in the innovation and employee involvement categories were perceived to be less important in goal setting. Looking at the individual measures, we see

that "R&D productivity" in the innovation category was rated as highly important by only 112 (44.3%) of the 253 firms, and "employee turnover" in the employee involvement category was rated as highly important by only 122 (48.2%) of the 253 firms.

The results of the study have important implications for those in the position of designing effective performance measurement systems. The first step is to get the right mix of key factors. If we were to develop a "hit" list of critical, non-financial factors to include in any performance measurement system by listening to Kaplan[1], Drucker[2], and Reichheld[3], we would include the following: market standing, innovation, productivity, customer service, and employee involvement. Although the responding executives in this study did identify market share, productivity, and customer service as highly important factors, they perceived innovation and employee involvement measures to be less important. This is clearly an area of concern if we believe what many business experts are saying about the increasing importance of innovation and human capital. It may well be that in the coming decade, intellectual capital will impact the bottom line more than booked, tangible assets. If this is the case, performance measurement systems must include leading indicators that tap human capital. This is one way managers will be able to manage and control knowledge.

THE IMPORTANCE-MEASUREMENT GAP

Our results show a substantial importance-measurement gap. That is, many companies that view non-financial performance factors as important are not capturing data on these factors. As one would expect, the importance-measurement gap is greatest for factors that are perceived to be unmeasurable or at best difficult to measure. For example, in the employee involvement category, although 192 (75.9%) companies rated "morale and corporate culture" as highly important, only 72 (37.5%) are measuring this factor. There is a similar finding for "core competencies"— 192 companies (75.9%) rated the factor as highly important, but only 69 (35.9%) are measuring this factor.

It is interesting to note that just as the categories of innovation and employee involvement received lower overall ratings of importance, responding firms indicated these two categories also have a low incidence of measurement. In particular, the non-financial performance factor least likely to be measured is "innovation." Although 160 firms (63.2%) rated the factor as highly important, only 35 firms (21.8%) are measuring this factor.

On the other hand, a number of other factors have a high rate of measurement. In the market performance category, 200 companies (79.1%) rated "market share" as highly important, and 182 firms (91.0%) are measuring this factor. "Market growth" was rated as highly important by 181 firms (71.5%), and 154 firms (85.1%) are measuring this factor. In the customer service category, "customer satisfaction" and "delivery performance/customer service" have measurement rates of 79.5% and 83.8%, respectively. In goal achievement, "productivity" has a measurement rate of 82.9%

     After a firm identifies the right mix of factors to include in the performance measurement system, it is critical that these factors get measured and reported. "What gets measured gets done" implies that the organization becomes what it measures. If you cannot measure something, you cannot control it, and control is essential. The results of this study show a substantial importance-measurement gap for a number of highly important factors, particularly in the categories of innovation and employee involvement. Many of these factors may be perceived to be unmeasurable or difficult to measure. However, the fact is that precise data collection may not be possible; a collection effort that provides even crude data can prove valuable. "What matters...is not the absolute magnitude in any area but the trend...that the measurements will give...no matter how crude and approximate the individual readings are by themselves."[4] Companies may have to experiment with measuring and interpreting different factors. The objective is to provide action-oriented information to managers—not to report balance sheet figures.

THE MEASUREMENT-USE GAP

The final step in the performance measurement process is the use of measurements in developing and monitoring strategic plans. In this study, we found evidence that a large number of businesses are collecting data that are not being used to inform managers in the planning process. We call this the measurement-use gap. Of course, the underlying assumption is that if companies are collecting the data on important factors, they intend to use the data to make business decisions. To illustrate the measurement-use gap, look at "delivery performance/customer service" in the customer service category (Fig. 1). While 197 (83.8%) of 235 study participants (who rated it highly important) indicated that their companies measure this factor, only 140 (71.1%) of 197 indicated that their firms actually use this information for planning purposes. In practical terms, this means that 28.9% of the firms are collecting information that serves no useful purpose in the planning process.

     The measurement-use gap appears to be most pronounced in the category of employee involvement.

Measures such as "employee satisfaction," "employee turnover," "internal recognition," and "morale and corporate culture" are not used in the planning process by more than 40% of the firms that collect data on these factors.

     Study results show that the measurement-use gap is the smallest in the market performance category. For "market growth," 132 (85.7%) of 154 responding firms measuring the factor are using the factor. Results are similar for "market share" in that 161 (88.5%) of 182 responding firms measuring the factor report that they are also using the data. These are measures that have been around for a while; hence, managers are able to interpret the data and translate the information into action items.

     The measurement-use gap appears to be moderate for the factors in the categories of customer service, innovation, and goal achievement. Roughly 25% of the companies who measure these factors do not use the results in their planning process.

     The underlying assumption is valid—if companies collect data on important performance factors, they intend to use the data to make business decisions. Why would companies identify factors as important, collect measurements on these factors, and then not use the information in the planning process? Certainly, in the case of the employee involvement category, the measures are "softer" than in categories such as market performance. The measurements may be more difficult to understand, and, for this reason, managers may have trouble in translating the information into action items. If, for whatever reason, a firm finds that it is using resources to collect data but fails to use the resulting information, this is an inefficient use of resources that must be checked. Either the information is not relevant, in which case the factor should be deleted from the performance measurement system, or, if the information is perceived to be critical and managers do not know how to use it, every effort must be made to understand the significance of the information.

COMPARING U.S. AND CANADIAN RESPONSES

We also wanted to examine the extent to which perceptions of the importance, measurement, and use of non-financial performance measures were similar across U.S. and Canadian firms.

     Both U.S. and Canadian respondents indicate that customer service and market performance categories are most important in setting company goals and that the other categories examined are at least moderately important. The only statistically significant difference between U.S. and Canadian firms is in their perception of the importance of the innovation category. U.S.

respondents indicate that these measures are more important in the goal-setting process. U.S. and Canadian firms also show similar patterns in the measurement and use of non-financial performance factors.

HOW THE SURVEY WAS DESIGNED

Questionnaires were mailed to the top executives of Fortune 500 firms in the United States and Post 300 firms in Canada. The names and addresses of study participants were compiled from two databases: Compact Disclosure and CANCORP Canadian Financials. One hundred and two of the Fortune 500 U.S. firms and 151 of the Post 300 Canadian firms responding to the mail survey, providing an overall response rate of 31.625%. This response rate is significantly higher than might be expected given previous research on survey response rates for companies of this size.[1] Involvement by the Canadian Institute of Chartered Accountants may account for this higher than usual response rate; previous research has shown that endorsement by a well-known external party yields significantly higher response rates.[2] Respondents were chairmen of the board (70), chief executive officers (85), and chief financial officers (98). Based on 1993 Compact Disclosure and CANCORP Canadian Financials data, the average number of individuals employed by responding U.S. firms was 23,835, and the average number of employees in the Canadian responding firms was 7,689.

[1]Dennis H. Tootelian and Ralph M. Gaedeke, Fortune 500 List Revisited 12 Years Later: Still an Endangered Species for Academic Research?" *Journal of Business Research*, Vol. 15, No. 4, August 1987, pp. 359-363.

[2]Linda Rochford, "Surveying a Targeted Population Segment: The Effects of Endorsement on Mail Questionnaire Response Rate," Journal of Marketing Theory & Practice, Vol. 3, Spring 1995, pp. 86-97.

For both U.S. and Canadian firms, market performance, customer service, and goal achievement are shown to be the most used and measured non-financial performance categories. However, consistent with U.S. firms' belief concerning the importance of the innovation category, the U.S. firms represented in this sample indicate that they are significantly more likely to both measure and use factors in the innovation category. Although there are several possible explanations for differences between U.S. and Canadian

firms as they relate to innovation, it is likely that differences are due, at least in part, to competitive influences. Previous research has shown that competitive pressure often serves as a catalyst for innovation and forces firms to adopt creative internal structures to be responsive to changing markets.[5]

GETTING PAST THREE RED FLAGS TO A DYNAMIC SYSTEM

The performance measurement process involves: (1) the identification of important financial and non-financial factors, (2) measurement of these factors, and (3) use of factors in developing and monitoring strategic plans. The results of this study, based on responses from the top executives of Fortune 500 and Post 300 firms, provide a comprehensive picture of the process of non-financial performance measurement—and show that U.S. and Canadian firms face similar challenges. We believe that study results highlight three red flags.

First, measures of innovation and employee involvement were not perceived to be as important as customer service and market standing—this is a concern. If we believe the business experts who are telling us that human capital and other intangible assets classed as intellectual capital are becoming the basis of competitive advantage and wealth creation, then it is imperative that measures of innovation and employee involvement be included in the performance measurement systems—that is, identified, measured, and used to design and monitor strategic plans. Although results show that U.S. firms view measures of innovation as more important in the goal setting process and are more likely to measure and use innovation factors, both U.S. and Canadian firms show substantial importance-measurement and measurement-use gaps.

Second, study results indicate a strong importance-measurement gap for certain factors. That is, although top executives believe that certain non-financial factors are highly important, a large number of firms are not capturing data on these measures. It is clear that some factors are more difficult to measure than others. But, even crude measurements on critical factors can provide valuable input to the control framework. To close the importance-measurement gap, companies may need to experiment with different measurement methodologies.

Third, results of the study suggest a substantial measurement-use gap. That is, a large number of companies are collecting data that are not being used by managers in the planning process. The reasons underlying the measurement-use gap should be investigated. If the firms are collecting data that are not useful, these factors should be deleted from the performance measurement system. If the data are on factors that are perceived to be critical, however, it may be that managers need help in learning how to use the information in the strategic planning process.

To develop a successful performance measurement system, managers must clearly understand the interests of the stakeholders (customers, employees, and investors), the strategic objectives of the company, and every aspect of the company's business processes. Only then can they be assured that the performance measurement system includes the right factors, both financial and non-financial. Long-term commitment to the system is required to assure that the factors are measured, understood, and used. The result can be a performance measurement system that is clearly linked to strategy, is dynamic, and is action-oriented.

[1] Robert S. Kaplan and David P. Norton, "The Balanced Scorecard—Measures that Drive Performance," *Harvard Business Review*, January-February, 1992, pp. 71-79; Norton (1993); "Putting the Balanced Scorecard to Work," *Harvard Business Review*, September-October, 1993, pp. 134-147; "Using the Balanced Scorecard as a Strategic Management System," *Harvard Business Review,* January-February 1996, pp. 75-85.

[2] Peter F. Drucker, *Managing for the Future*, New York: Truman Talley Books/Dutton, 1992: *Post-Capitalist Society*, Harper Business, New York, 1993: "The Age of Social Transformation," *The Atlantic Monthly*, November 1994, pp. 53-80.

[3] Frederick F. Reichheld, *The Loyalty Effect*, Harvard Business School Press, Boston, 1996.

[4] Drucker, *Managing for the Future*.

[5] Robert Simmons, *Levers of Control: How Managers Use Innovative Control Systems to Drive Strategic Renewal,* Harvard Business School Press, Boston, 1995.

Chapter 3
Cost Drivers and Basic Cost Concepts

Cases

3-1   Risk Aversion and Decision Making
3-2   Risk Aversion and Decision Making II
3-3   Cost Drivers and Strategy

Readings

Mike Anastas: The Changing World of Management Accounting and Financial Management

This article discusses the findings of Project Millennium, a qualitative market research project conducted for the Institute of Management Accountants. The project involved focus group studies of management accountants, consultants, and business executives to identify the role of management accounting and of the management accountant of the future.

Discussion Questions:
1.   What are the key findings of the Millennium Project?
2.   What are the implications of these findings for the education of management accountants?

Cases

3-1. Risk Aversion and Decision Making

John Smith is the production manager of Elmo's Glue Company. Because of limited capacity, the company can produce only one of two possible products. The two products are:

A) a space-age bonding formula that has a 15% probability of making a profit of $1,000,000 for the company and an 85% chance of generating $200,000 in profit, or

B) a reformulated household glue that has a 100% chance of making a profit of $310,000.

John gets a bonus of 20% of the profit from his department. John has the responsibility to choose between the two products. Assume John is more risk-averse than the top management of Elmo's Glue Company.

REQUIRED:

Which product will John choose? Why? Is this the product Elmo's would choose? Why or why not? How can Elmo's change its reward system to have John consistently make decisions which are consistent with top management's wishes?

3-2. Risk Aversion and Decision Making V

John Holt is the production supervisor for ITEXX, a manufacturer of plastic parts, with customers in the automobile and consumer products industries. On a Tuesday morning, one of ITEXX's sales manager's has just asked John to re-schedule his manufacturing jobs for the rest of the week to accommodate a special order from a new customer. The catch is that getting the customer requires fast turn-around on the order, and would mean not only delaying the current production schedule, but in addition running the production equipment all three shifts for the remainder of the week. This would make it impossible to complete the regularly scheduled maintenance on the equipment that John had planned for midweek. The sales manager is keen on getting the new customer, which could mean an important increase in overall sales and output at the plant. However, John is worried not only about the delay of the current jobs, but the chance that the delay in maintenance will cause one of the machines to fail, which would back-up the orders in the plant for at least a week, meaning a substantial delay for the new order as well as those currently scheduled.

REQUIRED:

Explain how you think John should resolve this problem. What would be a good policy for handling issues like this in the future?

3-3. Cost Drivers and Strategy.

Joe Costanzo is owner of a growing chain of grocery stores in the Richmond, Virginia and the Washington, D.C. area. Joe's stores specialize in organic and other specialty foods and other specialty products, which have attracted a strong following. As his business matures, Joe is now more interested in understanding how he can better manage the profitability of his stores. In particular, he is interested in understanding what drives the costs in his business.

REQUIRED:

As a potential consultant to Joe, develop a proposal for a consulting engagement which would focus on the profitability and cost driver issues Joe is concerned about. The proposal should address which types of cost drivers should be studied and why. Also, the proposal should identify what are likely to be the important cost drivers in this business.

The Changing World of Management Accounting and Financial Management

By Mike Anastas

Imagine that you have just entered a time capsule that transports you to your office as it will look in the year 2007. The controller is video conferencing with the company's director of operations in Central Europe. They are discussing various cost management strategies based on information they see on their computer screens.

As you observe the sparsely populated offices, you notice several video conferences taking place among on-site staff and managers working at home or in other far-flung locations. Participants are discussing the successful use of electronic data interchange and straight-through processing and are making decisions based on sales and production activity information that is updated instantly on their PCs.

You already know or have witnessed how much management accounting and financial management have changed in the last 10 years, but you couldn't have predicted all the changes you see in your office of the future. Every executive is conducting business on the Internet, accessing instant snapshots of accounting and financial data on their laptop computers as they manipulate various business scenarios and send results around the globe as only the most progressive companies do now. Also, electronic data interchange will be the standard rather than the exception, and straight-through processing will create strategic alliances between vendors and customers at every level of production.

These are among the images and predictions from Project Millennium, a qualitative market research project we conducted for the Institute of Management Accountants earlier this year (see sidebar). Participants in the research envision major changes in the responsibilities of accounting and financial managers as well as the work they do and the equipment they use. They also predict that there will be fewer management accountants, but they will be at more senior levels in the corporation. And they will share more in decision making for their companies along with other members of their cross-functional teams.

Some participants in Project Millennium tagged the management accountant and financial manager of the future an "internal consultant," someone with the curiosity and flexibility to change and motivate others to change. These internal consultants will add value by helping their organizations find ways to stay profitable and keep ahead of the competition.

Management accountants and financial managers of the future will be expected to have command of the latest information technology software as well as an overall understanding of the business. To be successful, they will be proficient in communicating ideas through written form and verbal presentations. Performance reviews in the future will be based on the ability to analyze information and situations and make decisions that drive the business rather than the ability to measure the business. The key will be their ability to stay ahead of change.

FEWER BUT MORE SENIOR PEOPLE

IMA members and other lenders in the industry predict a trend for more chief executive officers (CEOs) and chief Operating officers (COOs) to be recruited from the ranks of management accountants and financial managers because of an increasing emphasis on financial management and the need for people who can decipher financial data and present the results as strategic information. In fact, the most notable shift in the profession is away from analysis of the past toward strategic thinking about the future. "There are some who are predicting the disappearance of the financial function in corporations over time...but the upper-echelon people are getting much more heavily involved in the strategic direction of the organization. [It is hoped] it will be more analytical with a higher level of work product and less detail on record keeping."

Information technology is pushing management accountants and financial managers up the ladder as they become advisors or internal consultants to other managers in the company who have access to software to manage costs and budgets. As the end user takes responsibility for the task, the accountant becomes responsible for the system and process, but not for the final report. "Ten years from now, there may be fewer people in finance because the people in line management and the business units will possess the knowledge about costs and budgeting. They will be enabled by technology and decision analysis tools, along with a few management accountants and financial managers."

INTERNAL CONSULTANTS AND STRATEGISTS

Changes brought about by information technology, which freed management accountants and financial managers from tracking past performance, have put them in the enviable position of becoming "internal consultants" who create strategies and recommendations to guide management decisions. "Management accountants can be the bridge between functions and they can be key players because they have that overview that many others do not have." "The finance and accounting department is really the information center...to understanding where the organization is coming from and where it is going."

Senior accounting and finance professionals are in a central position to keep their companies on track. "The financial managers of the future will be looking at every aspect of a company's operations. They will be at the right hand of their CEO and COO to monitor the resources of the company, the people, the products, ideas and innovations, to make sure the company is focused and stays on the right track."

But to be effective internal consultants, financial professionals must master special consulting skills, especially communications and interpersonal relations. "Your interpersonal skills are going to have to be better than ever." "All the skills related to communication—speaking, listening, sending, receiving—will be paramount." "The ability to communicate, both verbally and in writing, and leadership skills will differen-

tiate between the extremely successful management accountants and others."

ABOUT PROJECT MILLENIUM

"Project MILLENNIUM: Customers and Future Markets...Looking Ahead to 2007." Was designed to help the IMA predict major changes and skills required for professionals in management accounting and financial management. Focus group discussions among IMA members and executives who employ IMA members were held in New York, Chicago, San Francisco, Dallas, Cleveland, Philadelphia, Tampa, and Atlanta between December 1996 and February 1997. Individual interviews were conducted among industry experts, consultants, and visionaries in information technology as well as officers of the IMA, major corporations, and other professional organizations. Some of their quotes illustrate this article.

What are some of the other predictions? Companies will continue to place a premium on those individuals who have a broad overview of business and who can use case studies as a basis for solving problems. "There's going to be more demand for people who can learn from case studies that show how to increase ongoing earnings per share."

Also, as organizations downsize and run on leaner staffs, there is a growing appreciation for individuals who propose new ideas and suggest taking risks, One IMA member in San Francisco calls these employees "intrepreneurs." "An 'intrepreneur' is someone who works for a company and is able and willing to take risks there, to gamble for the greater good."

And management accountants and financial managers have to start thinking in new ways. "Accountants tend to be pretty good at productivity and administration. In 2007 we will need people who are also good in creative entrepreneurial ideas and teamwork."

DECISION-MAKING TEAM MEMBER

Today more companies are relying on cross-functional teams to run their operations, and by 2007 nearly every company will be run by such strategic teams. Decision making often involves interaction with a variety of executives within an organization, and participation of accounting and finance people is essential because of their skills and disciplines. "The management accountant of 10 years from now will be more of a team player, an integral partner in operations...respected more for business acumen and decision-making...helping to lend order and structure to making the right business decisions." Professionals who are responsible for accounting will have migrated to be more information-based strategic business advisors...The accountant has to be one of the people around the table when strategic decisions are made."

Being effective as one of the decision-makers around the table means having an overview of the total business picture—beyond cost and budgets. "Management accountants with broad business perspectives will be a necessity...as integrators of all the business activities, things that are already happening, such as performance management, balanced scorecards, process improvement, ABC, ABM...because of our knowledge and role as the common denominator for business."

Management accountants and financial managers seem to welcome this new view of themselves. "We're no longer the bean counters. We're making decisions..." "We do a lot less book-keeping and lot more analysis and making decisions." "You don't just bring information to the table anymore, you're making decisions at the table."

In addition, the future of management accounting and financial management includes the adoption of new theories and approaches, such as strategic cost management, that require new ways of thinking. "Strategic cost management means controlling the costs of our suppliers, especially in heavy manufacturing. Not just to minimize costs but to maximize creativity, to get a better product or more functionality. The whole firm would be focused on how we can reduce costs and strengthen our position."

This shift in thinking not only will affect management accountants and financial managers who already are involved in the profession, but it will place new requirements on students preparing to enter the arena. Ideally, those coming into the field in the future will be well rounded and interested in more than fundamental skills. "Every student should have a more broad-based education...to be a more dynamic contributor to the team."

INITIATING AND IMPLEMENTING NEW TECHNOLOGY

Management accountants and financial managers will continue to be the primary consumers of new information technology in most organizations. Accounting was among the first functions to be automated with early spreadsheet programs. Consequently, accounting and finance managers generally are more well prepared than others to seek and evaluate new software. They connect the end user to the technology that accesses information. "The big success factor is realizing that accountants are informational managers." Mastery of technology is seen as essential for the future. "If you don't stay current with the technology, your career is in jeopardy.

The shift from looking backward to looking forward has been facilitated by new software. "The relevancy of historical information will decline as the importance of immediate information and projections increases. And technology is the primary driver of that." "With electronic commerce and technology...it's conceivable that in 10 years you will no longer have accounts receivable and accountants payable departments. We'd be out of that business."

Some large, multinational corporations still operate MS-DOS systems on networks, but the average organization is operating Windows-based PCs connected by corporate intranets and the Internet, which facilitates electronic data interchange and straight-through processing. These new methods of data exchange make the role of management accountants and financial managers even more critical. "With your PCs we can run circles around the mainframe that was controlled by the Data Processing Department."

But the downside is that corporate accountants often complain they are being asked to produce more information with fewer people. As data go online for every manager to see on a PC, there is a demand for instant information. That means management accountants must produce more financial analyses, not just masses of data, so leaders can build strategies and make decisions based on more precise information. "Many more companies will be using Online Analytical Processing (OLAP) to go beyond the general ledger and to slice and dice the data in all kinds of ways, such as detailed customer and sales analysis."

And management accountants and financial managers will be using sophisticated information technology to create predictive data that forecast demand, production, sales, costs, and reported earnings. For example, "We will be converting activity-based costs systems from feedback to 'feed-forward' systems so you can estimate as you implement so you can estimate as you implement strategies like commonality and minimum component counts."

STAYING AHEAD OF CHANGE

Most visionaries in accounting and finance believe the rate of change will accelerate as we move into the next century. Changes in management accounting and finance will require changes in the way individuals approach their work. "Employers will not be content with accountants who view themselves mainly as scorekeepers...they want people who can influence the score, not simply report the score. It's going to require a different mindset...a shift in the way we view our positions.

The shift from record keeping to strategizing and forecasting demands that individuals develop special skills to be effective. "The management accountant has to be more of a change agent and a sales person rather than just a reporter—someone who can sell the idea of what to do with the information."

By the year 2007, most organizations will be sourcing and selling around the world. "...A lot of our suppliers and customers are going to be overseas, and we better get prepared for it." "There are very few businesses out there not touched by the international dimension some way."

But many individuals feel ill-prepared to deal with the global market. "If I were starting out today, I would learn about global markets and learn a foreign language...the kinds of things you'll really be able to use on a day-to-day basis."

Another significant change in the next 10 years will be greater diversity in the accounting and finance departments. "People coming from every field you can imagine...there's much greater diversity in the workforce..."

And most companies will be using the new media and forms of communication now being used by large multinational organizations. "There will be less business face-to-face, more by e-mail and teleconferencing. Communications will have to be more effective and precise." "The Internet will play an important role in the way we educate ourselves."

One IMA member in Cleveland summed up her philosophy about change, and it seems to apply to everyone in the profession who wants to be successful and add value to their organizations. "Learning is a lifetime proposition. We should go to school to 'Learn how to learn,' to adapt and to change, not stand still..."

Chapter 4
Activity-Based Costing and Management

Cases
4-1   Blue Ridge Manufacturing (Activity-Based Costing)
4-2   Centerior Energy Corporation (Activity-Based Costing)
4-3   Tektronix (Activity-Based Costing)

Readings
Terrell L. Carter, Ali Sedaghat, and Thomas D. Williams: How ABC Changed the Post Office

The article describes the activity-based cost study and market strategy study conducted for the United States Post Office by Coopers & Lybrand. The specific focus of the analysis was the cost/benefit of including credit and debit card transactions in post offices. The ABC study projected costs for the credit/debit card program and found significant savings for adoption. The Post Service Board of Governors approved the plan in October 1994.

Discussion Questions:
1. What are the unit, batch, and product level activities at the Post Office, and what are the cost drivers for each?
2. What does the ABC model show about the relative costs of the different payment options: cash, check, credit card, and debit card?
3.   What are the limitations of the ABC analysis done of the Post Office as described in the article?

Cases

4-1. Blue Ridge Manufacturing Case

BACKGROUND:

Blue Ridge Manufacturing produces and sells towels for the U.S. "sports towel" market. A "sports towel" is a towel that has the promotion of an event or a logo printed on it. They're called sports towels because their most popular use is for distribution in connection with major sporting events such as the Super Bowl, NCAA Final Four, Augusta National Golf Tournament and the U.S. Open Tennis Tournament. Towels with college, NBA and NFL team logos, and promotions for commercial products such as soft drinks, beer, fast food chains, etc., are also big sellers.

The firm designs, knits, prints and embroiders towels. The firm knits all the towels it sells and tracks costs for towel production separately from the cost to customize the towels. Seventy-five percent of its orders include logo design, while the balance are print only and require the payment of a license fee for the logo used. However, about 15% of its orders include embroidery. Towels are made in three sizes: regular (18" x 30"), hand (12" x 20") and mid-range (15"x 24"). The normal production cycle for an order of white towels is three days. If a customer wants a colored towel, the basic white towel made by Blue Ridge is sent to a dyeing firm, which extends the production cycle of an order by three days. Also, occasionally, customers order towels in sizes other than the three standard sizes. These towels are called "special".

The firm now produces a "medium" quality towel. They have had some difficulty with the "staying power" of the material printed on these towels, which is attributed to the towel quality, the ink and the printing process. Customers have complained that the ink "lays on the surface" and it cracks and peels off.

Blue Ridge recently made a break-through in developing an ink that soaks into the towel, won't wash out and is non-toxic. A big advantage of this ink is that it avoids EPA disposal requirements because it can be "washed down the drain". Due to these characteristics of its new ink, Blue Ridge is considering upgrading the quality of the basic towel it produces because it will "take" the ink better, both the towel and the ink will last longer and the product will sell at a higher price. If it takes this step, the company will evaluate expanding its marketing and sales area with the objective of "going national".

CUSTOMERS:

Except for a few non-regional chains, Blue Ridge's sales are predominantly in the southeastern states. The company sells its products to 986 different customers. These customers differ primarily in the volume of their purchases, so management classifies each customer in one of three groups: large (8), medium (154) and small (824). Large customers are primarily national chains, small customers are single store operations (including pro shops at golf courses) and medium-sized customers are small chains, large single stores or licensing agents for professional sports teams and manufacturers of consumer products. T-1 gives the product and customer size statistics for 19X2.

Blue Ridge has a different approach to customers in each of its three categories. A small group of in-house sales people sell directly to buyers in the large customer category. Independent manufacturer representatives, on commission, call on the license holder or the manager of a store in the medium customer category. Ads placed in regional and national magazines and newspapers target customers primarily in the small-customer segment, who call or mail in their orders.

Blue Ridge does not give discounts and it ships all orders FOB point of origin.

49

MANUFACTURING:

Blue Ridge has a modern knitting and printing plant in the foothills of North Carolina's Blue Ridge Mountains. Upgrading the facilities over recent years was accompanied by the introduction of an ABC system to determine product costs. The cost accounting system is fairly sophisticated and management has confidence in the accuracy of the manufacturing cost figures for each product line. T-2 shows the firm's unit costs for various items.

Company management is committed to adopting advanced manufacturing techniques such as benchmarking and just-in-time (JIT). The corporate culture necessary for the success of such techniques is evolving and worker empowerment is already a major program. In addition, workers are allowed several hours away from regular work assignments each week for training programs conferring on budgets and work improvements and applying the ABC system.

PERFORMANCE:

The income statement in T-3 shows that the company is profitable. However, management has become concerned about the profitability of the customers in its three customer-size categories—large, medium and small. Different customers demand different levels of support. Management has no basis for identifying customers that generate high profits or to drop those that do not generate enough revenues to cover the expenses to support them. Under the previous accounting system, it wasn't possible to determine the costs of supporting individual customers.

With the introduction of ABC, it now may be possible to determine customer profitability. T-4a shows how the administrative and selling costs are assigned and re-assigned between various functions within the selling and marketing areas and to sub-activities in the selling and marketing areas. T-4b provides a list of selling and marketing activities and the activity base to use in assigning costs to each.

Required:

The managers of Blue Ridge Manufacturing have hired your consulting firm to advise them on the potential of using strategic cost analysis in assessing the profitability of their customer accounts.
Your analysis should include:

1. What is Blue Ridge's competitive strategy?

2. What type of cost system does Blue Ridge use, and is it consistent with their strategy?

3. Develop a spreadsheet analysis which can be used to assess the profitability of the three customer groups of Blue Ridge—large, medium and small customer account sizes. Use the information in Tables 1-4 to trace and allocate the costs necessary for the analysis.

TABLE 1
BLUE RIDGE MANUFACTURING

Product and Customer Size Statistics	Sales in Units by Customer Account Size			
	Large	Medium	Small	Total
Towel: Regular	27,250	16,600	10,550	54,400
Mid-Size	36,640	18,552	10,308	65,500
Hand	35,880	19,966	95,954	151,800
Special	480	3,426	594	4,500
Number of Units Sold	100,250	58,544	117,406	276,200
Number of Units Embroidered	5,959	6,490	29,394	41,842
Number of Units Dyed	20,536	9,935	12,328	42,798
Sales Volume	$308,762	$183,744	$318,024	$810,530
Number of Orders Received	133	845	5,130	6,108
Number of Shipments Made	147	923	5,431	6,501
Number of Invoices Sent	112	754	4,737	5,603
Accounts with Balance >60 Days	1	11	122	134

TABLE 2
BLUE RIDGE MANUFACTURING

Line 1 Direct Manufacturing Costs

	Quantity	Sales Price	Direct Materials	Direct Labor	Factory Overhead	Total
Towels: Regular	54,400	$3.60	$0.60	$0.37	$0.22	$1.19
Mid-Size	65,500	3.20	0.50	0.33	0.20	1.03
Hand	151,800	2.55	0.39	0.31	0.19	0.89
Special	4,500	4.00	0.67	0.48	0.29	1.44

Line 2 Direct Costs of Customizing

	Quantity	Cost	Direct Materials	Direct Labor	Factory Overhead	Total
Inking (based on passes)	552,400	—	$0.0030	$0.0045	$0.0742	$0.0817
Dyeing	42,798	$0.11	—	—	0.0000	0.1100
Embroidery	41,842	—	0.0026	0.1750	1.0994	1.2770

Direct Labor Wage Rate: $9.00 (Including Fringes)
Inking requires one pass for each color used, average two colors per towel.

51

TABLE 3
BLUE RIDGE MANUFACTURING

Income Statement For the Year Ending 19X2

Sales		Quantity Sold	Sales
Product Line: Towels		54,400	$195,840
Regular		65,500	209,600
Mid-Size		151,800	387,090
Hand		4,500	18,000
Special		276,200	$810,530
Less: Cost of Goods Manufactured			
Towels	30.2%	$244,308	
Customizing	12.7%	103,270	
Other Factory	2.1%	17,000	$364,578
Overhead			
Gross Profit	55.1%		$445,952
Less: Selling & Administration			
General Administration	21.0%	$170,000	
Selling Expenses	19.1%	155,000	325,000
Profit Before Taxes			$120,952
Taxes @ 30.0%			36,286
Net Profit, After Taxes			$ 84,666

BLUE RIDGE MANUFACTURING
Balance Sheet at Year-End—19X2

Cash	$ 8,000		
Accounts Receivable	14,200		
Inventory	26,000		
Equipment (Net)	174,000		
Buildings (Net)	245,900		
			$468,100
Accounts Payable	$ 28,000		
Loans	115,100	$143,100	
Stockholder's Equity	$240,000		
Retained Earnings	85,000	$325,000	$468,100

TABLE 4A
BLUE RIDGE MANUFACTURING

Costs Incurred in Each Function (Shipping, Sales, Marketing)

	Total	Shipping	Sales	Marketing	Other	Total Assigned
Administration	$170,000	$ 17,000	$ 37,400	$20,400	$ 56,100	$130,900
Selling	155,000	15,500	117,800	9,300	12,400	155,000
		$ 32,500	$155,200	$29,700	$ 68,500	$285,900

Selling and Administrative Activities:	Each function is used for the Following Activities, in Percent:			
	Shipping	Sales	Marketing	Other
Entering Purchase Orders		55		10
Commissions		10		
Shipping Activities	65			15
Invoicing				20
Cost to Make Sales Calls		30		10
Checking Credit				10
Samples, Catalog Info.	5		10	
Special Handling Charges	5			5
Distribution Management	10		10	
Marketing, by Customer Type		5		
Advertising/Promotion			30	
Marketing	15		50	5
Administrative Office Support				20
Licenses, Fees				5
	100	100	100	100

TABLE 4B
BLUE RIDGE MANUFACTURING

Cost Drivers for Allocating Costs of Activities to Customer Groups (Large, Medium, Small)

Activity	Cost Driver
Entering Purchase Orders	Number of Orders
Commissions	Direct
Shipping Activities	Number of Shipments
Invoicing	Number of Invoices
Cost to Make Sales Calls	Direct
Checking Credit	Percent Accounts >60 Days
Samples, Catalog Info.	Sales Dollars
Special Handling Charges	Management Estimate[1]
Distribution Management	Sales Dollars
Marketing, by Customer Type	Sales Dollars
Advertising/Promotion	Management Estimate[2]
Marketing	Number of Units Sold[3]
Administrative Office Support	Number of Units Sold[4]
Licenses, Fees	Direct

[1]20% to medium-sized customers; 80% to small-sized customers.
[2]25% to medium-sized customers; 75% to small-sized customers.
[3]Excluding Specials
[4]Excluding Specials

4-2. Centerior Energy Corporation

The challenge of operating efficiently is spelled out in the rate agreement. Our interim goal is to reduce annual operation and maintenance expense (other than fuel and purchased power) by $40 million to $100 million by 1991. No Company activity is off limits where cost cutting is concerned, except where cost-cutting would reduce the quality of our service to customers or endanger our employees or the public.

(From Centerior Energy Corporation 1988 Annual report)

BACKGROUND

Centerior Energy Corporation was created in 19X5 as a holding company for the Cleveland Electric Illumination Company (CEI) and Toledo Edison (TEd). CEI and TEd are electric utilities serving market areas in northeastern and northwestern Ohio, respectively. As a result of the formation of Centerior Energy, Centerior Service Company was formed to provide administrative and engineering services to CEI and TEd. Centerior Energy Corporation and Centerior Service Company operate under the rules and regulations of the SEC for public utility holding companies; Centerior Service Company, CEI, and TEd are regulated by the Federal Energy Regulatory Commission (FERC) and the Public Utilities Commission of the State of Ohio (PUCO).

The rate agreement referred to in the above excerpt became effective on February 1, 19X9. Additional rate increases were to follow in 19Y0 and 19Y1. The PUCO attached to this rate agreement a requirement that Centerior Energy not only establish fair and reasonable productivity standards for generating units but also reduce the costs of operating and maintaining the units' generating capacity. After the February 1, 19X9 rate increase, CEI's and TEd's prices to residential customers for 500 kilowatt-hours of service were $10.10 and $11.30 per kilowatt-hour, respectively. (See T-1 for a chart of typical electric billings as of January 1, 19X9 in selected northern cities.)

Although revenues had increased since 19X6, operating income at Centerior had decreased, due principally to growth in operation and maintenance expense as well as in depreciation and amortization. Centerior was especially concerned about managing the operation and maintenance expense because of its dramatic recent growth and its immediate demands for cash for current operating purposes. (See T-2 for three years' comparative results of operations for Centerior Energy.)

ACCOUNTING SYSTEMS

In the early 19X0s, TEd had developed concepts for activity accounting that accumulated costs at a relatively low level of aggregation to activities such as maintaining poles, operating boilers, and replacing transformers. In addition, TEd had developed allocation systems that assigned indirect costs on the basis of standards which reflected flexible activity levels. TEd's accounting system had been in place for about 35 years without major changes. Upper, middle, and lower management had become accustomed to managing their activities using reports that captured costs at the activity level.

CEI's accounting system, on the other hand, captured costs at a much higher level of aggregation. It was used to control labor and material costs at the operating department level on a monthly basis. These costs were assigned directly to departments rather than to activities. Indirect costs were accumulated at headquarters and allocated monthly to the operating departments. First-line managers were unaccustomed to receiving cost reports from the accounting system. For the most part, the accounting and work management systems were not compatible with each other. Accounting cost information was provided only to executive and middle management.

55

The manner in which the two operating companies budgeted for costs differed dramatically, reflecting differences in the cost systems. TEd's budget was prepared by estimating activity levels throughout the entire organization for the budget period. Costs were subsequently traced to activities across departmental lines. CEI budgeted at the department level, without the same emphasis on tracing the impact of one department's operating decisions on other units of the company.

MANAGEMENT ACCOUNTING RESPONSE

"There were really two parts of our charge to create a new accounting system for Centerior Energy," explained Jack Flick, the corporation's Manager of Accounting Systems. "First, as our part of the company-wide commitment to reduce operating costs, we were expected to implement a system or systems that would streamline the accounting functions within Centerior. Prior to the rate agreement there were 45 accountants at Centerior Service, 180 at CEI, and 65 at TEd, for a total of 290. Top management challenged us to create and implement a corporation-wide accounting system that would reduce that number.

"Second, the PUCO placed a challenge before us to manage our costs more effectively. To do that we had to think in terms of an overall cost management system that would satisfy the regulatory requirements. Our biggest hurdle was the immense difference in cost management traditions in the two operating companies, CEI and Toledo Edison. Even though Toledo Edison's system was based on concepts which we believed to be sound, its age—about 35 years—and its dedicated computer system—which was pretty inflexible—presented very real problems. It was not possible to make adjustments to the old system in order to fix it adequately for the 19Y0s.

"CEI was entirely different. Its accounting system was even older and conceptually never had reached the level of costing activities. Especially difficult for us were the problems created by the system of cost allocation. For example, repair departments were allocated actual costs of the warehouse on a monthly basis according to the number of actual requisitions. That meant that everybody tried to requisition warehouse items in the busy summer months and avoid requisitions in the winter when little work was done. Repair units would inflate their requisitions in the summer and stockpile parts. This is only one of a multitude of ways in which the costing system created management problems."

REQUIRED:

1. Based on the brief description of CEI's and TEd's accounting systems, identify their cost objects. How does any difference in cost objects relate to management control and cost management problems that may arise from the affiliation of the two companies?

2. Should accounting systems remain decentralized to the operating companies or be centralized at Centerior Service Company?

3. What are the benefits and costs of an activity-based approach to cost attribution, budgeting, and management performance evaluation throughout Centerior Energy?

TABLE 1
TYPICAL ELECTRIC BILLINGS RESIDENTIAL
PRICES PER KWH (JANUARY 1, 19X9)

New York	$.1272
Philadelphia	.1235
Akron	.1137
Gary	.1076
Pittsburgh	.1051
Newark, NJ	.1050
Chicago	.1014
Toledo*	.1001
Hartford	.0993
Cleveland*	.0927
Boston	.0884
Detroit	.0877
Buffalo	.0846
Dayton	.0828
Erie	.0812
Baltimore	.0751
Milwaukee	.0741
Columbus	.0718
Cincinnati	.0711
Washington, D.C.	.0507

TABLE 2
CENTERIOR ENERGY CORPORATION
RESULTS OF OPERATIONS

	For the years ended December 31,		
	19X8	19X7	19X6
Operating Revenues:			
Electric	$2,037,560	$1,911,985	$1,882,838
Steam heating	—	13,371	12,953
	$2,037,560	$1,925,356	$1,895,791
Operating Expenses:			
Fuel and purchased power	391,401	470,466	522,281
Other operation and maintenance	865,632	642,594	550,874
Depreciation and amortization	264,824	214,421	141,009
Taxes, other than federal income taxes	268,550	207,521	194,925
Perry Unit 1 and Beaver Valley Unit 2 deferred operating expenses	(188,209)	(87,623)	—
Federal income taxes	123,697	105,912	138,181
	1,725,895	1,553,291	1,547,270
Operating Income	$ 311,665	$ 372,065	$ 348,521

4-3. Tektronix

BACKGROUND

Tektronix, Inc. headquartered in Portland, Oregon, is a world leader in the production of electronic test and measurement instruments. The company's principal product since its founding in 1946 has been the oscilloscope (scope), an instrument that measures and graphically displays electronic signals. The two divisions of the Portables Group produce and market high and medium-performance portable scopes.

Tektronix experienced almost uninterrupted growth through the 1970s based on a successful strategy of providing technical excellence in the scope market and continually improving its products in terms of both functionality and performance for the dollar. In the early 1980s, however, the lower priced end of the division's medium-performance line of scopes was challenged by an aggressive low-price strategy of several Japanese competitors. Moving in from the low-price, low-performance market segment in which Tektronix had decided not to compete, these companies set prices 25 percent below the U.S. firm's prevailing prices. Rather than moving up the scale to more highly differentiated products, the group management decided to block the move.

The first step was to reduce the prices of higher-performance, higher-cost scopes to the prices of the competitors' scopes of lower performance. This short-term strategy resulted in reported losses for those instruments. The second step was to put in place a new management team whose objective was to turn the business around. These managers concluded that, contrary to conventional wisdom, the Portables Group divisions could compete successfully with foreign competition on a cost basis. To do so, the divisions would have to reduce costs and increase customer value by increasing operational efficiency.

PRODUCTION PROCESS CHANGES

The production process in the Portables Group divisions consisted of many functional islands, including etched circuit board (ECB) insertion, ECB assembly, ECB testing, ECB repair, final assembly, test, thermal cycle, test/QC, cabinet fitting, finishing, boxing for shipment, and shipment. The new management team consolidated these functionally-oriented activities into integrated production lines in open work spaces that allow visual control of the entire production area. Parts inventory areas were also placed parallel to production lines so that at each work station operators would be able to pull their own parts. This in essence created an early warning system that nearly eliminated line stoppages due to stockouts.

Additional steps that were taken in the early to mid 1980s to solve managerial and technical problems include implementation of just-in-time (JIT) delivery and scheduling techniques and total quality control (TQC), movement of manufacturing support departments into the production area, and implementation of people involvement (PI) techniques to move responsibility for problem solving down to the operating level of the divisions. The results of these changes were impressive: substantial reductions in cycle time, direct labor hours per unit, and inventory, and increases in output dollars per person per day and operating income. The cost accounting group had dutifully measured these improvements, but had not effectively supported the strategic direction of the divisions.

COST ACCOUNTING SYSTEM

DIRECT MATERIALS AND DIRECT LABOR

The total manufacturing cost of the newest portable scopes produced with the latest technologies has 75% direct materials, 3% direct labor, and 22% factory overhead. In most cases, direct materials and direct labor are easily traced to specific products for costing purposes. Prior to the mid 1980s, however, the divisions' attempts to control direct labor had been a resource drain that actually *decreased* productivity.

There were approximately twenty-five production cost centers in the Portable Instruments Plant. Very detailed labor efficiency reports were prepared monthly for each cost center and each major step in the production process. In addition, an efficiency rating for each individual employee was computed daily. Employees reported the quantity of units produced and the time required to produce them, often overestimating the quantity produced to show improved efficiency against continually updated standards. The poor quality of collected data resulted in semi-annual inventory-downs when physical and book quantities were compared.

"The inadequacy of our efficiency reporting system became clear when we analyzed one of our new JIT production lines," commented Michael Wright, Financial Systems Application Manager. "On a JIT manufacturing line, once the excess inventory has been flushed out, it is essentially impossible for any person to work faster or slower than the line moves. However, if one person on the line is having a problem, it immediately becomes apparent because the product flow on the line stops. Corrective action is then taken, and the line is started up again.

"On that line, the system told us that the efficiency of each of the workers was decreasing. However, stepping back from the detail of the situation allowed us to look at the overall picture. We found that the costs incurred on the line were going down and its product output was going up. Obviously, it was becoming more, not less, efficient."

The quantity of direct labor data collected and processed also was a problem. Production employees often spent twenty minutes per day completing required reports when they could have been producing output. Additionally, the accounting staff was processing 35,000 labor transactions per month to account for what amounted to 3 percent of total manufacturing cost.

"Transactions cost money," observed John Jonez, Group Cost Accounting Manager, "and lots of transactions cost lots of money."

In response to these problems, the group accounting staff greatly simplified its procedures. It abandoned the measurement of labor performance for each operation, and greatly reduced the number of variances reported. The number of monthly labor transactions fell to less than 70, allowing the staff to spend more time on factory overhead allocation and other pressing issues.

FACTORY OVERHEAD

The product costing system allocated all factory overhead costs to products based on standard direct labor hours. A separate rate was computed for each manufacturing cost center. This system led to rapidly increasing rates: the direct labor content of the group's products had been continually decreasing for years, while factory overhead costs were increasing in absolute terms.

"Because the costing system correlated overhead to labor, our engineers concluded that the way to reduce overhead costs was to reduce labor," commented Jonez. "The focus of cost reduction programs therefore had been the elimination of direct labor. However, most of this effort was misdirected, because there was almost no correlation between overhead cost incurrence and direct labor hours worked. Our system penalized products with proportionately higher direct labor, but it wasn't those products that caused overhead costs. We proved that. We attacked direct labor and it went down, but at the same time overhead went up.

"We therefore knew that we needed a new way to allocate overhead. More fundamentally, we needed a way for the cost accounting system to support the manufacturing strategy of our group. The objective was clear-to provide management with accounting information that would be useful in identifying cost reduction opportunities in its operating decisions as well as provide a basis for effective reporting of accomplishments."

APPROACH TO METHOD CHANGE

Initial Steps

The first step taken by Wright and Jonez in developing a new overhead allocation method was to establish a set of desirable characteristics for the method. They decided that it must accurately assign costs to products, thus providing better support for management decisions than the old method. It must support the JIT manufacturing strategy of the Portables Group. It also must be intuitively logical and easily understandable by management. And finally, it must provide information that is accessible by decision makers.

The next step was to interview the engineering and manufacturing managers who were the primary users of product cost information. These users were asked, "What is it that makes your job more difficult? What is it that makes certain products more difficult to manufacture? What causes the production line to slow down? What is it that causes overhead?" The answers to these questions were remarkably consistent-there were too many unique part numbers in the system. This finding revealed a major flaw in the ability of the direct labor-based costing method to communicate information critical for cost-related decisions. Manufacturing managers realized there were substantial cost reduction opportunities through the standardization of component parts, but there was no direct method to communicate this idea to design and cost-reduction engineers who made part selection decisions.

Although difficult to quantify, some costs are associated with just carrying a part number in the database. Each part number must be originally set up in the system, built into the structure of a bill of materials, and maintained until it is no longer used. Moreover, each part must be planned, scheduled, negotiated with vendors, purchased, received, stored, moved, and paid for. Having two parts similar enough that one could be used for both applications requires unnecessary duplication of these activities, and therefore unnecessary costs.

Standardizing parts results in several indirect benefits. Fewer unique part numbers usually means fewer vendors and greater quality of delivered parts. It also means smoother JIT production, fewer shutdowns of manufacturing lines, and greater field reliability. These observations led to a preliminary consensus on the need to develop a product costing method that would quantify and communicate the value of parts standardization.

COST ANALYSIS

"To confirm our assessment," stated Jonez, "we segmented the total manufacturing overhead cost pool. The costs of all cost centers comprising the pool were categorized as either materials-related or conversion-related based upon rules developed in conjunction with operating managers.(See T-1)

"Material-related costs pertain to procurement, scheduling, receiving, incoming inspection, stockroom personnel, cost-reduction engineering, and information systems. Conversion-related costs are associated with direct labor, manufacturing supervision, and process-related engineering. Application of the rules resulted in an approximately 55/45 split between materials overhead (MOH) and conversion overhead (COH). This finding further confirmed the inadequacy of the existing method, which applied all overhead based on direct labor."

The accounting analysts decided to focus their initial efforts on the MOH pool. To improve their understanding of the composition of the pool and thus assist them in developing a method for its allocation, Wright and Jonez consulted operating managers and further segmented it into:

1. Costs due to the value of parts,

2. Costs due to the absolute number of parts used,

3. Costs due to the maintenance and handling of each different part number and

4. Costs due to each use of a different part number.

The managers believed that the majority of MOH costs were of type (3). The costs due to the value of parts (1) and the frequency of the use of parts (2 and 4) categories were considered quite small by comparison.

The analysts therefore concluded that the material-related costs of the Portables Group would decrease if a smaller number of different part numbers were used in its products. This cost reduction would result from two factors. First, greater volume discounts would be realized by purchasing larger volumes of fewer unique parts. Second, material overhead costs would be lower. "It was the latter point that we wanted our new allocation method to focus on," commented Wright.

"Our goal," continued Jonez, "was to increase customer value by reducing overhead costs. Our strategy was parts standardization. We needed a tactic to operationalize the strategy."

(IMA Case)

REQUIRED:

1. Using assumed numbers, develop a cost allocation method for materials overhead (MOH) to quantify and communicate the strategy of parts standardization.

2. Explain how use of your method would support the strategy.

3. Is any method which applies the entire MOH cost pool on the basis of one cost driver sufficiently accurate for product decisions in the highly competitive portable scope markets? Explain.

4. Are MOH product costing rates developed for management reporting appropriate for inventory valuation for external reporting? Why or why not?

Table 1
Rules for Overhead Segmentation by Cost Center Classification
(1) *Production.* The overhead costs of any cost center containing direct labor employees are assigned 100 percent to the COH pool.
(2) *Group/Division/Product Group Support.* The total costs of any manufacturing staff cost center are assigned 50 percent to the COH pool and 50 percent to the MOH pool.
(3) *Group/Division/Product Group Support.* The total costs of any manufacturing support cost center (e.g., Material Management of Information Systems) are assigned 100 percent to the MOH pool.
(4) *Manufacturing Cost-Reduction Engineering.* The total costs of any cost reduction engineering cost center are assigned 100 percent to the MOH pool.
(5) *Manufacturing Process-Related Engineering.* The total costs of any process-related engineering cost center are assigned 100 percent to the COH pool.

How ABC Changed the Post Office

To meet its competition, the U.S. Postal Service had to change and offer customers credit/debit card service.

By Terrell L. Carter; Ali M. Sedghat, CMA; and Thomas D. Williams

The U.S. Postal Service is a unique federal entity in several respects. First, the USPS, in essence, operates in a manner similar to many private sector companies. The USPS provides a variety of services, generates revenues from these services and incurs costs and expenses as a result of its operations. Second, the USPS is unique in that it is open to private sector competition. Competition includes companies such as Federal Express, United Parcel Service, Mail Boxes Etc., and a host of other similar companies. Few other government agencies or departments operate in a similar business environment.

Retailers as well as USPS competitors have long accepted credit cards as payment options for goods and services. Moreover, new technologies are beginning to lead to a "cashless" world. Customers are seeking convenience and value, while businesses are striving for increased sales and guaranteed payment. Given the competitive forces facing the USPS and the rapid pace at which new technologies are becoming available, USPS management realized that it had to use innovative business methods to maintain and increase its market share against its competition and provide increased value to its customers while ensuring cost effectiveness.

Based on this evaluation of its position in the marketplace, the USPS engaged Coopers & Lybrand (C&L) to conduct activity-based cost studies of its key revenue collection processes and market strategy study for a na-

tional credit card and debit card program. To obtain an understanding of the cash, check, and credit/debit card activities, C&L reviewed USPS data and procedure manuals, interviewed USPS headquarters staff, and conducted telephone surveys of front window supervisors and district office accounting personnel. Using an activity-based cost modeling approach, C&L defined the cash and check process in terms of the activities that link together to make the processes. C&L also identified unit, batch, and product sustaining activities; resources for each of the activities; and the transaction volumes for each activity. Unit activity was the acceptance and processing of a payment by item. Batch activities involved close-out at the end of the day, consolidation, and supervisory review. Product activities included maintenance charges for bank accounts and deposit reconciliation (cash and checks) and terminal maintenance and training (credit and debit cards).

After building the cash and check cost models, C&L defined activity-based costs for the credit and debit card activities similarly. The components of the

TABLE 1
ANALYSIS OF ACTIVITIES

Cash Process Activities	Credit/Debit Card Activities	Check Process Activities
1. Receive cash	1. Process card transactions	1. Receive checks
2. Deposit cash	2. Close out point-of-sale (POS) terminal	2. Deposit checks
3. Maintain bank accounts (including cash concentration and funds mobilization)	3. Reconcile credit and debit card receipts	3. Maintain bank accounts (including cash concentration and funds mobilization)
4. Reconcile bank accounts	4. Process chargebacks	4. Reconcile bank accounts
	5. Maintain POS and telecommunications equipment	

Note: Cash is handled by USPS employees four times: 1. By the clerk when accepting payment from a customer. 2. By the clerk when counting the cash in the drawer daily. 3. By a supervisor when counting the cash before the bank deposit. 4. By another supervisor when counting the cash to verify before the deposit.

TABLE 2a
ACTIVITY-BASED COST MODEL FOR CASH PROCESSES

Unit Activities	Driver	Cost per Driver	Driver Quantities	Annual Cost
Accept cash	Number of cash transactions	$0.49	921,881,239	$451,173,288
Processing of cash by bank	Number of cash transactions	0.02	921,881,239	19,974,271
Batch Activities				
Close-out and supervisor review of clerk	Number of close-outs	5.79	28,029,443	162,255,662
Consolidation and deposit of unit's receipts	Number of deposits	16.16	9,902,381	160,016,636
Review and transfer funds-time	Number of accounts	1,884.47	7,490	14,114,698
Product Activities				
Maintenance charges for bank accounts	Number of accounts	114.32	7,490	856,286
Reconciling bank accounts	Number of accounts	1,935.94	7,490	14,500,182
	TOTAL COST			**$822,891,023**

TABLE 2b.
ACTIVITY-BASED COST MODEL FOR CHECK PROCESSES

Unit Activities	Driver	Cost per Driver	Driver Quantities	Annual Cost
Accept checks	Number of checks	$0.98	120,173,780	$117,627,298
Processing of checks by bank	Number of checks	0.06	120,173,780	7,335,089
Processing of returned checks	Number of bad checks	25.16	143,436	3,608,400
Batch Activities				
Close-out and supervisor review of clerk	Number of close-outs	2.67	28,029,443	74,887,229
Consolidation and deposit of unit's receipts	Number of deposits	2.07	9,902,381	20,505,861
Review and transfer funds-time	Number of accounts	250.20	7,490	1,873,980
Product Activities				
Maintenance charges for bank accounts	Number of accounts	14.91	7,490	111,641
Reconciling bank accounts	Number of accounts	251.80	7,490	1,185,971
	TOTAL COST			**$227,135,469**

cash, check, and credit/debit card activities are shown in T-1. The activity cost models for the cash and check activities are shown in T-2. The activity-based cost models for the credit card and debit card activities are shown in Table 3. C&L also conducted product pricing and profitability analyses of the credit/debit card test program.

In analyzing data from Phase 1 of the USPS credit card and debit card test market plan and the organizational costs associated with serving USPS customers through its 28,728 post office, 9,059 stations and branches, and 1,605 community postal units, C&L identified the following issues affecting costs, product pricing, competitiveness, and customer value.[1]

1. USPS provides a limited assortment of payment options relative to the competition:

- Cash and check payments are predominant USPS payment options,

- Competitors provide credit card payment options, and

- Most USPS transactions must occur at a post office

2. USPS generates a large volume of low-value cash transactions:

- The majority of transactions are $20 or less, and

- Transactions on a per-dollar basis are expensive to process.

3. USPS' check receipts processing is costly:

63

TABLE 3a
ACTIVITY-BASED COST MODEL FOR CREDIT CARD PROCESSES

Unit Activities	Driver	Cost per Driver	Driver Quantities	Annual Cost
Process credit card	Number of credit transactions	$0.80	357,796	$287,217
Payment of credit card fee	$ size of transactions	0.01	18,512,365	252,474
Processing chargebacks	Number of chargebacks	23.87	120	2,865
Batch Activities				
Close-out terminal	Number of close-outs	1.30	160,596	208,581
Reconciling daily receipts—district	Number of stations	65.84	1,500	98,767
Process from 1908	Number of 1908s	9.04	2,884	26,072
Product Activities				
Maintain equipment	Number of terminals	275.60	1,875	516,754
Training	Number of districts	22,311.84	5	111,559
	TOTAL COST			$1,504,289

TABLE 3b
ACTIVITY-BASED COST MODEL FOR DEBIT CARD PROCESSES

Unit Activities	Driver	Cost per Driver	Driver Quantities	Annual Cost
Process debit card	Number of debit transactions	$0.86	35,262	$30,260
Batch Activities				
Close-out terminal	Number of close-outs	0.12	160,596	19,746
Reconciling daily receipts—district	Number of stations	6.24	1,500	9,359
Process from 1908	Number of 1908s	0.86	2,884	2,470
Product Activities				
Maintain equipment	Number of terminals	26.11	1,875	48,965
Training	Number of districts	2,114.16	5	10,571
	TOTAL COST			$121,371

- Extra steps are required,

- Additional bank charges are incurred, and

- $3-$4 million is lost to bed checks.

4. Policies and procedures are not consistent.

5. Based on independent surveys, cash, check, and credit/debit card processes are not uniform.

PROJECTED COST MODEL FOR USPS

The ABC study also revealed hidden and indirect costs for each of the payment activities. Combining all of the costs resulted in the breakdown shown in T-4. C&L pointed out that "total incremental costs for a national credit/debit card program are immaterial in rela-

tion to total USPS payment processing costs that exceed $1 billion per year, based on the activity-based cost study data collected through the February/March 1994 time frame."[2] The cost data showed that the net benefit of accepting credit and debit cards would be negative through 1997. Projections showed that from

TABLE 4
PROCESSING COSTS

Activity Processing of		Cost Per Dollar Processed	
Cash	$20	$.045	$.048
Checks	$51	$.038	$.040
Credit Cards	$52	$.081	$.027
Debit Cards	$49	$.071	$.015

1998 through 2000, the net benefits of card acceptance would be $5.2 million, $15.6 million, and $28.8 million, respectively (see T-5).

In summarizing these findings, C&L reported that, "Credit and debit card processing costs are relatively high at the moment due to the normal impact of process start-up, low initial volume and high initial implementation costs. However, as volumes continue to grow, projected credit and debit card costs can become competitive with current cash and check processing costs."[3] C&L also reported that "credit and debit card processing costs for retail window transactions becomes cost effective once total card revenue exceeds 3%-4% of total revenues from retail transactions. As card volume continues to displace cash and check transactions, card costs become even more advantageous."[4]

TABLE 5
PROJECTED COST MODEL

Base Line	1994	1995	1996	1997	1998	1999	2000
Cash	822,856,044	879,004,435	938,710,365	1,003,001,968	1,071,923,013	1,145,819,941	1,225,066,230
Check	227,789,177	242,987,911	259,731,645	277,371,596	296,274,358	316,534,152	338,252,449
Total Cost	1,050,645,221	1,121,992,346	1,198,442,010	1,280,373,564	1,368,197,371	1,462,354,093	1,563,318,679
Card Program							
Cash	822,856,044	867,786,033	899,084,296	933,386,322	967,692,345	1,001,794,407	1,035,444,902
Check	227,789,177	238,356,354	250,021,816	259,526,699	269,039,899	278,505,217	287,864,197
Credit	1,511,405	18,948,017	46,924,315	69,641,084	96,614,272	127,254,140	161,39,635
Debit	125,709	3,112,999	13,839,778	21,074,881	29,567,163	39,187,991	49,833,387
Total Cost	1,052,282,335	1,128,203,403	1,209,870,205	1,283,628,986	1,362,913,679	1,446,741,755	1,534,482,121
Net Benefit (Cost)	(1,637,114)	(6,211,057)	(11,428,195)	(3,255,422)	5,283,692	15,612,238	28,836,558

COST PER DOLLAR

Base Line	1994	1995	1996	1997	1998	1999	2000
Cash	0.045	0.042	0.044	0.043	0.042	0.042	0.042
Check	0.037	0.035	0.036	0.036	0.036	0.035	0.035
Card Program							
Cash	0.045	0.042	0.045	0.045	0.045	0.046	0.047
Check	0.037	0.036	0.037	0.038	0.038	0.039	0.039
Credit	0.082	0.035	0.033	0.029	0.028	0.027	0.027
Debit	0.073	0.023	0.021	0.017	0.016	0.015	0.015

Note: The 1994 Model Totals were higher than actual Phase 1 Cost Models due to the incremental start-up costs of the national program. C&L stressed that data for this model would be subject to change as new data and information become available, and for the model to continue to be useful, it would have to be updated on a periodic basis to reflect ongoing program management modification.

COOPERS & LYBRAND'S RECOMMENDATION

Based on its analysis of the market test, a Gallup survey and market trends, C&L recommended that the USPS use a three-phase strategy to implement a national policy of accepting both credit and debit cards: Phase I—Market Test (which was already completed); Phase II—Mobilize and Market; Phase III—Modify,

Mobilize and market. This two-step phase began with an aggressive mobilization effort to implement nationwide acceptance of credit and debit cards for selected USPS products and services at retail windows beginning with larger offices. The potential benefits were identified as increased customer satisfaction, increased sales, and improved processing efficiency. The second step was an aggressive targeted marketing campaign designed to increase credit card usage at USPS retail windows. "Studies indicate that a targeted marketing campaign can have significant impact on consumer use of debit and credit cards. A recent study concluded that the value of increased sales more than covered the additional expense of advertising."[5] The potential benefits identified were increased credit/debit card volume, increased total sales, and reduced transaction costs.

Modify. This phase entailed implementing improved credit/debit card processing technology and procedures to increase the benefits and continue to reduce the costs of the national card program. C&L recommended installing online point-of-sale terminals and consolidating all card authorization and transaction processing. The national implementation would use standalone card verification terminals, and this phase would replace them with integrated equipment. The potential benefits identified would be improved processing efficiency, reduced processing costs, reduced transaction errors and rejects, and improved management information.

TABLE 6				
Through March 1997	Total Number of Transactions	Total Dollar Transactions	Average Ticket	Total Chargebacks*
Credit Cards	26,494,680	$1,276,263,936	$48	$61,723
Debit Cards	2,251,720	$ 118,529,332	$53	n/a

*Chargebacks are charges that customers dispute, which, after investigating, the card companies reverse. This becomes n expense to the merchant

THE BOARD APPROVES CARDS

Senior postal management decided on the basis of the C&L analysis and a decision analysis report (DAR) prepared by USPS Finance to propose to the USPS Board of Governors ("Board") that credit and debit cards be accepted nationally at USPS retail windows. Management recommended an aggressive two-year implementation. By the end of the second year, 33,000 post offices would be equipped with 50,000 card terminals and trained USPS personnel.[6] The DAR provided the following breakdown:

Expense investment (50,000 card terminals)
$25,893,000
Installation expense   3,825,000

Total investment (fiscal years 1995 and 1996)
$29,718,000
Operating costs in first full year (FY 97) $30,327,000

Customer service initiative with no claimed ROI

Potential cost savings and revenue enhancements not included.

It is important to note the last two points. The program, while virtually ensuring an ROI and cost savings, was not being proposed for the financial benefits. Instead, as USPS CFO Michael J. Riley said in his presentation to the Board, "It is important to note that

this is a customer service initiative which does not attempt to claim a return on investment. This is in spite of the fact that many retailers report savings from processing less currency and checks, as well as increased revenue from offering this growing retail payment option. We base our DAR on increased customer satisfaction."[7] In October 1994, the Board unanimously approved the proposal without any modifications.

THE ROLL-OUT

The next stop after Board approval was to get a contract in place for a credit card processor and a vendor to supply the 50,000 card terminals. A contract was competitively awarded the following spring to NationsBank with NaBanco, a national card processor, as its subcontractor.[8] NaBanco also would supply the terminals under a contract it had with a manufacturer in Atlanta, Microbilt, Inc. In April 1995, the roll-out began.

Since April 1995, the program has broadened in scope to include phone and mail orders for stamps including philately and vending machines. Because of demand, the contract recently was modified to increase the number of card terminals shipped to more than 67,000. From a customer service perspective, credit and debit card acceptance has been a runaway success, and even with such an aggressive implementation schedule it has been difficult to satisfy demand.

This project has been a very successful customer-driven initiative. Since the roll-out began, there have been more than 300 positive news articles covering this program. Not only do customers enjoy the convenience and flexibility of not having to carry as much cash, but USPS retail window clerks, who feel safer because there is less cash in their drawers, benefit as well. USPS clerks also like card acceptance because card transactions are more accurate than counting cash, so their liability is minimized.[9]

The USPS benefits because it gets funds the next day from card transactions at a very competitive discount rate. The payment infrastructure created by card acceptance has helped the USPS launch new products and market tests more quickly. Starting credit card acceptance later benefited the Postal Service because it could add debit card acceptance at the same time with one roll-out rather than two. The USPS is now the nation's largest debit card acceptor. The program has been highly successful in all of its aims, as these important statistics show (see T-6).

See Fig 1 for the growth trends in transaction and dollar-volume.

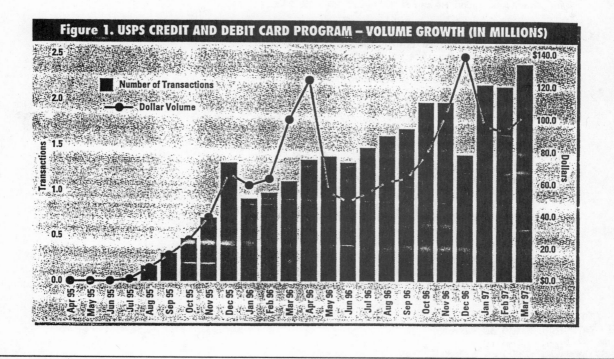

Figure 1. USPS CREDIT AND DEBIT CARD PROGRAM – VOLUME GROWTH (IN MILLIONS)

AS EASY AS ABC: MAXIMIZING VALUE

The popularity of activity-based costing and activity-based management is growing. In the private sector, hundreds of companies have adopted activity-based costing and management approaches to cost finding and cost accounting. These range from manufacturers such as John Deere to service firms such as American Express. Many have gone a step further and adopted activity-based management approaches.

Now, local and national public sector organizations are beginning to apply activity-based costing and activity-based management to the task of reinventing government. These organizations range from the road maintenance department in Indianapolis to enormous federal agencies such as the USPS as described here.

Earlier attempts at improving government operations have been largely unsuccessful. Activity-based costing and activity-based management approaches are allowing these government organizations to discover and take advantage of four elements missing from earlier performance improvement attempts. They include:

- Financial and performance information systems that enable and encourage managers to make strategic process improvements that maximize value to customers and taxpayers.
- A management and organizational structure built around processes or how the work gets done in an organization.
- A strategy for managing the human aspects of changing from a static bureaucracy to a dynamic, improvement-driven organization.
- A common financial and managerial language for different parts of an organization and all of a government's agencies.

Activity-based costing approaches are ever evolving. Nearly every organization applying these approaches discovers new uses. They go far beyond ABC's original purpose of calculating accurate product costs, all the way to activity-based management, a comprehensive management approach. The case of the USPS's national credit card and debit card program provides an excellent example of how effective activity-based approaches can be in facilitating strategic process improvements that maximize value to customers while ensuring economic viability and cost effectiveness.■

Terrell L. Carter is assistant treasurer, payment technologies, for the United States Postal Service. A 28-year career employee., Terry holds a B.S. degree in Computer Information Systems from Strayer College, Washington, D.C. and is an executive MBA fellow at Loyola College in Maryland. He is a member of the Treasury Management Association. He can be reached at (202) 268-2330.

Ali M. Sedaghat, CMA, DBA, KPMG Faculty Alumni Fellow, is an associate of accounting at Loyola College in Maryland. He earned his B.A. degree from Abadan Institute of Technology and MBA and DBA degrees from The George Washington University. He is a member of IMA's Baltimore Chapter, through which this article was submitted.

Thomas D. Williams is the financial management officer for the National Institute of Allergy and Infectious Diseases at the National Institutes of Health. A 15-year career employee of the federal government, Tom has extensive experience in domestic and international governmental budgeting, accounting, finance, and management. Tom is also an executive MBA fellow at Loyola College in Maryland.

Authors acknowledge valuable contributions by Julie Jack, Julie Moore, and Matthew Wong.

---

[1] "United States Postal Service Credit/Debit Card Strategy—Final Report," Coopers & Lybrand L.L.P., Washington, D.C., April 19, 1994, p. 8.

[2] Ibid., page 37.

[3] Ibid., page 3.

[4] Ibid., page 12.

[5] Ibid., page 31.

[6] 6,000 "contract" stations would not be included in the two-year implementation.

[7] "Credit-Debit Card Acceptance at the Retail Window," presentation to the Board of Governors, October 3, 1994.

[8] NaBanco is now First Data Merchant Services (FDMS).

[9] USPS window clerks must compensate the USPS for shortages, so errors in cash handling are costly to them.

Chapter 5
Target Costing, Theory of Constraints, and Life Cycle Costing

Cases
5-1   California-Illini Manufacturing (The Theory of Constraints)
5-2   Constraint Analysis

Readings

George Schmelze, Rolf Geier, and Thomas E. Buttross: **Target Costing at ITT Automotive**

This article provides a good example of an actual application of target costing. The example is of the production and sale of brake systems, an intensely competitive industry. The article explains how value engineering is used. Two important concepts of the article are (1) target costing is a moving target, and as prices fall in the industry, target costs and manufacturing costs are required to fall as well, and (2) target costing is a bottom-up, team-oriented process that requires cross-functional teams. Also, the article explains how ITT uses "tracking sheets" to manage the life cycle costs of the product.

Discussion Questions:
1. How are prices set at ITT Automotive?
2. How does ITT Automotive obtain information about a competitor's costs?
3. What are the target costing tools used at ITT Automotive?
4. How is the tracking sheet used in ITT Automotive's target costing system?

Cases

5-1. California-Illini Manufacturing

The California-Illini Manufacturing Company's (CI) plant operates in the rural central valley of California. It is family-owned and run. CI's plant manager, a grandson of the founder, went to school with many of the employees. Despite this family atmosphere, CI is the largest producer of plain and hard-faced replacement tillage tools in the United States. It averages annual sales of $13 million. Farmers use tillage tools to cultivate the land. Hard-facing, the application of brazed chromium carbide to leading edges, increases a tool's durability.

THE PRODUCTION PROCESS

Historically, CI grew from the founders' original blacksmith shop, and today the production process is still relatively simple. The plant manager described the process as "You simply take a piece of metal. And then you bang, heat, and shape it until it's a finished product. It really isn't a sophisticated process. We just do it better than anyone else." The production process is like a flow following a routing from one cost center to another in a sequence of move, wait, setup, and runtime for each process. Work-in-process inventories in the move and wait stage litter the plant. Economic lot size rules determine the size of each batch while production schedules push jobs onto the floor.

THE COST SYSTEM: MEASURING PERFORMANCE

CI uses standard unit costs to measure performance and profit potential. In this cost system, each materials and labor input is given a standard usage, and production managers are evaluated on their ability to meet or improve upon these standards. Differences from the standard were called "variances." For example, if a certain manufacturing operation required at standard 5 minutes, the operator would be expected to complete a lot of 100 parts in 500 minutes. If actually 550 minutes were required, there would be a 50 minute unfavorable variance. Also, using the operator's wage rate, the cost of the variance could be calculated.

CI'S IMPROVEMENT STRATEGY

The depressed market in the mid-1980s caused a 1986 net loss of close to $1.8 million. Inventory turns were down to one and a half, and cash flow was poor. Facing these conditions, management adopted a new strategy stressing improvements in accounting performance and reduction of inventories. Their strategies for improvement included: increasing productivity, cost cutting (overhead control), improving technology, and increasing prices.

1. **Productivity**. Productivity improvements centered on direct labor productivity measures. Output per direct labor hour was the crucial factor. Accordingly, improving efficiency, by definition, consisted of keeping direct labor busy producing as much product as possible during regular working hours. Actions supporting this strategy were 1) reducing idle manhours between jobs, 2) increasing batch sizes to maximize runtime, and 3) reducing setup times.

   The operational control system measured the "earned labor hours" for each department daily. While the plant manager only received these reports weekly, he was still aware of the daily figures. Budget reports, including variances, while processed monthly, were often two to three weeks late! Thus, they had little direct impact on day-to-day decisions. However, the plant manager knew what the accounting reports should be like from his daily earned labor hours information.

The short-term results of these efforts were impressive because plant efficiency measures rose about 15%. There were, however, some negative, unanticipated side effects in work-in-process levels, scheduling, and overtime.

First, work-in-process levels increased. In order to improve efficiency measures, departments kept processing large lots regardless of current demand. Once a machine had been set up, to economically justify large batches, the rationale was to provide for both current and future inventory needs. Consequently, finished goods grew from two to six-months' supply.

Second, the large batch sizes made scheduling difficult. They reduced plant flexibility by keeping machines on single jobs for long periods. Therefore, it was difficult to adjust for normal production problems and still maintain the production schedule. Machines were not readily available for special situations and expediting.

Finally, these large batches, while increasing productivity, created the need for overtime to maintain the schedule. Overtime in the finishing department, for example, increased by 15-20%, thus raising operating expenses. The larger lots reduced the variety of products produced each production period. This increased the lead time for custom orders could get stuck behind jobs with long runtimes. Overtime, then, became necessary to expedite out-of-stock orders. These factors combined with low sales volumes to create losses and more cash flow problems.

2. **Overhead**. Overhead improvement focused on two strategies. The first was direct cost reduction. The second concentrated on reducing unit costs by increasing volume. The higher volumes allowed overhead to be absorbed over more units. However, because CI's cost structure had large fixed obligations (like union contracted pension fund contribution), potential overhead savings were minimal.

The results of these strategies were unimpressive. The union didn't make many concessions, and few overhead savings occurred. Production volumes did increase, but the plant was producing to cover overhead rather than to satisfy immediate demand. Management hoped that increasing sales would eventually take care of the excess production. Unfortunately, this didn't happen. By 1989 inventories were 24% higher than in 1986. And, once again, there were cash flow and earnings problems.

3. **Technology.** CI considered the technology focus to be particularly troublesome. Concentrating on reducing unit costs through technology improvement often blocked out other aspects of the decision. Management's assumptions were that the savings from each decision flowed directly to the bottom line. However for CI this myopic view of unit costs encouraged mistakes.

Management's use of robots provided a vivid example of the problems. Robots were investigated as a means of decreasing the unit costs for the application knife. The anhydrous ammonia applicator knife was popular worldwide, to revitalize the soil with ammonia fertilizer after each harvest. Although CI led the industry in product quality, it was a high-cost producer. The primary reason was determined to be hand welding, using expensive piece rates, with manual electric arc welders.

After a unit-cost analysis, the savings in labor and applied overhead seemed to justify the introduction of welding robots (T1-2-3). Subsequent price reductions increased sales from 20,000 to more than 60,000 units in the first. At the new, lower, price the company seemed to still realize savings of $1.25 per unit.

Unfortunately, these savings were illusory. During the second year, other manufacturers became price competitive and sales volume dropped to 40,000 units; however, management still believed the robots saved the company money. At a 10% discount rate the three-year net present value was $63,730. A major problem was that labor savings disappeared as manual welders found work in other areas of the plant. In fact, the robots required additional new hires and caused increases in

72

utilities and maintenance costs. New operating expenses were greater than the increased throughput. Thus, management was misled by its focus on standard unit costs.

4. **Selling Prices.** Unfortunately, the market for the firm's products was very competitive. Due to such macroeconomic factors as government programs and foreign grain production, the domestic market was shrinking. Internationally, CI's high unit costs made foreign markets difficult to enter. Consequently, management perceived the marketplace to be mostly out of their control. Their main focus was on improving plant performance. Nonetheless, CI still tried to increase the sales volume in domestic markets and to find new foreign markets. As for the foreign markets they experienced some success and some failures.

In an attempt to find new international markets, the company successfully set up a working relationship with a John Deere distributor in Mexico and, unsuccessfully pursued a contract in Saudi Arabia. This failure was very revealing because Saudi Arabian soils were made to order for CI's product. The Saudi's cultivation process was particularly abrasive for tillage tools. Because of frequent breakdowns, crews with replacement parts had to constantly follow the field workers. But with CI's parts this practice wasn't necessary. Consequently, the Saudis were very enthusiastic about the company's products. Unfortunately, CI did not believe the 10% profit margins to be large enough. CI rejected the Saudi Arabia offer. This happened while at the same time the plant was having difficulty with operating expenses, overhead, and inventories. Thus, the accounting cost standards influenced market decisions as well as leading to questionable, limited improvements in manufacturing. All was not harmonious among management as well.

During this time, marketing and production meetings were frequent. Marketing pointed out that while quality was good, prices were too high and lead times were too inaccurate. On the other hand, production complained that marketing was constantly messing up their production schedules.

Using this combination of efficiency improvement, overhead reduction, unit-cost reductions and sales margins, management proceeded, over an 18-month period, to reduce domestic volume by 11.5% and to turn away significant foreign opportunities. Overall, decisions to improve the performance of the company using standard cost measurement failed. By February 1989, operating expenses were 20% greater than the disastrous 1986 figures. During the same period, inventories increased by 24%, and net profits continued to deteriorate.

At year-end CI hired a new Production Control/Inventory Control (PCIC) manager. However, the plant manager was suspicious when the PCIC manager came to him with revised schedules. The PCIC manager suggested processing job lots of 100 to 150 parts rather than the current 6,000. The plant manager questioned the PCIC manager's ability. "Clearly he isn't very knowledgeable. How can we make any money running only small lots? The setup costs will kill us!

Finally the PCIC manager gave the plant manager a copy of The Goal by E. Goldratt and J. Cox. After reading the first few pages, the plant manager recognized many similarities between his plant and the one described in this book.

REQUIRED:

1. What is the firm's competitive strategy? Does the strategy seem appropriate?

2. What motivated the cost reduction strategy? Did the cost reduction strategy work? Why?

3. How did CI's standard cost system affect the cost reduction strategy?

4. What is the role of work-in-process in the cost reduction strategy?

5. Is the new Production control/Inventory Control (PCIC) manager on the right track with the smaller lot sizes?

6. What steps is the PCIC likely to take now?

7. What type of cost system should be used at CI?

(IMA adapted)

TABLE 1
IMPACT OF ROBOTICS ON STANDARD COST
ANHYDROUS AMMONIA KNIVES

Department	Material: Before	After	Labor: Before	After	Overhead: Before	After	Total: Before	After
Cold Shear	$2.000	$2.000	$0.068	$0.068	$0.238	$0.238	$2.306	$2.306
Hot Forge			$0.127	$0.127	$0.445	$0.445	$0.572	$0.572
Heat Treat			$0.025	$0.025	$0.088	$0.088	$0.113	$0.113
Shot Blast			$0.025	$0.025	$0.088	$0.088	$0.113	$0.113
Arc Weld	$6.500	$6.500	$1.380	$0.250	$4.830	$0.875	$12.710	$7.625
Paint/Pack			$0.076	$0.076	$0.266	$0.266	$0.342	$0.342
Total	$8.500	$8.500	$1.701	$0.571	$5.954	$1.999	$16.155	$11.070
Selling Price							$18.150	$14.310
Gross Margin							12.353%	29.274%
Unit Profit							$1.995	$3.241

Note – OH/DL = 3.5/1

TABLE 2
IMPACT OF ROBOTICS ON STANDARD COST
ANHYDROUS AMMONIA KNIVES

Standard Cost Accounting Assumptions:

Year	Unit Savings	Unit Sales	+(–) Profits	Present Value (10%)
1	$1.245	6,000	$ 74,700	$ 67,909
2	$1.245	4,000	49,800	41,157
3	$1.245	4,000	49,800	37,415
Total			$174,300	$146,482
Initial investment				$ (60,000)
Net present value				$ 86,482

TABLE 3
IMPACT OF ROBOTICS ON STANDARD COST
ANHYDROUS AMMONIA KNIVES

Actual Results:

Year	Net Additional: Labor	Maintenance	Utilities	Total Additional: Expenses	Net Additional: Throughput	+(-) Profits	Present Value (10%)
1	$52,000	$2,000	$4,000	$ 58,000	$155,600	$97,600	$88,727
2	$92,000	$2,000	$4,000	$ 98,000	$ 39,400	($58,600)	($48,430)
3	$92,000	$2,000	$4,000	$ 98,000	$ 39,400	($58,600)	($44,027)
Total				$254,000	$234,400	($19,600)	($3,730)
Initial Investment							($60,000)
Net Present Value							($63,730)

5-2. Contrast Analysis

Silver Aviation assembles small aircraft for commercial use. The majority of Silver's business is with small freight airlines serving those areas where the airport size does not accommodate larger planes. The remainder of Silver's customers are commuter airlines and individuals who use planes in their businesses such as the owners of larger ranches. Silver recently expanded its market into Central and South America, and the company expects to double its sales over the next three years.

In order to schedule work and keep track of all projects, Silver uses a network diagram. The diagram for the construction of a single cargo plane is shown in Exhibit A. The diagram shows that there are four alternative paths with the critical path being ABGEFJK.

Bob Peterson, President of Coastal Airlines, has recently placed an order with Silver Aviation for five cargo planes. At the time of contract negotiations, Peterson agreed to a delivery time of thirteen weeks (five working days per week) for the first plane with the balance of the planes being delivered at the rate of one every four weeks. Because of problems with some of the aircraft Coastal is currently using, Peterson has contacted Grace Vander, Sales Manager for Silver Aviation, to ask about improving the delivery date of the first cargo plane. Vander replied that she believed the schedule could be shortened by as much as ten working days or two weeks, but the cost of construction would increase as a result. Peterson said he would be willing to consider the increased costs, and they agreed to meet the following day to review a revised schedule that Vander would prepare.

Because Silver Aviation has assembled aircraft on an accelerated basis previously, the company has compiled a list of crash costs for this purpose. Vander used the data shown on the Crash Cost Listing in Exhibit B to develop a plan to cut 10 working days from the schedule at a minimum increase in cost to Coastal Airlines. Upon completing her plan, Vander was pleased that she could report to Peterson that Silver would be able to cut 10 working days from the schedule. The associated increase in cost would be $6,000. Presented below is Vander's plan for the accelerated delivery of the cargo plane starting from the regularly scheduled days and cost.

Completion Time	Activity Crashed	Additional Cost per Day	Total Direct Cost
65 days			$65,100
64	HJ by one day	$400	65,500
63	FJ by one day	400	65,900
61	GH by two days	500	66,900
59	CD by two days	700	68,300
58	EF by one day	800	69,100
56	DE by two days	800	70,700
55	BG by one day	1,000	71,700

REQUIRED:

Evaluate the accelerated delivery schedule prepared by Grace Vander.

1. Explain why Vander's plan as presented is unsatisfactory.

2. Revise the accelerated delivery schedule so that Coastal Airlines will take delivery of the first plane two weeks ahead of schedule at the least incremental cost to Coastal.

3. Calculate the incremental costs Bob Peterson will have to pay for this revised accelerated delivery. (CMA 6/87)

Target Costing at ITT Automotive

By George Schmelze, CPA; Rolf Geier; and Thomas E. Buttross, CMA

Intense competition and pressure from customers to reduce prices has forced many companies to reduce their costs to survive. These companies have found that most costs are committed once production begins, and, therefore, the costs must be reduced earlier in the product life cycle, particularly while the product is in the planning and design stages. Target costing is a proven, effective method of reducing production costs throughout the product life cycle, without reducing quality or functionality and without increasing the time it takes to design and develop a product. At ITT Automotive, the brakes area has been using target costing for three to four years, and it provides an excellent model that other areas of the company are beginning to emulate.

Target costing is a proactive, strategic cost management philosophy that is price-driven, customer-focused, design-centered, and cross-functional.[1] Unlike traditional cost control systems, which do not control costs until production has commenced, the target costing philosophy requires that aggressive cost management occur in the product planning stage, the product design stage, and the production stage. By designing lower costs into the product, companies realize the best sources of cost savings—before the product reaches the production stage. These cost savings cannot be realized, however, with traditional costing systems, such as standard costing systems and activity-based costing systems.[2]

Target costing transcends the functional areas of a company. For target costing to be successful, integration is needed in the form of cross-functional teams comprising engineering, product design, production, purchasing, sales, finance, cost accounting, cost targeting, and, in many cases, customers and suppliers. Upper-level management support is crucial to the success of target costing because resources need to be allocated to the target costing area, and the cross-functional teams must be empowered to make many critical decisions.

Target costing differs from traditional "cost-plus" costing. Rather than the selling price being a function of estimated costs, the target cost is a function of the selling price and a desired profit. Furthermore, with target costing, the target cost is determined before the product is designed. The target costing equation is as follows:

$$\text{Target Price} - \text{Target Profit} = \text{Target Cost}$$

Various factors are considered when computing the future selling price of the proposed product including functionality of the product, projected sales volumes, and quality. For example, management strategy may call for a price that maintains or increases market share.

Due to intense competition, many companies have little flexibility when setting a price. When market conditions are extremely competitive, the price may be driven by the market. In other cases, the target cost of the downstream company is the target price of the upstream company. Where selling price and profit margin are fixed by competitive pressures and management policies, respectively, reducing the firm's production costs may be the only source of increased earnings.

Once the target cost is computed, it must be assigned to final assembly, subassemblies, and components before design can begin. After the product is designed, estimated costs of production are compared with target costs. If the estimated costs are higher than the target costs, value engineering is employed to help the company achieve its target. Value engineering is a process in which the cross-functional team attempts to reduce costs during the design and preproduction stages without compromising quality and functionality by determining the optimal processes, materials, and machinery needed for production.

Estimated costs are compared with the targets throughout the product life cycle. Once the product reaches production, however, cost maintenance (as opposed to cost reduction) generally becomes the objective.

TARGET COSTING AT ITT AUTOMOTIVE

To illustrate the process of target costing, let's look at the target costing practices at ITT Automotive. ITT Automotive, one of the world's largest suppliers of auto parts, produced sales of $4.8 billion in 1994, which represented an increase of more than 34% compared to 1993. In 1995, sales were approximately $5.7 billion. Products produced include brake systems and components, wiper handling systems and components, fluid handling systems and components, structural systems and components, electric motors, switches, and lamps. More than 35,000 employees work for the company, with the vast majority of these employees located in the United States and Germany.

The brakes area has used target costing extensively for the last few years because of an extremely competitive environment. For example, the price of anti-lock brake systems, which currently sell for about $200, is expected to drop to $100 by the year 2000. Furthermore, the functionality of the product is expected to increase.

Establishing the target price and target margin. At ITT Automotive, price is generally set externally, either by competitive pressure or by the customer's target costing system. For example, the price that Mercedes-Benz offers ITT Automotive for an anti-lock brake system (ABS) is Mercedes-Benz's target cost.

The first step in the process occurs when ITT Automotive receives an invitation to bid from the customer. Due to the competitive nature of this industry, ITT Automotive cannot use "cost-plus" pricing when setting the price. The price that the company generally will quote is a price that already has been set by market conditions. An analysis then is performed to determine if the product fits ITT Automotive's strategic goals and if the volume can be produced. Financial information including internal rate of return (IRR) and return on investment (ROI) also are calculated to ensure that ITT Automotive can earn a proper return. If productivity increases (reductions in price) are expected by the customer, the analysis must include an explanation concerning how the productivity increases will be achieved.

To determine whether the price is feasible, a permanent cost targeting group made up of employees with backgrounds in engineering, cost accounting, and sales receives the quote. Keeping in mind that the product being quoted will not be produced for several

years, the ITT Automotive cost targeting group makes a determination concerning whether enough value engineering can be accomplished before the product is produced in order to meet the quoted price. Other factors considered by the cost targeting team when determining the feasibility of a price include previous quotes issued, economic factors such as anticipated inflation and interest rates, competitor pricing, and cost structure.

Because ITT Automotive does not produce automobiles, it does not have information concerning prices (and costs) of competitors' component parts. Information from a tear-down analysis of a competitor's product, however, may provide ITT Automotive with information that is useful in determining a competitor's costs and, by adding a reasonable margin, the competitor's price. Tear-down analysis, sometimes referred to as reverse engineering, is an analytical process in which a company will examine in detail a competitor's product. During tear-down analysis, a competitor's product is torn apart by engineers, component by component. An indication of the competitor's design, estimated cost structure, quality, functionality, and possible processes used to build the product are garnered from this process. From this analysis, ITT Automotive may be able to improve designs or processes in order to reduce cost without losing functionality (or to increase functionality and quality without increasing costs). The information garnered from this study is recorded on a standardized document that compares each competitor's product with ITT Automotive's product. This information is useful for price setting because the tear-down analysis provides information concerning the estimated cost structure of the competitor.

Price setting is an iterative process. The cost targeting team will try to find ways to reduce costs in order to accept a bid without comprising ITT Automotive's expected return. For example, the cost targeting team may consult with the design engineers who may suggest that some new process or technology will be available when the product is produced that will reduce the cost of the product.

Assigning the target cost. The target cost is the target price minus the target margin. Finding the target cost is a relatively straightforward calculation; the difficulty for most companies is reaching the target cost in order to meet the company's profit objectives. The target cost should include all costs related to the new product. At ITT Automotive, target costs include direct materials, direct labor, tooling costs, depreciation, promotion, service, and working capital.

Once the target cost has been computed, specific targets are assigned first to final assemblies, then to subassemblies, and then finally to individual components. This work is performed by individuals in the permanent cost targeting group. Although the setting of the targets is a cross-functional procedure, the ITT Automotive team believes that it is critical for someone who is independent to first set the targets. Once the targets are set initially in cost targeting, feedback is given to the cost targeting area from various members of the cross-functional team, including purchasing and production, concerning targets that are considered unreasonable. This step allows the cross-functional team to be involved in the target-setting process without bogging down the process.

Individual targets are set for each component that is purchased, along with targets for burden and labor. The target costs are tracked throughout the product's life cycle, beginning with the design of the product, continuing when tooling is released, and not concluding until the product is discontinued.

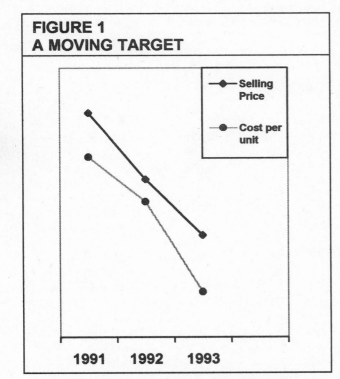

FIGURE 1
A MOVING TARGET

Selling Price

Cost per unit

1991   1992   1993

In many situations, the price that ITT Automotive will receive for the product will become lower each year. Thus, the target costs will have to be lower each year to provide the company with the same return from year to year. Eventually the margin will become too small, and new products will have to be developed. Fig. 1 shows a typical target costing situation, where cost targets are lower each year fueled by productivity increases. The targets are met by using cross-functional teams, setting early cost targets, engaging in value engineering (including tear-down analysis of competitor products and concurrent engineering and production), and forming partnerships with suppliers.

Then these targets are compared with quotes (or estimated costs for items such as depreciation). If the targets are not met, costs are reduced through value engineering and value analysis.

SOME TARGET COSTING TOOLS USED AT ITT AUTOMOTIVE

Achieving the target cost requires companies to take a disciplined approach toward value improvement. Value improvement occurs when functionality and quality are held constant while costs are reduced or when quality and functionality are increased while price is held constant,[3] At ITT Automotive, achieving the target cost is accomplished through several techniques including the use of cross-functional teams, setting early cost targets, value engineering, and forming partnerships with suppliers.

The target costing process, however, does not end in the early stages of the product life cycle. Once the product reaches production, cost maintenance is practiced through profit improvement planning and value analysis. These techniques help individuals in all of the functional areas take ownership for meeting cost targets throughout the product's life cycle.

Target costing cannot be successful without the involvement of an effective cross-functional team. Team participants at ITT Automotive include product design, engineering, purchasing, manufacturing, finance, and cost targeting. Participation from the team is expected throughout the product life cycle.

One byproduct of the use of cross functional teams is increased understanding of processes and product design by members of the cross-functional team. Members of the cross-functional team at ITT Automotive must have knowledge of processes and design to contribute in a meaningful way to the target costing process. For example, purchasing personnel must have a working knowledge of how the product is designed to make optimal decisions concerning the purchase of components and parts. Similarly, the cost targeting personnel must have a basic understanding of the prices of component parts and subassemblies in order to make decisions concerning the allocation of target costs.

Value engineering is another important component of target costing at ITT Automotive. The objective of value engineering is to reduce costs without reducing functionality or quality without increasing costs before the product reaches the production line. During value engineering, the cross-functional team will try to determine optimal processes, materials, and equipment for designing, engineering, and producing the product.[4] The value engineering philosophy recognizes that decisions made early in the design process affect price and product costs. At ITT Automotive, members of the cross-functional team are empowered to find the most optimal processes, materials used, tooling and capital investment requirements and to decide whether to make or outsource the product. Tear-down analysis also is performed during value engineering.

Target costing should result in improved relationships with suppliers. At ITT Automotive, key suppliers are considered an integral part of the target costing team. This arrangement allows the suppliers to take "ownership" of the target costing process. These suppliers should be consulted early in the product life cycle, and they should play a significant role in product design and development.

Occasionally, a supplier may have a difficult time in meeting the target cost. In cases where the supplier is having this type of problem, ITT Automotive will ask for a detailed analysis of the supplier's cost to help the supplier reduce costs. This analysis is extremely detailed and provides the starting point for ITT Automotive to suggest some "value analysis" that will help the supplier reduce its costs.

Cost tracking sheets are used in the cost targeting area to keep track of the "targets" and to compare the targets with actual costs. At ITT Automotive, these sheets are used to assign the target cost from the final product to final assemblies, subassemblies, and components. Each tracking sheet becomes more specific until, finally, the individual components are tracked.

The tracking sheets track the cost of the product throughout the product life cycle: at the design stage (DS), when the tooling is in place (TS), and finally, when the product reaches production (PS). Setting early targets helps ITT Automotive investigate and try to remedy problem situations. For example, if the quote of a certain supplier is higher than the target, the cross-functional team may decide to visit the supplier to determine why there is a difference between the target and the quote. Fig. 2 shows a hypothetical example of this process. Investment in capital equip-

FIGURE 2
COST TRACKING SHEETS

ABS System

Description	Design Stage Target	Design Stage Quote	Tool Stage Target	Tool Stage Quote	Production Stage Target	Production Stage Quote
Control Unit	a	a + 1	a	a + 5	a	a − 1
Motor etc.	x	x	x	x	x	x
Production Cost	x	x	x	x	x	x
Other	x	x	x	x	x	x
Total Cost	x	x	x	x	x	X

Control Unit-Final Assembly

Description	Design Stage Target	Design Stage Quote	Tool Stage Target	Tool Stage Quote	Production Stage Target	Production Stage Quote
Bracket	X	X	X	X	X	x
ECU	X	x	x	x	x	x
Piston Assembly	b	b + 2	b	b + 1	b	b − .1

Piston Assembly-Subassembly

Description	Design Stage Target	Design Stage Quote	Tool Stage Target	Tool Stage Quote	Production Stage Target	Production Stage Quote
O-ring	x	x	x	x	x	x
Valve	x	x	x	x	x	x
Spring	x	x	x	x	x	x

Cost tracking sheets are prepared for the final product, final assemblies, and subassemblies, the latter includes tracking of individual components

ment, which can be quite substantial, also is tracked through the use of cost tracking sheets.

ITT Automotive periodically conducts meetings with the cross-functional team to hold them responsible for the targets that were set and to develop, through brainstorming, ways to further reduce costs. At these "profit improvement planning" meetings, a "checklist" of problems are discussed among the cross-functional team. Before the meeting, each member of the team is handed a document detailing each of the problem areas, the person(s) responsible for eliminating the problem, comments on why the problem is occurring, and a suggested completion date for solving the problem. During the meeting, the person responsible for the area where the problem is occurring will discuss the steps that are being taken to solve the problem and receive suggestions from members of the cross-functional team.

Value analysis at ITT Automotive is used on products that are not yielding an adequate return. The results of value analysis may not be as great as the results from value engineering because value analysis is performed during the production stage—after ITT Automotive is locked into a good portion of its costs. The results from value analysis, however, can be dramatic.

Readers interested in more information about target costing can look forward to the research monograph, *Target Costing and Value Engineering* by Robin Cooper and Regine Slagmulder, to be published by the IMA Foundation for Applied Research, Inc., in early 1997. It is the first in a series of five books by Cooper on Japanese cost management practices. CAM-1 (Consortium for Advanced Manufacturing-International) recently issued *Target Costing: The New Frontier in Strategic Cost Management*, which provides practical insights on how to use target costing for profit planning and cost management. It can be ordered (C1/$50) by calling (800) 638-4427, ext. 278, or faxing (201) 573-9507.

TARGET COSTING MARKET SHARE

ITT Automotive uses target costing to maintain its profitability and increase its market share during these extremely competitive times in the automotive industry. Although the process is difficult at times, and costly resources are needed to have an effective target costing system, companies such as ITT Automotive have found the investment critical to meeting their corporate objectives successfully.

Target costing basically is a bottom-up, team-oriented philosophy. It is a very structured method of setting and achieving goals. For target costing to be successful, setting up cross-functional teams is not enough. Most important, there must be senior management support for the process. Senior management must allocate the necessary resources to the project and must empower the cross-functional teams to make critical decisions. Other requirements include setting early cost targets, performing competitive analysis and value engineering, forming partnerships with suppliers, and applying pressure to everyone in the value chain to reduce costs.

George Schmelzle, CPA, is an assistant professor of accountancy at the University of Detroit, Mercy. He was a faculty intern at ITT Automotive in the summer of 1995. He is a member of the Detroit Chapter of the IMA, through which this article was submitted. He can be reached at (312) 993-3327.

Rolf Geier heads the target costing/value analysis team in the brakes department at ITT Automotive. Additional credits are given to Gerd Klostermann. He is head of the target costing/value analysis team in Europe with worldwide responsibilities.

Thomas E. Buttross, CMA, is an assistant professor of accountancy at Indiana University, Kokomo. He is a member of the Detroit Chapter of IMA. He can be reached at (317) 455-9471.

[1]*Target Costing—The New Frontier in Strategic Cost Management,* The Consortium for Advanced Manufacturing-International (CAM-1), Bedford, Tex., 1995.
[2]Activity-based costing can provide valuable input for the target costing product design stage. Product designers can use cost tables that include actual cost data from the ABC system as well as pro forma amounts for processes not currently used by the company. See Takeo Yoshikawa, John Innes, and Falconer Mitchell, "Cost Tables: A Foundation of Japanese Cost Management," *Journal of Cost Management,* Fall 1990, Vol. 4, No. 3, pp. 30-36.
[3]The personal computer is a good example of the latter. Although the price of computers has remained constant the past few years, functionality has increased dramatically.
[4]*Implementing Target Costing—Management Accounting Guideline #28,* a joint research project of the Society of Management Accountants of Canada, the Institute of Management Accountants, and the Consortium for Advanced Manufacturing-International, 1995.

Chapter 6
Total Quality Management

Cases
6-1   Analysis of Quality Cost Reports

Readings
***David M. Buehlmann and Donald Stover:* How Xerox Solves Quality Problems**
This article reports the processes Xerox developed to identify and solve quality
problems and the results of applying the processes to improve customer billing accuracy
at the company's Omaha District office. Included in the article are determinations of cost
of billing errors and lost revenues that result from failing to meet customer
requirements, an Ishikawa diagram, and a six-step problem-solving processes.

Discussion Questions:
1   How were cost of nonconformance and cost of lost opportunity determined?
        Should they be measured differently?
2.   What were the main causes of billing quality problems at Xerox's Omaha District
        office?
3.   Did the Omaha office solve the billing errors problem?

Cases

6-1. Critical Success Factors

(Analyzing Quality Cost Report) Bergen, Inc., produces telephone equipment at its Georgia plant. In recent years, the company's market share has been eroded by stiff competition from Asian and European competitors. Price and product quality are the two key areas in which companies compete in this market.

Two years ago, Jerry Holman, Bergen's president, decided to devote more resources to the improvement of product quality after learning that his company's products had been ranked fourth in product quality in a recent survey of telephone equipment users. He believed that Bergen could no longer afford to ignore the importance of product quality. Holman set up a task force that he headed to implement a formal quality improvement program. Included on this task were representatives from engineering, sales, customer service, production, and accounting. This broad representation was needed because Holman believed that this was a companywide program, and that all employees should share the responsibility for its success.

After the first meeting of the task force, Sheila Haynes, manager of sales, asked Tony Reese, production manager, what he thought of the proposed program. Reese replied, "I have reservations. Quality is too abstract to be attaching costs to it and then to be holding you and me responsible for cost improvements. I like to work with goals that I can see and count! I'm nervous about having my annual bonus based on a decrease in quality costs; there are too many variables that we have no control over."

Bergen's quality improvement program has now been in operation for two years. The company's most recent cost report is shown below.

BERGEN, INC
Quality Cost Report
(in thousands)

	12/31/x7		12/31/x8	
Prevention costs:				
Machine maintenance	$215		$160	
Training suppliers	5		15	
Design reviews	20	$ 240	95	$ 270
Appraisal costs:				
Incoming inspection	$ 45		$ 22	
Final testing	160	205	94	116
Internal failure costs:				
Rework	$120		$ 62	
Scrap	68	188	40	102
External failure costs:				
Warranty repairs	$ 69		$ 23	
Customer returns	262	331	80	103
Total quality cost		$ 964		$ 591
Total production cost		$4,120		$4,510

87

As they were reviewing the report, Haynes asked Reese what he now thought of the quality improvement program. "The work is really moving through the production department," Reese replied. "We used to spend time helping the customer service department solve their problems, but they are leaving us alone these days. I have no complaints so far, and I'm relieved to see the new quality improvement hasn't adversely affected our bonuses. I'm anxious to see if it increases our bonuses in the future."

REQUIRED:

1. By analyzing the company's quality cost report, determine if Bergen, Inc's quality improvement program has been successful. List specific evidence to support your answer. Show percentage figures in two ways; first, as a percentage of total production cost; and second, as a percentage of total quality cost. Carry all computations to one decimal place.

2. Discuss why Tony Reese's current reaction to the quality improvement program is more favorable than his initial reaction.

3. Jerry Holman believed that the quality improvement program was essential and that Bergen, Inc., could no longer afford to ignore the importance of product quality. Discuss how Bergen, Inc., could measure the opportunity cost of not implementing the quality improvement program.

How Xerox Solves Quality Problems

By David M. Buehmann, CPA and Donald Stover

Management accountants agree that it is important to support quality improvement as a business strategy and to measure the company's total cost of quality to focus management's attention on this issue. However, one key area that has been ignored is: What processes should a company use to identify and solve a specific quality problem?

Xerox Corporation developed two processes to identify and solve specific quality problems—the problem solving process (PSP) and the quality improvement process (QIP). All employees receive training in these two processes to help them identify and solve quality problems through participation on quality improvement teams (QITs). These processes recently were used to improve customer billing accuracy at the company's Omaha District office.

PROBLEM IDENTIFIED

Xerox's regular customer satisfaction surveys indicated that 18% of the Omaha District's customers were dissatisfied with billing accuracy. Further, 40% of these customers were dissatisfied with the process of correcting billing errors. Overall customer satisfaction, which is a key objective used to evaluate Xerox performance, was being affected negatively by billing errors. Some at the Omaha District office believed that this fact alone was enough to justify a major effort to improve billing accuracy.

Additional analysis was performed before the decision was made to form a quality improvement team to consider the billing errors problem. As a second measure, the billing error rate was calculated at 3.54%—a daunting number in an age of zero defects.

Last, the Omaha District calculated the cost of nonconformance (CON) (the cost to fix the billing errors) and the cost of lost opportunity (CLO) (the lost revenues that result from failing to meet customer requirements). They were $121,688 and $73,794, respectively, for the six-month test period.

How were the CON and CLO calculated? The CON is found in the accounting records—but only with difficulty. This is because the accounting records do not report many of the costs of poor quality separately. For example, the salaries of people answering customer complaints about billing errors along with the related postage, computer time, and clerical support costs are not reported in the accounts separately. Consequently, a sample of billing errors was drawn and an analysis made of the relevant costs of correcting the errors that resulted in an average cost of $106 per billing error. Multiplying this $106 figure by the number of billing errors during the six-month test period resulted in the total cost of nonconformance of $121,688.

From an accounting measurement perspective, Xerox's attempt to measure the CLO is particularly instructive. Frequently, even managerial accountants shy away from measuring opportunity costs on the grounds that these costs are too subjective.[1] Yet lost customers can have a significant impact on a company's future success.[2]

Fortunately, the Omaha District already had on file prior customer satisfaction surveys for the customers who cancelled their rental/maintenance agreements during the six-month test period.[3] These surveys indicated that 1.85% of the cancellations were influenced significantly by billing errors. Applying this percentage to the annual revenue from cancelled rental/maintenance agreements and multiplying by four years (the average life remaining or cancelled contracts) results in the CLO of $73,794.

Certainly the accuracy of this measurement of the cost of lost opportunity can be criticized because billing errors were not the sole cause of the contract cancellations. Further, Xerox's opportunity cost on these cancellations was lost profit, not lost revenue.[4]While these criticisms are valid, failure to place any measure on the CLO implies that zero is a more accurate measure of the loss. We could argue that zero cost of CLO, is on the face, unsupportable. Also, when considering that a lost customer may never be regained and also may share its dissatisfaction with others, Xerox's measurement of CLP appears rather conservative.

FORMING THE TEAM

It was clear that billing errors had an impact on many departments. It also was obvious that the billing department only had partial responsibility for the billing process because it received its input data from other departments.

Consequently, the district business manager selected a cross-functional quality improvement team representing all interested contributing departments. The seven person team contained representatives from customer relations, marketing support, service, business operations, and sales. One of the members was a trained facilitator of quality improvement teams.

They named themselves the "Billing Bloopers QIT" and advertised themselves as "98 years of Xerox experience working together to improve billing quality."

Appointing people to a QIT for the purpose of studying a predetermined problem is unusual at Xerox. Normally, volunteers in a functional area from a team to study a problem they have determined is important to their area. Generally, volunteer teams are highly motivated because they want to participate and because they selected a problem that they deemed important.. However, the billing error problem cut across functional areas so it was unlikely that any functional area team would address it. Additionally, the problem was so important to meeting customer satisfaction objectives that the Omaha District business manager took the risk of appointing a team even though it might not be as motivated as a volunteer team.

FIGURE 1
ISHIKAWA DIAGRAM: BILLING QUALITY QIT

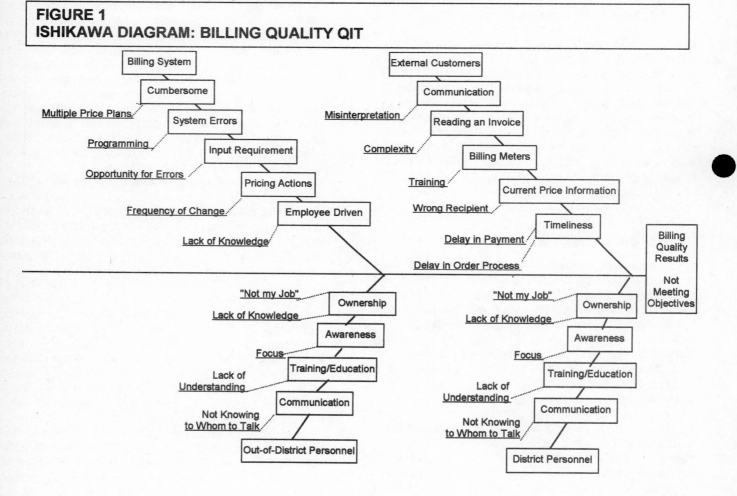

Table 1
NINE-STEP QUALITY IMPROVEMENT PROCESS

Step	Result
1. Identify Output	Captain Xero Educational Communicator
2. Identify Customer	Primary—District Personnel Secondary—Customer Service Support Center
3. Identify Customer Requirements	Understand billing quality objectives and provide examples of causes and methods of correction
4. Translate Requirements into Supplier Specifications	Communicate definition and measures of billing quality, publish billing problems weekly, and communicate periodic results and targets
5. Identify Steps in Work Process	Produce flowchart
6. Select Measurements	Number and types of billing adjustment causals.
7. Determine Process Capability	Relate types of errors to Captain Xero issue dates.
8. Evaluate Results	Were results achieved? If not, begin problem-solving process.
9. Recycle	Solve problem and re-enter quality improvement process as needed.

At the first two team meetings, management's fear about less than optimal motivation proved to be a real issue. Several team members raised questions such as, "Why am I here?" Or, "I service machines—I have nothing to do with billing," and "billing is an administrative issue, not my issue."

It was interesting to observe the change in attitude as this diverse team met to discuss the billing problem. The team facilitator allowed them to vent their concerns. Gradually, the team members began to understand their role in the billing process as well as the significance of the billing problem. You almost could see the light bulbs going on.

After two meetings, the Billing Bloopers QIT assumed ownership of the billing problem and became a highly motivated team. To this day, the team retains its sense of solidarity (despite its cross-functional membership) through continued monitoring of the billing error rate as well as from the corporate level recognition of its success.

PROBLEM-SOLVING PROCESS

All Xerox employees are trained in a six-step problem-solving process that is used to attack any quality problem. The Billing Bloopers QIT met one hour per week for two months and followed this process.

Step 1: *Identifying and Selecting the Problem*. The district business manager reviewed the regular customer satisfaction surveys before forming the quality improvement team. The billing error rate of 3.54% was unacceptable. In other situations, the quality improvement team defines the problem to study after reviewing and prioritizing the problems in its responsibility area.

Step 2: *Analyzing the Problem*. Several charts and graphs are available to assist the quality improvement team with this step. The Ishikawa Diagram or fishbone framework was selected to guide team members' discussions (Fig. 1). Team members listed all those who might have an impact on billing errors and the likely causes of these errors.

Normally, a Pareto chart also would be used next in the analysis to illustrate the most frequent causes of billing errors. The Billing Bloopers QIT did not do this because it became clear during the team's discussions that district personnel caused most of the errors and that they made errors due to lack of knowledge about correct billing input. Therefore, the team decided to concentrate on the lower right-hand corner of the chart.

Step 3: *Generating Potential Solutions*. A brainstorming session focused on various methods of educating district personnel about correct billing input. The team concluded that efforts to educate employees had to be attention getting; focus on a specific, manageable, issue; and be available on a regular basis to ensure a high level of awareness.

Step 4: *Select and Plan Solution*. As a result of the ideas developed in the brainstorming session, the quality improvement team reached almost immediate consensus to develop a cartoon hero similar to Batman. Captain Xero cartoons would be published weekly to educate all district personnel about billing. Each week a single, key piece of information would be selected to inform district personnel about billing input.

Steps 5 and 6: *Implement and Evaluate Solutions*. To implement the Captain Xero program, the quality improvement team began the quality improvement process (Fig. 2). Because the problem-solving process and the quality improvement process are complementary, the teams shift back and forth as needed. Results of this process are presented in T-1.

QUALITY IMPROVEMENT PROCESS

The first three steps in the quality improvement process were identified quickly from previous discussions.

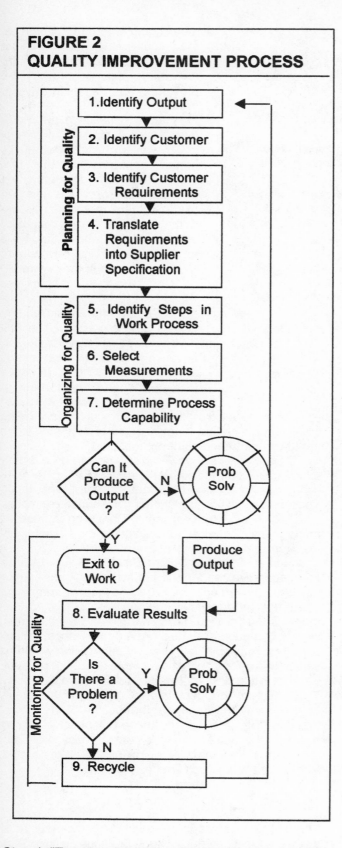

FIGURE 2
QUALITY IMPROVEMENT PROCESS

could address them first. The quality improvement team prepared a flowchart to identify clearly the steps involved in preparing and distributing Captain Xero. Overall, the key measure to monitor the success of the QIP was the billing error rate, but the QIT also measured the specific types of billing errors addressed by the cartoon to determine its effectiveness.

As indicated in Fig. 3, all aspects of the billing errors problem improved in both six-month periods after the birth of Captain Xero. Billing errors were reduced an overall 52% from 3.54% to 1.71%. Customer satisfaction with billing accuracy increased from 81.5% to 87.2% and with billing error correction from 60% to 77.4%. There was also a 54% reduction in the net cost of quality. Stated another way, an investment of about $7,000 in prevention resulted in the company saving more than $112,000 in the second six-month period.[5]

Captain Xero was so well received in the Omaha District office that it has since been circulated to many other locations within Xerox.

THE FUTURE

Can it be said that the Billing Bloopers QIT solved the billing errors problem? No. According to QIP Step 9, "Recycle," there must be continuous improvement and monitoring of quality. Should billing errors stop decreasing, the quality improvement team would begin meeting again to apply the problem-solving and quality improvement processes for a fresh look at the problem.

A more stringent goal of a 1.3% billing error rate is set for the next six-month period. We believe the Omaha District office is on track to achieve this goal because of its desire to continuously improve the quality of customer billing.

The outmoded, but frequently used, approach of putting together a temporary team to develop a quick-fix for quality and then disband the team and consider quality "solved" is inappropriate and shortsighted. Xerox believes that the key to success is continuous improvement, a factor on which all managers are evaluated.

Step 4, "Translate Requirements," required the use of a Pareto chart to identify which particular billing errors were made most frequently so that Captain Xero

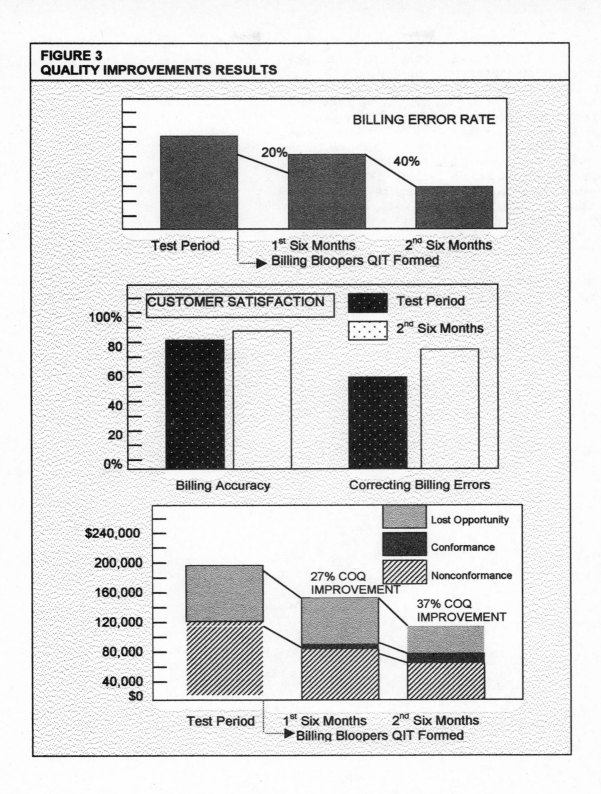

FIGURE 3
QUALITY IMPROVEMENTS RESULTS

BILLING ERROR RATE

20%   40%

Test Period   1st Six Months   2nd Six Months
Billing Bloopers QIT Formed

CUSTOMER SATISFACTION   Test Period   2nd Six Months

100%
80
60
40
20
0%

Billing Accuracy   Correcting Billing Errors

Lost Opportunity
Conformance
Nonconformance

$240,000
200,000
160,000
120,000
80,000
40,000
$0

27% COQ IMPROVEMENT
37% COQ IMPROVEMENT

Test Period   1st Six Months   2nd Six Months
Billing Bloopers QIT Formed

[1] Charles Horngren and George Foster, *Cost Accounting*, 7th ed. Prentice Hall, Inc., 1991, p. 377.

[2] Frederick Rercheld and Earl Sasser, "Zero Defections: Quality Comes to Services," *Harvard Business Review*, September-October 1990, pp. 105-111

[3] Xerox considers the "annuity stream" from rental/service contracts of critical importance to its success. Consequently, this revenue stream rather than product sales was the focus of CLO. Xerox is in constant contact with rental-service customers to retain their business.

[4] Xerox evaluates managers on meeting their revenue targets. To maintain this key corporate focus, the CLO used the lost revenue as its measure.

[5] The prevention cost included not only the cost of preparing and distributing Captain Xero but the cost of the time of the Billing Bloopers QIT.

Chapter 7
Cost Estimation

Cases

Readings

Adel M. Novin: Applying Overhead: How to Find the Right Bases and Rates

This article shows an actual application of regression analysis for determining multiple overhead rates using the spreadsheet software LOTUS 123 (the steps and the results are very similar to EXCEL which has regression under TOOLS/ADD-INS/DATA ANALYSIS in contrast to LOTUS which has regression under DATA). The article explains the interpretation of the R-squared and t-values and provides a good discussion of when regression analysis is useful.

Discussion Questions:
1. What is regression analysis used to accomplish in this article?
2. What are the steps to perform a simple regression analysis?
3. What does Table 7 tell you? Which cost driver would you pick for each cost type --
    maintenance, packaging, materials handling, storage, and production scheduling?

Ken M. Boze: Measuring Learning Costs

This article shows the importance of the costs of system change-over, a part of which is the cost of learning a new system. The costs are considered from a couple of different perspectives: (1) infrequent significant change, (2) frequent smaller changes, and (3) parallel systems. There are a number of recommendations for controlling costs, especially those related to employee productivity, when system change-overs are made.

Discussion Question
1. What are the different methods of implementation described in the article, and what
    are the implications for learning costs for each method?

See Also: "**Accounting for Magic**", for a cost estimation spreadsheet (Chapter 12), and a regression application in "**Overhead Control Implications of Activity Costing**" (Chapter 16).

Cases

7-1. The High-Low Method and Regression Analysis

The Brenham General Hospital was approached by Health Food, Inc. (HFI) which specializes in the preparation of meals for institutional patients. HFI stated that it would prepare all inpatient meals to provider specifications and deliver them on time for $11.50 per meal. The hospital was facing a steady decline in bed occupancy and was determined to hold the line on costs wherever possible.

Hospital management did not have a clear idea what the present system of providing meals to patients was costing. Hospital staff gathered the information below, which covered expenses for the dietary department for the past year.

The hospital has 120 beds. It is open year-round and has a 33% percent occupancy rate. Patients are served an average of 2.8 meals per occupancy day.

It was determined that the dietitian provided valuable counseling and advising services. Should the hospital eliminate in-house meal preparation, it would want to retain her services. Also, the administration wanted to keep and maintain the kitchen and equipment.

REQUIRED:

1. Using the high-low method and regression analysis, determine the variable and fixed costs of the in-house meal service.
2. Which cost estimation method would you choose and why?
3. Should the hospital administration accept the offer of the outside company? Why or why not?

	Dietitian	Other staff	Food Costs	Maintenance	Patient Equipment	Days
January	$ 2,875	$ 3,122	$ 9,674	$ 1,401	$ 1,649	1,382
February	$ 2,875	$ 2,908	$ 9.184	$ 1,322	$ 1,415	1,312
March	$ 2,875	$ 2,655	$ 8,302	$ 1,322	$ 1,313	1,186
April	$ 2,875	$ 2,600	$ 7,084	$ 1,288	$ 1,105	1,012
May	$ 2,875	$ 2,433	$ 6,398	$ 1,200	$ 1,089	914
June	$ 2,875	$ 2,083	$ 4,338	$ 1,133	$ 1,011	604
July	$ 2,875	$ 1,809	$ 3,612	$ 1,093	$ 900	516
August	$ 2,875	$ 2,322	$ 6,275	$ 1,122	$ 1,112	896
September	$ 2,875	$ 1,434	$ 6,734	$ 1,235	$ 1,103	962
October	$ 2,875	$ 2,700	$ 9,002	$ 1,302	$ 1,300	1,286
November	$ 2,875	$ 2,798	$ 8,456	$ 1,300	$ 1,442	1,208
December	$ 2,875	$ 2,600	$ 7,798	$ 1,322	$ 1,396	1,114
TOTAL	$34,500	$29,464	$86,857	$15,040	$14,835	12,392

7-2.   The Pump Division

The Pump Division has one plant dedicated to the design and manufacture of large, highly technical, customized pumps. Typically the contract life (production cycle) is one to three years. Most original equipment (OE) orders are obtained by preparing and submitting a bid proposal from a cost estimate analysis and conducting negotiating sessions with the customer. Sometimes orders are accepted as loss leaders in order to establish a position in the more profitable aftermarket business.

The contracts generally are fixed price. When coupled with the highly technical specifications and the length of the "in process" time, there is a high risk of job cost overruns. Company policy is to record revenue and costs on a completed contract basis, rather than as a percent of completion.

After a major decline in profitability, combined with several unfavorable year-end surprise inventory adjustments, new plant management decided to undertake a review of the operation to identify the key factors that affect inventory control. Management analysis revealed the following:

- The cost estimating function reported to the sales department.
- Final job costs varied significantly from original cost estimates. It was difficult to determine the source of variances until analyses were made upon completion of the jobs.
- The negotiated pricing of a contract was almost always on the basis of "whatever it takes to get the order," particularly when there was excess productive capacity in the industry.
- Progress payments/advanced payments were secured on some contracts, but such payments often were dropped if pricing competition was severe.
- When inflation was at double-digit levels, the company attempted to insert escalation clauses into contracts based on government indexes. However, most often, this resulted in fixed-price contracts with some estimate of inflation included.
- During the audit at the end of each year, a lower-of-cost-or-market analysis was made on major jobs in process. It was this exercise that revealed unfavorable inventory adjustments in recent years. Two examples are shown below:

(In Thousands)	Job 1	Job 2
Original cost Estimate	$2,113	$1,800
Costs Incurred to Date:		
Manufacturing	2,100	—
Engineering	373	100
Estimate to Complete	367	2,500
Total Current Estimate	2,840	2,600
Lower-of-cost-or-market: Contract Sales Price	2,520	2,000
Less 10% Allowance for Normal Profit Margin	(252)	(200)
Inventory Value	2,268	1,800
Inventory Reserve Adjustment (loss)	$ (572)	$ (800)

On job 2, the engineering department determined that the pump would not meet specifications in accordance with the original cost estimate and re-engineered the pump. This led to an increased estimate before the job entered the manufacturing stage.

REQUIRED:

1. What courses of action might be appropriate for the plant manager and his controller relating to (a) estimating costs, and (b) application of the lower of cost or market rule?
2. What is the significance of progress payments/advanced payments and escalation clauses on the performance of the operation?
   (IMA, 1986)

7-3.   Laurnet Products

Laurent Products is a manufacturer of plastic packaging products with plants located throughout Europe and customers worldwide. "There is no doubt that the need to continue to grow sales is an important corporate objective and one which we need to always have in mind," remarked Arnoud Baynard, managing director. "Not only is this important in terms of continuing to increase sales revenue overall but it is an essential part of our commitment for next year's budget. Resisting group pressure and allowing ourselves this time to test the market for other new segments has brought some order into this phase of our development. The segment penetration achieved so far and the opportunity to build on this most successful initiative augers well for the future. Thank you, George, for a comprehensive summary of the market result to date" concluded Arnoud. "It seems as though this initiative is one which will help us meet out short and longer-term objectives." Arnoud Baynard's summary concerned a strategy overview provided by George St. Marc, marketing director of the company.

MARKETING STRATEGY

During the past ten years Laurent Products has successfully developed a line of packaging materials and a unique bagging system which present an important opportunity to increase the productivity of checkout counters in grocery stores. The plastic bags manufactured by Laurent are produced in several sizes, different plastic film colors, and may have attractive multi-color printed designs on one or both sides to meet the specification of a particular grocery store. The company concentrated its efforts in selling to the top twenty grocery market chains in Europe. By limiting its marketing efforts to a relatively few, very large multi-outlet grocery chains (which have centralized purchasing groups), the company achieved low marketing and selling costs but high market penetration. Last year the company reached a market share of 65% in the large grocery chain market and, in turn, relatively large customer order sizes. Two market segments are evident in the large grocery chain market. In the first (called the value added segment) customers buy the company's product primarily because of its advantage in reducing operating costs at checkout counters. The advantages provided by the Laurent bagging system include the lower cost of bags and labor costs of running the checkout counter as well as improved customer service. Frequently, the store operations personnel in this segment are active in making the buying decision. The second segment is referred to as being price sensitive as the customers purchase these products primarily on the basis of price. For these customers, purchasing managers are the key decision-makers in the buying decision.

RECENT COMPETITION

Laurent's success in the grocery chain market has attracted an increasing number of competitors into the market. While the company had been very successful in bringing out a series of new product types with innovative labor-saving features for the grocery stores, the competitors have eventually been able to develop quite similar products. The result has been increased competition with a substantial reduction in Laurent's prices (dropping 26% last year), and a major decline in the firms' profit margin. The size of the price sensitive segment is growing rapidly while the value added market segment is shrinking in size. The company faces an increasingly competitive market situation characterized by significant excess producer capacity.

WHOLESALE MARKET INITIATIVE

As a result of the increased competition in the grocery chain market, George has proposed to begin to focus on the small independent grocery stores who purchase bags from large wholesale distributors. The potential sales for this wholesaler segment is about the same size as the grocery chain market (20 billion bags per year versus 25 billion bags per year), but includes a much larger number of independent store customers. At this time less than 15% of the bags sold in the wholesaler market are made of plastic. The independent grocery stores differ from the large grocery chains in that they purchase their grocery bags from wholesalers and distributors. Compared to the grocery chains, there are many more independent grocery store outlets widely dispersed over a large geographical area. The pilot marketing studies run last year by Laurent indicate that the customer order sizes for the wholesaler segment tend to be relatively small, and that the number of different product variations (in terms for example of print color, film color, and print type) tend to be relatively large in comparison with the grocery chain market. These studies also indicate that prices (and corresponding profit margins) are much higher than in the price sensitive segment currently served by the company.

MANUFACTURING

To support domestic and export sales, the company has located a number of plants throughout Europe to best support the geographical spread of the supermarket and hypermarket outlets of its various customers. "In the early years," explained Marcel Ray, manufacturing director, "capacity had, by necessity, always chased demand. The rapid growth in sales during the past few years and the need to make major decisions concerning new plant locations and process investments had understandably contributed to this capacity following the demand situation. However, with sales starting to level off this problem of capacity has now corrected itself."

Investments in manufacturing had been to support two principal objectives; to increase capacity and to reduce costs. The cost reduction initiatives principally concerned material costs and reduced processing times. "Current initiatives" explained Marcel "are continuing these themes. Our capacity uplifts will take the form of equipment similar to our existing machines. Over the years we have deliberately chosen to invest in machines which are similar to existing equipment in order to capitalize on the fact that the process is relatively simple and that products can, with relatively few exceptions, be processed on any machine in the plant. The only major restriction is the number of colors which a machine can accommodate on a single pass. Future investment proposals now being considered are based on this rationale."

In order to make best use of total capacity at all sites, customer orders are collated at the head office site in Lyon. They are then allocated to plants to take account of current plant loading, available capacity, customer lead times, and transport distances between the plant and a customer's required delivery location. As a result, forward loading on a plant is only two or, at most. three days ahead. Plants then schedule these orders into their production processes in order to meet customer call-offs and individual equipment loading rules.

Once the printing details are agreed with a customer, a plate is produced and checked. In line with a call-off schedule, the plates are allocated to machines. Color changes (where necessary) are also part of the setup details. T-1 provides an actual schedule of orders for four different bagging lines which is representative of the operations in the Paris Plant (and also for the company's other plants).

CONCLUDING REMARKS

In reviewing the proposed marketing initiatives regarding the wholesaler market, Arnoud Baynard, commented, "Since sales in our traditional markets are leveling off, the new marketing initiative appears to be an important step in giving us a fresh impetus to sales volume growth. We have now reached a point in our company where we do not have to endure capacity shortage problems. In fact, with the drop in sales last year, the company currently has excess capacity with which to pursue the wholesaler market. So, our main concern is to improve the decline in the profit performance that has occurred during the past year, and the new marketing initiatives should help to restore the profit margins and hence to secure this necessary, overall improvement.

REQUIRED

1. Discuss briefly Laurent's competitive position and strategy.
2. What are the implications of the marketing and manufacturing initiatives undertaken by Laurent?
3. How does Laurent's strategy deal effectively with global competition in its business. How should it?
4. Using the data in Table 1 and appropriate methods of analysis such as regression, analyze the effect of order size and product variety on the productivity and cost structure of the Paris plant.

TABLE 1

Machine Number	Prod. Order Quantity	Print Type Complexity	Per unit Downtime & Setup	Per Unit Runtime	Total Setup & Downtime	Total Runtime	Total Variable Cost/Unit
2	480	1	0.002	0.042	1.100	20.300	7.04
2	489	1	0.000	0.043	0.070	21.200	6.99
2	480	1	0.005	0.042	2.600	20.100	6.99
4	180	1	0.004	0.040	0.700	7.200	6.97
4	2160	2	0.002	0.035	4.700	76.600	6.94
4	1377	2	0.002	0.040	3.100	55.700	6.95
4	120	2	0.004	0.040	0.500	4.800	6.97
4	540	2	0.003	0.041	1.400	22.300	6.97
4	360	2	0.014	0.041	5.100	14.800	6.98
4	1080	2	0.011	0.038	12.000	40.600	7.01
4	300	2	0.004	0.043	1.100	12.900	7.03
4	2400	2	0.005	0.035	11.000	82.900	7.05
4	81	2	0.046	0.041	3.700	3.300	7.09
8	360	1	0.002	0.043	0.800	15.300	7.82
8	120	1	0.002	0.043	0.200	5.200	7.83
8	120	1	0.007	0.042	0.800	5.000	8.17
8	60	1	0.008	0.042	0.500	2.500	8.83
8	240	1	0.008	0.043	1.900	10.200	7.94
8	60	1	0.005	0.047	0.300	2.800	7.97
8	240	1	0.000	0.058	0.200	14.000	8.1
8	120	1	0.018	0.043	2.200	5.200	8.09
8	60	1	0.018	0.043	1.100	2.600	7.93
8	480	1	0.011	0.044	5.100	20.900	8.23
8	240	2	0.005	0.041	1.300	9.900	7.91
8	537	2	0.005	0.042	2.500	22.700	7.87
8	420	2	0.006	0.042	2.500	17.700	7.89
8	1182	2	0.015	0.042	17.700	49.200	7.89
8	60	2	0.055	0.048	3.300	2.900	8.83
8	180	2	0.012	0.042	2.200	7.600	7.9
8	60	2	0.042	0.040	2.500	2.400	7.9
8	240	2	0.007	0.043	1.600	10.300	7.86
8	60	2	0.008	0.042	0.500	2.500	7.93
8	41	2	0.029	0.046	1.200	1.900	7.96
8	60	2	0.042	0.047	2.500	2.800	8
8	120	2	0.012	0.047	1.400	5.600	8.08
8	60	2	0.062	0.042	3.700	2.500	7.9
8	60	2	0.043	0.043	2.600	2.600	8
8	360	2	0.011	0.043	3.900	15.400	8.01
8	120	2	0.020	0.047	2.400	5.600	7.97
8	180	2	0.014	0.049	2.600	8.900	8.15
8	60	2	0.023	0.043	1.400	2.600	8.27
8	60	2	0.040	0.040	2.400	2.400	8.55
8	60	2	0.042	0.043	2.500	2.600	8.66
8	60	2	0.047	0.047	2.800	2.800	8.17
8	60	4	0.048	0.042	2.900	2.500	8.06
8	60	4	0.015	0.042	0.900	2.500	8.55
8	60	4	0.058	0.042	3.500	2.500	8.11
8	120	4	0.017	0.045	2.000	5.400	8.17
8	60	4	0.057	0.040	3.400	2.400	8.06
13	120	1	0.005	0.039	0.600	4.700	6.98
13	717	1	0.004	0.041	3.100	29.500	7
13	1500	1	0.006	0.043	9.500	64.100	7.08
13	2475	1	0.009	0.034	22.500	83.000	7.2
13	240	1	0.010	0.048	2.400	11.400	7.25
13	882	2	0.018	0.030	15.700	26.600	6.47
13	1677	2	0.011	0.036	18.600	60.500	7.04
13	243	2	0.002	0.046	0.500	11.100	7.05

Applying Overhead: How to Find the Right Bases and Rates

Determine the relationship between overhead costs and various cost drivers with the help of regression analysis.

By Adel M. Novin

Direct labor no longer may be the most effective base for applying factory overhead costs to various jobs and products. With today's highly automated systems, labor-related costs constitute only a small portion of total manufacturing costs, and overhead costs now correlate more with factors such as machine hours and material quantities. Accordingly, many companies are beginning to identify application bases that better reflect the causes of overhead costs in their unique manufacturing environments.

Selection of proper application bases also has received a boost from the recent growth in activity-based costing (ABC), ABC applies accumulated costs for each activity to products and jobs using a separate base for each activity. Thus, it is crucial to select the right bases (cost drivers) for applying the costs of various activities to products and jobs.

SEARCHING FOR A PROPER BASE

Theoretically, the factory overhead cost application base should be a principal cost driver—an activity (or activities) that causes factory overhead costs to be incurred. In other words, there should be a strong cause-and-effect relationship between the factory overhead costs incurred and the base chosen for their application. Selecting the proper base requires knowledge of the relationships between the overhead costs and various cost drivers such as machine hours, direct labor hours, direct labor costs, space occupied, pounds handled, invoices processed, number of component parts, number of setups, units produced, and material costs or material quantities.

Using an objective technique, regression analysis, rather than experience or observation of activities can be helpful in ascertaining the relationship between the overhead costs and various cost drivers. Regression analysis has not been explored fully in practice, possibly due to its computational complexities coupled with a lack of easily accessible computer software. With the widespread use of microcomputers and spreadsheet programs, however, regression analysis now can be performed rather easily. The regression analysis described below was done using Lotus 1-2-3 (Version 2 and higher).

Regression analysis is one of the few quantitative techniques available for: (1) determining and analyzing the extent of the relationship between overhead costs and various cost drivers and (2) estimating the linear or curvilinear relationship between overhead costs and cost drivers. One of the values provided by regression analysis, the coefficient of determination or R Squared, measures the extent of the relationship between the two variables. More specifically, the value of R Squared indicates the percentage of variation in the dependent variable (overhead costs in this case) that is explained by variation in the independent variable (the cost driver). The value of R Squared is always between zero and 100%. The closer its value is to 100%, the stronger the relationship between the two variables.

Regression analysis can help us investigate the strength of the relationship between the overhead cost and various cost drivers. In simple terms, the cost driver that receives an R-Squared value closest to 100% will be the most accurate predictor of overhead costs. The following section will illustrate this concept.

To find the proper application base, the first step is to identify the various cost drivers that might explain changes in overhead costs. Suppose that in searching for an application base for overhead costs, we have found three possible cost drivers—direct labor hours, machine hours, and number of production setups.

Regression analysis requires actual data on selected variables for several periods. Suppose we have data from 12 consecutive months (with outliers excluded) on overhead costs, direct labor hours, machine hours, and number of production setups, as shown in T-1. The table duplicates the Lotus 1-2-3 worksheet exactly.

With three possible cost drivers, three different regression analyses should be performed, following the steps in T-2 each time. Of course, a different output-range should be selected for each variable.

T 3 presents the regression output obtained from Lotus 1-2-3 for the three regression analyses. According to the R-Squared values, machine hours explain about 77% of changes in variable overhead costs, while the number of set-ups and direct labor hours explain 39% and 29%, respectively. Thus, it appears that the most proper base for application of overhead costs in our example is machine hours because it has the strongest relationship with overhead costs.

CONSTRUCTION OF A SINGLE OVERHEAD RATE

Referring to the regression results in T-3, "Constant" represents an estimate of the fixed portion of the overhead cost, while "X Coefficient(s)" represents an estimate of the variable rate of the overhead costs. For example, based on the regression results for machine hours, the estimated linear relationship between monthly overhead costs (OH) and machine hours (MH) can be presented by the following simple regression line: OH = \$72,794 + \$74.72 MH, where \$72,794 is an estimate of total monthly fixed overhead costs and \$74.72 is the rate for the application of variable overhead costs (i.e., \$74.72 per machine hour).

We then come to the question of how to assign the fixed portion of overhead costs to products and jobs. There are two possible approaches. Under the first, a separate base that reflects the demands made by products and jobs on a firm's fixed resources is used to apply fixed costs to products and jobs. This base may be determined by engineering methods such as time and motion studies. In this case, there would be two rates based on two different bases for the application of overhead costs, one for fixed overhead and one for variable overhead costs. This approach is strongly suggested when fixed overhead

represents a major portion of overhead costs because it is more scientific than the second method.

TABLE 1
DATA FOR REGRESSION ANALYSIS

	A	B	C	D
	FOH	DIR LABOR	MACHINE	NO. OF
1	COSTS	HOURS	HOURS	SETUPS
2				
3	155,000	985	1,060	200
4	160,000	1,068	1,080	225
5	170,000	1,095	1,100	250
6	165,000	1,105	1,200	202
7	185,000	1,200	1,600	210
8	135,000	1,160	1,100	150
9	145,000	1,145	1,080	165
10	150,000	1,025	1,090	180
11	180,000	1,115	1,300	204
12	175,000	1,136	1,400	206
13	190,000	1,185	1,500	208
14	200,000	1,220	1,700	212

Under the second approach, a company may decide to apply fixed overhead to products and jobs using the same base as that identified for the variable overhead costs. In this case, the overall overhead rate may be determined by regression through origin, which forces fixed costs to zero. To perform regression through origin on machine hours, follow steps 1 through 4 of T-2 (using the range of observations

TABLE 2
STEPS TO PERFORM SIMPLE REGRESSION ANALYSIS

1) Having the Lotus worksheet with data (i.e., Table 1) on the screen, type /DR to activate the regression analysis program.

2) Having the cursor on the "X-Range" option, press the return key, and type the range of observations for direct labor hours (e.g. B3.B14). Press the return key. "X-Range" will always be used to denote the range for the cost driver (independent variable).

3) Move the cursor to the "Y-Range" option, press the return key, and then type the range of observations for overhead costs (e.g. A3.A14). Press the return key. The "Y-Range" will always be used to denote the range for the costs (dependent variable).

4) Move the cursor to the "Output-Range" option, press the return key, and then type in the desired starting cell for the results (e.g., A20).

5) Move the cursor to the "Go" option, and press the return key to run the regression analysis. At this point the regression results will appear on the screen.

TABLE 3
REGRESSION OUTPUT FROM LOTUS 1-2-3

REGRESSION RESULTS FOR OVERHEAD COSTS WITH DL HOURS
Regression Output:

Constant		919.02
Std Err of Y Est		17,267.60
R Squared		0.29
No. of Observations		12
Degrees of Freedom		10
X Coefficient(s)	148.74	
Std Err of Coef.	74.35	

REGRESSION RESULTS FOR OVERHEAD COSTS WITH MACHINE HOURS
Regression Output:

Constant		72,793.81
Std Err of Y Est		9,799.08
R Squared		0.77
No. of Observations		12
Degrees of Freedom		10
X Coefficient(s)	74.72	
Std Err of Coef.	12.91	

REGRESSION RESULTS FOR OVERHEAD COSTS WITH NUMBER OF SETUPS
Regression Output:

Constant		74,033.14
Std Err of Y Est		15,909.72
R Squared		0.39
No. of Observations		12
Degrees of Freedom		10
X Coefficient(s)	465.00	
Std Err of Coef.	182.47	

TABLE 4
REGRESSION RESULTS FOR OVERHEAD COSTS WITH MACHINE HOURS THROUGH ORIGIN

Regression Output:

Constant		00.00
Std Err of Y Est		15,966.99
R Squared		0.33
No. of Observations		12
Degrees of Freedom		11
X Coefficient(s)	130.48	
Std Err of Coef.	3.58	

TABLE 5
MULTIPLE REGRESSION RESULTS FOR OVERHEAD COSTS WITH MACHINE HOURS AND NUMBER OF SETUPS

Regression Output:

Constant		19,796.43
Std Err of Y Est		4,951.11
R Squared		0.95
No. of Observations		12
Degrees of Freedom		9
X Coefficient(s)	65.44	322.21
Std Err of Coef.	6.74	58.66

for machine hours instead of direct labor hours for the "X-Range"), then move the cursor to the "Intercept" option, press the return key, and select the "Zero" option. According to the results, shown in Table 4, OH = $130.48MH. That is, the overhead rate is $130.48 per machine hour, with no separate fixed portion. This method of allocating fixed overhead costs to products and jobs is not as scientifically accurate as the engineering method; however, it is much simpler to use and does not distort cost allocation significantly when fixed overhead is a relatively small portion of total overhead costs.

CONSTRUCTION OF MULTIPLE OVERHEAD RATES

In a complex manufacturing environment, variable overhead costs may be driven by several equally important factors. Under such circumstances, the use of more than one base for the application of variable overhead costs to products and jobs results in a more accurate cost estimate. For example, the cost of one activity, material handling, may be applied to products based upon both the number of material requisitions and the number of parts per material requisition. To accommodate the use of more than one independent variable, we would need to perform a multiple regression, which Lotus 1-2-3 also allows for. Thus, we can construct more than one overhead rate.

Continuing our prior example, suppose that we want to apply overhead costs based on the two cost drivers with the strongest relationship to overhead cost—machine hours and number of setups. To perform multiple regression analysis, follow the same steps as for performance of simple regression, except that the "X-Range" will consist of the range of observations for both machine hours and number of setups (that is, C3.D14).

T-5 presents the results for the multiple regression. "Constant" represents an estimate of the fixed overhead cost, while "X Coefficients" represent an estimate of the variable rates of the overhead costs. For example, the estimated relationship between

TABLE 6
MULTIPLE REGRESSION RESULTS FOR OVERHEAD COSTS WITH MACHINE HOURS AND NUMBER OF SETUPS THROUGH ORIGIN

Regression Output:

Constant		00.00
Std Err of Y Est		5,285.53
R Squared		0.93
No. of Observations		12
Degrees of Freedom		10
X Coefficient(s)	69.99	390.72
Std Err of Coef.	6.47	41.10

the overhead costs (OH) and the two driving factors, machine hours (MH) and number of setups (NS), can be expressed by the following multiple regression line: OH = $19,796.43 + $65.44 MH + $322.21 NS, where $19,796.43 is an estimate of the total monthly fixed overhead costs, and $65.44 and $322.21 are the estimated variable overhead costs per machine hour and per setup, respectively. The value of R Squared for the multiple regression line is 95%, which is greater than that of the simple regression line based solely on machine hours (77%). This fact implies that the application of variable overhead costs based on both machine hours and number of setups would result in more accurate cost estimates

Here, again, total fixed overhead costs may be applied to jobs and products either using a different base determined by engineering methods such as time and motion studies or using the same base as for variable overhead (machine hours and number of setups). Use of a separate base for the application of fixed costs would result in a total of three overhead rates, one for fixed overhead and two for variable overheads.

If we decide to apply fixed overhead using the identified bases for variable overhead costs (machine hours and number of setups), then we should use multiple regression through origin. The steps to perform multiple regression through origin are the same as those used to perform regular multiple regression, except that the "intercept equal to zero" option must be selected, as is done for simple regression through origin. Referring to the results in T-6, the estimated relationship between the overhead costs (OH) and the two driving factors, machine hours (MH) and

number of setups (NS), with zero fixed costs, can be expressed by the following multiple regression line: OH = $69.99 MH + $390.72 NS. That is, overhead costs will be applied to products and jobs based on $69.99 per machine hour and $390.72 per setup.

It is important to remember that the variable overhead rates computed by regression analysis (the "X Coefficients") are estimates derived from our 12 observations. The reliability of the estimated variable overhead rates can and should be determined by computing the t-test value for each rate. The t-test value equals the "X Coefficients" over the "Std Err of Coef." As a general rule, if the absolute value of the t-test for any variable rate is greater than two, then the estimated overhead rate is considered highly reliable. Referring to Table 3, for example, the value of the t-test for the variable overhead based on machine hours is about 5.8 (74.72/12.91), which tells us that the rate can be relied upon. The overhead sites determined from regression analysis, after adjusting for expected future inflation, would be usable as long as no major change in the cost structure and manufacturing process has occurred.

RATES FOR ACTIVITY-BASED COSTING

For more accurate product costing, firms are beginning to use activity-based costing for computing overhead costs. under this system, accumulated costs for each activity are applied to products and jobs using a separate base for each activity. in a manner similar to that described above, regression analysis can be used to investigate the strength of the relationship between various activities and cost drivers in order to determine the proper base(s) and rate(s) for applying the cost of each activity to products and jobs.

We also may use regression analysis to classify a large number of activities into a few groups (cost pools) based on common bases. Suppose that through use of simple regression analysis, we have computed the R-Squared values for the pairs of activities and cost drivers shown in T-7. Based on the R-

TABLE 7
R-SQUARED VALUES FOR VARIOUS PAIRS OF ACTIVITIES AND COST DRIVERS

	Maintenance	Packaging	Materials Handling	Storage	Production Scheduling
Machine Hours	.85	.46	.68	.45	.82
Pounds of Material	.38	.88	.90	.75	.43
Labor Hours	.30	.28	.38	.22	.43

Squared values, we may group the five activities into two cost pools. It appears that the principal cause of the packaging, materials handling and storage activities costs is pounds of materials. Thus, the cost pool consisting of the accumulated costs of these three activities can be applied to products and jobs based on number of pounds of materials used. Similarly, the accumulated costs of maintenance and production scheduling, which have a high correlation with machine hours, can be applied to products and jobs based on machine hours. In this way, all costs included in each cost pool will have the same cause-and-effect relationship with the chosen cost allocation base.

As business becomes increasingly more competitive, decision makers are demanding more accurate cost figures from cost accounting systems. For accurate costing, it is crucial that factory overhead and activity costs be applied to various products and jobs using bases that reflect principal causes of the overhead costs. Regression analysis has proved to be a practical, effective, and objective method for selecting proper cost application bases.

In addition to its usefulness for determining proper application bases, regression analysis is a practical method for developing single or multiple overhead rates for the application of overhead costs to products and jobs. With the widespread use of microcomputers and spreadsheet programs such as Lotus 1-2-3, regression analysis can be performed easily.

Measuring Learning Costs

When systems change, how humans learn directly affects productivity.

By Ken M. Boze, CPA

Certificate of Merit, 1993-94

Management accountants are in a unique position to foster change by improving accounting, data gathering, internal control, or information processing systems. But often learning costs associated with change are grossly underestimated. Change, seen as an improvement by management, may be viewed by employees as adding complexity, causing resistance or even refusal to learn the new system.

As Nathan Weaks[1] notes, "The key (to being valuable) is convincing managers we can solve more problems than we create."

Change always has a cost, and systems changes are not exception to this rule. Many of these costs, which are easily quantifiable, are transparent to change agents. Learning costs, however, sometimes are not as visible to managers and therefore can contribute to overall dissatisfaction with a project that might not meet expectations. Managers and management accountants need to understand better the relationship between system change, the learning curve, and productivity.

The first step in the training scenario is that employees must learn new procedures. These procedures could involve data entry, information processing, or user analysis. When examined quantitatively and under ideal circumstances, the changes may promise benefits vastly exceeding costs. Sometimes the true costs exceed the benefits, and frustrated managers might contemplate foregoing the changes.

The next step may be to educate the person being "helped" by listing the benefits and advantages of the changes. Accountants may market their ideas with logic, assuming the changes will be welcomed after they are understood.

The system users then may try the changes, only to confirm their previous sentiments that they are not worth the efforts. At this point the movement toward change may deteriorate to frustrated finger pointing.

Instead of becoming more valuable to the system user, the accountant becomes a political antagonist.

GREAT LEAP FORWARD VS. EVOLUTIONARY APPROACH

Often, successful change occurs through crises, as when an important customer is deciding to take its business elsewhere. During crisis, employees marshal their survival skills, putting in the necessary overtime and home time to retrain themselves. Change occurs at painfully high costs for both the individual and the company.

J. W. Wilkinson[2] defines this type of system change as a "Great Leap Forward." Such a change attempts to cover great technological distances in a single bound, moving from an out-of-date, ineffective system to advanced capabilities quickly. Successful great leaps make good press. The unsuccessful scarcely appear except in the financial obituaries. He states:

> "...(this) approach entails several risks. Attempting to move forward too far too fast can lead to costly failure. The leap may be too complex for the systems analysts and programmers to handle successfully. Or, the leap may provide a sophisticated system that the unsophisticated are not prepared to accept and use effectively."

In an accounting setting this type of change may occur when a timeworn accounting system, viewed with disdain, cannot deliver critical facts necessary for pressing decisions when customers are leaving and plants are shutting down. Users may demand to throw out the old system for "one that works." Hence, a great leap forward occurs.

The downside for this approach in bureaucracies, both inside and outside government, is that well-known firms engaged to deliver new accounting systems may develop systems that never work as promised or are never fully implemented.

A more common path to system changes is the evolutionary approach.[3] This approach moves through a series of stages over time, developing each stage into a somewhat more advanced system. Manageable change comes in small doses. The evolutionary approach may seem to avoid many problems of the great leap because it avoids throwing out the old system . It does not imply changing the old system constantly or adopting the frequent updates provided by, for example, software manufacturers if these updates cause significant productivity problems.

Unfortunately, evolutionary changes also entail risks. Adjustments may occur so often that employees are constantly high on the learning curve, the promised benefits never materializing.

Many young accounting staffers try to stay on the cutting edge by learning the latest programs or system advances. Proficiency with a particular system usually coincides with an increased responsibility for output and efficiency. As staffers mature professionally, however, they no longer have the luxury of enough time to learn new system implementations, but they are expected to be productive because they are "experienced."

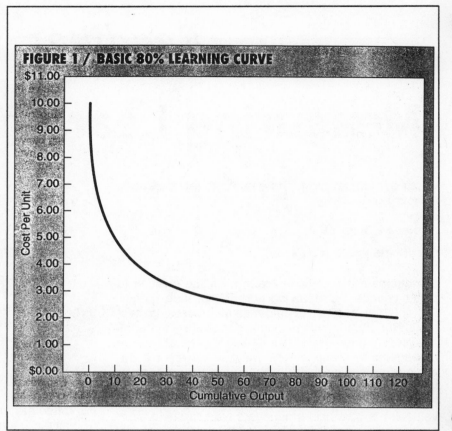

FIGURE 1 / BASIC 80% LEARNING CURVE

THE EVOLUTIONARY PROCESS AND THE LEARNING CURVE

The chemical industry serves as an example of the evolutionary process where highly automated production depends heavily on capital investment. The capital investment, in turn, incorporates learning from current research and previous production systems, which have evolved into cost-efficient, mechanical processes.

A study performed by M.B. Liberman in 1984 found that cost efficiencies are a direct result of learning.[4] Liberman statistically fit the traditional "learning curve" observed by T. P. Wright in 1936 to several decades of cost and price data for the chemical industry.[5] The learning curve explained cost changes more significantly than any other factor studied previously, including company size.

Also discovered was that the slope of the learning curve, that is, the rate at which learning is transformed into cost improvements, depends a great deal on research and development (R&D) expenditures and capital intensity. The more automated the system and the more spent on R&D (learning), the greater the efficiency improvements for a given period.

Liberman states that the learning curve (also called cost curve, efficiency curve, productivity curve, learning theory, and so on) is used extensively in industry as a tool for production planning, cost forecasting, and delivery schedules.

Accounting systems are following the chemical industry's pattern of automating data collection and evaluation processes. Yet, we see little attention paid to the learning costs of accounting system changes. Both collecting and inputting data and interpreting the results involve learning.

SUBCONSCIOUS LEARNING

Recent discoveries about memory loss and training indicate the human brain stores learning in different areas. People who cannot learn on the conscious cognitive level, due to disease or brain injury, can learn at the subconscious level to be efficient at repetitive jobs such as data entry.[6]

Many training programs target the conscious level, yet it is the subconscious level, the instinctive level, that determines efficiency. It is at this level where procedures are stored from repetition and on-the-job training.

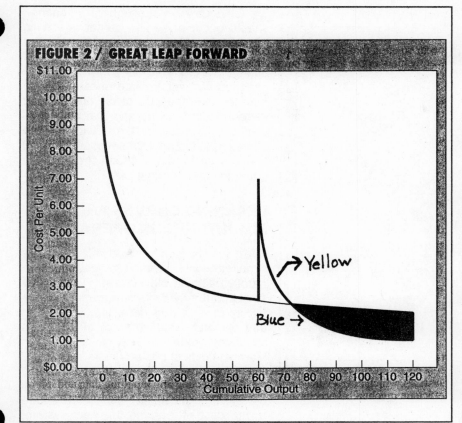

FIGURE 2 / GREAT LEAP FORWARD

Yellow

Blue →

Cost Per Unit (vertical axis): $0.00 to $11.00

Cumulative Output (horizontal axis): 0 to 120

Y = Cost per unit.
X = The attempt number or units produced to date.
a = The cost of the first unit or successful attempt.
b = The learning elasticity.

This equation can be graphed very easily and incorporated into system change evaluations.

The 80% learning curve is standard for many activities and can serve as an average in forecasting learning costs. For each doubling of output, the cost of the new output is 80% of the cost of the prior output. The learning elasticity for this curve is about .32.

Movement down the curve occurs by eliminating hesitation and mistakes, automating certain tasks, and system users making changes. A new curve is created when there are major changes because new procedures must be learned and old ones eliminated. A disruption in an established routine may cause costs to increase and efficiency to decrease temporarily as users either hesitate to undertake the new routine or adopt the new routine in error.

Directly addressing this problem is Lotus. By preserving its keystroke sequences in updated versions of its 1-2-3 spreadsheet program, it still dominates the spreadsheet market over programs providing better output or features. Other software producers may have fizzled as they enhanced their programs and in the process changed keystroke sequences used instinctively by longtime users.

MEASURING LEARNING

The learning curve graphically portrays costs and benefits of experience. It plots cost per unit of additional output on the vertical axis and cumulative output on the horizontal axis. It is a geometric curve, decreasing quickly at first, then leveling. As a person attempts a new task, learning occurs quickly and the curve is steep. With each additional repetition, learning occurs at a decreasing rate and the learning curve flattens. Some call this flat part of the learning curve a "learning plateau," where improvement is small. The equation for the learning curve is:

$$Y = a\,X^{-b}$$

Where:

THE LEARNING CURVE AND THE GREAT LEAP FORWARD

Figure 2 shows the great leap forward approach to system changes. Two learning curves are overlaid. The first starts high and on the left, representing learning costs of the old system. The second appears about midway through the graph and represents a new system or major change.

The heavy line represents actual costs per unit as expertise grows with an old system. Then a major change is made, and the curve spikes with the change. The yellow area above the old curve and below the new one represents increased learning costs due to the change. The blue area on the right below the old curve and above the new curve, represents the benefits of the change.

The optimal modification strategy compares anticipated change costs to benefits, changing only when net benefits are positive. Figure 2 shows a positive net benefits change. In this example, the benefits clearly outweigh the costs. Nonetheless, costs are very high in the short run.

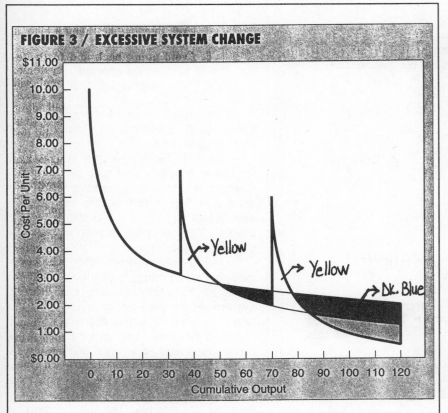

FIGURE 3 / EXCESSIVE SYSTEM CHANGE

Obviously, subsequent change should occur at some optimal rate such that costs do not stay high on the learning curve. The benefits of the first change may extend well past subsequent changes and accumulate positively. Also note that the changes cause the learning plateau to drop away and that more efficiency is possible than without the changes. Changes that necessitate small learning costs may steepen the long-run learning curve, or cost path, significantly.

LEARNING CURVES AND SIMULTANEOUS OPERATIONS

The Wilkinson study suggests simultaneously running a new system parallel with an old system.[7] The theory says that if a new system goes through a full cycle with real data, you will detect and eliminate problems not evident with simulated data. Figure 4 shows the learning costs of this process.

The learning cost spike turns into more of a tower. The costs of running the old system, shown in yellow, are added to the cost of learning the new system, shown in orange. Not only is learning taking place with the new system, but learning continues with the old

THE LEARNING CURVE AND FREQUENT CHANGES

Figure 3 shows what happens when changes occur at frequent intervals. Two changes are plotted rather close together.

The graph demonstrates the benefits of the first change in dark blue and of the second change in light blue. The learning costs are shown in yellow. It is possible to pile change on change and get a net cost curve that climbs like a staircase or place changes so close the graph looks like a saw cutting into profits. In these cases, learning costs always exceed any realized benefits unless conditions stabilize.

This example is constructed to highlight that the cost savings of any change may be reduced by subsequent changes. Because the second change occurs quickly, the benefits of the first change are cut short by the savings lost while learning is taking place on the second change. The total reduced benefits of these changes may never equal learning costs if changes occur frequently or if the life of the system is short.

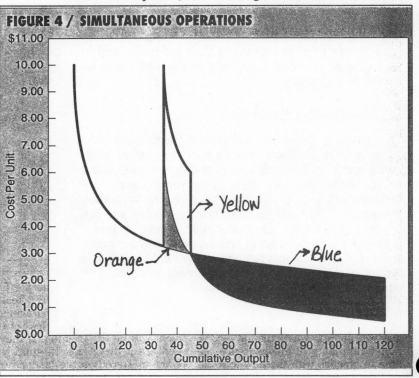

FIGURE 4 / SIMULTANEOUS OPERATIONS

112

system. Because costs are quite steep, the process is frequently cut short by making the transition too soon or never adopting the new system fully. This example shows visually that the benefits, in blue, can indeed be greater than the learning costs of running two systems simultaneously.

PRACTICAL IMPLICATIONS

In practice, learning costs are often underestimated for hands-on exercises and training. Benefits are overestimated due to new efficiencies never being fully realized when more changes are made. Or, changes are never learned and implemented.

As with many forecasting activities, measuring and calculating these amounts are difficult, yet it is possible. One consultant suggested that a "Rule of Twos" may apply here. The rule is: "It always costs twice as much, takes twice as long, and delivers half of what the experts tell you it will." Or, you can use the learning curve equation.

Table 1 is included to aid in quantifying costs and designing training programs. It shows the productivity from additional exercises or attempts at a new procedure or process using the standard 80% learning curve described earlier. The middle column shows the incremental productivity increase, and the right column shows the cumulative productivity increase.

The first attempt is expensive. The second yields a 20% time reduction. It takes five attempts to get about a 40% reduction from the first attempt and eight or nine to reach the 50% point. Additional improvement is small beyond that.

The data tell us training programs should contain at least eight to 10 exercises for each activity, which should move the individual well down the learning curve. Added time between training and practical application shifts the learning curve up, as does time away from the job. Therefore, it is important users apply what they learn quickly and get plenty of practice. Training should be timed with this in mind. When changes are made, allow liberal hands-on, low-pressure, consistent training time.

When changes are initiated from the outside, the intiator must appreciate these *lost productivity* learning costs. It is important to include more than just the cost of training sessions in the budget, but to maintain credibility with system users, anticipate initially less productivity as well.

RECOMMENDATIONS

Here are some recommendations for management accountants to put into practice when they are instituting systems changes at their companies:

	TABLE 1 EXPECTED IMPROVEMENT WITH 80% LEARNING CURVE	
Attempt Number	Expected Productivity Increase from Prior Attempt	Expected Cumulative Improvement from First Attempt
2	20.0%	20.0%
3	12.2	29.8
4	8.8	36.0
5	6.9	40.4
6	5.7	43.8
7	4.8	46.6
8	4.2	48.8
9	3.7	50.7
10	3.3	52.4
11	3.0	53.8
12	2.8	55.1
13	2.5	56.2
14	2.4	57.2
15	2.2	58.2
16	2.1	59.0
17	1.9	59.8
18	1.8	60.6
19	1.7	61.3
20	1.6	61.9
21	1.6	62.5
22	1.5	63.0
23	1.4	63.6
24	1.4	64.1
25	1.3	64.5
26	1.3	65.0
27	1.2	65.4
28	1.2	65.8
29	1.1	66.2
30	1.1	66.6
31	1.1	66.9
32	1.0	67.2
33	1.0	67.6
34	1.0	67.9

1. Avoid trying to stay current with the most recent technology by constantly making changes. Realize the benefits of learning by using a system for a reasonable period of time without making a major change.

2. When you do change or modify systems, make the new links to humans as similar as possible to the old links. Use similar key-stroke sequences and functions, or keep manual processes very similar to old routines. Encourage the users' inputs. This practice results in moving the users down the learning curve toward lowered costs.

3. Lower expectations of the benefits from short seminars that teach about new ways of dealing with the system yet have little or no "hands-on practice." Doing it once, or being told how to do it, without sufficient practice, is not enough.

4. Recognize that the "Rule of Twos" may well apply to your situation.

5. Schedule plenty of low-pressure time to practice with the new system and allow for decreased efficiency during the changeover. Realize that the longer between training and implementation, the less efficient will be the training. If they don't use it, they do lose it—quickly. Once mastered on the instinctive level, though, like riding a bike. It will always be there.

6. Avoid going back and forth between the old and new systems. Recognize that certain stimuli will trigger automatic responses (flashbacks) where someone will "do it the old way" without thinking, thus increasing learning costs by decreasing productivity.

7. Realize that the longer someone has been doing something, the harder it will be for him or her to change. The first system a person learns is probably the most eficient one. The more experienced employees may have the most difficulty changing.

8. Allow individuals who are under pressure to produce and who have little time or motivation to change to use whatever is best fo them. Concentrate on automating changes while keeping human links as similar to the old ways as possible. Have the system make changes instead of having individuals learn new ways. Sometimes it is easier to teach a machine than a person.

In summary, remember that system changes have a hidden cost and implementation plans should take such costs into account. The old ways will fade with time if they are not used. Helping the older and more experienced employees build bridges with the new methods may yield more benefits to you in office politics, loyalty, and allies than any amount of money your initial suggestions saved the firm.

Ken M. Boze, Ph.D., CPA, is associate professor, School of Business, University of Alaska Anchorage, Anchorage, Alaska, He can be reached at (907) 786-4144.

[1] S. Jayson, "Playing on the Management Team," MANAGEMENT ACCOUNTING, March 1993, p. 24.

[2] J. W. Wilkinson, *Accounting and Information Systems,* 2nd ed. John Wiley & Sons: New York, 1986, p. 764.

[3] Ibid.

[4] M. B. Liberman, "The Learning Curve and Pricing in the Chemical Processing Industries," *Rand Journal of Economics*, Vol. 15, No. 2, Summer 1984.

[5] T. P. Wright, "Factors Affecting the Cost of Airplanes," *Journal of Aeronautical Sciences,* Vol. 3. No. 4, 1936, pp. 122-128.

[6] D. Stiff, "Amnesia Studies Show Brain Can Be Taught at Subconscious Level," *The Wall Street Journal*, October 5, 1993.

[7]

Chapter 8
Cost-Volume-Profit Analysis

Cases

Readings

Richard A. Lord: Interpreting and Measuring Operating Leverage

The paper presents an extended coverage of operating leverage. It develops the relationship between operating leverage and changes in fixed and variable costs. It also shows that there is not a simple, direct relationship between operating leverage and the level of fixed costs. Also, alternative measures of operating leverage are considered, and the differences between the measures are explained.

Discussion Questions:
1. What is the significance of the results in this paper for the use of the concept of operating leverage in the strategic analysis of firms?
2. Is operating leverage affected by changes in both fixed and variable costs or of fixed costs only? Explain your answer.
3. What are the problems in using a point-to-point (elasticity-based) measure of operating leverage?

116

Cases

8-1. Cost-Volume-Profit Analysis and Strategy

Mr. Carter is the manager of Simmons Farm and Seed Company, a wholesaler of fertilizer, seed, and other farm supplies. The company has been successful in recent years primarily because of great customer service—flexible credit terms, customized orders (quantities, seed mix, etc), and on-time delivery, among others. Global Agricultural Products, Inc., Simmons' parent corporation, has informed Mr. Carter that his budgeted net income for 19x7 will be $120,000. The budget was based on data for the prior year and Mr. Carter's belief that there would be no significant changes in revenues and expenses for the coming period.

After the determination of the budget, Carter received notice from Simmons' principal shipping agent that it was about to increase its rates by 10%. This carrier handles 90% of Simmons' total shipping volume. Paying the increased rate will result in failure to meet the budgeted income level, and Mr. Carter is understandably reluctant to allow that to happen. He is considering two alternatives. First, it is possible to use another carrier whose rates are 5% less than the old carrier's original rate. The old carrier, however, is a subsidiary of a major customer; shifting to a new carrier will almost certainly result in loss of that customer and sales amounting to $70,000.

Assume that prior to the recent rate increase, the shipping costs of the principal carrier and the other carriers were the same, and that costs of the other carriers are not expected to change.

As a second alternative, Simmons can purchase its own trucks thereby reducing its shipping costs to 85% of the original rate. The new trucks would have an expected life of 10 years, no salvage value and would be depreciated on a straight line basis. Related fixed costs excluding depreciation would be $2,000. Assume that if Simmons purchases the trucks, Simmons will replace the principal shipper and the other shippers.

Following are data from the prior year:

Sales	$1,500,000
Variable costs (excluding shipping)	1,095,000
Shipping costs	135,000
Fixed costs	150,000

REQUIRED:

1. Using cost-volume-profit analysis and the data provided, determine the maximum amount that Mr. Carter can pay for the trucks and still expect to attain budgeted net income.
2. At what price for a truck would Mr. Carter be indifferent between purchasing the new trucks and using a new carrier?
3. Mr. Carter has decided to use a new carrier, but now is worried its apparent lack of reliability may adversely affect sales volume. Determine the dollar amount of sales that Simmons can lose because of lack of reliability before any benefit from switching carriers is lost completely.
4. Describe what you think is the competitive strategy of Simmons Farm and Seed Company. What should be the strategy? How would the use of a new carrier affect the strategy?
5. Can Mr. Carter use value chain analysis to improve the profits of Simmons Farm and Seed Company? If so, explain how briefly.

8-2. Cost-Volume-Profit Analysis and Cost Estimation

The following requirement is based on information in the Atlantic City Casino case, case 2-33 at the end of Chapter 2. Re-read the case and complete the requirements below.

REQUIRED:

1. Using the data provided in the case, build a cost estimation model to predict net income based on total revenues. Then, use this model to determine an estimate of the industry-wide breakeven point in sales revenue. Evaluate the reliability and precision of the estimation method you have chosen.
2. Develop a cost estimation model to predict casino revenues based on square feet of casino floor space. Use this model to determine the expected full-year revenue for casino number nine. Evaluate the precision and reliability of the method you have chosen.
3. Repeat part (2) above, using number of rooms to predict room revenues, and number of restaurants to predict food and beverage revenues for the full year for casino number nine.

8-3. Cost-Volume-Profit Analysis and Strategy II

Melford Hospital operates a general hospital, but rents space and beds to separately-owned entities rendering specialized services such as pediatrics and psychiatric care. Melford charges each separate entity for common services such as patients' meals and laundry, and for administrative services such as billings and collections. Space and bed rentals are fixed charges for the year, based on bed capacity rented to each entity.

Melford charged the following costs to pediatrics for the year ended June 30, 19X2:

	Patient Days (variable)	Bed Capacity (fixed)
Dietary	$ 600,000	—
Janitorial	—	$ 70,000
Laundry	300,000	—
Laboratory	450,000	—
Pharmacy	350,000	—
Repairs and maintenance	—	30,000
General and administrative	—	1,300,000
Rent	—	1,500,000
Billings and collections	300,000	—
Total	$2,000,000	$2,900,000

During the year ended June 30, 19X2, pediatrics charged each patient an average of $300 per day, had a capacity of 60 beds, and had revenue of $6,000,000 for 365 days. In addition, pediatrics directly employed the following personnel:

	Annual Salaries
Supervising nurses	$25,000
Nurses	20,000
Aides	9,000

Melford has the following minimum departmental personnel requirements based on total annual patients days:

Annual Patient Days	Aides	Nurses	Supervising Nurses
Up to 21,900	20	10	4
21,900 to 26,000	26	13	4
26,001 to 29,200	30	15	4

These staffing levels represent full-time equivalents. Pediatrics always employs only the minimum number of required full-time personnel. Salaries of supervising nurses, nurses, and aides are therefor fixed within ranges of annual patient days.

Pediatrics operated at 100% capacity on 90 days during the year ended June 30, 19X2. It is estimated that during these 90 days the demand exceeded 20 patients more than capacity. Melford has an additional 20 beds available for rent for the year ending June 30, 19X3. Such additional rental would increase pediatrics' fixed charges based on bed capacity.

119

REQUIRED:

1. What is the strategic role of CVP analysis for Melford hospital?

2. Determine the minimum number of patient days required for pediatrics to breakeven for the year ending June 30, 19X3, if the additional 20 beds are not rented. Patient demand is unknown, but assume that revenue per patient day, cost per patient day, cost per bed, and salary rates will remain the same as for the year ended June 30, 19X2.

3. Assume that patient demand, revenue, revenue per patient day, cost per patient day, cost per bed, and salary rates for the year ending June 30, 19X3 remain the same as for the year ended June 30, 19X2. Prepare a schedule of increase in revenue and increase in costs for the year ending June 30, 19X3, in order to determine the net increase or decrease in earnings from the additional 20 beds if pediatrics rents this extra capacity from Melford.

Interpreting and Measuring Operating Leverage

Richard A. Lord

ABSTRACT: This paper has two objectives. First, the relationship between changes in the degree of operating leverage and break-even point with changes in fixed and variable costs is explored. It is shown that changes in these measures are positively related to changes in both fixed and variable costs. In fact, the present study shows that it is possible for fixed costs to rise while unit variable costs fall and, still for both the degree of operating leverage and breakeven point to decrease. This is contrary to the impression given in many accounting and finance texts. Second, the study examines alternative methodologies for calculation of the degree of operating leverage and the interpretation of the different signs and magnitudes of the measures. There are important differences in the several methods of computing the degree of operating leverage which can produce misleading notions about the firm's operating characteristics.

Most business majors study the concept of break-even analysis at some point in their accounting training. Many of these students are also exposed to the notions of operating leverage and degree of operating leverage in their courses on managerial accounting and finance. It is often implicitly suggested that operating leverage is a simple measure of the extent to which a firm is employing fixed costs in its production function. This paper explores two aspects of the firm's degree of operating leverage.

First, the theoretical relationship between changes in a firm's operating characteristics (unit price, level of output, unit variable cost, and fixed costs) and its degree of operating leverage is developed. It is found that conventional measures of degree of operating leverage do not necessarily rise as fixed costs increase accompanied by a decrease in unit variable costs, but that changes in the degree of operating lev-

erage are positively related to increases in cost, whether fixed or variable. Even more interesting, it is found that (for a given level of demand) each firm has a natural rate of substitution at which it can increase fixed costs while lowering variable costs without any change in the degree of operating leverage or break-even point. In fact, it is possible to find a firm taking on higher levels of fixed costs with lower unit variable costs and have its degree of operating leverage and break-even point decrease.

The second area of concern is the difference between measures of degree of operating leverage as they are computed in practice, as compared to how they appear in most textbooks. There are two computational nuances to consider. One is the simple difference between point elasticities and point-to-point elasticities. The other is the tendency of point-to-point measures of degree of operating leverage to produce numerical results less than one for small changes in unit output. This is of extreme importance for researchers attempting to employ degree of operating leverage as a simple linear or curvilinear proxy for a firm's operating leverage.

The relationship between fixed and variable cost technology, operating leverage, and the break-even point is first outlined. Then, a theoretical analysis of degree of operating leverage is developed. Next, the empirical performance of the various methods to calculate the degree of operating leverage are presented, and in the final section, conclusions are summarized.

RELATIONSHIP BETWEEN FIXED COST, VARIABLE COST, AND OPERATING LEVERAGE

The principles of fixed and variable costs are usually introduced to students early-on in cost and managerial accounting, as well as microeconomics courses. While these concepts are simple to understand, practitioners know what they—especially fixed costs—are elusive in real life.

After exposure to the idea of fixed and variable costs, some students in managerial accounting and finance are introduced to the concept of operating leverage. Characteristic is the statement from Garrison and Noreen (1994, p. 295) that "If a company has high operating leverage (that is, a high portion of fixed costs in relation to variable costs), then profits will be very sensitive to changes in sales." Similar definitions can be found in managerial accounting texts by Hansen and Mowen (1994, 350) and Hilton (1994, 339). They are also common in finance texts—for instance the popular volume by Brigham (1994, 426). To demonstrate this relationship, authors show a couple of hypothetical income statements. These examples usually leave the student convinced that firms with high fixed costs and low variable costs will have high levels of operating leverage.

Notice, however, that the word "portion" in Garrison and Noreen's definition makes the operating leverage dependent on the level of the firm's rate of output, which, in turn, depends on quantity demanded. For instance, imagine a firm with a production function involving a given (annual) fixed cost and a per-unit variable cost. If it produced only one unit this year, it would clearly have very high fixed costs relative to variable costs, hence it would have a high level of operating leverage. As output begins to rise, however, the firm's level of operating leverage would begin to fall. This definition of operating leverage depends as much (or more) on the exogenous level of demand as it does on the endogenous fixed and variable cost technology the firm has chosen to employ.

Most textbooks also present alternative measures to quantify the relationship between the amounts of fixed cost and unit variable cost in a firm's production technology and the risks associated with demand for the product. The most common and most simple is, of course, the break-even point (BE). Cost accounting texts usually include a lengthy discussion of cost-volume-profit (CVP) analysis. Many managerial accounting texts also feature a presentation of degree of operating leverage (DOL). For instance, Garrison and Noreen (1994, 296) and Hansen and Mowen (1994, p. 350) both include a discussion of DOL, while Hilton (1994) does not. In this work, we will concentrate on the properties of DOL as a measure of the relative amounts of fixed and unit variable costs employed by the firm in production (with occasional references to the BE).

When a discussion of DOL is included in accounting texts, the most popular definition is:

$$DOL_1 = [(p-v)Q]/[(p-v)Q - F], (1)$$

where p is the unit price of goods sold, v is the unit variable cost, F is the periodic fixed cost of the firm,

and Q is the unit output or quantity demanded for the period. From a practical point of view, this presentation is not very useful, as the parameters necessary for the calculation are usually unobservable.

A more workable alternative presented by Brigham (1994, 440) in his finance text, which we will dub DOL_2 is:

$$DOL_2 = \% \Delta \text{ EBIT} / \% \Delta Q, (2)$$

where EBIT is the firm's earnings before interest and taxes $((p-v)Q - F)$. Again, since Q is often unobservable to outside analysts, equation (2) is often presented as

$$DOL_3 = \% \Delta \text{ EBIT} / \% \Delta \text{ Sales (\$), (3)}$$

where sales are pQ. Such definitions occur less frequently in the managerial accounting texts, but they do occasionally appear. For instance, see Hansen and Mowen, (1994, 350) and Maher et al. (1991, p. 917).

It is obvious from equations (2) and (3) that DOL is what an economist would call an elasticity measure. As defined above, DOL, is a point estimate of the elasticity measure whereas DOL_2 and DOL_3 are arc elasticities or estimates of the elasticity made from actual, observed changes.

We wish to determine to what extent these elasticity measures of operating leverage tell us about changes in the endogenous level of fixed and variable cost in the firm's production function. By observing changes in the various measures of DOL, what can we predict about shifts in the production function?

ESTIMATES OF DOL WITH OBSERVABLE OPERATING PARAMETERS

In most textbook presentations, it is assumed that unit price (p), unit variable cost (V), and fixed costs (F) are unchanging parameters and that DOL is a function of unit output (Q). Under these conditions, equations (2) and (3) are interchangeable since, with prices given, the change in unit sales and dollar sales are identical. The analysis implicitly assumes that p is determined in a perfectly competitive economy and is not a function of Q and that there are no downward sloping demand curves. If there were, the calculations would be much more complex.

Equation (1) is based on the (presumably observable) levels of three parameters (p, v, and F) and the variable (Q). The reader can quickly confirm the relationship between the break-even point and DOL, noting where Q>BE, then DOL_1>1, and if Q<BE, then DOL_1<0. This relationship is obvious from the graphs usually presented in the CVP analyses of most accounting texts explaining operating profit or loss as a function of units sold (see Horngren et al. 1994, p. 64). Another, more informative graphical relationship

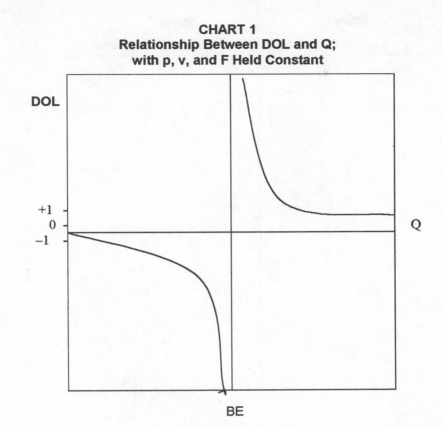

CHART 1
Relationship Between DOL and Q;
with p, v, and F Held Constant

$$\{Q = F/(p - v\}$$

between DOL_1 and Q (assuming the parameters p, v, and F are given) is presented in chart 1, showing that DOL converges to plus or minus infinity as output approaches the BE point.

Let's consider how the level of DOL_1 would change in response to changes in its various subcomponents. First, it is obvious from chart 1 that DOL, decreases as the variable Q increases (given the parameters p, v, and F). This result holds whether Q is above or below the BE point (the one exception being the jump from negative to positive infinity as you "cross" the BE point). To be precise, the partial derivative for DOL_1, with respect to Q is:

$$\delta DOL_1/\delta Q = -F(p - v)/[((p - v)Q - F)^2]. \quad (4)$$

As long as $(p - v) > 0$, this derivative is negative.

Now let's consider what would happen if the parameters of the function change, which is, of course, very possible in the real world. First, what if there were a change in price, assuming constant v, F and Q? In this case,

$$\delta DOL_1/\delta p = -FQ/[((p - F)^2]. \quad (5)$$

then, DOL_1 decreases with increases in price. It should also be noted that where $p<v$, $0 < DOL_1 < 1$, a result that is impossible on chart 1, which was based on the assumption $p > v$.

The parameters of most interest are the fixed and variable costs. The partial derivatives in each case are,

$$\delta DOL_1/\delta v = -FQ/[((p - v)Q - F)^2], \quad (6)$$

and

$$\delta DOL_1/\delta F = (p - v)Q/[((p - v)Q - F)^2], \quad (7)$$

These two derivatives imply that DOL_1 increases with an increase in either fixed or variable cost (assuming $p > v$).

It is also interesting to note the interrelationships between these measures at any given level of output. The measures $\delta DOL_1/\delta p$ and $\delta DOL_1/\delta v$ have exactly the same magnitude but opposite signs. Also, the ratio between $\delta DOL_1/\delta v$ and $\delta DOL_1/\delta F$, is $F/(p - v)$, which is equal to the BE point. Similarly, the ratio between $\delta DOL_1/\delta v$ and $\delta DOL_1/\delta Q$ is $-Q/(p - v)$ and that between $\delta DOL_1/\delta F$ and $\delta DOL_1/\delta Q$ is $-F/(p - v)$.

Consider two firms, manufacturing the same product, where both sell their output for $8.00 per unit, and both have annual demand for 200 units. Firm A employs a technology involving fixed costs of $400 per year and variable costs of $4.00 per unit. Firm B, on the other hand, has a variable cost of only $3.00 per unit, but has annual fixed cost of $500. Both of these firms have a $DOL_1 = 2$, even though Firm B clearly uses a higher ratio of fixed costs to unit variable costs in its production function.

CHART 2
Rate of Substitution Fixed and Variable Costs

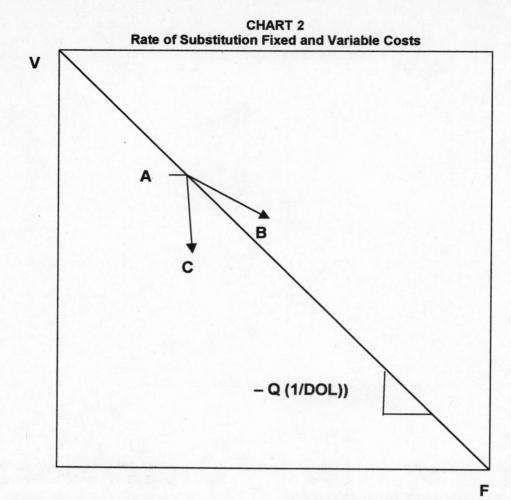

$$- Q\,(1/DOL))$$

Interestingly, these two different technologies have the same DOL_1 and BE point at every level of output. There is in fact, an associated family of fixed vs. variable cost production functions that would all have the same DOL_1 at every level of output. This set of technologies is linear in fixed cost vs. variable cost space (see chart 2). Technologies above and to the right of the line have higher levels of DOL_1 than those on the line, and technologies below and to the left have lower levels of DOL_1 (at a given level of demand). If fixed costs are changed as a function of variable costs when a new production technology is introduced, the slope of this line is,

$$\delta DOL/\delta v = \{[(pQ - vQ - F)(-Q)]$$
$$-[(pQ - vQ)(-Q - \delta F/\delta v)]\}$$
$$/[(pQ - vQ - F)^2].$$

Setting $\delta DOL/\delta v = 0$ and solving for $\delta F/\delta v$, $\delta F/\delta v = [(pQ - vQ - F)/(p - v)] - Q$. Then, substituting DOL_1 back into the expression, $\delta F/\delta v = -Q(1 - (1/DOL_1))$. When the firm substitutes fixed for variable cost at this rate, DOL_1 will remain constant for a given level of output. If the firm adds new fixed costs at a higher rate than the corresponding reduction in variable costs,

DOL_1 will rise for a given level of demand. This would be a shift from point A to point B on chart 2. These are the cases usually presented in numerical examples of operating leverage, DOL or BE point. This gives students the impression that these measures rise with an increase in the ratio between fixed cost and unit variable cost. Notice, however, that it would be possible to shift from point A to point C, raising fixed costs and lowering variable costs, yet DOL would fall at all levels of output.

ELASTICITY MEASURES OF DOL

Next, consider the arc elasticity measures of DOL represented by equations (2) and (3). First make the usual assumptions that price, fixed cost, and unit variable cost are constant and that only the output is allowed to fluctuate. Consider a firm with a unit selling price of $8.00, unit variable cost of $4.00 ($p - v$ = 4.00), and fixed costs of $400 per year, implying a BE point of 100 units (these same initial conditions will be used in all subsequent examples).

124

Suppose that annual sales are at 97 units, (which is below the BE point), and that sales grow at one percent per year. Results for Q, EBIT and each of the three estimates of DOL are presented in table 1. As predicted by equation (4), each DOL measure falls as Q increases (with the exception of the jump over BE). Also, DOL never falls in the range between zero and one. The relationship between the different DOLs is clear with DOL_2 and DOL_3 tracking DOL_1 exactly. This is not surprising, as these were the conditions under which equations (2) and (3) were derived from equation (1).

It is necessary to point out a potential problem in the calculation of DOL_2 and DOL_3. As stated above, equation (1) is a point estimate of the DOL, while equations (2) and (3) and based on actual ex post changes in the variables. Normally, formulas for percentage change are presented as either,

$$\% \Delta Q = (Q_2 - Q_1)/Q_1, \quad (8)$$

or,

$$\% \Delta Q = (Q_2 - Q_1)/Q_1 +, Q_2)/2)., \quad (9)$$

If the percentage changes used to calculate DOL_2 and DOL_3 were estimated by equation (8), DOL_2 and DOL_3 would appear to lag DOL_1 by one period. If equation (9) were employed to estimate the percentage changes used to calculate DOL_2 and DOL_3, the estimates would be an "average" of the current and preceding estimates of DOL_1. Therefore, care must be taken to line up the estimated percentage changes used in calculating DOL_2 and DOL_3 with the point es-

timate of elasticity. This can be done, in this example, by using the final value of the variables (where the point estimate is made) as the denominator of the fraction,

$$\% \Delta Q = (Q_2 - Q_1)/Q_2, \quad (10)$$

The results of the calculations of DOL_2 and DOL_3 in table 1 show that estimating the percentage changes using equation (10) will align all the estimates of DOL.

Dugan and Shriver (1992) conducted an empirical study of elasticity-based measures of DOL using accounting data. One of their efficiency tests of a measure of DOL was the percentage of results greater than one. This follows a suggestion by O'Brien and Vanderheiden (1987). Assuming most firms operate above their BE point, this seems to be a reasonable approach. The very notion of this test, however, suggests that, in practice, estimates of DOL_2 and DOL_3 tend to produce a considerable number of observations less than one (which, according to the logic in the last section, would imply a unit sales price less than variable cost) and even less than zero (which implies the firm is operating below the BE point). Clearly, in practice, the estimates of DOL_2 and DOL_3 over time do not behave as anticipated in chart 1 and T-1. This is because the parameters, p, v, and F, are not constant. However, our earlier estimates of partial derivatives (in equations (5), (6), and (7)) should give us some insight into the sensitivity of changes in estimates of DOL_2 and DOL_3 to changes in the parameters.

TABLE 1
MEASURES OF DOL WITH Q INCREASING AT 1 PERCENT
(p, v, and F_v constant)

Period	Q	EBIT	DOL_1	DOL_2	DOL_3
1	97.00	−12.00	−32.33	—	—
2	97.97	−8.12	−48.26	−48.26	−48.26
3	98.95	−4.20	−94.19	−94.19	−94.19
4	99.94	−0.24	−1632.50	−1632.50	−1632.50
5	100.94	3.75	107.60	107.60	107.60
6	101.95	7.79	52.35	52.35	52.35
7	102.97	11.87	34.71	34.71	34.71
8	104.00	15.98	26.02	26.02	26.02
9	105.04	20.14	20.86	20.86	20.86
10	106.09	24.34	17.43	17.43	17.43

TABLE 2
LEVELS OF DOL$_1$ WITH CHANGES IN Q AND v
(p and F constant)

| | | | | v | | | |
	3.94	3.96	3.98	4.00	4.02	4.04	4.06
104	18.99	20.84	23.12	26.00	29.74	34.78	41.99
106	14.18	15.16	16.31	17.67	19.28	21.24	23.68
108	11.40	12.01	12.71	13.50	14.41	15.45	16.67
Q 110	9.58	10.00	10.48	11.00	11.58	12.24	12.98
112	8.31	8.62	8.96	9.33	9.74	10.19	10.69
114	7.37	7.61	7.86	8.14	8.45	8.78	9.14
116	6.64	6.83	7.03	7.25	7.49	7.74	8.01

Therefore, we will consider, analytically, the cases where these parameters are allowed to fluctuate. Notice that in equations (2) and (3), we cannot hold output constant, as this would result in a value of zero in the denominator. Therefore, we cannot conduct a true sensitivity analysis of the impact of the changes in parameters on DOL$_2$ and DOL$_3$ in isolation.

For our examples, we will assume base levels for the parameters of p = $8.00, v = $4.00, and F = $400 (the initial BE = 100 units). We will then consider cases with values above and below the base level for each parameter in turn. Since unit output must also vary in order to calculate DOL$_2$ or DOL$_3$, we will consider values of output around an initial base level of 110 units (in the profitable region of output). This base level of unit output was chosen for two reasons. First, it is near the BE point, so changes in the level of DOL will be large for a change in the variable or parameter (this would arguably be the area of most interest to a firm's manager). Second, according to equation (4), this also happens to be the point at which $\delta DOL/\delta Q =$

−1. This should make it a bit more convenient to distinguish the impact of a change in output from the impact of the change in the parameter of interest.

Results for the cases where unit variable costs are allowed to fluctuate along with unit output are presented in T-2 and 3. The levels of DOL$_1$ are presented in T-2 and the levels of DOL$_2$ and DOL$_3$ are shown in T-3 (in this case, since unit price is constant, these values are identical). In T-2, it is possible to see the impacts of changes in unit output and unit variable cost in isolation. In the column with v = 4.00, we can observe the impact of changes in output on DOL$_1$. Notice that as Q decreases below the base level of 110 units, the levels of DOL$_1$ increase by slightly more than two for each two-unit decrease in output. Also, as output increases above the base level by units of two, DOL$_1$ decreases by increments of slightly less than two. As noted earlier, $\delta DOL/\delta Q = -1$. In this case, the slight discrepancies are, of course, based on the convexity of the curve (as seen in chart 1).

TABLE 3
LEVELS OF DOL$_2$ AND DOL$_3$ WITH CHANGES IN Q AND v
(p and F constant)

| | | | | v | | | |
	3.94	3.96	3.98	4.00	4.02	4.04	4.06
104	13.84	17.06	21.02	26.00	32.48	41.23	53.71
106	8.42	11.04	14.09	17.67	21.95	27.14	33.59
108	2.13	5.47	9.23	13.50	18.39	24.04	30.64
Q 110							
112	15.06	13.32	11.41	9.33	7.05	4.53	1.74
114	10.36	9.68	8.94	8.14	7.28	6.34	5.31
116	8.44	8.07	7.67	7.25	6.80	6.31	5.78

TABLE 4
LEVELS OF DOL$_2$ AND DOL$_3$ WITH SMALL CHANGES IN Q
(p and F constant)

				v			
	3.94	3.96	3.98	4.00	4.02	4.04	4.06
109.88	−121.37	−81.63	−37.70	11.13	65.69	127.08	196.68
109.92	−186.32	−127.08	−61.63	11.08	92.32	183.69	287.18
109.96	−381.01	−263.31	−133.31	11.06	172.28	353.51	558.73
Q 110.00							
110.04	397.89	281.65	153.33	10.96	−147.94	−326.38	−528.25
110.08	203.09	146.34	81.61	10.92	−67.94	−156.46	−256.55
110.12	138.13	99.87	57.67	10.88	−41.30	−99.85	−166.01

In the row with Q = 110, we can see the impact of changes in unit variable cost in isolation. At the initial levels of output $\delta DOL_1/\delta v$ = 27.5. Since variable cost is changing in increments of 2 cents, one would theoretically anticipate changes in the level of DOL$_1$ by 0.55 (27.5 × .02) across each column. Note that as unit variable cost increases above $4.00, the changes in DOL are slightly greater than 0.55, and as v decreases below $4.00, the changes in DOL$_1$ are slightly less than 0.55 (again, this is due to the convexity in the relationship between v and DOL$_1$). Also note that the values of DOL$_1$ rise steadily along each row and column as the level of unit output falls and the level of unit variable cost rises.

The values for DOL$_2$ and DOL$_3$, in T-3, were calculated by taking the percentage change from the initial base position (p = 8.00, v = 4.00, F = 4.00, Q = 110, and DOL$_1$ = 11.00) to the new level of output and unit variable cost using equation (10). As stated above, it is not possible to calculate levels of DOL$_2$ and DOL$_3$ in the case where output does not change. Also, notice that in the column with v = 4.00, the re-

sults in T-2 and T-3 are identical. This is, of course, the same result seen in T-1.

What is most interesting is to observe the differences between T-2 and T-3 for the results in the quadrants off the center row and column. In the extreme corner of each northern quadrant (lower unit output), the values of DOL$_1$ and DOL$_2$ are both higher than the initial level of DOL$_1$ = 11.00. In the northeastern quadrant, values of DOL$_2$ are greater than corresponding values of DOL$_1$. However, in the northwestern quadrant, values of DOL$_2$ are less than DOL$_1$. In the southern quadrants, we observe the opposite conditions: values are below DOL$_1$ = 11.00, while DOL$_2$ > DOL$_1$ in the southwestern quadrant and DOL$_2$ < DOL$_1$ in the southeastern quadrant.

The other notable feature of T-3 is that if one looks down the columns, as unit output rises, DOL$_2$ does not steadily fall. There is an obvious "ridge" in the level of DOL$_2$, where it falls then rises then begins to fall again. Most of these dips appear near the center row, but in the column with v = 4.04, it can be seen further down the column.

TABLE 5
LEVELS OF DOL$_2$ AND DOL$_3$ WITH CHANGES IN Q AND v
AT HIGH INITIAL LEVELS OF Q
(p and F constant)

				v			
	3.94	3.96	3.98	4.00	4.02	4.04	4.06
204	0.93	1.27	1.61	1.96	2.32	2.68	3.01
206	0.43	0.93	1.43	1.94	2.47	3.00	3.55
208	−1.05	−0.08	0.92	1.93	2.96	4.01	5.08
Q 210							
212	4.77	3.83	2.87	1.89	0.90	−0.12	−1.15
214	3.29	2.83	2.36	1.88	1.39	0.90	0.38
216	2.79	2.49	2.18	1.86	1.54	1.21	0.88

TABLE 6
LEVELS OF DOL$_1$ WITH CHANGES IN Q AND F
(p and v constant)

				v			
	3.94	3.96	3.98	4.00	4.02	4.04	4.06
104	18.91	20.80	23.11	26.00	29.71	34.67	41.60
106	14.13	15.14	16.31	17.67	19.27	21.20	23.56
108	11.37	12.00	12.71	13.50	14.40	15.43	16.62
Q 110	9.57	10.00	10.48	11.00	11.58	12.22	12.94
112	8.30	8.62	8.96	9.33	9.74	10.18	10.67
114	7.36	7.60	7.86	8.14	8.44	8.77	9.12
116	6.63	6.82	7.03	7.25	7.48	7.73	8.00

These two differences in the outcomes are caused by two separate computational nuances. The source of the first bias is again an arc elasticity problem. Both measures of DOL are based on equation (2), which can be rewritten as: DOL = [(EBIT$_2$ − EBIT$_1$)/EBIT$_2$/[(Q$_2$ − Q$_1$)/Q$_2$], but in calculating DOL$_1$, it is implicitly assumed that p$_1$, v$_1$, and F$_1$ are equal to p$_2$, v$_2$, and F$_2$ throughout:

$$DOL_1 = \{[(p_2 - v_2)Q_2 - F_2]$$
$$- \ [(p_2 - v_2)Q_1 - F_2]\} \times \phi, \quad (11)$$

where $\phi = (Q2 - Q1)/(Q2 \times EBIT2)$.
DOL$_2$, however, is in fact:

$$DOL_2 = \{[(p_2 - v_2)Q_2 - F_2]$$
$$- \ [(p_1 - v_1)Q_1 - F_1]\} \times \phi, \quad (12)$$

In tables 2 and 3, $p_2 = p_1$ and $F_2 = F_1$, but $v_2 \neq v_1$. For instance, in the northeastern quadrant, $v_2 > v_1$—therefore, DOL$_2$ > DOL$_1$. Similar reasoning, of course, explains the biases in the distant corners of the other three quadrants.

The second flaw, the existence of "a valley and a ridge" in the data near the row associated with the base level of output (Q = 110, is also due to a problem involved in estimations of elasticity from point-to-point. Notice that very small changes in unit output create relatively large changes in EBIT as they are leveraged in the numerator, since they are multiplied by the operating margin. In T-3, these effects are hidden, since at an output level of Q = 110, we are so near the BE point that small changes in output cause relatively large changes in DOL$_2$. In T-4, we see a case featuring must smaller changes in unit output, and here the very large positive and negative levels of DOL$_2$ associated with small changes in unit output are clear. It is also important to keep in mind that this problem can be quite serious at levels of output far from the BE point, as the level of sensitivity to changes in unit output is even lower. Results for calculations of DOL$_2$ for the area around an initial output level of 210 units are shown in T-5. Here the negative results for DOL$_2$ are evident. Also, notice that for several observations, 0 < DOL$_2$ < 1. According to standard theory, this should occur in cases where p <v, which is, of course, unlikely, but such results will obviously be quite common when equations (2) or (3) are employed to calculate DOL.

TABLE 7
LEVELS OF DOL$_2$ AND DOL$_3$ WITH CHANGES IN Q AND F
(p and v constant)

				v			
	3.94	3.96	3.98	4.00	4.02	4.04	4.06
104	14.18	17.33	21.19	26.00	32.19	40.44	52.00
106	8.83	11.36	14.27	17.67	21.68	26.50	32.39
108	2.84	6.00	9.53	13.50	18.00	23.14	29.08
Q 110							
112	14.52	12.92	11.20	9.33	7.30	5.09	2.67
114	10.11	9.50	8.85	8.14	7.39	6.58	5.70
116	8.29	7.96	7.62	7.25	6.86	6.44	6.00

TABLE 8
LEVELS OF DOL1 WITH CHANGES IN Q AND p
(v and F constant)

					v			
		7.94	7.96	7.98	8.00	8.02	8.04	8.06
	104	41.99	34.78	29.74	26.00	23.12	20.84	18.99
	106	23.68	21.24	19.28	17.67	16.31	15.16	14.18
	108	16.67	15.45	14.41	13.50	12.71	12.01	11.40
Q	110	12.98	12.24	11.58	11.00	10.48	10.01	9.58
	112	10.69	10.19	9.74	9.33	8.96	8.62	8.31
	114	9.14	8.78	8.45	8.14	7.86	7.61	7.37
	116	8.01	7.74	7.49	7.25	7.03	6.83	6.64

TABLE 9
LEVELS OF DOL$_2$ WITH CHANGES IN Q AND p
(v and F constant)

					v			
		7.94	7.96	7.98	8.00	8.02	8.04	8.06
	104	53.71	41.23	32.48	26.00	21.02	17.06	13.84
	106	33.59	27.14	21.95	17.67	14.08	11.04	8.42
	108	30.64	24.04	18.39	13.50	9.23	5.47	2.13
Q	110							
	112	1.74	4.53	7.05	9.33	11.41	13.32	15.06
	114	5.31	6.34	7.28	8.14	8.94	9.68	10.36
	116	5.78	6.31	6.80	7.25	7.67	8.07	8.44

TABLE 10
LEVELS OF DOL$_2$ WITH CHANGES IN Q AND p
(v and constant)

					v			
		7.94	7.96	7.98	8.00	8.02	8.04	8.06
	104	41.17	37.75	31.05	26.00	22.02	18.77	16.03
	106	27.18	23.85	20.53	17.67	15.12	12.79	10.58
	108	21.64	18.83	16.16	13.50	10.70	7.53	3.61
Q	110							
	112	2.97	6.26	8.18	9.33	10.04	10.46	10.69
	114	6.70	7.36	7.82	8.14	8.37	8.51	8.60
	116	6.70	6.95	7.12	7.25	7.34	7.39	7.42

The estimates for levels of DOL_1 and DOL_2 associated with changes in unit output and fixed costs are summarized in T-6 and 7 respectively. At the initial conditions, the elasticity $\delta DOL_1/\delta F = 0.275$, which means that changes of \$2.00 in the fixed costs should cause changes of approximately 0.55 in the level of DOL_1 (notice, as stated above, that $[DOL_1/\delta v]/[\delta DOL_1/\delta F] = F/(p - v)$). The results are clearly very close to those for changes in variable cost summarized in T-2 and 3. As expected, rising levels of DOL_1 are associated with falling levels of output and rising costs. We also notice the same biases in the estimates of DOL_2, where small changes in output cause extreme results, and also the arc estimation problems for values of DOL_2 associated with larger changes in output.

Results for the levels of DOL_1, and DOL_2, and DOL_3, when both unit output and unit price change, are presented in T-8, 9, and 10 respectively. Again, the familiar patterns occur. In this case, DOL_1 increases with decreases in unit price. In fact, as discussed above, $\delta DOL_1/\delta p = -DOL_1/\delta v$, and comparison reveals that T-8 and 9 are mirror images of T-2 and 3. The results for both DOL_2 and DOL_3 reveal the extreme values for small changes in unit output. Both are also biased by the arc elasticity problem for larger changes in unit output. An interesting feature of T-10 is that the results from elasticity DOL_3 are closer to those for DOL_1 than are estimates of DOL_2. This helps reduce this bias to an extent, as DOL_3 is, in fact, the most commonly used method in practice.

SUMMARY

Many textbook presentations of DOL and the BE point leave the impression that these measures increase unambiguously when a firm increases fixed expenses and lowers unit variable costs in its production function. We demonstrate that DOL increases with a rise in either fixed or variable costs, not just fixed costs. From this observation, it is not difficult to conceive of a case where a firm would actually increase fixed costs and lower variable costs in its productive technology, but have DOL and the BE point fall. We find that so long as the firm substitutes higher fixed costs for variable cost at the rate $\delta F/\delta v = -Q(1 - (1/DOL))$, at any given level of Q, DOL and the BE point will remain unaltered. However, if the rate of substitution between fixed and variable cost changes at a different rate, DOL and the BE point could either rise or fall.

We have also attempted to demonstrate the possible computational biases associated with two simple elasticity measures of DOL (DOL_2 and DOL_3). The first fundamental problem is that these are point-to-point methodologies which should always produce different results than those estimated by the single point esti-

mate methodology (DOL_1). The second notable problem is that for "small" changes in unit output, it is very likely that estimates made by the point-to-point methods will produce levels of DOL lower than one, even for firms operating above the BE point. In fact, the likelihood of observing measures of DOL less than one increases, the higher the unit output is above the BE point. This clearly creates a serious problem for empirical researchers attempting to employ DOL as a proxy for a firm's operating leverage.

It seems that the discussion of operating leverage is normally intended as a simple ex post method to estimate the relative level of annual fixed and unit variable costs a firm employs in its production function. We have shown that drawing such inferences from measures of DOL is problematic. The insights developed here also have important Implications for all attempts to relate cost volume-profit analysis or break-even analysis to the level of firm fixed costs and variable costs. It is also important that users of the point-to-point elasticity measures of DOL (DOL_2 and DOL_3) understand the potential hazards of this methodology, particularly the tendency to produce DOL measures less than one.

REFERENCES:

Brigham, E. F. 1994. *Fundamentals of Financial Management*, 7th Edition. Fort Worth, TX: Dryden-Press.

Dugan, M. T., and K. A. Shriver. 1992. An empirical comparison of alternative methods for the estimation of the degree of operating leverage. *Financial Review* (May): 309-321

Garrison, R. H., and E. W. Noreen, 1994. *Managerial Accounting: Concepts for Planning, Control, and Decision-Making*, 7th Edition. Burr Ridge, IL: Irwin.

Hansen, D. R., and M. M. Mowen. 1994. *Management Accounting*, 3rd Edition. Cincinnati, OH: South-Western.

Hilton, R. W. 1994. *Managerial Accounting*, 2nd Edition. New York, NY: McGraw-Hill.

Horngren, C. T., G. Foster, and S. M. Datar, 1994. *Cost Accounting: A Managerial Emphasis*, 8th Edition, Englewood Cliffs, NJ: Prentice Hall.

Maher, M. W., C. P. Stickney, R. L. Weil, and S. Davidson. 1991. *Managerial Accounting: An Introduction to Concepts, Methods, and Uses*, 4th Edition.. San Diego, CA:: Harcourt Brace Jovanovich.

O'Brien, T. J., and P. A. Vanderheiden. 1987. Empirical measurement of operating leverage for growing firms. Financial Management (Summer): 45-53.

Chapter 9
Strategy and the Master Budget

Cases
9-1   The Master Budget and Sales Forecasting

Readings
Kenneth A. Merchant: **How Challenging Should Profit Budget Targets Be?**
The article argues for using highly achievable budget targets, and explains six key advantages for doing so, including the favorable effect on the managers commitment and confidence. The article also explains some of the risks of using highly achievable budget targets. The concept of risk is illustrated with probability distributions, with a relatively low risk environment having a probability distribution with lower variance.

Discussion Questions:
1. Explain each of the six advantages of highly achievable budget targets mentioned in the article. Can you think of any in addition?
2. What are the risks of highly achievable budget targets mentioned in the article? Can you think of any in addition?

Cases

9-1. The Master Budget and Sales Forecasting

(Sales forecast, CMA adapted) Bailment Company is a temporary employment firm that has offices throughout the United States. Bailment is a well established company in a highly competitive industry. It provides both clerical and professional workers to a broad range of customers. The temporary workers are hired for the day, a week, or a month at rates commensurate with each worker's skill level.

Bailment top management wants to develop a forecasting system in order to estimate revenue and to plan workforce levels. Management wants to forecast its revenues for each quarter during the current year as well as the annual revenue for each of the next five years.

Kathy Gregsen, Budget Analyst in the Bailment Accounting Department, has been given the responsibility for this project. She has determined that Bailment has historical data by month for at least the last 10 years. Her cursory review of the monthly revenue history indicates that Bailment business may have a pronounced seasonal pattern. She also suspects that the business may be cyclical in nature.

Gregsen has concluded that she would like to develop a statistically based sales forecasting system. She is considering the applicability of simple linear regression analysis and/or time series analysis. One of the things she would like to do is compare Bailment revenue to the Index of Industrial Production and to Gross National Product (GNP).

REQUIRED:

1. Kathy Gregsen needs to identify all of the things required to develop a forecasting system. Identify the typical things Gregsen needs in order to develop a forecasting system.

2. For each of the two statistical techniques identified by Kathy Gregsen, i.e., simple linear regression analysis and time series analysis.

   a. Describe the technique, being sure to include the purpose of the technique.

   b. Identify the variable and/or data required to use the technique.

   c. Explain how Gregsen will be able to evaluate the results of the analysis.

   d. Discuss the strengths and weaknesses of the techniques in general.

   e. Discuss the strengths and weaknesses of the technique in terms of its relevance for varying lengths of forecasts and its reliability in forecasting cyclical turning points.

How Challenging Should Profit Budget Targets Be?

By Kenneth A. Merchant

Certificate of Merit, 1989-90

It is a basic axiom of management that budget targets should be set to be challenging but achievable. But to establish that target, managers must first determine what "challenging but achievable" really means. Should profits be targeted at some easily obtainable goal, a realistic middle ground, or at a point so high that hope of attainment is slim?

There is no one right answer, given the number of purposes for which budgets are used: planning, coordination, control, motivation, and performance evaluation. Some may argue that planning purposes are served best with a best-guess budget, one that is as likely to be exceeded as missed[1] Others may propose that, for optimum motivation, budget targets should be highly challenging, with only a 25% to 40% chance of achievement.[2]

There is one target-level choice, however, that serves the combination of purposes for which budgets are used quite well in the vast majority of organizational situations. Therefore, it provides an effective compromise. That choice is to set budget targets with a high probability of achievement—achievable by most managers 80% to 90% of the time—and then to supplement these targets with promises of extra incentives for performance exceeding the target level.[3] This prescription for the optimal budget target level, which is nearest point A in Fig. 1, is made assuming that Fig. 1 represents the probability distribution of forthcoming profits for an effective management team working at a consistently high level of effort.

These targets with an 80% to 90% probability of achievement are labeled properly "highly achievable" for most managers, but because of the assumption described in the preceding paragraph, the targets are at least somewhat challenging. They are not "easy." Even talented, experienced profit center managers must work hard and effectively to give themselves a good chance of achieving these targets.

THE ADVANTAGES OF USING HIGHLY ACHIEVABLE BUDGET TARGETS

Choosing budget targets with such a high probability of achievement provides many advantages to corporation, including the following:

1. *Managers commitment to achieve the budget targets is increased.* When targets are set to be highly achievable, the corporation can assess profit center managers high penalties for failing to achieve the targets at least many more years than not. These penalties can include loss of reputation, loss of autonomy, inability to get funding proposals approved, and sometimes even loss of job. Corporations can allow managers few or no excuses for not achieving the targets because the high achievability is designed to protect the managers to a considerable extent from the effects of unfavorable circumstances that were unforeseen at the time performance targets were set.

Because profit center managers face the risk of high penalties for performance shortfalls and do not have the safety net of excuses, they become highly committed to achieve their targets. This commitment causes them to prepare their budget forecasts more carefully and to spend more of their time managing rather than inventing excuses to explain their failures.

Firms that switch their budgeting philosophy to using highly achievable targets instead of "stretch" or "best guess" targets note the increase in commitment quite quickly. Comments a profit center manager in a large U.S. chemical corporation which made the switch:

> "Two years ago, our budgets were just best-effort forecasts. Today they are commitments. There is a vast difference. It's better to run this way. We have discipline. People used to

make projections, but they forgot about them until they had to make another projection. Nobody ever came back and slapped their hand Now people are challenged to put the things in place that are required to make the projections happen. The plans have begun to have credibility. Our spending plans are based on realistic projections."

Conversely, when budget targets are set at highly challenging levels, the danger exists that managers will not be committed to try to achieve their targets. For example, in a small publicly held electronics firm, which until recently had used a stretch target budgeting philosophy, profit center managers had started earning bonuses when their division's reported profit exceeded 60% of the budgeted level. But all too often, the profit center and corporate budgets were not achieved. In the words of the chief financial officer: "The system had some fudge in it. The managers were still in bonus territory, so they didn't have to worry about meeting the budget. It was like a wish, too easily blown off."

The corporation now has changed to what is known as "minimum performance standard" budget targets and its managers' commitment to these new targets has increased sharply. Since the change, the profit centers have achieved virtually all their budget targets every quarter.

The danger of lack of commitment to achieve targets is particularly acute if something goes wrong early in the year and loss of commitment leads to lower motivation. In the words of a manager whose entity had not achieved its budget targets for several years, "After the first few months of the year, we began to look at our goals as 'pie in the sky.' [The goals] didn't inspire us to do different things. They were just demoralizing."

2. *Managers' confidence remains high.* Regardless of the level of budget achievability, in the minds of most managers budget achievement defines the line between success and failure. Budget targets are the most specific and tangible goals managers are given, and most people define personal success in terms of their high degree of achievement of predetermined targets. As one manager put it, "If I were to miss my budget, I would feel like a failure. When I exceed my budget, I feel proud."

It is to the corporation's advantage

to have its managers feel like winners. Managers who feel good about themselves and their abilities are more likely to work harder and to take prudent risks.

3. *Organizational control costs decrease.* Most corporations use a management-by-exception control philosophy where negative variances from budget signal the need for investigation and perhaps intervention in the affairs of the operating units. If budget targets are set to be highly achievable, negative variances are relatively rare, and top management or staff attention is directed to the few situations where the operating problems are most likely and most serious.

This point is illustrated in Fig. 1. The probability distribution of profit outcomes shifts to the left (lower profit) for a lazy or ineffective manager. What was a highly achievable target for an effective, hardworking manager (point A) is not as highly achievable for an ineffective or lazy manager. Budget misses of two or three years send a strong signal that something is wrong and that top management intervention is necessary. Budget misses also provide objective rationales for relieving poor managers of their jobs.

4. *The risk of managers engaging in harmful earnings management practices is reduced.* Managers who are likely to achieve their budget targets are less likely to engage in costly actions designed to boost earnings in the short term. These actions include making potentially risky operating decisions (such as delaying preventative maintenance) and en-

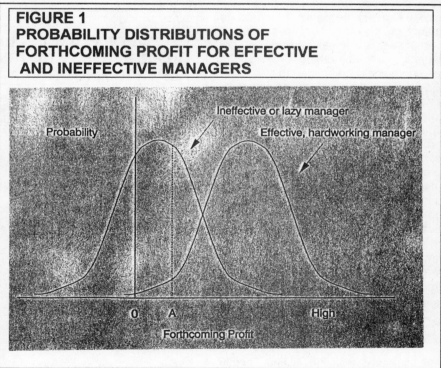

FIGURE 1
PROBABILITY DISTRIBUTIONS OF
FORTHCOMING PROFIT FOR EFFECTIVE
AND INEFFECTIVE MANAGERS

gaging in deceptive accounting practices (such as altering judgments about reserves).

Highly achievable budget targets also lessen the incentives some managers have to reduce current period income. Those individuals who are facing stretch targets they consider nearly impossible to achieve may "take a bath"; they may take costly actions to position their entities for the subsequent accounting period. For example, they may defer sales and incur as many discretionary expenses as possible in the current period.

5. *Effective managers are allowed greater operating flexibility.* Highly achievable budget targets allow managers whose entities are performing well to accumulate some slack resources. Most managers will use this slack so that they do not have to respond to unforeseen, unfavorable short-term contingencies in costly ways, such as a suspension of productive long-term investments or a layoff. Some managers also will use the slack in productive, creative ways to fund "skunkworks" that may have high payoffs.

6. *The corporation is somewhat protected against the costs of optimistic revenue projections.* Budgets with optimistic revenue projections often induce managers to acquire resources in anticipation of activity levels that may not be forthcoming. Some of these resources, particularly people, can be difficult to eliminate when reality sets in. As one corporate president expressed it: "I think we ought to have a semiaggressive plan, but one that is achievable. We want to make it every year. It's too hard to adjust on the downside, to slough off commitments of expenses or not launch something you're psychologically committed to."

7. *The predictability of corporate earnings is increased.* When budget targets are likely to be achieved, the consolidated budget provides a highly probable lower bound of forthcoming corporate profits. This earnings predictability is valuable, particularly to managers of publicly held corporations. Earnings are usually less predictable in corporations whose business units face similar business risks, so this earnings-predictability advantage of highly achievable budget targets is higher in undiversified rather than diversified, firms.

A RISK IN USING HIGHLY ACHIEVABLE BUDGET TARGETS

The primary risk in using highly

achievable budget targets is that managers may not be challenged to perform at their maximum. They may be satisfied with mediocrity—their levels of aspiration may be too low—and their motivation may slack off after the budgeted profit targets are achieved.

This problem of lack of challenge is potentially more serious when planning uncertainty is relatively high (and the inability to make adjustments for the effects of factors over which the managers had little or no control is relatively low). This is because the distance between the highly achievable target levels and the best-guess (or even higher) target levels is much greater than when planning uncertainty is low. This is shown in Fig. 2. The tall curve shows a profit probability distribution in a relatively low uncertainty environment. The highly achievable budget level (B1) is not far from the most likely performance level (P). The shorter, flatter curve shows a distribution in a relatively uncertain environment. In this case, the highly achievable budget level (B2) is far below the most likely performance level.

Even in environments of high uncertainty, however, this lack-of-challenge problem is not inevitable. Most profit center managers have risen through the ranks because they are good performers with strong internal drives for competition and self-satisfaction. Furthermore, the "winning" feeling generated from budget achievement in prior periods is likely to increase, not decrease, the managers' levels of aspiration.

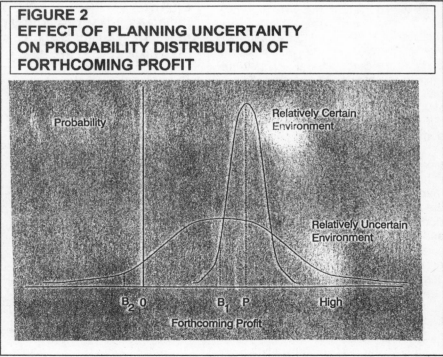

FIGURE 2
EFFECT OF PLANNING UNCERTAINTY ON PROBABILITY DISTRIBUTION OF FORTHCOMING PROFIT

136

Furthermore, even when the risk of less than optimal challenge does exist, it can be minimized by giving managers incentives to strive for and to produce profits in excess of their budget targets. These incentives can be provided in combinations of many forms of rewards, including extra bonuses, recognition, autonomy, command over resources, and increased prospects for career advancement.

Profit center managers also can be asked to turn in more profit than originally was budgeted. This is a common occurrence in U.S. corporations.[4] These orders, combined with the highly achievable original targets, make the budget somewhat flexible. The highly achievable targets protect the profit center managers from the effects of unfavorable influences not explicitly expounded in the budget forecasts. The requests for profits above budgeted levels can be used to adjust for the effects of unforeseen good fortune on the measures of operating results. They can protect the corporation from the negative effects of excessive easy performance targets, such as managers' lagging ambition and the creation of excessive slack.

Only in a few organizational situations is it not desirable to set highly achievable profit budget targets. One exception is caused by organizational need. A company in grave difficulty may want to set less achievable budget targets as a signal to its managers that a certain higher level of performance is necessary for the corporation to survive or for the profit center to stave off divestment.

A second exception occurs when it is desirable to correct for a profit center's windfall gain. Sometimes when managers have been lucky in a prior period, perhaps earning large and mostly undeserved bonuses, a more challenging budget target can be set as an effective way of making compensation more fair across the multiyear period. Here, though, care must be taken to guard against unwarranted management turnover because current period expected compensation probably will fall below competitive market levels.

In virtually all other situations, it is desirable to set highly achievable profit budget targets while allowing the managers few excuses for not achieving the targets but providing them significant additional rewards for exceeding the targets. Setting targets that are highly achievable, but not too easy takes considerable managerial skill. Upper-level managers must know enough about the profit centers' capabilities and business prospects to be able to judge the probability of budget success reasonably well in order to make this budget philosophy work properly. But when they implement this combination of mechanisms effectively, they will ensure that all the purposes for which budgets are used—planning, coordination, control, motivation, and performance evaluation—are served well.

Kenneth Merchant is professor of accounting at the University of Southern California.

[1] For example, see M. E. Barrett and L. B. Fraser III, "Conflicting Roles in Budgeting for Operations," *Harvard Business Review*, July-August 1977, pp. 137-146.

[2] For example, see R. L. M. Dunbar, "Budgeting for Control," *Administrative Science Quarterly*, March 1971, pp. 88-96.

[3] This finding emerged in a recent intensive study of 12 divisionalized corporations and some related fieldwork. Ten of the 12 corporations participating in the research study had used highly achievable budget targets for some time. One had recently changed its budgeting philosophy. It formerly used "stretch" budget targets but changed to have its targets reflect "minimum performance standards." One firm was still using stretch budget targets, but most of the managers in the firm were recommending that this philosophy of budgeting be changed. (For a detailed report of the findings of this study, see K Merchant, *Rewarding Results: Motivating Profit Center Managers*, Harvard Business School Press, 1989.)

[4] For example, Merchant (1989) found that profit center managers in seven of the 12 firms studied were sometimes given direct orders from upper management to turn in greater profits than were budgeted. In some of these firms, the orders were given virtually every quarter.

Chapter 10
Decision Making with a Strategic Emphasis

Cases

10-1   Decision Making Under Uncertainty
10-2   Profitability Analysis
10-3   Make or Buy
10-4   The Superior Valve Division

Readings

John K. Shank and Vijay Govindarajan: **Making Strategy Explicit in Cost Analysis: The Baldwin Bike Case**

This case discussion is a classic in strategic cost management. The authors effectively show how an apparently direct application of contribution margin analysis to resolve a special order decision is incomplete without consideration of strategic implications. The case and discussion are an excellent way to see the importance of a strategic approach to decision making, and thus to decisions like the special order decision.

Discussion Questions:
1. What is the proper decision for Baldwin Bicycle based on a contribution margin analysis?
2. What is the proper decision for Baldwin Bicycle based on a strategic analysis?
3. Contrast your answers in parts 1 and 2 above. What do you think Baldwin Bicycle should do?

Cases

10-1. Decision Making Under Uncertainty

Exquisite Foods Incorporated (EFI) sells premium foods. Three independent strategies are being considered to promote a new product, *Soufflés for Microwaves*, to dual-career families. Currently the contribution margin ratio on EFI's foods is 65%, which is expected to apply to the new product. EFI's policy for promoting new products permits only one type of advertising campaign until the product has been established.

STRATEGY ONE

The first strategy concentrates on television and magazine advertising. EFI would hire a marketing consultant to prepare a 30-second video commercial and a magazine advertisement. The commercial would air during the evening to address the working market, while the magazine advertisement would be placed in magazines read by career-minded individuals. This advertising campaign would provide EFI $230,000 expected contribution from sales.

STRATEGY TWO

The second strategy promotes the product by offering 25% off coupons in the Sunday newspaper supplements, with a projected 15 percent redemption rate on sales revenue. EFI would hire a marketing consultant for $5,000 to design a one-quarter page, two-color coupon advertisement. The coupon would be distributed in the Sunday newspaper supplements at a cost of $195,000. Based on prior experience, EFI expects the following additional sales from this form of advertisement.

Expected sales	Probability
$500,000	10%
600,000	25
700,000	35
800,000	20
900,000	10

STRATEGY THREE

The third strategy offers a $.50 mail-in rebate coupon attached to each box of *Soufflés for Microwaves*. EFI would hire a marketing consultant for $5,000 to create a one-sixth page, one-color rebate coupon. Printing and attaching costs for the rebate coupon are $.07 per package, and EFI is planning to include the rebate offer on 500,000 packages. Although 500,000 packages may be sold, only a 10 percent redemption rate is expected. EFI expects the following additional sales from this type of promotion:

Expected sales	Probability
$400,000	10%
450,000	30
500,000	35
550,000	20
600,000	5

REQUIRED:

1. Exquisite Foods Incorporated (EFI) wishes to select the most profitable marketing alternative to promote *Soufflés for Microwaves*. Recommend which of the three strategies presented above should be adopted by EFI. Support your recommendation with appropriate calculations and analysis.
2. What selection criteria, other than profitability, should be considered in arriving at a decision on the choice of promotion alternatives?

10-2. Profitability Analysis

Sportway, Inc. is a wholesale distributor supplying a wide range of moderately priced sporting equipment to large chain stores. About 60 percent of Sportway's products are purchased from other companies while the remainder are manufactured by Sportway. The company has a Plastics Department that is currently manufacturing molded fishing tackle boxes. Sportway is able to manufacture and sell 8,000 tackle boxes annually, making full use of its direct labor capacity at available work stations. Presented below are the selling price and costs associated with Sportway's tackle boxes.

Selling price per box		$86.00
Costs per box		
Molded plastic	$ 8.00	
Hinges, latches, handle	9.00	
Direct labor ($15.00/hr.)	18.75	
Manufacturing overhead............	12.50	
Selling and administrative cost ..	17.00	65.25
Profit per box.............................		$20.75

Because Sportway believes it could sell 12,000 tackle boxes if it had sufficient manufacturing capacity, the company has looked into the possibility of purchasing the tackle boxes for distribution. Maple Products, a steady supplier of quality products, would be able to provide up to 9,000 tackle boxes per year at a price of $68.00 per box delivered to Sportway's facility.

Bart Johnson, Sportway's product manager, has suggested that the company could make better use of its Plastics Department by manufacturing skateboards. To support his position, Johnson has a market study that indicates an expanding market for skateboards and a need for additional suppliers. Johnson believes that Sportway could expect to sell 17,500 skateboards annually at a price of $45.00 per skateboard. Johnson's estimate of the costs to manufacture the skateboards is presented below.

Selling price per skateboard		$45.00
Costs per skateboard		
Molded plastic	$5.50	
Wheels, hardware	7.00	
Direct labor ($15.00/hr.)	7.50	
Manufacturing overhead..............	5.00	
Selling and administrative cost	9.00	34.00
Profit per box.............................		$11.00

In the Plastics Department, Sportway uses direct labor hours as the application base for manufacturing overhead. Included in the manufacturing overhead for the current year is $50,000 of factory-wide, fixed manufacturing overhead that has been allocated to the Plastics Department. For each unit of product that Sportway sells, regardless of whether the product has been purchased or is manufactured by Sportway, there is an allocated $6.00 fixed overhead cost per unit for distribution that is included in the selling and administrative cost for all products. Total selling and administrative costs for the purchased tackle boxes would be $10.00 per unit.

REQUIRED:

1. Prepare an analysis based on the data presented that will show which product or products Sportway Inc. should manufacture and/or purchase to maximize profitability and show the associated financial impact. Support your answer with appropriate calculations.
2. Identify the strategic factors Sportway should consider in its product decisions. (CMA 6/90)

10-3. Make or Buy

Robert Products Inc. consists of three decentralized divisions, Bayside Division, Cole Division, and Diamond Division. The president of Robert Products has given the managers of the three divisions authority to decide whether to sell outside the company or among themselves at an internal price determined by the division managers. Market conditions are such that sales made internally or externally will not affect market or transfer prices. Intermediate markets will always be available for Bayside, Cole, and Diamond to purchase their manufacturing needs or sell their product.

The manager of the Cole Division is currently considering the two alternative orders presented below.

- The Diamond Division is in need of 3,000 units of a motor than can be supplied by the Cole Division. To manufacture these motors, Cole would purchase components from the Bayside Division at a price of $600 per unit; Bayside's variable cost for these components is $300 per unit. Cole Division will further process these components at a variable cost of $500 per unit.
- If the Diamond Division cannot obtain the motors from Cole Division, it will purchase the motors from London Company which has offered to supply them to Diamond at a price of $1,500 per unit. London Company would also purchase 3,000 components from Bayside Division at a price of $400 for each of these motors; Bayside's variable cost for these components is $200 per unit.
- The Wales Company wants to place an order with the Cole Division for 3,500 similar motors at a price of $1,250 per unit. Cole would again purchase components from the Bayside Division at a price of $500 per unit; Bayside's variable cost for these components is $250 per unit. Cole Division will further process these components at a variable cost of $400 per unit.

The Cole Division's plant capacity is limited, and the company can accept either the Wales contract or the Diamond order, but not both. The president of Robert Products and the manager of the Cole Division agree that it would not be beneficial in the short or long run to increase capacity.

REQUIRED:

1. Determine whether the Cole Division should sell motors to the Diamond Division at the prevailing market price, or accept the Wales Company contract. Support your answer with appropriate calculations.
2. What strategic factors should Robert Products consider as the Cole and Diamond divisions make their respective decision?
   (CMA 6/88)

10-4. The Superior Valve Division

In 19X2, the Superior Valve Division of the Able Corporation found itself in a position typical of fast-growing companies. Although sales revenues were increasing rapidly, capital equipment allocations from Able were less than desired, and profits were variable. Jerry Conrad, the general manager of the division, enrolled that year in a seminar on contribution margin income sponsored by the American Management Association (AMA). According to Conrad, "Before I went to that seminar, my knowledge of contribution margin income was limited to casual comments that I overheard at group general managers' meetings. A large acquisition in the automotive aftermarket industry had always used a contribution margin approach in its accounting systems. All other segments of the Able Corporation used the full costing method, but this company was allowed to keep its contribution margin cost system because a forced change of systems at the time of acquisition would have been too disruptive."

Jerry believed that the full cost reports used in his division were accurate. He and Frances Kardell, the Division Controller, were confident they knew the total manufacturing cost of each of their products. However, Jerry did not have the same confidence in his staff's ability to determine how volume changes would affect profits. He was convinced that better utilization of plant and equipment and a more effective pricing structure would lead to substantially improved earnings. The division was not as profitable as others in the industry or other similar-size divisions in the corporation that had comparable manufacturing processes.

THE CONTRIBUTION MARGIN APPROACH

A main point of the AMA seminar was that product lines do not produce profits; they produce contribution margin (sales revenue minus variable costs), which can become profits only after fixed costs are covered. The seminar also underscored not only the importance of cost behavior analysis but also the arbitrariness of many fixed cost allocations. Jerry immediately saw in contribution margin a new approach to solving Superior Valve's problems with both product mix and pricing decisions.

Jerry discussed the subject of contribution margin with Todd Talbott, the Group Controller. After hearing the advantages and disadvantages of the approach, Jerry recommended that his division's product costing system be overhauled for the third time since Able Corporation acquired Superior Valve 20 years ago. Todd agreed to support a change in the management reporting system, but he pointed out that the contribution margin approach was contrary to the reporting philosophy of the corporation and, for external purposes, did not comply with GAAP, S.E.C. reporting requirements, and Internal Revenue Service directives on inventory valuation.

When the decision to proceed was made, Frances and her accounting staff used regression analysis to classify manufacturing costs, other operating costs, and selling and general administration costs as either variable, fixed, or mixed. Mixed costs were separated into their variable and fixed components. Fixed costs then were identified as either discretionary (amounts to be expended based on decisions made annually or at shorter intervals) or committed (usually not subject to change in the short-run). A booklet on contribution margin which Jerry gave to his staff stated that fixed expenses are a function of time, and variable expenses (1) vary directly with changes in volume and (2) are usually expressed as a percentage of sales dollars or direct labor dollars.

SPECIAL ORDER

The Wadsworth Company, which was experimenting with various components of its product line, offered to purchase 6,000 Hydro-Con multi-function control valves from Superior for $160 each. Wadsworth would need 500 units per month with delivery commencing at the start of the new year. The special order would be in addition to the 80,000 units that Ralph Darwin, the division's Marketing Manager, expected to sell at the regular $200 price. Ralph considered the order to represent an excellent opportunity to increase long-term sales volume because it would be a new application for the product. He negotiated a flat $48,000 commission with the selling distributor.

Jerry was concerned that cutting the price of the valve would set an undesirable precedent. He pondered the special deal for several days before going to see Ralph. "The price is below our full cost of $175 per unit," he said. "If we accept the Wadsworth proposal, the firm can always expect favored treatment."

Jerry asked Daria Good, the Manufacturing Manager, and Frances to join this discussion in Darwin's office. When they arrived, he asked, "What is the division's capacity for making Hydro-Con Control?" Good's reply was "One hundred thousand (100,000) units per year, if we don't retool any machines dedicated to another product line."

Frances presented the following standard cost data for Hydro-Con valves:

Raw material	$ 35
Purchased components	30
Direct labor	12
Manufacturing overhead	44
Total standard cost	$121

After distributing copies of the budgeted income statement for the upcoming fiscal year, Frances revealed the variable overhead for the 80,000 unit Hydro-Con budget was $2,400,000. Of the budgeted fixed manufacturing costs, $400,000 was discretionary, with the remainder committed to basic capacity charges. Variable "other operating expenses" totaled $4 per unit; a 10% distributor commission ($20 per unit) comprised the variable portion of selling and general administration expenses. The Controller further indicated that manufacturing adjustments represented production variances and scrap, which she expected to vary with the number of valves produced. At the budgeted volume level, fixed other operating expenses would add an average of $16 to unit cost. Basic service costs such a production control, engineering administration, and accounting totaling $880,000 were allocated to Hydro-Con; the remaining fixed other operating expenses were directly related to the product line and were discretionary in nature.

As the discussion continued, Ralph reviewed next year's budget. Of the total fixed selling, general, and administrative expense, $160,000 was earmarked for future advertising space in several trade publications and an upcoming trade show. The remainder of the budget related to salaries and other firm commitments.

The Hydro-Con budget was designed to fully recover all costs at the 80,000 unit production level. The other product line budgets also were designed to fully recover costs at budgeted volume levels, and all fixed costs were expected to remain unchanged until the current maximum capacities were surpassed. Jerry asked his Division Controller what effect the Wadsworth offer would have on profits. But Daria had not yet studied the effects volume changes would have on division operations.

PRODUCT LINE ELIMINATION

Superior Valve's Marketing Department prepared a sales order plan by product line for each new year in both units and dollars. The Production Control Department then used the order plan to develop a sales shipment plan for each of the division's three plants. Ralph Darwin had very little marketing information to use in developing the Made to Order (MTO) Hydraulic Control product line plan. However, he knew that the line's compound growth pattern over the last three years had been quite disappointing, and he saw little prospect for substantial sales growth in the short-term future.

Ralph recommended the division consider eliminating the Made to Order line. Daria had assured him that the MTO-dedicated machinery could be retooled to produce either of the standard lines. Darwin was convinced he could develop a market for the additional standard product in a relatively short time, and he strongly believed the division should concentrate on its two basic product lines. "After all," he commented, "that's where we're most successful." However, until the additional market for the standard product was developed, the elimination of MTO would mean the elimination of 30 manufacturing jobs.

At the last staff meeting of the year, Jerry Conrad told Ralph he would study the product line elimination proposal after he made a decision on the Hydro-Con special order. He assigned the proposal top priority for the new year.

REQUIRED:

1. Assume that inventories will not change during the year. Prepare budgeted contribution approach product line income statements for the year ending 6/30/19X3. Categorize fixed costs as either discretionary or committed.
2. Should Jerry Conrad decide to accept the Wadsworth Company special order? If so, what will be the new Hydro-Con return on sales?
3. Should the Superior Valve Division eliminate the Made to Order product line if there were no alternative uses for its production capacity?
4. If all resulting standard products could be sold, how should the M-T-O capacity be allocated? (Assume only the capacity currently being used to produce 20,000 M-T-O units would be used to produce additional standard products.)
5. Identify the strategic factors that Superior Valve should consider.
6. What changes, if any, should be made to the division's cost system? Why?
7. What ethical issues, if any, should the division consider in connection with the decision to eliminate MTO?

TABLE A

Superior Valve Division
Budgeted Income Statement for the Year Ending 6/30/19X3
($000)

	Hydro-Con	Pneu-trol	Made to Order	Total Division
Revenue	$16,000	$13,000	$ 5,000	$34,000
Material	5,200	3,900	1,300	10,400
Direct Labor	960	1,235	1,000	3,195
Overhead	3,520	2,990	1,531	8,041
Total Cost of Sales @ Standard	9,680	8,125	3,831	21,636
Gross Margin	6,320	4,875	1,169	12,364
Adjustments	800	520	554	1,874
Net Manufacturing Margin	5,520	4,355	615	10,490
Other Oper. Exp. Expenses	1,600	1,560	750	3,910
Selling & General Administration	1,920	1,560	600	4,080
Operating Income	$ 2,000	$ 1,235	$ (735)	$ 2,500

TABLE B

Superior Valve Division
Product Line Data

	Pneu-trol	MTO
Unit selling price	$ 50.00	$ 250.00
Variable overhead per unit	$ 6.50	$ 50.55
Total discretionary fixed overhead	$225,000	$100,000
Variable other operating cost per unit	$ 1.50	$ 5.00
Variable selling and general admin. per unit	$ 5.00	$ 25.00
Committed fixed other operating costs	$970,000	$550,000
Committed fixed selling & general admin.	$160,000	$ 75,000

Product Line	Present Max. Capacity in Units	Machine Hrs./Unit
Hydro-Con	100,000	6
Pneu-trol	350,000	2
MTO	50,000	5

Demonstrating Strategic Versus Conventional Analysis

A Peek at the SCM Themes

In this chapter we present a short case (dealing with a private label opportunity for a bicycle manufacturer) that supports a strategic analysis as well as a relevant cost analysis. The chapter demonstrates the conventional analysis and then a strategic analysis drawing upon the three themes described in chapter 2. When the analysis is presented in the strategic terms, the managerial insights can differ dramatically. This case is an excellent example of the need for managers to be aware that cost analysis must explicitly consider strategic issues and concerns. This concept represents a very natural extension of the managerial accounting framework that became popular about thirty years ago (Anthony, 1956; Horngren, 1962). Managerial accounting replaced cost accounting as a framework for financial analysis for decision making by demonstrating that the cost accounting framework lacked decision relevance. The cost accounting framework failed to take into account the advances in decision analysis that had become popular in the 1950s. In the past twenty years there has been another dramatic extension of decision analysis to take explicit account of strategic issues.[1]

It is now time for management thinking about cost analysis to move forward again to incorporate this newly enriched decision analysis paradigm. Strategic accounting will supplant managerial accounting as a framework for decision making by demonstrating that managerial accounting lacks strategic relevance. These points are illustrated by the following case concerning the Baldwin Bicycle Company.

THE CASE OF BALDWIN BICYCLE COMPANY

In May 1983, Suzanne Leister, marketing vice president of Baldwin Bicycle Company, was mulling over the discussion she had had the previous day with Karl Knott, a buyer from Hi-Valu Stores, Inc. Hi-Valu operated a chain of discount department stores in the northwest. Hi-Valu's sales volume had grown to the extent that it was beginning to add house-brand (also called private-label) merchandise to the product lines of several of its departments. Mr. Knott, Hi-Valu's buyer for sporting goods, had approached Ms. Leister about the possibility of Baldwin's producing bicycles for Hi-Valu. The bicycles would bear the name "Challenger," which Hi-Valu planned to use for all of its house brand sporting goods.

Baldwin had been making bicycles for almost forty years. In 1983, the company's line included ten models, ranging from a small beginner's model with training wheels to a deluxe twelve-speed adult's model. Sales were currently at an annual rate of about $10 million. The company's 1982 financial statement appears in Exh. 1. Most of Baldwin's sales were through independently owned retailers (toy stores, hardware stores, sporting goods stores) and bicycle shops. Baldwin had never distributed its products through department store chains of any type. Ms. Leister felt that Baldwin bicycles had the image of being above average in quality and price, but not a top of the line product.

Hi-Valu's proposal to Baldwin had features that made it quite different from Baldwin's normal way of doing business. First, it was very important to Hi-Valu to have ready access to a large inventory of bicycles, because Hi-Valu had had great difficulty in predicting bicycle sales, both by store and by month. Hi-Valu wanted to carry these inventories in its regional warehouses, but did not want title on a bicycle to pass from Baldwin to Hi-Valu until the bicycle was shipped from one of its regional warehouses to specific Hi-Valu store. At that point, Hi-Valu would regard the bicycle as having been purchased from Baldwin and would pay for it within thirty days. However, Hi-Valu would agree to take title to any bicycle that had been in one of its warehouses for four months, again paying for it

EXHIBIT 1
FINANCIAL STATEMENTS
(Thousand of dollars)

BALDWIN BICYCLE COMPANY
Balance Sheet
As of December 31, 1982

Assets		Liabilities and Owners Equity	
Cash	$ 342	Accounts payable	$ 512
Accounts receivable	1,359	Accrued expenses	340
Inventories	2,756	Short-term bank loans	2,626
Plant and equipment (net)	$3,635	Long-term Note payable	1,512
	$8,092	Total-liabilities	$4,990
		Owners' equity	3,102
			$8,092

Income Statement
For the Year Ended December 31, 1982

Sales revenues	$10,872
Cost of sales	8,045
Gross margin	2,827
Selling and administrative expenses	2,354
Income before taxes	473
Income tax expense	218
Net income	255

within thirty days. Mr. Knott estimated that, on average, a bicycle would remain in a Hi-Valu regional warehouse for two months.

Second, Hi-Valu wanted to sell its Challenger bicycles at lower prices than the name brand bicycles it carried and yet earn approximately the same dollar gross margin on each bicycle sold. The rationale was that Challenger bicycle sales would take away from the sales of the name brand bikes. Thus, Hi-Valu wanted to purchase bicycles from Baldwin at lower prices than the wholesale prices of comparable bicycles sold through Baldwin's usual channels.

Finally, Hi-Valu wanted the Challenger bicycle to be somewhat different in appearance from Baldwin's other bikes. While the frame and mechanical components could be the same as used on current Baldwin models, the fenders, seats, and handlebars would need to be somewhat different, and the tires would have to have the name Challenger molded into their sidewalls. Also, the bicycles would have to be packed in boxes printed with the Hi-Valu and Challenger names. Ms. Leister expected these requirements to increase Baldwin's purchasing, inventorying, and production costs over and above the added costs that would be incurred for a comparable increase in volume for Baldwin's regular products.

On the positive side, Ms. Leister was acutely aware that the bicycle boom had flattened out, and this trend plus a poor economy had caused Baldwin's sales volume to fall during the past two years.[2] As a result, Baldwin currently was operating its plant at about seventy-five percent of one shift's capacity. Thus, the added volume from Hi-Valu's purchases possibly could be very attractive. If agreement could be reached on prices, Hi-Valu would sign a contract guaranteeing to Baldwin that Hi-Valu would buy its house-brand bicycles only from Baldwin for a three-year period. The contract would then be automatically extended on a year-to-year basis, unless one party gave the other at least three months' notice that it did not wish to extend the contract.

Suzanne Leister realized that she needed to do some preliminary financial analysis of this proposal before having any further discussions with Karl Knott. She had written on a pad the information she had gathered to use in her initial analysis; this information is shown in Exh. 2.

This short but very rich case is particularly useful for illustrating strategic accounting because the conclusions that emerge from a relevant cost analysis diverge so widely from the conclusions suggested by a strategic cost analysis. In order to contrast the two perspectives, we will first present the relevant cost analysis—an exercise in financial analysis for a potential extra chunk of business.

RELEVANT COST ANALYSIS OF THE HI-VALU OFFER

A relevant cost perspective would typically consider cost behavior as a starting point. From the facts of the case, it is not difficult to deduce that the incremental cost of producing a Challenger bicycle is about $69 (material, direct labor, and about $9+ of variable overhead). The idea here is to back out the allocated share of fixed manufacturing overhead from the unit cost. In terms of the management decision, the point is that a $92+ selling price provides much more incremental profit than the standard cost of $84+ might

EXHIBIT 2
DATA PERTINENT TO HI-VALU PROPOSAL
(Notes Taken by Suzanne Leister)

1. Estimated first-year costs of producing Challenger bicycles (average unit costs, assuming a constant mix of models):

Materials	$39.80*
Labor	19.60
Overhead (@ 125% of labor)	24.50[†]
	$83.90

    *Includes items specific to models for Hi-Valu, not used in our standard models.
    [†]Accountant says about 40% of total production overhead cost is variable; 125% of DLS rate is based on volume of 100,000 bicycles per year.

2. Unit price and annual volume: Hi-Valu estimates it will need 25,000 bikes a year and proposes to pay us (based on the assumed mix of models) an average of $92.29 per bike for the first year. Contract to contain an inflation escalation clause such that price will increase in proportion to inflation, caused increases in costs shown in item 1, above; thus, the $92.29 and $83.90 figures are, in effect, constant-dollar amounts. Knott intimated that there was very little, if any, negotiating leeway in the $92.29 proposed initial price.

3. Asset-related costs (annual variable costs, as percent of dollar value of assets):

Pretax costs of funds (to finance receivables or inventories)	18.0%
Record keeping costs (for receivables or inventories)	1.0
Inventory insurance	0.3
State property tax on inventory	0.7
Inventory-handling labor and equipment	3.0
Pilferage, obsolescence, breakage, etc.	0.5

4. Assumptions for Challenger-related added inventories (average over the year):

    Materials: two months' supply.
    Work in process: 1,000 bikes, half completed (but all materials for them issued).
    Finished goods: 500 bikes (awaiting next carload lot shipment to a Hi-Valu warehouse).

5. Impact on our regular sales: Some customers comparison shop for bikes, and many of them are likely to recognize Challenger bike as a good value when compared with a similar bike (either ours or a competitor's) at a higher price in a nonchain toy or bicycle store. In 1982, we sold 98.791 bikes. My best guess is that our sales over the next three years will be about 100,000 bikes a year if we forego the Hi-Valu deal. If we accept it, I think we'll lose about 3,000 units of our regular sales volume a year, since our retail distribution is quite strong in Hi-Valu's market regions. These estimates do not include the possibility that a few of our current dealers might drop our line if they find out we're making bikes for Hi-Valu.

The information about overhead in item 1 can be used to infer that fixed manufacturing overhead is about $1.5 million per year.

suggest. Since the fixed costs are already being covered by the regular business, they need not be covered again.

A second element of the relevant cost analysis typically would be the cost of carrying the incremental investment needed to support the incremental sales. This calculation has two components: the incremental working capital investment (no incremental fixed assets are required) and the annual carrying charge percentage. The extra investment can be estimated fairly readily as shown in Exh. 3.

The major judgment in this calculation is the number of bikes in the consignment inventory. We do not try to formalize that uncertainty any more carefully here because the issue is not central to the point of this chapter. However, choosing the annual carrying charge rate is clearly a major element in the analysis. Several basic ideas are involved:

Capital is not free

The relevant charge is the cost of capital plus incremental carrying costs (insurance, handling, taxes, etc.).

Cost of capital is some form of weighted average across the debt and equity capital sources used by the firm.

Any specific number chosen is, at best, a rough approximation because the true cost of capital cannot be observed.

If incremental debt costs 18%, before tax, a first-cut weighted average cost of capital (after tax) might be 13% assuming 1/3 debt and 2/3 equity in the capital structure—1/3 × (18% × 0.5) + 2/3 (15%).

Incremental carrying cost seems to be about 4% a year (before tax) for inventory and 0% for receivables, rejecting part of the case note as being just an allocation of common costs.

Combining carrying costs and cost of capital, an after-tax charge of 15% for inventory and 13% for receivables is a reasonable first cut.

Combining these two components (incremental working capital investment and annual carrying charge) of the carrying cost calculation produces an annual cost number somewhere between about $56,000 (for a $400,000) investment) and about $131,000 (for a $900,000 investment). A midrange estimate is about $100,000 or $4 per bike (over the estimated 25,000 Challenger bicycles). The range here is from about $2 to about $5 per bicycle. This amount is well below the $11.50 after-tax marginal contribution ([$92 − $69] × 5), even at the high end of the investment and carrying cost range.

A third element of the relevant cost analysis would typically be an erosion or cannibalization charge for the lost sales of regular Baldwin bikes as a direct result of Hi-Valu's entry into the market. The two main judgments here are how much the charge should be, assuming it is relevant and whether this is a relevant charge against the project. If a charge is to be assessed, it should be the lost profit contribution from the lost sales. It is possible to calculate that the regular business yields a contribution of about $44 per bicycle (sales price of ~$110[$10.8M/99K] less variable cost of ~$66 [$8.0M − 1.5M*/99K]). Thus, if 3,000 units are lost, the impact on profit would be about $130,000. (3,000 × ~$44). Partly offsetting this, the incremental working capital investment (calculated earlier) would decline somewhat.

Whether or not an erosion charge is relevant is arguable. Assuming that 3,000 customers who otherwise would have bought a Baldwin bicycle buy a Challenger bicycle, the lost profit is certainly real to Baldwin. On the other hand, it probably is reasonable to assume that Hi-Valu will find someone to make Challenger bikes and that Baldwin's sales will drop somewhat as a result, regardless of what Baldwin does. Thus, the sales are lost once Hi-Valu enters the market, regardless of Baldwin's actions. Baldwin's base volume has become 96,000 units instead of 99,000 and the erosion charge is not incremental to the Challenger deal. The marketing dimension of a relevant cost analysis supports the idea that one cannot stop new products from eroding the sales of old products. A firm can only choose whether or not to sell the new products. In this context, focusing on the erosion is not only arrogant (our products are impervious to

EXHIBIT 3
CALCULATING THE EXTRA INVESTMENT REQUIRED TO SUPPORT INCREMENTAL SALES

Raw Material (2 months' stock)	
~4,000 bikes × ~$40 =	~$160,000
Work in process (1,000 units)	
"Half finished" implies about $55 semi finished cost	
(100% of material plus half of labor and variable overhead)	
~1,000 bikes × ~$55 =	~$55,000
Finished units in the factory	
~500 bikes × $69 =	~$35,000
Finished units in the Hi-Valu warehouse	
Per case facts, about 2 months' supply, on average	
~4,000 bikes × ~$69 =	~$280,000
(The range here is probably from ~$100,000 to ~$550,000)	
Accounts receivable (30 days sales)	
~2,000 bikes × ~$92 =	~$185,000
Less a trade credit offset	
Assume 45 days credit from the materials suppliers	
~3,000 bikes × ~$40 =	(~$120,000)
Net Extra Investment	
Range = ~$400,000 to ~$900,000)	~$595,000

153

decline unless we cannibalize them) but also short-sighted (we lose the opportunity to sell new products but sales of the old products decline anyway). Thus, a strong argument can be made to exclude the erosion charge.

Summarizing the components of the cost analysis, we can calculate the incremental profitability as follows:

1. Incremental profit contribution for 25,000 bikes = ~$288,000, after tax:

$$($92 - $69) \times 25,000 \times 0.5.$$

2. The incremental capital charge would be about $100,000, after tax.
3. Incremental residual income after tax is about $188,000 per year on a $600,000 investment. Thus, this is a very attractive return.

This calculation is clearly only a first approximation of the incremental return because it ignores the time value of money. A multiperiod, discounted cash flow approach would be preferable, Also, it leaves open the time period for the project. However, refining this calculation does not change the basic message that the Hi-Valu deal is very attractive from a short-run, incremental financial analysis perspective.

If there are caveats in the analysis, they center around the following issues:

The consigned inventory issue. (Does Baldwin have to tolerate this sort of imposition on normal business terms by Hi-Valu?)

The capacity issue. (Is it wise for Baldwin to tie up most of its excess capacity, unused though it currently is, for several years at well below normal prices?)

The long-run/short-run cost issue. (Is it really appropriate to ignore fixed overhead in a project that uses almost 20% of Baldwin's capacity over a three-year period?)

The uncertainty of Hi-Valu's demand. (What happens to the incremental analysis if Hi-Valu takes fewer than 25,000 bikes or more than 25,000?)

The incremental debt capacity issue. (Can Baldwin borrow an incremental $400,000—$900,000 to finance the project?)

Only the last one of these potential concerns requires additional analysis. The other four are more qualitative than quantitative. The debt capacity issue does require explicit attention.

The $2.6 million level of short-term debt is very high for a year-end balance sheet for a company like Baldwin. December 31 should be a point in the year of nearly maximum liquidity for a manufacturer of a seasonal, consumer durable product like bicycles. Production for the Christmas season should be shipped and paid for by that date, and the production buildup for spring should not be started. One clue to this liquidity crunch is the high level of inventory still on hand at this slack time of year. The $2.7M of inventory represents about 120 days' supply (2.7/8.0 × 365) at a time of the year when very little stock should be on hand. Much of this inventory is likely to be slow moving or even obsolete product. And, it is all financed with short-term debt.

Even though the incremental residual income from the project looks very attractive, it is problematic whether the firm could justify borrowing another $600,00 or so for the Hi-Valu project. One imaginative thought in this regard is reworking some of these bicycles as Challengers. Thinks approach would save much of the material cost per bicycle and also substitutes rework labor for new assembly labor. If the idea is feasible, it probably involves an incremental cost of much less than $69 per bicycle, so that the financing need is reduced. Our experience with the case indicates that managers who get this far in the analysis are sufficiently attracted by the high incremental profit to lead them to argue that the financing problem would not be insurmountable, even if trouble-some, and even if reworking existing inventory isn't deemed practical.

On balance, this analysis comes down to very attractive incremental short-run profits, coupled with some qualitative caveats that somewhat mitigate this attractiveness and a major financing concern that may or may not be deemed binding. The case is sufficiently rich that managers very seldom go outside this relevant cost framework in considering the decision. The case reinforces many basic managerial accounting themes such as:

Cost behavior analysis

Profit contribution analysis

Long-run versus short-run product and customer profitability

Inventory and receivables carrying cost

Working capital management

Project return on investment (ROA) versus residual income)

Balancing quantitative and qualitative issues in a decision

154

Also, this case treats these themes in a context that involves sufficient marketing complexity (the erosion issue and the private label volume enhancement idea for makers of branded products) and sufficient uncertainty (the short-term debt crunch and the structure of the consigned inventory provision) to support excellent discussion with senior management groups. We have used the case more than sixty times in programs for a dozen major corporations and in the Amos Tuck Executive Program. The relevant framework emerges in virtually every discussion.

STRATEGIC ANALYSIS OF THE HI-VALU OFFER

We are not aware of many cases in which the strategic cost analysis yields such totally different insights from the managerial accounting analysis. Because the two perspectives diverge so widely in this case, it is an excellent example of how dangerously narrow our conventional viewpoint can sometimes be. It is interesting to note that virtually none of the points mentioned in this section of the chapter have been raised by the more than 1,000 senior-level managers with whom we have used the case. This observation is not a criticism of these managers; rather, it is a comment on the prevailing narrow conception of cost analysis among U.S. businesses.

Our strategic analysis starts by looking at the value chain positioning of the Challenger bicycle in the marketplace. How much penetration is it likely to achieve? This question follows the fundamental logic of marketing strategy: segmentation and positioning. The case is silent on the segmentation issue and on the differing basic economics of two very different customer groups—a middle-America retailer (Baldwin's normal customer) versus a discount chain (Hi-Valu). But it is not difficult to speculate with reasonable accuracy about the implications for Baldwin of two very different value chain configurations regarding product distribution. The fact that the case is totally silent on these issues is further evidence of what contemporary managerial accounting authors see as relevant concerns. Based on general knowledge or retailers' profit margins and some estimating of freight costs, it is possible to construct the strategic cost comparison outlined in Exh. 4.

Going to the next stage in the value chain, is this difference of $67 reflective of a commensurate difference in value to the consumer? It should be noted that the bicycles differ only in cosmetic ways. The basic

EXHIBIT 4
THE DISTRIBUTION STEP IN THE VALUE CHAIN

	One of Baldwin's Current Dealers		Hi-Valu Stores
Purchase cost	$110		$ 92
Freight cost	10	(Truckload shipping)	8
Delivered cost	120		100
Necessary margin as percent of sales price	(Independent retailer) 40%	(Discount merchandiser	25%
Implied retail price	$200		$133

elements that drive the value of the bicycle are identical (weight to strength relationship in the frame, derailleur, crankshaft, gears, and brakes). Other elements of real value (free assembly, point of sale merchandising, service) or perceived value (brand image, dealer image) obviously differ between the two products. But, do they differ by $67 on a $200 purchase? This is a real issue.

It is also possible to develop a simple market segmentation of the distribution stage in the value chain, based on general knowledge about bicycle retailing, as shown in Exh. 5. This segmentation immediately raises the issue of whether Hi-Valu's positioning of the Challenger will attract customers from the cheap bicycle segment or the value bicycle segment. This distinction is critical for Baldwin. Challenger sales taken from low-end dealers (customers who trade up in quality for the same price) are totally new sales for Baldwin, but Challenges sales taken from mid-range dealers (customers who trade down in price for comparable quality) constitute a direct attack on Baldwin's mainstream business and on its mainstream dealer network.

Drawing again upon general knowledge of trends in retailing over the past few decades, it is very likely that a big share of Challenger sales will come from people who otherwise would have shopped in a neighborhood toy store, hardware store, sporting goods store, or small department store. Forty years ago, virtually all bicycles sold in the United States were value bicycles. Specialty shops pushing premium-priced bicycles did not exist and discount chains pushing the cheap, low-end bikes were just emerging. Sears, Roebuck and J. C. Penney were already well established, but they were not yet perceived as a catastrophic threat to "mom and pop" retailers.

Our strategic analysis must also consider strategic positioning issues. Over the past thirty years the bicycle business has developed almost exactly as Porter's competitive strategy framework would predict (Porter, 1980). One can compete successfully by being different and commanding a premium price for that differentiation, such as BMW automobiles. Or, one can

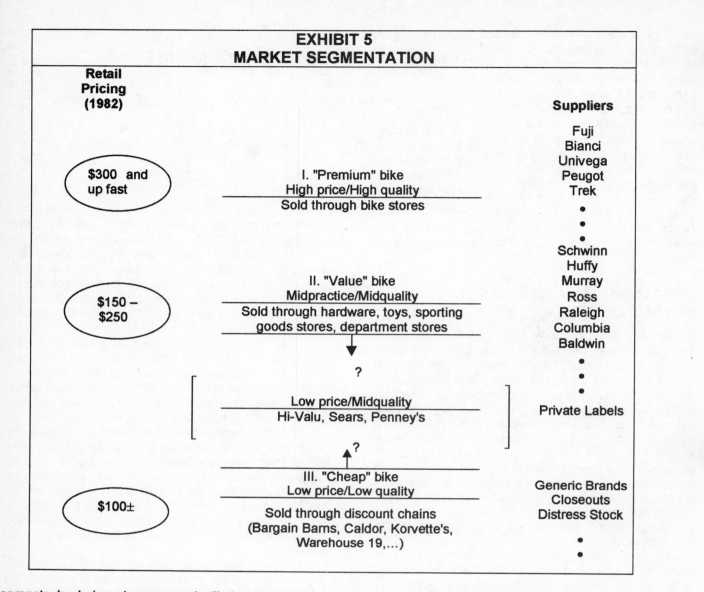

EXHIBIT 5
MARKET SEGMENTATION

Retail Pricing (1982)

Suppliers

Fuji
Bianci
Univega
Peugot
Trek
•
•
•
Schwinn
Huffy
Murray
Ross
Raleigh
Columbia
Baldwin
•
•
•

$300 and up fast

I. "Premium" bike
High price/High quality
Sold through bike stores

$150 – $250

II. "Value" bike
Midpractice/Midquality
Sold through hardware, toys, sporting
goods stores, department stores

?

Low price/Midquality
Hi-Valu, Sears, Penney's

Private Labels
•
•
•

?

III. "Cheap" bike
Low price/Low quality

$100±

Sold through discount chains
(Bargain Barns, Caldor, Korvette's,
Warehouse 19,...)

Generic Brands
Closeouts
Distress Stock
•
•

compete by being cheaper, and offering reasonable quality for the low price, such as Toyota automobiles. A manufacturer who is neither identifiably better nor demonstrably cheaper will wither away over time, such as AMC automobiles. Porter refers to such firms as being "stuck in the middle" because they do not have a sustainable competitive advantage. Such firms may survive for a long time if the business is sufficiently attractive (automobiles, for example) and if growth rates and investment rates do not force a quick shake out of the weaker players (as they have done in microcomputers, for example). But, firms that lack a sustainable competitive edge eventually will wither.

This focus on the value chain and strategic positioning highlights that, by putting Hi-Valu into the bicycle business, Baldwin is not only creating another direct competitor to its regular customers but also offering that competitor a much better price than it offers its regular customers. Baldwin can, of course, argue that the Challenger bicycle is different, but what will Hi-Valu tell its customers? And, what will the customers believe? In agreeing to this offer, Baldwin almost certainly would further erode the already declining market position of its regular customers. In all probability, this is not a short-run, tactical profit enhancement opportunity. It is very likely a strategic repositioning with major long-run implications.

Just because the Hi-Valu offer is a strategic opportunity to reconfigure the value chain rather than a tactical short-run profit boost does not mean it is necessarily unattractive for Baldwin. In fact, this sort of strategic repositioning may be just what Baldwin needs. As emphasized in the third element of the SCM framework, cost driver analysis can play a significant role in evaluating this strategic opportunity. Examining which cost factors drive the overall profit-

EXHIBIT 6
RETURN ON EQUITY

	Margins (P/S)	×	Asset Intensity (S/A)	Leverage (A/E)	=	Return
Baldwin, 1981	$255K/$10.8M		$10.8M/$8.0M (1.35)	$8.0M/$3.0M (2.67)	=	$255K/$3.0
Average of U.S. manufacturing (early 1980s)	(2 + %) 5%		1.5	2	=	(8 + %) 15%
Baldwin with the Hi-Valu deal in 1982, at best	−$400K/$12.8 3%		$12.8M/$8.6M (1.49)	$8.6M/$3.0M	=	13%

ability of Baldwin is one way to assess the attractiveness of its current strategic niche. Exh. 6 shows return on equity (profit/equity) in terms of margins (profit/sales), asset intensity (sales/assets), and leverage (assets/equity) and suggests that Baldwin currently is marginally profitable, at best.

Baldwin is earning only about half of the average of all manufacturing firms, even though it is much more heavily leveraged. A good case could be made that Baldwin presents too much basic business operating risk to justify such a high level of financial risk (leverage). Either Baldwin's lenders are inattentive or they have been forced into the current situation by supposedly short-term loans that become long term when inventory was not converted into sales. This strategic assessment of risk and return relationships makes it much harder to argue that Baldwin is a reasonable candidate for further loans.

Another use of cost driver analysis is to flesh out the likely results, over time, of Baldwin's move into the lower price segment of the market. The company's basic economic structure currently is as follows:

Contribution margin per unit $44 (40% of sales).

Fixed cost base (annually):
Manufacturing: ~$1.5M } $3.9M
Selling and administration   ~2.4M

Break-even point = 89K units ($3.9M/$44), is about two-thirds of one shift capacity.

Profit (before tax) at 99K units would be about $440K (10,000 × $44). This estimate is quite close to the $474K earned in 1981.

Profit (before tax) at one shift capacity of 133K units = 44,000 × $44 = $1.9M. This is an excellent return on equity.

Asset investment:
Inventory = 120 days (obviously more an advocate or just in case than just in time)
Accounts receivable = 45 days, which is typical
Property turnover = 10.8/3.6 = 3×, which is reasonable

Fixed cost percentage of sales:
Manufacturing = 1.5/10.8 = ~14%
Selling and administrative = 2.4/10.8 = ~22%

Gross margin = ~26% of sales (2.8/10.8), a very low figure for a consumer durables manufacturer.

Selling and administrative cost = ~22% of sales, which seems very high for a low-margin manufacturer.

This analysis clearly suggests that Baldwin is geared up for a much higher level of sales than it is now achieving and that reasonable profit levels hinge on much higher volume levels. In SCM terms, Baldwin has committed to a strategy dependent on scale economies that are not being achieved. Bicycle sales in the United States reached a peak of 15 million units in 1973 and had declined to 10 million units in 1982, so it is not surprising that Baldwin looks like a company that sorely needs much more volume. Doesn't this requirement suggest that the extra volume provided by Hi-Valu would be an ideal option?

Not necessarily. The Hi-Valu project is very likely to alienate Baldwin's current dealers. It is usually unwise to try to be a significant supplier simultaneously in two price segments with a substantially identical product, although some industries try this ploy. The liquor companies seem to make it work. ("The only difference between $5 vodka and $10 vodka is $5 and a Russian-looking label.") But, this strategy has been a poor one for many other firms. Fram oil filters (Bendix) lost their ability to command a premium price when they became so readily available in discount chains. Chevrolet and Oldsmobile were totally different automobiles in the 1950s. Many people believe that much of General Motors' current decline can be traced to the decision to stop differentiating its cars in ways other than cosmetic trim and price. GM even lost a court case over Oldsmobile's use of Chevrolet engines in its cars. Oldsmobile saw this practice as a normal part of its common parts manufacturing strategy. Consumers saw it as breaking faith with the Oldsmobile tradition. The Toro Company almost went bankrupt in 1980 when it solved an excess inventory

EXHIBIT 7
BALDWIN'S SITUATION

It is profitable, but only modestly so.
It is heavily leveraged—probably too heavily.
Its strategic niche is slowly eroding away.
A solution presents itself (the Hi-Valu offer).

Plus	Minus
Looks like great incremental return on investment	Looks extremely profitable for Hi-Valu. Can Baldwin negotiate a better deal? (Probably yes, but should it try?)
Utilizes excess capacity.	Raises major ethical issues about Baldwin's responsibility to its current customers.
Opens new channel of distribution for Baldwin that is a growth market.	Barely break even on full cost basis.
	Major cash flow crunch: Can Baldwin borrow an additional $600K?
	At best, puts company ROE at average level.
	Strategically very risky.

What looks like a good opportunity from a short-run relevant cost perspective looks like a disaster from a strategic perspective.

---

problem by flooding discount chains with its supposedly premium snow blowers. It almost lost its dealer network in the process.

Baldwin's dealers cannot stop the firm from supplying Hi-Valu, but they do not have to cooperate by offering the $200 Baldwin bicycle as the stalking horse for the $133 Challenger bicycle. If they normally stock two or three brands to give their customers a choice, they can add Huffy, Ross, Murray, or Schwinn and drop Baldwin from the set. This response would, in effect, drive Baldwin much more heavily toward the growing low-end bike segment and away from the declining mid-value segment. What would this change in Baldwin's sales mix do for its basic economics? In SCM terms, what cost drivers became critical in trying to serve the low-end segment?

- Contribution margin would only be $23 (25% of sales) instead of $44, and it would be likely to fall steadily because of competition from the Taiwanese and the Koreans.

- The break-even point would be 170K units ($3.9M/$23) or about 130% of one shift capacity. (Break-even point greater than capacity is one pretty sure strategic danger signal.)

- If there are good reasons to stay with a one shift operation and if the firm wants to earn 15% ROE, on a $3M equity base, it must earn $450K after tax or $900K before tax. This requires ~39K bicycles (at $23 contribution each).

- This leaves ~94K bicycles to pay for fixed overhead (133K − 39K). At $23 per bicycle this allows ~$2.2M for overhead (94K × $23).

- Thus, the firm will have to cut its fixed costs by more than 40%, in the short run (from $3.9M to $2.2M) just to earn an average return on equity.

- As prices come under continuing pressure from foreign manufacturers, unless Baldwin can cut variable costs, margins will fall and overhead will have to be cut even more.

Can Baldwin realistically expect to compete as a supplier of low-cost bikes once the attraction of its mid-brand image has been eroded? What would be the possible source of its cost advantage? It could not plan to compete on scale advantages or learning curve advantages or technological leadership. Very few U.S. firms have learned to play this continual cost reduction game well, especially when starting from a weakened position such as Baldwin faces. Thus, the cold reality is that Baldwin is caught between the proverbial rock and hard place. Its position is summarized in Exh. 7.

Exh. 8 summarizes the strategic options from a financial perspective. How can cost analysis help the firm to understand the relative attractiveness of the strategic alternatives?

Baldwin clearly cannot plan to stay in their current niche indefinitely nor can they move entirely to the Hi-Valu niche. What other strategic alternatives do they have? How could cost analysis help the firm to assess

---

EXHIBIT 8
STRATEGIC COST ANALYSIS FOR BALDWIN

Alternative #1. Do not accept the Hi-Valu deal
ROE is inadequate (~8%).
Middle market is slowly shrinking.
Even if Baldwin rejects the Hi-Valu offer, someone else will do it, thereby further
  eroding Baldwin's current niche. So, even its current ROE of 8% is vulnerable

Alternative #2. Current niche plus Hi-Valu deal
ROE is still average (~13%) at best.
Great threat to the core business. If their dealers drop Baldwin products, the projected
  ROE of 13% is seriously open to question. Baldwin might be forced to go 100% to Hi-Valu's
  niche, where the basic economics are marginal at best.
What if Baldwin's current dealers ask for a deal similar to Hi-Valu's?
Going private label is a strategic shift; what are the organizational implications of diluting
  the strategic thrust?
An ethical issue: Is the difference in price of $133 versus $200 reflective of a difference
  in value to the customer?

Alternative #3. Go 100% to Hi-Valu's niche.
Basic economics are marginal, unless able to cut fixed costs by more than 40%, just in the short run.
Baldwin's ability to compete long run against foreign competition as a low-cost producer is very doubtful.

---

the relative attractiveness of these options? Two additional strategic alternatives would be:

1. Go entirely to the premium segment.

2. Try to find new product opportunities in the value niche (mountain bikes, etc.).

There is not enough information in the case for a strategic financial analysis of any of these options. Unless the firm can find a sustainable niche somewhere, its future is bleak. Some bicycle firms did find new prosperity in the mid-1980s with the emergence of the off-road bicycles, which sold almost 3 million units in 1986. But, the market research, product development, market development, and manufacturing retooling required to enter and succeed in this new niche probably would take far more money than Baldwin could muster. The firm has used up most of its slack in chasing fond hopes of resurgence in a gradually dying market segment. Strategically, it is dead in the water and it may not know it. Other strategic options for the firm could be developed here, but that is not the intent of this analysis.

The difficulty of finding an appropriate strategic response in this situation, even for a well-positioned firm, is demonstrated by the decline of the traditional market leader, Schwinn, into bankruptcy in 1992.

In summary, this strategic analysis, based heavily on concepts articulated in marketing strategy and in competitive strategy and using cost analysis designed to complement and reinforce the strategic view, pres-

ents a totally different perspective on the Baldwin Bicycle case. If we had access to the company's internal cost records and the records of its competitors and its customers, we could attempt a value chain analysis to see exactly where Baldwin got so far off the track, but that is not possible in this case.

What is possible, however, is to contrast this rudimentary strategic cost analysis with the relevant cost analysis to show how different the business problem looks from these two perspectives. Although the three elements of the SCM theme are all present here, the case is too limited to permit a careful exposition of any of them. A much more careful exposition of all three themes follows in chapters 4 through 14.

Cost analysis must be supplemented by strategic analysis, as the Baldwin case demonstrates, in order to understand the real business problem. This approach means that the cost analysis concepts must be explicitly tied to the strategic context of the business problem. In that sense, strategic cost analysis must now begin to go beyond the cost accounting framework it replaced thirty years ago.

---

[1] A modified version of this chapter appeared as "Making Strategy Explicit in Cost Analysis; A Case Study," by John K. Shank and Vijay Govindarajan; *Sloan Management Review*, 29, 3 (Spring 1988), pp. 19-30. Copyright 1988 by the Sloan Management Review Association. All rights reserved. Reprinted by permission of the publisher.

[2] The case study of Baldwin Bicycle Company was adapted from R. N. Anthony and J. S. Reece, Accounting: Text and Cases (Homewood, Ill; Richard Irwin, 1983), pp. 742-44.

Chapter 11
Capital Budgeting

Cases

Readings

Wilton L. Accola: **Assessing Risk and Uncertainty in New Technology Investments**

This article develops a framework for managers to use in assessing new technology investments, based on both nonquantitative risk factors and quantifiable financial returns and risk factors.

The framework extends the conventional two-dimensional risk-return model to a three dimensional approach in which the third dimension is the nonquantifiable, uncertain factors.

The analytical hierarchy process (AHP), which is used for assessing nonquantifiable data, is the underlying model of the framework.

Discussion Questions
1. What approaches are often used in assessing investments in new technology?
2. Why are these approaches inadequate or impractical?
3. How does the proposed model incorporate an assessment of nonquantifiable uncertainties, quantifiable financial returns, and risk parameter in evaluating capital investment projects?
4. How does the method explained in this article differ from previous models which have used the AHP method in investment decision making?

Note: See also the article selected for Chapter 19, "Does ROI Apply to Robotics Factories?"

Cases

11-1. Capital Investment Analysis

MACRS (CMA adapted) Beloit Company manufacturers motorized utility equipment and trucks. Beloit's Assembly Department employs about 200 workers who are covered by a labor contract that will expire on December 31, 19x5. During negotiations with Beloit for a new contract, the union has presented a proposal covering the next four years (19x6-x9). This proposal calls for an increase in wage rates of $2.00 per hour at the beginning of 19x6 and an additional $1.00 per hour at the beginning of 19x8. Employee benefits will be 40 percent of regular wages (total wages exclusive of any overtime premium) under the terms of the union proposal. Management is concerned that the increase in labor costs will eliminate most of its profits.

Beloit's long-range plans call for expansion of the product line in the near future. Management is working with outside consultants on the design of a new automated plant that will double present capacity. The new plant is to be operational in January 20x0, at which time the existing facility will be sold.

The assembly activity in the new plant will be highly automated. Now, in response to the union proposal, management wants to examine the possibility of automating the existing Assembly Department. Because the system has already been designed and developed, the vice-president of Production is confident that the equipment could be acquired and installed in late 19x5 to be operational in January 19x6.

The Controller has been asked to provide an economic analysis of the proposal to automate the existing Assembly Department based on the labor costs included in the union proposal. The Controller has accumulated the following data.

- The sales revenues for the next four years are expected to be relatively stable.
- Production volume is uniform throughout the year. Currently, a total of 40,000 labor hours is worked annually in the Assembly Department, of which 3,000 labor hours are subject to an overtime premium of 50 percent of the wage rate.
- The wage rate under the current labor contract is $20 per hour.
- The new equipment will be purchased and installed in the Assembly Department in December 19x5 at a cost of $3,000,000. The company will claim the four percent reduced investment tax credit in the year the equipment is placed in service; there is no reduction in asset basis when the reduced investment tax credit is claimed. For financial reporting, the equipment will be depreciated using the straight-line method over the four-year life. For tax Purposes, this is three-year equipment and will be depreciated using the MACRS personal property rates presented below.

MACRS Tables for Three-Year property
Year 1 — 33.33%
Year 2 — 44.45%
Year 3 — 14.81%
Year 4 — 7.41%

- The labor hours worked in the Assembly Department will be reduced to 15,000 annually with the new equipment, and because of increased efficiency, overtime will be eliminated.
- Annual maintenance costs will increase by $12,000 with the new equipment.

- The existing facility can be sold for $1,600,000 at December 31, 19x9. However, if the Assembly Department is automated, the plant can then be sold for $2,000,000. The basis for tax purposes of the existing facility on December 31, 19x9, exclusive of the new equipment, will be $1,400,000, whether or not the Assembly Department is automated.
- Beloit Company is subject to a 40 percent income tax rate of all income.
- Management assumes annual cash flows occur at the end of the year for evaluating capital investment proposals. The company uses a 15 percent after-tax discount rate.

REQUIRED:

Based on the labor costs included in the union proposal, calculate the net present value at December 31, 19x5, of Beloit Company's proposal to automate the Assembly Department.

11-2. Capital Investment Analysis II

(From Management Accounting Campus Report, contributed by Nabil Hassan) The Nabil Company makes a microcomputer desk that it sells for $50 under a contract to a large computer retailer. The company operates one shift in its Ohio plant. The annual normal capacity is 100,000 units.

Direct labor is paid at the rate of $8.00 per hour. An employee can produce a desk in four hours. Eight board feet of hard board costing $0.25 per board foot are used in each desk. Indirect manufacturing costs (manufacturing overhead) at normal capacity of 100,000 units are described by the following budget line:

Total Costs = Fixed Costs + Variable Cost Per Unit
Total Costs = $25,000 + $0.30/unit

Some years ago, The Nabil Company installed a saw which presently has a carrying value (book value) of $20,000 and is being depreciated $2,000 a year. At the time of installation, it was estimated that the saw would have no scrap value at the end of its useful life because the scrap value would equal its dismantling costs.

At present, a sales agent from The Hassan Company is encouraging The Nabil Company to replace the old saw, currently in operation, with its new computer-controlled saw. An advantage of the new machine is that it will cut direct labor time substantially; the time required to produce one desk will fall from four hours to two hours. However, because the new saw is more powerful than the present machine, it is expected that utility costs will increase by $0.10 per unit.

The new saw will cost $100,000, including installation charges and transportation. The estimated useful life of the new saw is 10 years; it will be depreciated by the straight-line method. At the end of 10 years, the salvage value is estimated to be $10,000.

The Hassan Company agrees that if Nabil will buy the new saw, they will buy the old saw for $4,000 with the no dismantling costs to be charged to Nabil. The income tax rate is 50%. The Nabil Company management expects a return on investment of 15%. For income tax purposes, the loss on trade-in of the old machine is allowable as a tax deduction.

REQUIRED:

As financial analyst for The Oilers Company you are charged with analysis of the purchase of the new equipment. In the preparation of a report for the president, you will need to determine for consideration by management:

1- The contribution margin per unit, under current operating conditions;
2- The standard overhead rate (applied rate) per unit under current operating conditions:
3- The budget line for indirect manufacturing costs (manufactured overhead), assuming the new saw is purchased and installed;
4- The manufacturing overhead standard rate (applied rate) of the new machine if normal capacity of 100,000 units is expected to remain the same;
5- The contribution margin per unit assuming the sales price remains unchanged, if the new saw is purchased and installed;
6- The net additional investment of the machine, assuming The Oilers Company decides to install the new saw;
7- The expected net additional cash flow per year if the new saw is installed—assume the company sells all that it produces;
8- The present value index (profitability index) of the new equipment; and
9- Comment on the importance of the profitability index.

Assessing Risk and Uncertainty in New Technology Investments

By Wilton L. Accola
Wilton L. Accola (deceased) formerly Assistant Professor at University of Memphis.

SYNOPSIS: Recently, much attention has focused on the shortcomings of traditional capital budgeting models in evaluating new technology investments. Critics argue that such models particularly those based on discounted cash flows, lead managers to favor less promising investments over strategic new technology investments because many benefits of the strategic investment are highly uncertain and cannot be quantified. Furthermore, the riskiness of a new technology investment is difficult to assess because outcome probabilities are difficult to estimate. Consequently, several writers have concluded that traditional capital budgeting models are inadequate for evaluating new technology investments.

This paper provides a theory-based framework for evaluating nonquantifiable uncertainties and multiple aspects of risk in capital investments and makes the following contributions:

- The two-dimensional risk-return framework is extended to include a third dimension, nonquantifiable uncertainty. This expanded framework enables managers to formally evaluate all significant nonquantifiable uncertainties relevant to the resource allocation decision.
- The proposed evaluation approach makes a clear distinction between quantifiable returns, quantifiable risks, and nonquantifiable uncertainties. If a clear distinction is not made when evaluating benefits, the quantifiable part of the benefit may be counted twice—once in the quantifiable return and once when nonquantifiable benefits are evaluated. The approach proposed in this paper reduces the possibility of double-counting.
- A composite measure of quantifiable risk is introduced in this paper. By capturing multiple aspects of risk, this composite measure provides managers with more risk information than models which define risk in terms of a single parameter. The composite risk measure also reflects the objectives of the firm.

An important function of a management accounting information system is to provide managers with models that evaluate all relevant information needed for making capital allocation decisions. Ideally, the management accounting information system should provide information and models useful for (1) predicting the future cash flows of prospective investment alternatives, (2) assessing the riskiness of these future cash flows, and (3) assessing the nonquantifiable uncertainties surrounding the estimation of future cash flows.[1]

Recently, much attention has focused on the shortcomings of management accounting information systems in evaluating new technology investments.. The special problems encountered in measuring benefits and risks of computer-integrated-manufacturing (CIM) investments have been of particular concern. Critics argue that quantitative models, particularly discounted cash flow (DCF) models, lead managers to favor less promising investments over strategic new technology investments because many benefits of the strategic investments are highly uncertain and cannot be quantified. Furthermore, the riskiness of a new technology investment is difficult to assess because outcome probabilities are difficult to estimate. Consequently, several writers concluded that traditional quantitative models are inadequate for evaluating new technology investments.

Models enabling managers to evaluate qualitative criteria have been proposed for use in evaluating CIM investments. The Analytical Hierarchy Process (AHP) model, which can be used to assess non-quantifiable data, has received support as a practical aid for evaluating CIM investments. Automan (Weber 1989), a computerized AHP decision aid jointly sponsored by the Institute of Management Accountants and the U.S. Department of Commerce, was developed specifically to evaluate CIM investment decisions (Weber 1989). Expert Choice, developed by Decision Support Software, Inc., is also used for evaluating multiple criteria investment decisions.

Despite the growing interest among managers in AHP and other multiple criteria models, the use of such models may produce undesirable outcomes if these models are applied in inappropriate ways. This paper develops a theory-based framework for evaluating multiple dimensions of risk and uncertainty. Although this paper refers to the AHP model as a means of implementing the proposed framework, other multiattribute weighting techniques also may be used to implement this framework.[2]

I. PROBLEMS IN EVALUATING NEW TECHNOLOGY INVESTMENTS

Traditional capital budgeting models have been limited to assessing quantifiable financial information and usually disregard nonquantifiable benefits. The ultimate financial productivity of a new technology investment is affected to a considerable extent by nonquantifiable benefits (Kaplan 1986).

Benefits often associated with CIM investments—consistency with business strategy, improved competitive position, improved delivery and service, improved product quality, and reduced product development time—often are difficult to quantify. A survey of American high-technology companies and users of managerial accounting information reveals that more than half of the respondents did not attempt to quantify these benefits (Howell et al. 1987). In Japan, 71 percent of advanced manufacturing companies surveyed justify investments on the basis of difficult-to-quantify benefits (Scarbrough et al. 1991).

Mensah and Miranti (1989) classified CIM benefits into two categories—primary benefits and secondary benefits. Because the primary benefits of automation are based on cost savings, they are reasonably estimable from historical data. These include: (1) direct labor savings, (2) direct material savings, (3) savings from the reduction in set-ups, (4) savings from higher quality products, and (5) savings from reduced materials and in-process inventories.

Secondary benefits are much more difficult to quantify and are often highly uncertain. These benefits include: (1) increased market demand due to improved process control/product reliability, (2) improved product performance, (3) additional manufacturing capabilities/flexibility, (4) rapid learning effects, and (5) improved employee morale.

DIFFICULTIES IN APPLYING DCF TECHNIQUES

Despite these difficulties, several authors attempted to demonstrate how discounted cash flow analysis can be applied to automation projects. Most of these research studies appeared in engineering journals and focus on the economics of specific equipment configurations. Generally, such attempts failed to develop quantitative criteria for evaluating qualitative benefits and/or are based on assumptions which may not hold in practice (Mensah and Miranti 1989).

ARBITRARILY HIGH HURDLE RATES

The use of arbitrarily high hurdle discount rates to account for the high risk inherent in new technologies has often led managers to fund investments which are less desirable strategically than investments in new technology (Kaplan 1986; Sullivan and Reeve 1988). Arbitrarily high hurdle thresholds favor short-term projects over long-term projects with large cash flows in the middle to late part of the project's life. Sullivan and Reeve(1988) pointed out that when high hurdle rates are combined with an incomplete analysis of qualitative benefits, few strategic projects are adopted. They concluded that companies using risk-adjusted hurdle rates to evaluate investments incorporate subjective risk assessments into the analysis twice—once through the use of a high discount rate and again by omitting many of the difficult-to-quantify benefits.

Other authors objected to the use of risk-adjusted discount rates on theoretical grounds (Ronen and Sorter 1972).. A major theoretical weakness involves use of a single measure to reflect both expected cash flows and the riskiness of the expected cash flows. Because there are many different determinants of risk, it is difficult to capture all the aspects of a project's riskiness through a single modification of the discount rate (Ronen and Sorter 1972). In practice, adjustments to the discount rate are affected by managers' attitudes toward risk rather than by an explicit representation of the risks inherent in the investment alternatives (Ronen and Sorter 1972). For these reasons, models used should enable managers to measure and evaluate expected cash flows separately from the risks associated with them. In choice situations involving multiple aspects of risk, models with multiple risk parameters should be used to explicitly represent all significant aspects of risk existing in the choice alternatives.

OTHER RISK MEASUREMENT APPROACHES

Multiple-dimensional risk models represent expected cash flows and their associated risks separately. Two dimensional risk-return models, as typified by Hillier's method (1963) and the Capital Asset Pricing Model, combine a return measure with a single measure of risk.

Many different risk measures have been used as parameters for multiple-dimensional risk models. Two major types of risk measures used as model parameters are *moment-oriented and dimension-oriented measures* (Schoemaker 1979; Aschenbrenner 1984). **Moment-oriented** models assume that data are available to estimate multiple outcomes of alternatives and their related probabilities; **dimension-oriented** models are based on risk "dimensions" and often require less data.

Moment-oriented approaches include Hillier's use of standard deviations to measure the riskiness of cash flows (Hillier 1963; Washburn 1992), variance (Norgaard and Killeen 1990) and confidence limits (Libby and Fishburn 1977). Most sophisticated risky choice capital budgeting models are based on a moment-oriented definition of risk, requiring estimation of the probability distribution of cash flows (Norgaard and Killeen 1990).

Dimension-oriented risk measures are often used when the probability distribution of cash flows is difficult to estimate. These measures are not based on an entire probability of cash flows. Instead, they capture various dimensions of risk present in the choice situation.

An important risk dimension that should often be considered in CIM investment decisions is the possibility of a ruinous loss. The amount of capital investment as a percentage of total assets of the firm may be used to represent the possibility of a ruinous loss. The larger the proportion of resources committed to a capital project, the greater the risk of insolvency. The probability of losses exceeding a certain percentage of total equity also may be used to measure the ruinous loss dimension.

The widespread use of the payback method for evaluating capital projects (Mao 1970; Scapens and Sale 1981; Howell et al. 1987; Pike 1983, 1988), may be attributed to its usefulness as a dimension-oriented risk measure. Payback period often is used as a measure of liquidity risk.

Another risk dimension relevant to capital budgeting decisions is the failure to achieve a target return. Examples of risk measures that capture this dimension include semivariance and the probability of below-target returns. Unlike moment-oriented risk parameters which define risk as an aspect of the entire probability distribution, these measures define risk in terms of only the negative side of a probability distribution. Semivariance, as a measure of downside risk, specifically considers situations where one or more outcomes for an alternative are lower than some critical amount (usually, a target return). Semivariance, unlike variance or standard deviation, does not consider the possibility of a large favorable outcome to be risky. Another measure of downside risk, the probability of below-target returns, associates greater risk with a higher probability of failing to achieve a target return. This measure is an important risk parameter when it is difficult for managers to estimate a reliable probability distribution of cash flows (Mao 1970).

Although many different quantitative risk measures—both moment- and dimension-oriented—have been used as parameters for risk return tradeoff models, these models primarily use a single measure, such as variance, beta or semivariance, to represent an investment's riskiness (Libby and Fishburn 1977). For some capital budgeting decisions, models with multiple risk parameters may better represent the risk that exists in the situation than simpler models with a single risk parameter.

A restrictive characteristic of both moment- and dimension-oriented risk measures is the requirement that risk must be quantified. The dimension-oriented approach requires quantification of the particular risk dimension being measured. A requirement of the moment-oriented approach is that probability distributions of risky cash flows can be reasonably estimated. In some situations, such as new technology investment decisions, probability distributions are difficult to estimate and quantification of all uncertainties is impossible. In such situations, such as new technology investment decisions, probability distributions are difficult to estimate and quantification of all uncertainties is impossible. In such situations, it may be necessary to use a model that considers nonquantifiable risk and return, to obtain a more complete evaluation of the project's riskiness.

STRATEGIC INVESTMENT

Because traditional capital budgeting models fail to measure qualitative benefits, some authors suggest that certain investments be classified as "strategic" and implemented regardless of financial justification (Haspeslaugh 1982; Logue 1981). These authors define strategic investments as those necessary for the firm's survival. The "best" alternative is not necessarily the optimal alternative as ranked by net present value or internal rate of return, but the one that enables the firm to survive threats from competitors. Because a CIM investment is a strategic investment, these authors argue that it should be adopted regardless of the discounted cash flow projections.

The problem with such an approach is the difficulty firms have in distinguishing between strategic and nonstrategic investments. Not every CIM investment is necessary for the survival of the firm. To properly define and evaluate a strategic investment, criteria must be developed to determine the degree to which an investment opportunity contributes to the firm's survival.

ANALYTICAL FRAMEWORK

Several authors proposed variations of an analytical model, the Analytical Hierarchy Process (AHP), to supplement discounted cash flow techniques in evaluating new technology investments (Arbel and Seidmann 1984; Canada and Sullivan 1989; Neises and Bennett 1989; Stout et al. 1991). Subjective estimates of uncertain benefits for which probabilities cannot be reasonably estimated can be formally incorporated into the analysis through the use of AHP. Rather than requiring decision makers to put a dollar amount on benefits that are by their nature difficult to quantify, AHP enables decision makers to measure the perceived importance of these benefits.

Previous AHP studies focused primarily on use of the AHP model to combine quantitative and qualitative benefits into an overall rating of new technology investments (Canada and Sullivan 1989; Neises and Bennett 1989; Stout et al. 1991). Harper et al. (1992) recommend that AHP users and researchers take care to create hierarchical structures that are grounded in theory. This paper extends previous AHP studies by proposing that AHP can be used to measure non-quantitative benefits. However, previous AHP models can be susceptible to management manipulation because they combine managers' less reliable subjective estimates of qualitative data with quantitative data into a single overall rating.

The framework proposed in this paper requires decision makers to separately evaluate non-quantifiable uncertainties and quantitative measures of financial risk and return. Managers must first estimate the annual cash flows about which they have the greatest confidence: the cost of new process equipment and benefits expected from labor, inventory, floor space, and cost-of-quality savings. The quantitative financial risk and return dimensions of the proposed three-dimensional framework are based on these estimates. After the quantifiable costs and benefits are estimated, the non-quantifiable benefits are subjectively evaluated using AHP and represented as the third dimension of the proposed framework—nonquantifiable uncertainty.

II. A FRAMEWORK FOR EVALUATING MULTIPLE DIMENSIONS OF RISK AND UNCERTAINTY

The appropriateness of any particular risky choice model depends on the nature of the decision and whether the model captures the significant parameters of risk and uncertainty relevant to that particular decision. When available information is insufficient to generate probability distributions of cash flows required for moment-oriented risky choice models, models that capture decision makers' assessments of non-quantifiable uncertainties and other aspects of risk may be more appropriate.

Within the capital budgeting field, one-dimensional discounted cash flow models and two-dimensional risk and return models have dominated. It has become clear, however, that these models are incomplete. In most new technology investment situations, risk is multi-dimensional and cannot be completely represented with a single risk measure.

The approach proposed in this paper extends the two-dimensional risk and return framework to include a third dimension—nonquantifiable uncertainty. In addition, the quantitative risk dimension is a composite measure, incorporating multiple risk parameters. It provides decision makers with more risk information than single-parameter models. Fig. 1 illustrates how non-quantifiable uncertainties and quantifiable financial return and risk dimensions may be evaluated using this approach.

The proposed framework, unlike single-criterion ranking methods such as net present value, does not provide a single optimal alternative. Rather, an "efficient plane"—the shaded region in Fig. 1—provides a set of alternatives that dominate all alternatives below the plane. Alternative A provides many non-quantifiable benefits, has no risk and a small quantifiable return. Alternative B has no uncertain benefits, no risk and a quantifiable return slightly better than Alternative A. Alternative C also has no uncertain benefits, but is very risky, yet provides the highest quantifiable return. Alternative D provides the same amount of uncertain benefits as Alternative A, but is much more risky and provides a higher quantifiable return.

Selection of an alternative from the set of alternatives on the efficient plane depends on the decision maker's preferences for risk and uncertainty. A decision maker averse to risk and uncertainty selects an

FIGURE 1
A THREE-DIMENSIONAL FRAMEWORK FOR EVALUATING
RISKY CAPITAL PROJECTS

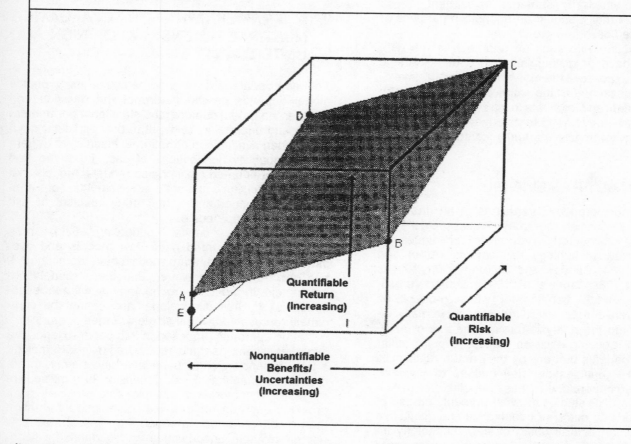

alternative on the efficient plane located on or near B.A risk- and uncertainty-seeking decision maker selects the alternative on the efficient plane close to D. Alternative E is sub-optimal because E is below the efficient plane. Alternative A, located on the efficient plane, is better than alternative E; both alternatives A and E have the same amount of quantifiable risk and nonquantifiable benefits, but A's quantifiable return is higher than E's.

The efficient plane slopes downward as non-quantifiable uncertainty increases, based on the assumption that the quantifiable returns for investments with large non-quantifiable benefits are less than the quantifiable returns for investments with few non-quantifiable benefits. However, the exact slope of the efficient plane will vary, depending on the set of alternatives being considered by a company.

This framework may be used to evaluate alternatives without non-quantifiable uncertainties. If only quantifiable risk and return are considered, the three-dimensional framework collapses into a two-

dimensional risk-return tradeoff framework with all alternatives being represented on the surface on the right side of Fig. 1.

HIERARCHICAL STRUCTURE

The proposed framework requires decision makers to use a hierarchical structure to evaluate a set of alternatives (see panels A, B, and E in Fig. 2.) Each dimension—quantifiable risk, quantifiable return, and on quantifiable benefits (uncertainty)—is represented separately. Managers begin by first estimating quantifiable risk and return for each alternative. After the quantifiable dimensions are computed, AHP is used to subjectively evaluate the non-quantifiable benefits.

In the proposed framework, ratings for each investment alternative are given for each major dimension—quantitative risk; quantitative return, and non-quantifiable uncertainties. Many previously AHP models compute a single, overall rating for each investment alternative rather than rating each investment alternative on each major dimension. The single over-all rating approach combines subjective estimates of non-quantifiable factors with quantifiable data. This rating process for three alternatives is illustrated in Fig. 2.

MEASUREMENT OF NON-QUANTIFIABLE BENEFITS (UNCERTAINTY)

Because introduction of non-quantifiable benefits into the decision model is a primary focus of this paper, the use of AHP for this purpose is discussed first. The hierarchy for non-quantifiable benefits in Fig. 2 has only two levels, but AHP can accommodate many

levels. At the bottom level of the hierarchy (panel F), managers weigh each investment alternative with re-spect to each non-quantifiable benefit—product reli-ability, product performance, flexibility, and employee morale. At the top level, (panel E) managers make pairwise comparisons between each of the non-quantifiable benefits to assign priority weights to each benefit based on its importance in meeting corporate objectives. Because the priority weights for the four non-quantifiable benefits are percentages, they must sum to 1. A rating with respect to non-quantifiable benefits is computed for each alternative based on the bottom level scaled values for each alternative and the priority weights.

FIGURE 2
CALCULATIONS FOR RISK, RETURN, AND UNCERTAINTY DIMENSIONS

Panel A: Quantifiable Return

ROI
(Ratio Scale)

Project 1	= 30%
Project 2	= 35%
Project 3	= 40 %

Panel B: Quantifiable Risk

Quantifiable Risk	Priority Weights
Ruinous Loss (RL) (investment % of assets)	.5
Liquidity Parameter (L) (Payback)	.4
Variability Parameter (V) (Std. Dev.)	.1

Project	Risk	Scaled Values (ratio scale)
1	RL	.50
2	RL	.25
3	RL	.25
1	L	.63
2	L	.25
3	L	.12
1	V	.57
2	V	.29
3	V	.14

(Continued on next page)

Figure 2
(Continued)

Panel C: Calculations for Scaling Quantitative Risk Parameters

Ruinous Loss Parameter:

	Investment as a Percentage of Total Assets (Investment/Total Assets)	Scaled Values
Project 1	40%	.40/80 = .50
Project 2	20%	.20/80 = .25
Project 3	<u>20%</u>	.20/80 = .25
	80%	1.00

Liquidity Risk Parameter:

	Payback Period	Scaled Values
Project 1	5 years	5/8 = .63
Project 2	2 years	2/8 = .25
Project 3	<u>1 year</u>	1/8 = <u>.12</u>
	8 years	1.00

Variability Risk Parameter:

	Standard Deviation of Quantifiable Returns	Scaled Values
Project 1	.2 Std. Dev	.2/.35 = .57
Project 2	.1 Std. Dev	.1/.35 = .29
Project 3	<u>.05 Std. Dev</u>	.05/.35 = <u>.14</u>
	.35 Std Dev.	1.00

Panel D: Calculations for the Composite Quantitative Risk Measure for Each Alternative

Risk Parameter	Bottom-Level Scaled Values		Priority Weights		Adjusted Values
Project 1:					
Ruinous Loss	.5	X	.5	=	.25
Liquidity Risk	.63	X	.4	=	.25
Variability Risk	.57	x	.1	=	.06
		Composite Risk Measure for Project 1			.56
Project 2:					
Ruinous Loss	.25	X	.5	=	.13
Liquidity Risk	.25	X	.4	=	.10
Variability Risk	.29	x	.1	=	<u>.03</u>
		Composite Risk Measure for Project 2			.26
Project 3					
Ruinous Loss	.25	X	.5	=	.13
Liquidity Risk	.12	X	.4	=	.05
Variability Risk	.14	x	.1	=	<u>.01</u>
		Composite Risk Measure for Project 3			.19

FIGURE 2
(Continued)

Panel E: Non-quantifiable Benefits (Uncertainties)

Non-quantifiable Benefit	Priority Weights
Product Reliability (PR)	.2
Product Performance (PP)	.2
Flexibility (F)	.4
Employee Morale (M)	.2

Project	Benefit	AHP Scaled Value (Interval Scale
1	PR	.67
2	PR	.22
3	PR	.11
1	PP	.75
2	PP	.20
3	PP	.05
1	F	.80
2	F	.10
3	F	.10
1	M	.60
2	M	.30
3	M	.10

Panel f: Calculations for the Overall Non-quantifiable Benefits Rating for Each Alternative

Risk Parameter	Bottom-Level Scaled Values		Priority Weights		Adjusted Values
Project 1:					
Product Reliability	.67	X	.2	=	.14
Product Performance	.75	X	.2	=	.15
Flexibility	.80	X	.4	=	.32
Employee Benefits	.60	X	.2	=	.12
Project 1's Overall Rating for Non-quantifiable Benefits					.73
Project 2:					
Product Reliability	.22	X	.2	=	.04
Product Performance	.20	X	.2	=	.04
Flexibility	.10	X	.4	=	.04
Employee Benefits	.30	X	.2	=	.06
Project 2's Overall Rating for Non-quantifiable Benefits					.18
Project 3:					
Product Reliability	.11	X	.2	=	.02
Product Performance	.05	X	.2	=	.01
Flexibility	.10	X	.4	=	.04
Employee Benefits	.10	X	.2	=	.02
Project 3's Overall Rating for Non-quantifiable Benefits					.09

A number of steps must be completed before ratings for each investment alternative can be generated. First, a manager compares each pair of investment alternatives. In each such pair-wise comparison, the manager indicates the strength of his/her preference for one alternative over another by selecting a numeric value ranging from 1 to 9. A description of the degrees of preference associated with the AHP numerical scale values is presented in T-1.

The results of the manager's pair-wise comparisons of three investment alternatives regarding the non-quantifiable benefits of product reliability are presented in T-2. The manager judged Project 1 to be moderately preferred over Project 2 with respect to product reliability, assigning a value of 3 to this comparison. In the second comparison, the manager strongly preferred Project 1 over Project 3 with respect to product reliability, assigning a value of 6 to this comparison. Finally, Project 2's product was judged to be slightly more reliable than Project 3's, and a value of 2 was assigned to this comparison.

Only three pair-wise comparisons must be obtained directly from managers, the rest are supplied by the AHP computer program.[3] Because any alternative is, by definition, equally preferred when compared to itself, the AHP computer program places "1s" along the three diagonal slots in the pairwise comparison matrix, as shown in T-3. It is not necessary for the manager to fill in the bottom part of the matrix because these three entries are reciprocals of, and

therefore can be inferred from, the corresponding entries in the upper part of the matrix which were input by the decision maker.

After all values for the matrix are supplied, the computer program checks the consistency of the manager's input values and generates weights (scaled values) for each project.[4] The AHP-generated scaled values show that the decision maker believes Project 1, with a scaled value of .67, provides the greatest non-quantifiable product reliability benefits; Project 2 is second with scaled value of .22; and Project 3, with a scaled value of .11, is least preferred. Panel E of Fig. 2, reflects these scaled AHP values for product reliability from the bottom-level of the hierarchy for non-quantifiable benefits.

In this example, the manager's pairwise comparisons were consistent. If comparisons are inconsistent, the AHP program requires the manager to change his input values until his comparisons became consistent.

The same steps are used to generate the AHP scaled values for product performance, flexibility, and employee morale. After generating the bottom-level scaled values for each remaining nonquantifiable attribute, managers use the AHP program to make pairwise comparisons between each non-quantifiable attribute to generate the top-level priority weights. The steps and AHP scale used to generate the priority weights are the same as those used to generate the scaled values.

After all scaled values and priority weights in the

TABLE 1
AHP MEASUREMENT SCALE

Description of Degree of Preferences	Numerical Value
Extremely preferred	9
Very strongly preferred	7
Strongly preferred	5
Moderately preferred	3
Equally preferred	1
Note: Intermediate values can be used to provide additional levels of discrimination.	

TABLE 2
PAIRWISE COMPARISON DATA ENTERED INTO THE AHP
COMPUTER PROGRAM BY THE DECISION MAKER

	Non-quantifiable Benefits—Product Reliability			
	Project 1	Project 2	Project 3	Weights
Project 1		3	6	
Project 2			2	
Project 3				

TABLE 3
COMPUTATIONS BY THE AHP COMPUTER PROGRAM
Non-quantifiable Benefits—Product Reliability

	Project 1	Project 2	Project 3	Weights
Project 1	1	3	6	.67
Project 2	1/3	1	2	.22
Project 3	1/6	1/2	1	.11
				1.00

non-quantifiable benefits hierarchy have been computed for each alternative, as illustrated in panel F of Fig. 2. First, the bottom-level scaled values for each alternative are multiplied by the priority weight for the same benefit. These adjusted values for each alternative are then summed to compute a non-quantifiable benefits rating for each alternative. The ratings represent in relative terms the amount of non-quantifiable benefits of each investment alternative compared to the non-quantifiable benefits of the other alternatives. Project 1, with a rating of .73, is believed to possess the most potential for realizing non-quantifiable revenue uncertainties. Project 3, with an overall rating of .09, has the least potential among the three alternatives. Project 2's non-quantifiable benefit rating of .18 is between Project 1's and Project 3's.

MEASUREMENT OF QUANTIFIABLE RISK

The hierarchy for evaluating quantifiable risk in Fig. 2 consists of two levels. At the bottom level of the hierarchy, scaled values for quantifiable risk parameters—ruinous loss, liquidity, and variability—are estimated for each alternative. The bottom-level scaled values are computed by summing values for the quantitative risk parameters and expressing these values as a percentage of the sum as shown in panel C of Fig. 2.

At the second level of the quantifiable risk hierarchy, management's priority weights establish the relative importance of each risk parameter. In Fig. 2, the priority weight assigned to the ruinous loss parameter (investment as a percentage of total assets) is .5. Compared with the priority weights assigned to the variability parameter, .1, and the liquidity parameter, I4, the ruinous loss parameter is more important in determining an alternative's final rating with respect to quantifiable risk. Because the priority weights are expressed as percentages, the priority weights for the three risk parameters sum to 1.

Priority weights are management's subjective weights based on the context of the decision and/or differences in corporate policy. Companies with cash flow problems may assign a large priority weight to the liquidity parameter. Small companies may consider the ruinous loss parameter very important, because a single bad investment may result in financial dissolution. Priority weights may be subjectively estimated by managers or computed by an AHP computer program discussed in the section on using AHP to measure nonquantifiable benefits.

After all scaled values and priority weights in the quantifiable risk hierarchy are computed, a composite risk measure can be calculated for each alternative as shown in panel D of Fig. 2. First, the bottom-level scaled values for each alternative are adjusted for the priorities for each risk parameter by multiplying each parameter's bottom-level scaled values by the parameter's priority weight. These adjusted values for each alternative are then summed to compute a composite risk measure for each alternative. Project 1 is the riskiest of the three alternatives with a composite risk measure of .56; projects 2 and 3 are less risky with composite risk measures of .26 and .19 respectively.

MEASUREMENT OF QUANTIFIABLE RETURN

The choice of financial return measure(s) used in the framework depends on company policy and on whether enough reliable information is available to accurately compute a given measure. The quantitative return measure reflects only the costs and revenues which can be reasonably estimated. One such quantitative financial performance measure, return on investment, is illustrated in Fig. 2. Other measures, such as net present value or internal rate of return, can also be used in this framework if enough reliable information is available. This framework does not limit the analysis to only one quantitative financial perform-

175

ance measure or to any particular type of financial performance measure. Just as multiple quantitative risk measures can be combined to measure quantifiable risk, multiple quantitative financial measures can be combined within this framework to measure financial performance.

Return on investment was chosen as the quantitative financial measure for illustration purposes in this paper for three reasons: (1) in many new technology investment situations, not enough reliable information about future cash flows is available to compute dis-

counted cash flow measures, (2) short-term quantitative financial performance measures such as return on investment are complemented in the proposed framework by longer term non-quantifiable factors such as improved quality and increased flexibility, and (3) income-based return measures are widely used in practice by advanced manufacturing firms (Howell et al. 1987). Because only return on investment is used in this paper, the quantitative returns illustrated in the graph in Fig. 3 are the original return on investment percentages for each project. No scaling and adjust-

FIGURE 3
GRAPHICAL PRESENTATION OF EXAMPLE

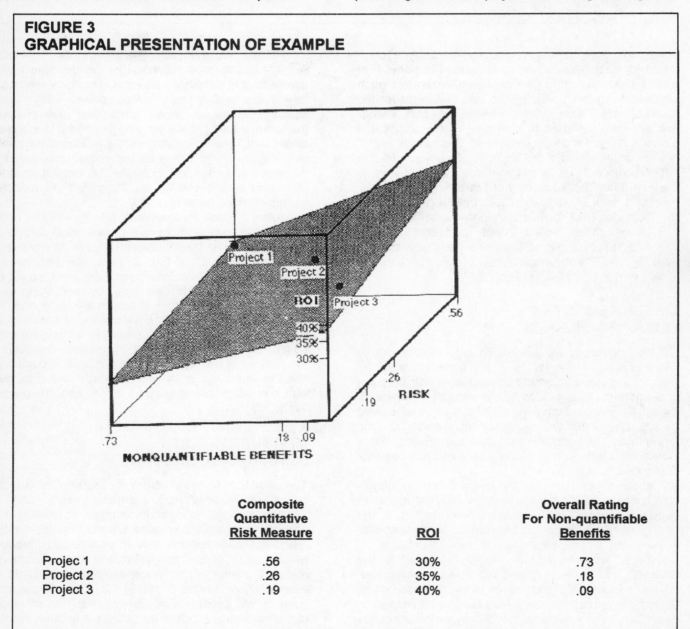

	Composite Quantitative Risk Measure	ROI	Overall Rating For Non-quantifiable Benefits
Projec 1	.56	30%	.73
Project 2	.26	35%	.18
Project 3	.19	40%	.09

ing for priority weights is needed when a single measure is used. If multiple quantitative performance measures are used, each measure must be scaled and adjusted for priority weights.

The three alternatives are graphed in the three-dimensional framework in Fig. 3. Because only three alternatives with different levels of quantifiable risk and return and nonquantifiable benefits are compared in the example, all three alternatives lie on the efficient plane. If more alternatives are included in the evaluation, the sub-optimal alternatives will be graphed below the efficient plane. Selection of an alternative from the set of alternatives on the efficient plane is left to the decision maker's trade-off preferences between quantifiable risk, quantifiable return, and non-quantifiable uncertainty.

FRAMEWORK BASED ON DECISION CONTEXT

In figure 2, the quantitative risk parameters—investment as a percentage of total assets, payback period, and standard deviation of returns—all represent different aspects of risk relevant to the projects being evaluated. Managers may use different sets of quantitative risk parameters and uncertainty attributes to evaluate different situations The choice of quantitative risk parameters and uncertainty attributes for inclusion in the framework should be based on two criteria—**representativeness** and **independence**. To fully represent the risks and uncertainties which exist in the actual investment decision, the framework should capture all significant aspects of risk and uncertainty relevant to the project alternatives under consideration. The risk parameters and uncertainty attributes included in the framework must be independent of each other so each measures a different aspect of risk and/or uncertainty. For example, variance and standard deviation should not be included as risk parameters in the same framework because they measure the same aspect of risk—variability in cash flows.

Selection of non-quantitative factors for the framework is determined by the decision context. If all factors can be reasonably estimated for a set of alternatives, the evaluation may be based solely on quantifiable risk and return factors. In other investment situations, certain factors may be partially quantifiable and partially non-quantifiable. For example, cost savings from producing more reliable products, such as reductions in rework costs, inspection costs, and warranty costs, may be estimated and included in the quantitative risk and return measures. The effect of producing more reliable products on market demand and revenue, however, may be so uncertain that reasonable estimates cannot be made. This effect would be subjectively evaluated by managers as a non-

quantifiable uncertainty. Similarly, some aspects of employee morale and additional manufacturing capabilities/ flexibility may be quantifiable while other aspects of these factors are highly uncertain and non-quantifiable.

MEASUREMENT SCALES

In this framework, each attribute is measured using the scale that provides the most information about the attribute. The quantitative return dimension is measured on the highest scale, the *ratio scale*. A **ratio scale** provides more information than the other scales—both the difference between values and the ratio of any two values are meaningful, and the value of zero means none. For example, a financial return of 40 percent is twice as much as a 20 percent return, and a zero percent return means no return.

Non-quantifiable uncertainties are measured on the second highest scale, the *interval scale*. On an **interval scale**, the difference between values is meaningful, but the ratio is not meaningful. The AHP scale used to measure non-quantifiable uncertainties is an interval scale; it captures the strength of a decision maker's preference for one alternative over a second alternative. AHP requires that decision makers assign a value of 1 if the two alternatives are equal, and a value of 2 if one alternative is slightly preferred over the other. But an alternative assigned the value of 2 is not twice as good as an alternative assigned a value of 1.[5]

Risk parameters included in the composite risk measure can be either ratio-scaled or interval-scaled measures. For example, variability in cash flows is measured on a ratio scale if standard deviation is used; a cash flow with a standard deviation of 6 is six times as variable as a cash flow with a standard deviation of 1. On the other hand, variability is measured on an interval scale if variance is used; a cash flow with a variance of 6 has greater variability than a cash flow with a variance of 1 but cannot be interpreted as being six times as variable. Regardless of whether risk parameters are ratio- or interval-scale measures, transformations (multiplication, division) or parameters do not change their measurement scales. The quality of the original measurement scale is preserved even though the magnitude of the original measurement is increased by multiplication or decreased by division.

Although ratio-scale measurements of risk parameters are preserved when the parameters are combined into a composite risk measure, an interval-scale interpretation of the composite risk measure is generally appropriate. A composite measure that represents a multidimensional concept, such as risk, is more difficult to interpret than a measure, such as standard deviation, that measures a single observable aspect—cash flow variability—of a multidimensional concept.

Comparing the sizes of two boxes illustrates this problem. A box with a length of 8 feet, height of 6 feet, and width of 4 feet is twice as long, high, and wide as a box that is 4 feet long, 3 feet high and 2 feet wide. Separately, each of these measures—length, height and width—suggest that the first box is only twice as large as the second box. However, when their sizes are compared using a three-dimension measure, volume, the larger box is 8 times as large as the smaller one. Likewise a ratio-scale interpretation of the composite risk measure cannot be inferred from the ratio-scale measures of individual risk parameters. Ratio-scale interpretations of the composite risk measure is further complicated because different risk parameters measure different attributes—time (payback period), variability (standard deviation), dollars (investment as a percentage of total assets).

The nature of the attribute being measured makes ratio-scale interpretations difficult for both single- and multi-dimensional risk measures. Risk is a highly idiosyncratic attribute, based on decision makers' perceptions rather than observable phenomena. Observable phenomena—time, dollars, and variability—can be measured on an absolute measurement scale; different decision makers using the same measurement method will come to the same conclusions. For example, few people would disagree that a payback period of 8 years is twice as long as a 4-year payback period or that a cash flow with a standard deviation of 6 is six times as variable as a cash flow with a standard deviation of 1. In contrast, the measurement of risk perceptions is based on a relative scale. One decision-maker may consider a project with a payback of 8 years twice as risky as a project with a 4-year payback, while another believes the project with the 8 year payback is eight times as risky as the one with the 4-year payback. Consequently, both single- and multi-dimensional measures of a perceptually-based attribute can, at best, be interpreted as interval-scale data.

I. SUMMARY AND DISCUSSION

This paper identified the limitations of using traditional models in evaluating new technology investments. A review of risky choice decision models suggests that evaluating an investment based on a single risk parameter may be inadequate in some decision situations. Models used in evaluating new technology investments should consider all risk aspects and non-quantifiable uncertainties relevant to the investment decision. If decision models do not completely capture and represent all factors relevant to the investment decision, managers may reject alternatives that

should be accepted and/or accept those that should be rejected. This paper developed a framework that enables managers to formally include an assessment of nonquantifiable uncertainties, quantifiable financial returns and multiple risk parameters in their evaluation of capital projects, while maintaining a distinction between factors that can be quantified and factors that only can be subjectively assessed. The proposed framework expands the two-dimensional risk-return framework to a three-dimensional framework, including nonquantifiable uncertainty as the third dimension. In addition, a composite measure of quantifiable risk consisting of multiple risk parameters was introduced in this paper. This composite risk measure provides managers with more risk information than single- and two-parameter risky choice models.

The framework does not replace discounted cash flow techniques. Rather, it may be used to supplement discounted cash flow techniques when enough information is available to make reliable cash flow projections. For some investment decisions, all revenues, costs, and associated probabilities can be reasonably estimated. In such cases, only quantitative risk and return measures need be evaluated; non-quantifiable uncertainties would not be included in the analysis.

Although this paper illustrates how the proposed framework can be used to evaluate new technology investments, the framework is not limited to new technology investment decisions. It may be used to evaluate more traditional investments involving non-quantifiable legal uncertainties and/or multiple aspects of risk such as mining operations, chemical and nuclear plants, and new product lines for drug companies. The proposed framework is flexible, allowing different risk parameters and uncertainty attributes to be included in the framework depending on the risks and uncertainties present in the investment decision. As new technologies are installed, more information about the benefits and costs of the new technologies becomes known. Consequently, some uncertainties surrounding the new technologies may become reasonably estimable so that traditional quantitative capital budgeting models may adequately capture more of the relevant factors in quantitative terms. Quantification of some non-quantifiable factors does not diminish the need for a framework to evaluate non-quantifiable uncertainties.

---

[1] A risky alternative may contain two separate components—risk and nonquantifiable uncertainty. Risk is defined as the *known* probability distribution of outcomes (expected cash flows); uncertainty exists when the probability distribution of outcomes (expected cash flows) is unknown and/or potential outcomes cannot be specified (Knight 1948; Luce and Raiffa

178

1957). Some authors refer to nonquantifiable uncertainty as ambiguity (Einhorn and Horgarth 1986)

[2] Other methods for obtaining decision makers' weights for multiple attributes include multiattribute stochastic decision models (Bernardo and Upton 1980), conjoint analysis (Wind and Saaty 1980), the Simple Multiattribute Rating Technique (SMART), the Holistic Orthogonal Parameter Estimate (HOPE) procedure, rank weighting techniques, policy capturing techniques, and subjectively dividing 100 points (Adelman et al. 1984; Stillwell et al. 1983). Some of these techniques are less practical than AHP for evaluating nonquantifiable uncertainties because they are inefficient and have restrictive assumptions (Wind and Saaty 1980)

[3] When only three alternatives are considered as in this example, it is not difficult for individuals to make consistent comparisons. However, when the number of alternatives increases this task becomes more difficult; AHP forces consistency among the pairwise comparisons.

[4] A manager's input values are consistent if all the columns of the input matrix have the same proportional values. The proportional values for each column of the input matrix in T-3 are computed by totaling the values in each column and then expressing each value as a percentage of the column total:

	Project 1		Project 2		Project 3	
	Input Values	Proportions	Input Values	Proportions	Input Values	Proportions
Project 1	1	1/1.5 = .67	3	3/4.5 = .67	6	6/9 = .67
Project 2	1/3	.33/1.5 = .22	1	1/4.5 = .22	2	2/9 = .22
Project 3	1/6	.16/1.5 = .11	1/2	.5/4.5 = .11	1	1/9 = .11
	1.5	1.00	4.5	1.00	9	1.00

In this example, the proportional values—.67, .22, and .11—are the same for each column. Consequently, the AHP program generates scaled values (weights) of .67 for Project 1, .22 for Project 2, and .11 for Project 3. If the proportional values for each column are not the same, the AHP program warns the manager that his input values are inconsistent and requires changes in input values until comparisons become consistent.

[5] Transformations of interval-scaled data (multiplication, division) will not convert the original data to a ratio scale. The AHP-generated scaled values for nonquantifiable benefits are based on an interval scale because the values (preferences) that are input into the AHP input matrix are interval-scale data. AHP cannot transform interval-scaled inputs into ratio-scaled output values.

REFERENCES:

Adelman, L. P., Sticha, and M. L. Donnell. 1984. The Role of Task Properties in Determining the Relative Effectiveness of Multiattribute Weighting Techniques. *Organizational Behavior and Human Performance* 33 (April): 243-262.

Arbel, A., and A. Seidmann. 1984. Performance Evaluation of Flexible Manufacturing Systems. IEEE *Transactions on Systems, Man, and Cybernetics* 14 (July-August): 606-617.

Aschenbrenner, K. M. 1984. Moment- Versus Dimension-Oriented Theories of Risky Choice: A (Fairly) General Test Involving Single-Peaked Preferences. *Journal of Experimental Psychology: Learning, Memory, and Cognition* 10 (July): 513-535.

Bernardo, J. J., and D. E. Upton. 1980. A stochastic Multiattribute Heuristic Model of Investor Choice. *Decision Sciences* 11 (July): 425-438.

Canada, J. R., and W. G. Sullivan. 1989. *Economic and Multiattribute Evaluation of Advanced Manufacturing Systems*. Englewood Cliffs, NJ: Prentice Hall.

Einhorn, H. J., and R. M. Hogarth. 1986. Decision Making Under Ambiguity. *The Journal of Business* 59 (October): 5225-5250.

Harper, Jr., and R. M., N. G. Apostolou, and B. P. Hartman. 1992. The Analytic Hierarchy Process: An Empirical Examination of Aggregation and Hierarchical Structuring. *Behavioral Research in Accounting* 4: 96-112.

Haspeslaugh, P. 1982. Portfolio Planning: Uses and Limits. *Harvard Business Review* 60 (January-February): 58-74.

Hillier, F. S. 1963. The Derivation of Probalistic Information for the Evaluation of Risky Investments. *Management Science* 9 (April): 441-460.

Howell, R. A., J. D. Brown, S. R. Soucy, and A. H. Seed. 1987. *Management Accounting in the New Manufacturing Environment*. Montvale, NJ: National Association of Accountants.

Kaplan, R. S. 1986. Must CIM be Justified by Faith Alone? *Harvard Business Review* 64 (March-April): 87-95.

Knight, F. H. 1948. Quoted by S. Cunningham (1967) in The Major Dimensions of Perceived Risk. *Risk Taking and Information Handling in Consumer Behavior*, edited by D. L. Cox. Boston, MA: Harvard University.

Libby, R. and P. C. Fishburn. 1977. Behavioral Models of Risk Taking in Business Decisions: A Survey and Evaluation. *Journal of Accounting Research* 2 (Autumn): 272-292.

Lintner, J. 1965. The Valuation of Risk Assets and the Selection of Risky Investments in Stock Portfolios and Capital Budgets. *The Review of Economics and Statistics* 47 (February): 13-37.

Logue, D. E. 1981. Some Thoughts on Corporate Investment Strategy and Pure Strategic Investments. *Readings in Strategy for Corporate Investment*, edited by F. G. J. Derkinderen and R. L. Crum. Boston, MA: Pitman.

Luce, R. D., and H. Raiffa. *1957. Games and Decisions*. New York, NY: Wiley.

Mao, J. C. T. 1970. Survey of Capital Budgeting: Theory and Practice. *Journal of Finance* 25 (May): 349-360.

Mensah, Y. M., and P. J. Miranti. 1989. Capital Expenditure Analysis and Automated Manufacturing Systems: A Review and Synthesis. *Journal of Accounting Literature* 8: 181-207.

Neises, S. J., and R. E. Bennett. 1989. Automan—Decision Support Software. *Management Accounting* 71 (November): 58-60.

Norgaard, R., and T. Killeen. 1990. Applied Capital Budgeting with Cash Flow Dependencies. *Decision Sciences* 21 (Summer): 572-587.

Pike, R. H. 1983. A Review of Recent Trends in Formal Capital Budgeting Processes. *Accounting and Business Research* 13 (Summer): 201-208.

———, 1988. An empirical Study of the Adoption of Sophisticated Capital Budgeting Practices and Decision-Making Effectiveness. *Accounting and Business Research* 18 (Autumn): 341-351.

Ronen, J., and G. H. sorter. 1972. Relevant Accounting. *Journal of Buysiness* 45 (April): 258-282.

Scapens, R. W., and J. T. Sale. 1981. Performance Measurement and Formal Capital Expenditure Controls in Divisionalised Companies. *Journal of Business Finance and Accounting* 8 (Autumn): 389-419.

Scarbrough, P., A. J. Nanni, and M. Sakurai. 1991. Japanese Management Accounting Practices and the Effects of Assembly and Process Automation. *Management Accounting Research* 2 (March): 27-46.

Schoemaker, P. J. H. 1979. The Role of Statistical Knowledge in Gambling Decisions; Moment vs. Risk Dimension Approaches. *Organizational Behavior and Human Performance* 24 (August): 1-17.

Stillwell, W. G., F. H. Barron, and W. Edwards. 1983. Evaluating Credit Applications: A Validation of Multiattribute Utility Weight Elicitation Techniques. *Organizational Behavior and Human Performance* 32: 87-108.

Stout, D. E., M. J. Liberatore, and T. F. Monahan. 1991. Decision Support Software for Capital Budgeting. *Management Accounting* 73 (July): 50-53.

Sullivan, W. G., and J. M. Reeve. 1988. Xventure: Expert Systems to the Rescue. *Management Accounting* 4 (October): 51-58.

Washburn, A. 1992. Present Values with Renewals. Management Science 38 (June): 846-850.

Weber, S. F. 1989. Automan: *Decision Support Software for Automated Manufacturing Investments, User Manual.* Gaithersburg, MD: U.S. Department of Commerce.

Wind, Y., and T. L. Saaty. 1980. Marketing Applications of the Analytical Hierarchy *Process. Management Science* 26 (July): 641-658.

Chapter 12
Job Costing

Cases

Readings

Thomas L. Barton and Frederick M. Cole: Accounting for Magic

This articles describes the cost estimation, production control, and accounting systems used at Sally Industries, Inc, a small manufacturer of entertainment robots. The production control system focuses on direct labor costs, which are an important element of product costs for Sally. Computer spreadsheets are used to estimate costs for proposed robotic products, and other software systems are used to accumulate cost data for products in process.

Discussion Questions:
1. Using Tables 1, 2 and 3, explain how the cost estimating spreadsheet at Sally is used to project product costs.
2. What are the advantages of the time management and production control system? Why is the payroll module such a critical part of the system?

182

Cases

12-1. Under or Over-Applied Overhead

Valport Company employs a job cost system based on the full absorption of actual costs. Factory overhead is applied on the basis of machine hours (MH) using a predetermined overhead rate. The current fiscal year rate of $15.00 per MH is based on estimated factory overhead costs of $1,200,000 and an estimated activity level of 80,000 machine hours. Valport's policy is to close the over/under application of factory overhead to the Cost of Goods Sold.

Operations for the year ended November 30, 19X8 have been completed, and all accounting entries have been made for the year except the application of manufacturing overhead to the jobs worked on during November, the transfer of costs from Work-in-Process to Finished Goods for the jobs completed in November, and the transfer of costs from Finished Goods to Cost of Goods Sold for the jobs that have been sold during November. Summarized data that have been accumulated from the accounting records as of October 31, 19X8 and for November 19X8, are presented below.

Work-in-Process		November 19X8 Activity		
Job No.	Balance 10/31/X8	Direct Materials	Direct Labor	Machine Hours
N11-007	$ 87,000	$ 1,500	$ 4,500	300
N11-013	55,000	4,000	12,000	1,000
N11-015	-0-	25,600	26,700	1,400
D12-002	-0-	37,900	20,000	2,500
D12-003	-0-	26,000	16,800	800
	$142,000	$95,000	$80,000	6,000

Operating Activity	Activity Through 10/31/X8	November 19X8 Activity
Factory overhead incurred		
Indirect materials	$ 125,000	$ 9,000
Indirect labor	345,000	30,000
Utilities	245,000	22,000
Depreciation	385,000	35,000
Total incurred overhead	$1,100,000	$96,000
Other items		
Material purchases	$965,000	$98,000
Direct labor costs	$845,000	$80,000
Machine hours.........................	73,000	6,000

Account Balances at Beginning of Fiscal Year	12/01/X7
Materials inventory `	$105,000
Work-in-Process inventory..............	60,000
Finished goods inventory...............	125,000

Material purchases and materials inventory consists of both direct and indirect materials. The balance of the Materials Inventory account as of November 30, 19X8, is $85,000.

Jobs N11-007, N11-013, and N11-015 were completed during November 19X8. All completed jobs except Job N11-013 had been turned over to customers by the close of business on November 30, 19X8.

REQUIRED:

1. Valport Company uses a predetermined overhead rate to apply factory overhead to its jobs. When overhead is accounted for in this manner, there may be over- or underapplied overhead.

    a. Explain why a business uses a predetermined overhead rate to apply factory overhead to its jobs.

    b. How much factory overhead would Valport have applied to jobs through October 31, 19X8?

    c. How much factory overhead would be applied to jobs by Valport during November 19X8?

    d. Determine the amount by which the factory overhead is over- or underapplied as of November 30, 19X8. Be sure to indicate whether the overhead is over- or underapplied.

    e. Over- or underapplied overhead must be eliminated at the end of the accounting period. Explain why Valport's method of closing over-or underapplied overhead to the Cost of Goods Sold is acceptable in this case.

2. Determine the balance in Valport Company's finished goods inventory at November 30, 19X8.

12-2. Under or OverApplied Overhead II

Constructo Inc. is a manufacturer of furnishings for infants and children. The company uses a job cost system and employs a full absorption accounting method for cost accumulation. Constructo's work-in-process inventory at April 30, 19X8 consisted of the following jobs.

Job No.	Items	Units	Accumulated Cost
CBS102	Cribs	20,000	$ 900,000
PLP086	Playpens	25,000	420,000
DRS114	Dressers	25,000	250,000
			$1,570,000

The company's finished goods inventory, which Constructo evaluates using the FIFO (First-in, first-out) method, consisted of five items.

Item	Quantity and Unit Cost	Accumulated Cost
Cribs	7,500 units @ $ 64 each	$ 480,000
Strollers	13,000 units @ $ 23 each	299,000
Carriages	11,200 units @ $102 each	1,142,400
Dressers	21,000 units @ $ 55 each	1,155,000
Playpens	19,400 units @ $ 35 each	679,999
		$3,755,400

Constructo applies factory overhead on the basis of direct labor hours. The company's factory overhead budget for the fiscal year ending May 31, 19X8, totals $4,500,000, and the company plans to expend 600,000 direct labor hours during this period. Through the first eleven months of the year, a total of 555,000 direct labor hours were worked, and total factory overhead amounted to $4,273,500.

At the end of April, the balance in Constructo's Materials Inventory account, which includes both raw materials and purchased parts, was $668,000. Additions to and requisitions from the materials inventory during the month of May included the following.

	Raw Materials	Purchased Parts
Additions	$242,000	$396,000
Requisitions:		
Job CBS102	51,000	104,000
Job PLP086	3,000	10,800
Job DRS114	124,000	87,000
Job STR077		
(10,000 strollers)	62,000	81,000
Job CRG098		
(5,000 carriages)	65,000	187,000

During the month of May, Constructo's factory payroll consisted of the following.

Account	Hours	Cost
CBS102	12,000	$122,400
PLP086	4,400	43,200
DRS114	19,500	200,500
STR077	3,500	30,000
CRG098	14,000	138,000
Indirect	3,000	29,400
Supervision		57,600
		$621,100

Listed below are the jobs that were completed and the unit sales for the month of May.

Job No.	Items	Quantity Complete
CBS102	Cribs	20,000
PLP086	Playpens	15,000
STR077	Strollers	10,000
CRG098	Carriages	5,000

Items	Quantity Shipped
Cribs	17,500
Playpens	21,000
Strollers	14,000
Dressers	18,000
Carriages	6,000

REQUIRED

1. Describe when it is appropriate for a company to use a job cost system.

2. Calculate the dollar balance in Constructo's work-in-process inventory account as of May 31, 19X8.

3. Calculate the dollar amount related to the playpens in Constructo's finished goods inventory as of May 31, 19X8.

4. Explain the proper accounting treatment for overapplied or underapplied overhead balances when using a job cost system.

Accounting for Magic

A potent mix of art, technology, and professional management

By Thomas L. Barton and Frederick M. Cole

By some twist of fate, you and your family find yourselves riding on an oversized bicycle with E.T., the Extraterrestrial. The bicycle twists and turns as you attempt to outmaneuver and outrun the government scientists and police officers trying to capture E.T. and subject him to some lethal experimentation. Will you make it? Can you save E.T.? Pedal faster!

Whew! The police are gone...but where are you now? Surrounded by 20-foot exotic plants...in some strange land like you've never seen before. E.T.'s home planet? Dreaming?

No...this is reality. It's the reality of "E.T.'s Adventure" ride at Universal Studios Florida theme park in Orlando, Fla. And you didn't imagine those 20-foot plants! They're real...sort of...just as real as the NASA technicians in space suits. All are entertainment robots, those lifelike creations you've seen performing at Walt Disney World and other major theme parks.

Many of the robots in the E.T. ride and other attractions at MCA Universal Studios were built 150 miles north of Orlando at Sally Industries, Inc., in Jacksonville. Sally is one of a handful of U.S. companies that builds these magical creatures and their props. It's a very specialized business called animatronics that merges art, technology, and professional management to make imagination come alive.

Each robot is an exacting mix of latex, wires, tubes, and a distinctive form of artistry that must be nurtured and managed carefully. This creative, labor-intensive work is performed in a business environment of fixed-price contracts and production schedules that *must* be adhered to. Although it sounds like the construction industry, how many contractors do you know who build humanoids that can sing and play the piano or Mayan ruins that spew forth fog and smoke—and speak?

This is construction with a critical difference: Many of Sally's artisans would be just as comfortable painting a sunset as they would features on a robot-scientist's face. Sally's management control system recognizes that reality in its *time management and production control* subsystem, which it uses to keep schedules on target.

For a small, specialized company like Sally to continue to prosper, it must manage its costs and revenues carefully. Unanticipated cost overruns on a major project such as MCA Universal could be especially damaging. It's no surprise, then, that the *cost estimation* phase of Sally's management control system is tightly drawn.

Both the *cost estimation* and the *time management and production control* systems are PC based because Sally needs the flexibility, power, ease of use, and low cost that PC can provide. In each case, the PC application has been successful and has played a significant role in Sally's managed growth and profitability. These two systems interface with each other and the company's general accounting system during the entire production process.

COST ESTIMATION

Entertainment robots are expensive. A simple one with limited movements, off-the-shelf parts, and a standard design may sell for $15,000. More complicated models with custom designs and complex body movements can run as much as $60,000. An entire scripted 10-minute show featuring a sextet of singing robots wearing fancy costumes and performing on a custom-built stage might cost a quarter of a million dollars.

Because of the enormous number of variables per robot character, before pricing a project Sally management carefully estimates the cost of the components through its *cost estimation system,* which basically is a Lotus 1-2-3 template designed by Sally's former Vice President of Finance Tom Turnage and which the company runs on an 80386 PC. Through the use of macros, information can be pulled into spreadsheets quickly and easily, with little searching, so design element changes can be costed individually.

To illustrate how this system works, let's follow the progress of an entertainment robot based on the his-

TABLE 1
RATE SCHEDULE SETTINGS,
HENRY VIII SPREADSHEET

Dept	Max	Min	Avg.	Amended 11/1XX Avg. with O/T	O/H	Total
Mechanical	8.00	7.00	7.50	7.68	8.45	16.13
Pneumatic	8.50	8.25	8.38	8.57	9.43	17.81
Art	9.00	4.25	6.63	6.78	7.46	14.09
Scenic	9.80	5.00	7.40	7.58	8.33	15.73
Electronics	18.00	12.50	15.25	15.61	17.17	32.42
Programming/Audio	7.25	7.00	7.13	7.29	8.02	15.15
Shop Admin	11.40	4.50	7.95	8.14	8.95	16.90
OVERALL OVERTIME	4.76%					

IMPORTANT NOTE: All numerical information is artificial and is not intended to reflect actual performance, prices, or costs.

torical figure, King Henry VIII. Suppose that a new theme park, Merrie Old England, Inc. (MOE), is negotiating with Sally to build Henry VIII as a cornerstone of one of its shows. MOE is exact about what it wants in Henry's appearance and body movements. Sally's salespeople accumulate these specifications and give them to company management for cost estimation

Sally's management costs out its robots as the sum total of direct labor, direct materials, and shop overhead on a full absorption basis. Shop overhead is assigned to product using a predetermined rate with direct labor as the base.

Direct labor is the most important direct cost component, so it is considered first in a project's cost estimation spreadsheet. A macro pulls direct labor rate information from another spreadsheet into the rate schedule settings part of the project spreadsheet. Direct labor is broken down into the seven functional areas—mechanical, pneumatic (compressed air to power movements), art, scenic, electronics, programming & audio, and shop administration—to control the individual phases of the job and because labor rates can vary markedly between labor tasks.

An average labor rate is calculated for each task and adjusted for overtime. The overtime factor is based on management's estimate of overtime hours per week for the project contained in another part of the spreadsheet. Then the predetermined overhead amount is added to the adjusted labor rates to yield a total conversion cost.

For instance, in T-1, the Rate Schedule Settings for Henry VIII, suppose that the labor rate for art ranges from a high of $9 to a low of $4.25, with an average of $6.63. The overtime factor for this project is 4.76% of total labor hours, calculated from the estimate of overtime hours per week. Thus the labor rate

adjusted for overtime is: $6.63 + ($6.63 × 4.76% × 0.5) = $6.78 (0.5 is the overtime premium). Assuming a predetermined overhead rate of 110%, the conversion cost rate for art on this project is $14.09 per direct labor hour of art.

The project costs are clustered around various parts, aspects, or characteristics of the robot or show. One such cluster is displayed in T-2, Design Element Costs. Here the estimated direct labor hours and materials for each of Henry's "elements" are specified. The labor estimates have been honed from Sally's experience in building entertainment robots.

The first element (line 1) in T-2 is design, with 15 mechanical hours, five pneumatic hours, and 9.5 art hours. The hours are costed out automatically in a cell formula that calls the conversion cost rate from T-1 for each task and multiplies it times the hours for the task. The total labor dollars amount for design is $465 (including overhead), displayed in the "Labor $" column and "Design" row.

Many of Sally's robots begin as standard designs and are modified according to customer specifications. Henry VIII is a good example. Henry's face and body will be augmented to reflect his enormous body size. He also will be able to blink his eyes, turn his head left and right, and rotate his left wrist, among other things. The first step in estimating Henry's costs, then, is to "call" the standard robot elements from another spreadsheet by invoking a macro. Then, the standard elements are modified for Henry. His "expanded body" (line 7) is a normal robot body with extra girth. The hours and materials for each task were adjusted upward to reflect the extra labor and materials needed for the modification. Whereas a normal body might cost $1,000, Henry's body costs $3,463.

188

TABLE 2
DESIGN ELEMENT COSTS, HENRY VIII SPREADSHEET

"ITEM" number 1 Description				Base character with Expanded Head and Body							
"ELEMENTS"	Mat $	Lab $	Total	Mech M hrs	Mech M mat	Pnu P hrs	Pnu P mat	Art A hrs	Art A mat	T & A T hrs	T & A T mat
1. Design	0	465	465	15.0	—	5.0	—	9.5	—	—	—
2. —	0	0	0	—	—	—	—	—	—	—	—
3. Character:	0	0	0	—	—	—	—	—	—	—	—
4. Expand std face	2540	916	3456	—	—	—	—	65.0	2540	—	—
5. Basic art fab-human	275	218	493	—	—	—	—	15.5	275	—	—
6. Royal Costume	1500	585	2085	—	—	—	—	41.5	1500	—	—
7. Expand body	2400	1063	3463	—	—	—	—	75.5	2400	—	—
8. Frame-no moves	200	710	910	44.0	200	—	—	—	—	—	—
9. Triple axis head	490	492	982	25.0	240	5.0	250	—	—	—	—
10. Head turn L/R	325	206	531	10.0	175	2.5	150	—	—	—	—
11. Mouth	165	116	281	5.0	140	2.0	25	—	—	—	—
12. Human 2-way eyes	420	504	924	—	—	22.0	320	8.0	100	—	—
13. Eye blink	145	248	393	—	—	10.0	100	5.0	45	—	—
14. Right shoulder	275	229	504	12.0	175	2.0	100	—	—	—	—
15. Right wrist triax	240	174	414	8.0	100	2.5	140	—	—	—	—
16. Left wrist rotate	350	116	466	5.0	200	2.0	150	—	—	—	—
17. Left fingers	400	922	1322	55.0	250	2.0	150	—	—	—	—
18. Stand/sit	600	1298	1898	75.0	350	5.0	250	—	—	—	—
19. Torso twist	225	229	454	12.0	125	2.0	100	—	—	—	—
20. Body Bow	400	426	826	22.0	250	4.0	150	—	—	—	—
21.	0	0	0	—	—	—	—	—	—	—	—
33. Test & Adjust	200	254	454	—	—	—	—	—	—	15.0	200
TOTAL COST	11150	9172	20322	288.0	2205	66.0	1885	220.0	6860	15.0	200
PROJECTED RETAIL	13118	10790	23908								

The procedure is repeated for all elements of a design.

At the bottom of T- 2, Henry's element costs are totaled ($20,322), and these totals are transferred to a third part of the spreadsheet (T- 3). Note that the T- 2 totals also are expressed in "projected retail" dollars using a markup percentage.

T- 3 is a summary of the project costs and retail prices for Henry VIII. The total estimated cost of $25,558 is the $20,322 of element cost previously discussed (T- 2) plus $5,236 of audio and motion control equipment summarized in a cost cluster in another part of the spreadsheet. Some project spreadsheets will contain a number of cost clusters, especially if the project includes multiple characters, scenery, and props.

In T- 3, a markup percentage was applied to the total cost to yield a contract amount ($30,068). The contract amount less the estimated costs is the gross margin of $4,510. For some situations, the contract amount will be set independent of the spreadsheet.

Once work has begun on a project, Sally management will use the detailed budget to monitor the project costs until completion. The direct labor hours become the basis for the time management and production control system, and the cost totals are posted to the general ledger budgetary accounts.

TIME MANAGEMENT AND PRODUCTION CONTROL

People are Sally's most valuable asset, and management of their time is at the core of Sally's production control system. The time management and production control system acts as an elaborate time clock, tracking each employee's hours by task within a project. It allows employees to virtually assign themselves to tasks while maintaining strict accountability for their precious time.

The time management and production control system is programmed in compiled BASIC and is installed on a dedicated 80286 PC located in the middle of the shop floor. The day's information is stored in system RAM and written to the hard drive every few minutes. The PC is connected to an uninterruptible power supply to enable RAM information to be saved before the system can experience a shutdown from a loss of power.

As production workers arrive in the morning, each one logs onto the time management system, and the arrival time is written to the database. The next screen displays a menu of projects available to be worked on. The employee chooses a project, and a menu of tasks for that project is displayed. The employee then logs

TABLE 3
SUMMARY COSTS AND RETAIL PRICES, HENRY VIII SPREADSHEET

Henry VIII   Contract Number: 7777
Preliminary Lotus   Filename   Henry
January 10, 19xx   Average Overtime
                Hours/Week   2

```
= = = = = = = = = = = = = = = = = = = = = = = = = = = =
=          signed                         date       =
=                                                     =
=                                                     =
======================================
```

Contract amount $30,068   100.00%
Estimated costs   25,558   85.00%
Gross margin $ 4,510   15.00%

	Mat $	Lab $	Total	Mech M hrs	Mech M mat	Pnu P hrs	Pnu P mat	Art A hrs	Art A mat	Scenic S hrs	Scenic S mat	Elec E hrs	Elec E mat	Audio Au hrs	Audio Au mat	T&A T hrs	T&A T mat
Grand Totals Costs	14585	10973	25558	288	2205	67	2120	220	6860	0	0	55	1400	0	1800	15	200
Projected Retail	17159	12909	30068														
Markup on Cost = 17.65%																	

IMPORTANT NOTE: All numerical information is artificial and is not intended to reflect actual performance, prices, or costs.

onto one of the tasks, and the start time for the task is written to the database.

An employee might work on this task for only a few minutes or for the rest of the day. If he or she stops working on that task, it may be that the paint has to dry, or the task is completed, or it's lunchtime, or it's the end of the day. Suppose it is 10 a.m. and the employee is waiting for the paint to dry on Henry VIII's face. He or she logs off this task and onto another one. In the meantime, the budgeted hours for the first task have been updated for this morning's work, and the budgeted hours remaining on all tasks are displayed on the terminal. At lunchtime, each worker is automatically logged off his or her task then logged back on an hour later.

At the end of the workday, the employees log themselves off the system, and their departure times are written to the database. Now the database contains the arrival and departure time for each production worker for that day plus the amount of time each worker spent on each project and task. This information is summarized in a Lotus spreadsheet weekly and then posted to Sally's payroll module in its accounting system. There it is automatically transferred to the job cost module and the general ledger accounts.

For a relatively small company such as Sally, the time management and production control system represents a significant investment in resources: a dedicated computer, custom programming, and a commitment by management and workers to its successful operation. Nevertheless, the system has paid for itself in a number of ways:

1. Workers are very conscious of how they use their time—especially as they log themselves in and out—and they can see how their time fits into the time budgeted for the project. They "work smarter."

2. Because the system is *on-line, real-time,* shop management knows the work status of each task and project at any instant. Managers can "manage smarter.

3. The system flags on the main screen any task and project that is over budget. Management can give these items special attention.

4. Time records are more accurate. Workers don't have to rely on their memories to complete a time sheet daily or weekly.

ACCOUNTING INTERFACE

The flowchart in Figure 1 shows how the cost estimation system, the time management and production control system, and the general accounting system interface.

The direct labor hours budgeted for each task in a project are input to the time management and production control system manually from hard-copy output of the cost estimation system. Hard copy also provides the basis for the preparation of a Lotus spreadsheet to summarize the budgeted revenues and costs and the assignment of this information to monthly accounting periods. Then the monthly budgetary information is posted to the company's general ledger system.

The time management and production control system provides hard copy that is used in the preparation of another Lotus spreadsheet summarizing hours worked by project and worker. This information is posted to the payroll module of the general accounting system where it automatically is distributed to the job cost module and to the general ledger accounts.

Sally's general accounting system is a PC-based software package designed primarily for contractors. The package differs from most contractor construction accounting packages in that it incorporates an inventory of raw materials. Most contractors simply order

190

building materials from wholesale suppliers as the materials are needed, which approximates just-in-time production (JIT). Sally on the other hand, maintains an inventory or raw materials consisting of standard production bushings; bearings; pneumatic cylinders; hoses; prosthetic devices such as hands, arms, and legs; and a large list of other materials including resin, plaster, clay, and paint needed in the manufacture of robots and their attendant props and scenery.

IN CONTROL

We know it's difficult to think of management control systems when you're trying to save E.T. from mortal peril. But the next time you see one of Sally's magical creations, pause for a moment, try to look beyond the makeup and props, and consider how a "lowly" system can be a critical cog in the complex wheel that brings you such an entertaining experience. Neither Sally nor any other company can endure without effective management control. The many, many hours that Sally's crew has invested in developing the cost estimation and time management and production control systems pay off every day in that enchanted twinkle in the eye of a singing bear or that exuberant grin on a pint-sized "ghostbuster" scoring a hit on villainous Prime Evil.

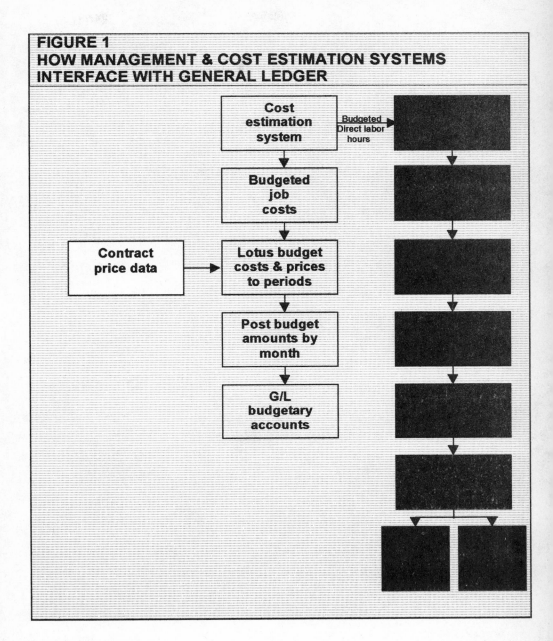

FIGURE 1
HOW MANAGEMENT & COST ESTIMATION SYSTEMS INTERFACE WITH GENERAL LEDGER

Cost estimation system

Budgeted Direct labor hours

Budgeted job costs

Contract price data → Lotus budget costs & prices to periods

Post budget amounts by month

G/L budgetary accounts

Chapter 13
Process Costing

Cases

13-1   Process Costing and Spoilage

Readings

Robert J. Bowlby: How Boeing Tracks Costs, A to Z
This articles explains the change in Boeing's costing approach, from one based on job-costing to a process approach.

Discussion Questions:
1. Explain what Boeing means by process accounting.
2. What are the advantages of the process accounting approach at Boeing?
3. How does the new process accounting approach affect each business unit□s incentives and tools to control costs?

Cases

13-1. Process Costings and Spoilage

Ranka Company manufacturers high quality leather products. The company's profits have declined during the past nine months. Ranka has used unit cost data that were developed eighteen months ago in planning and controlling its operations. In an attempt to isolate the causes of poor profit performance, management is investigating the manufacturing operations of each of its products.

One of Ranka's main products is fine leather belts. The belts are produced in a single continuous process in the Bluett Plant. During the process leather strips are sewn, punched, and dyed. Buckles are attached by rivets when the belts are 70 percent complete as to direct labor and overhead (conversion costs). The belts then enter a final finishing stage to conclude the process. Labor and overhead are applied continuously during the process.

The leather belts are inspected twice during the process: (1) right before the buckles are attached (70 percent point in the process) and (2) at the conclusion of the finishing stage (100 percent point in the process). Ranka uses the weighted average method to calculate its unit costs.

The leather belts produced at the Bluett Plant wholesale for $9.95 each. Management wants to compare the current manufacturing costs per unit with the prices which exist on the market for leather belts. Top management has asked the Bluett Plant to submit data on the cost of manufacturing the leather belts for the month of October. This cost data will be used to evaluate whether modifications in the production process should be initiated or whether an increase in the selling price of the belts if justified. The cost per equivalent unit which is being used for planning and controlling purposes is $5.35 per unit.

The work-in-process inventory consisted of 400 partially completed units on October 1. The belts were 25 percent completed as to conversion costs. The costs included in the inventory on October 1 were as follows:

Leather strips	$1,000
Conversion costs	300
	$1,300

During October 7,600 leather strips were placed in production. A total of 6,800 good leather belts were completed. A total of 300 belts were identified as defective at the two inspection points—100 at the first inspection point (before buckle is attached) and 200 at the final inspection point (after finishing). This quantity of defective belts was considered normal. In addition, 200 belts were removed from the production line when the process was 40% complete as to conversion costs because they had been damaged as a result of a malfunction during the sewing operation. This malfunction was considered an unusual occurrence, and consequently, the spoilage was classified as abnormal. Defective (spoiled) units are not reprocessed and have zero salvage value. The work-in-process inventory on October 31 consisted of 700 belts which were 50 percent complete as to conversion costs.

The costs charged to production during October were as follows:

Leather strips	$20,600
Buckles	4,550
Conversion	20,700
	$45,850

REQUIRED:

1. In order to provide cost data regarding the manufacture of leather belts in the Bluett Plant to the top management of Ranka Company, determine for the month of October:

    a. The equivalent units for each factor of production.

    b. The cost per equivalent whole unit for each factor of production.

    c. The assignment of total production costs to the work-in-process inventory and to goods transferred out.

    d. The average unit cost of the 6,800 good leather belts completed and transferred to finished goods.

2. If Ranka Company decided to repair (rework) the 300 defective belts which were considered normal spoilage, explain how the company would account for the rework costs.

   (CMA adapted)

How Boeing Tracks Costs, A to Z

When Boeing's internal customers clamored for better cost information, the company decided to empower its business units by giving them more responsibility for their own costs.

By Robert J. Bowlby

A few years ago, two of Boeing's internal customers, engineering and operations, told the finance department they weren't getting the cost information they needed to manage airplane design and production. They lacked relevant economic information on which to base their decisions.

When we heard that, we knew we had to do something to remedy the situation. Boeing's cost-accounting system worked for tax and financial accounting and could be used to determine product cost and profitability at an airplane model level. But we realized that at an operating level, we were giving our engineering and operations organizations budgets for only a few cost elements.

Further, the cost information we provided individual managers didn't align with their responsibilities or areas they could control or influence. Engineering and operations couldn't use the cost information they routinely received to perform reliable economic design trade studies or to make economically sound investment decisions. They had to generate such information almost exclusively by special analysis.

At Boeing, we've committed ourselves to continuously improving our processes so we can stay ahead of the competition and maintain or increase our long-term market share. We are rethinking and reshaping our corporate strategies, the cornerstone of which is "Customer In," a concept that means we continually seek input from our internal and external customers through internal feedback, customer-satisfaction surveys and market research.

With this type of strategy, finance must be a partner in all aspects of a business, from marketing and product design to production and customer support.

One of finance's most important jobs is to help create a systematic framework of financial and nonfinancial information and measures that contribute to making the decisions that ensure the enterprise's success.

Therefore, to improve the cost-management process, Boeing finance, operations and engineering decided to team together to study and rethink our managers' real information needs with respect to unit costs. The team spent some time identifying and reviewing "best practices" by studying industry, academia and our own internal practices. We came up with several key concepts aimed at improving the relevancy of our cost-management information.

FRONT-END ALIGNMENT

First, we decided to align our accounting practices to support the way we manage the enterprise. This includes being flexible and responsive enough so that we can change or redirect the system to enhance continuous process improvement, even in the middle of an accounting period.

Also, we realized we had to routinely provide the financial data that management needs to improve our processes and ultimately our products. We agreed that this data, which includes the costs of such items as materials, labor and energy, should represent the sum of all the resources actually used to build the part or assembly and that the area building that part or assembly must assume the responsibility for generating and tracking the data. From these key concepts, along with others like activity-based analysis, Boeing finance has been progressing toward implementing a modified process cost-accounting system.

Using process accounting means significantly changing cost-management practices and cost-assignment techniques. Part of the problem is that our current system was designed when our primary business was producing military aircraft. Our production methods, the makeup of our costs and the information we need about them have changed a lot since then.

Over time, our traditional job-cost system and cost-accounting practices have caused more and more costs that we'd traditionally categorized as overhead to be unloaded onto an ever-smaller direct-labor base. This evolved to the point where between 70 percent to 80 percent of the costs assigned to the final cost objectives of a manufacturing or engineering line organization were allocations from common overhead pools. Building and equipment maintenance, depreciation costs and the costs of industrial-engineering support activities and other support functions were lumped together in general overhead pools.

In today's factory, it's not uncommon to find that depreciation, technology, energy and nondirect labor expenses are often individually more significant than direct-touch or shop labor. The 20 percent to 30 percent of our costs that were mostly direct-touch labor assigned to the final cost objectives were the only cost elements the manufacturing or engineering line organizations had responsibility for and could directly link to the products they make. This meant that any process-improvement or cost-reduction initiative made by the line organization that didn't involve direct-labor savings wasn't directly reflected, or maybe not reflected at all, in the costs allocated to it. In many cases, the line organization couldn't be sure if total company costs would decrease or increase as a result of its actions.

To better manage the other 70 percent to 80 percent of the costs, traditional cost accounting and cost management separately identified significant chunks of the overhead cost and managed them individually. But, identifying separate cost elements, such as depreciation computing and nondirect labor, and trying to budget and control each one separately, didn't show the ways in which these cost elements interacted with one another.

These old accounting practices meant the overhead, the manufacturing or engineering line organization did receive was based on the direct-labor dollars it incurred. Because technology-related costs were buried in overhead, this approach tended to move the dollars from areas with higher technology costs into units with the larger direct-labor elements. What we needed were ways to better align more of our costs directly to what we really do—designing and assembling airplanes and manufacturing parts and assemblies for them.

THAT BILL HAS YOUR NAME ON IT

Aligning costs to operating decisions is an important component of the new management and operating philosophy we're striving to implement. The changes we're going through are substantial. We are moving from a functional enterprise to one organized around product processes, and from a company that allocates its resources by organization to one that aligns them to product processes. And we are replacing part/resource management with product-focused process management.

This new philosophy will allow us to match resources to small, focused product groups. These small business units will then contain one or more product-focused process units. Costs incurred at a broader level in the company will not become the responsibility of the product- or service-producing unit. Rather, these broader-level costs will be the responsibility of the general-purpose processes, such as the sales and marketing organization or the central tax staff. These groups will be accountable from the costs they are adding to the final product shipped to our customers.

By way of comparison, think about a typical activity-based costing model, which you could use to develop the cost drivers for overhead and manufacturing activities. The overhead drivers include the square footage, the headcount, direct-labor hours, and the number of products. Manufacturing's drivers are the unit volume, the number of shifts and the weighted unit volume. With an ABC model, you would use these drivers to link the overhead activities to the manufacturing processes and the manufacturing processes to products.

With process accounting, we trace the overhead costs to product-related manufacturing processes based on the business unit's responsibility for and ability to control and influence the costs that result from operating that process. This is important for several reasons. Under traditional accounting, a business unit can spend less money and thus help the company meet its overall cost-reduction targets. But it's the direct, measurable, cause-and-effect link back to the business unit's products that was missing. Reducing a few direct heads was about the only action the business-unit manager could take to actually see the business unit's costs, or rather the 20 percent to 30 percent of business-unit costs, go down.

Our new process-accounting approach has changed that situation dramatically. Today, the organization can exercise significant influence and control over the costs it incurs. In fact, the basic ground rule for assigning costs is the organization must be able to take some action on that cost element and see a predictable change in the overall costs being charged to it.

The costs the business unit is accountable for and can control now include those for detail and supplier parts, computing, depreciation, support labor and direct labor, and other nonlabor costs. The business manager has a much broader sphere of influence in

A FRACTION OF THE COSTS

Boeing's new cost-accounting system allows individual business units to portray their planned unit costs in today's environment and how they might compare to the unit costs upper management wants to achieve. The business units calculate their costs with the help of numerator and denominator charts like the ones below. The total dollar cost divided by good parts out equals the cost for good part shipped. Typical elements included under total costs are shown in the numerator chart. The denominator chart shows how we calculate our costs for good parts shipped.

In this example, the expected production, from the denominator table, is 13,439 units of output. The cost to product 13,439 units is estimated at $58.517 million (numerator table). Dividing 13,439 units into $58.517 million yields an expected average unit cost of $4,354.

Boeing's Cost Numerator...

Cost Element	Product Plan Costs (in $ thousands)
Touch Labor	12,150
Support Labor	9,223
Raw Materials	15,113
Equipment Depreciation	2,990
Equipment Maintenance	2,357
Tooling Depreciation	1,983
Tooling Maintenance	1,317
Distributed Material	503
Shop Supplies	915
Computing	6,662
Facilities Cost	3,552
Miscellaneous	1,752
Total	**$58,517**

...and Output Denominator

Part Number	Quantity	Product Weighting Factor	Units of Output
A	158	2.10	332
B	405	3.30	1,337
C	288	13.60	3,917
D	528	5.30	2,798
E	332	13.20	4,382
F	673	1.00	673
	2,384		13,439

which to exercise control and make improvements within the business unit.

But tracing this bigger bucket of costs to the business units is only part of the solution. The business units now need some tools with which they can manage their costs. Once they identify the resources they consume, they must analyze them and learn to recognize their process and resource cost drivers and the relationship among them by continually asking why a certain item or process costs what it does. Business units need to understand their cost drivers to increase product quality, cut costs, improve customer response time and so on. Our business units will use their unit cost targets and ad-hoc analysis techniques for the data they will track internally (see box on page 22).

As you can see from the example shown in the box, our basic approach is to compare and weight the individual parts produced in a product process, based on the differences between the parts or part families. We calculate the relative differences in the resources required to produce the different parts. Then we multiply the result—the product weighting factor for each part or product—by the expected production quantity for each part. The result is the business unit's expected production expressed in equivalent output units.

IT'S ALL RELATIVE

The normal procedure for determining these factors is to first identify the typical or base part or part family. Often that turns out to be the part that is the simplest. We give the base part a value of 1, 10 or 100, depending on the scale we want to use.

Then we review the other parts we produce, compare their features' relative value to the base part and determine their values. Take airplane skin panels, for example. We might assign a simple panel a value of one. A panel with a window could have a value of five, while a panel with an unusual shape could be a nine, and so on. The method also allows us to calculate the relative value of adding to or modifying various features.

Determining the relative value is probably the most complicated part of the whole process, but it's an essential aspect of process accounting. It's important to understand what's driving our current production costs, as well as the relative value of the parts being produced and the impact of process improvements and future production plans.

Individual business units can now project their costs for expected future levels of production. The production-producing business units will now be able

199

to better understand how they fit into the total company production and cost picture.

With this knowledge, Boeing can relate many aspects of the total business to one another in a manner that allows us to take actions at all levels of the company—actions with predictable results and a common focus. For example, we can now begin to trace the hidden costs of capacity to individual business units, and this brings up some different, interesting questions. What is the unit's excess capacity! What's the cost of holding inventory! Who's accountable for excess capacity and why!

Also, process accounting supports other concepts in our continuous process-improvement strategy, including total accountability, responsibility and control: flexibility; and total cost tied to customer value. With our process-accounting tools in hand, we can begin to answer the next round of questions we're asking ourselves in our continuing quest for quality.

Chapter 14
Cost Allocation: Service Departments and Joint Product Costs

Cases
14-1   Southwes*ern Bell Telephone (Revenue Allocation)
14-2   Mali Rice Growers (Cost Allocation)

Readings
Dennis P. Tishlias: **Reasonable Joint Cost Allocations in Nonprofits**
This article demonstrates the use of four alternative methods for allocating joint costs in nonprofit organizations. An example is provided of a hypothetical nonprofit with two program functions and one fund raising function. The three functions share a joint activity, a joint mailing, with a total cost of $100,000. The four allocation methods are (1) activity-based allocation, (2) equal sharing, (3) allocation based on stand-alone costs, and (4) allocation in proportion to cost savings. Stand-alone costs are the costs each function would incur if it performed the mailing alone.

Discussion Questions:
1.   Explain each of the four methods used in the example.
2.   Which of the four methods would you prefer, and why?
3.   What is the role of stand-alone costs in using each of the methods, and why are stand-alone costs important to consider?

202

Cases

14-1. Southwestern Bell Telephone

In the fall of 1989, the Texas Division of Southwestern Bell Telephone Company (SWBT) was facing considerable earnings uncertainty. Nine months had passed since the Texas Public Utilities Commission (PUC) had initiated an inquiry into SWBT's earnings in Texas. The Company was trying to negotiate a settlement but was having difficulty reaching an agreement with the commission staff and other interested parties. One group was proposing a decrease in SWBT revenues that would result in a 76% reduction in the company's Texas revenues and adversely affect Southwestern Bell Corporation's stock price.

At the same time that the PUC was investigating alleged overearnings related to SWBT's Texas intrastate operations, company officers in Texas were trying to meet budgeted net income objectives. These targets were necessary to keep earnings growing at a conservative yet steady rate. With actual data already available for much of the year, it was apparent that the overall target for 1989 might not be met. One of the main causes of this probable shortfall was the decrease SWBT was experiencing in revenues from long distance telephone calls. This decrease was due largely to increased payments in the form of settlements to other local exchange telephone companies in Texas. SWBT's management was searching for alternatives to the settlement process that would allow the company to retain its fair share of long distance revenues without financially ruining smaller telephone companies operating in the state.

INDUSTRY BACKGROUND

In January 1984, SWBT and six other regional telephone companies were divested from American Telephone and Telegraph Company (AT&T). In addition to retaining ownership of Western Electric (manufacturing), Bell Labs (research and development), and AT&T Information Systems, AT&T was allowed to retain ownership of interstate long distance services and a portion of intrastate long distance. Under the provisions of the Justice Department's Modified Final Judgment decree, each state was divided into Local Access Transport Areas (LATAs). Texas was divided into seventeen LATAs in addition to the standard metropolitan statistical area of San Angelo, which belongs solely to General Telephone (GTE).

Long distance calling between LATAs (interLATA) may be provided only by interexchange carriers (IXCs) such as AT&T, MCI, and Sprint. Local exchange carriers (LECs) such as SWBT and GTE provide basic telephone service and long distance calling within each LATA (intraLATA). In Texas, there are 59 LECs. SWBT is by far the largest, serving approximately 6.6 million telephone lines.

Because IXCs access their customers through LEC facilities, LECs charge IXCs for using their local networks. Theoretically, these per-minute-of-use charges are based on LEC costs. However, state commissions often inflate the rates to subsidize basic telephone rates, thus keeping them priced below cost.

INTERSTATE INTRALATA LONG DISTANCE

When a customer of an LEC makes an intrastate intraLATA long distance (toll) call, completion of the call often requires the use of another LEC's facilities. For example, a call from Dallas to Denton is an intraLATA toll call that originates in a Southwestern Bell area (Dallas) but terminates in a GTE area (Denton). The originator of the call is billed by Southwestern Bell, which must reimburse GTE for costs incurred in assisting in the call.

In Texas, this reimbursement is currently handled through a toll revenue pooling agreement among the LECs.

The pooling of intraLATA toll revenues is administered by the Texas Exchange Carrier Association (TECA). Each LEC reports monthly to the TECA administrator not only its billed toll revenues but also its expenses and investment incurred in providing toll service. TECA combines the revenue, expense, and investment information for all 59 LECs and calculates a rate of return equal to billed revenues less expenses (including taxes) divided by investment. Each LEC is allowed to recover its expenses plus the pool rate of return on its investment.

In 1987 the pool rate of return was approximately 19%. Although SWBT billed $555.3 million in toll revenues, it was allowed to retain only the total of its expenses ($285.4 million) and return ($147.9 million). The $122 million difference between what SWBT billed and what it was allowed to keep was paid to the pool administrator for disbursement to those companies whose costs exceeded their billed revenues.

CONCERNS WITH THE POOLING PROCESS

Southwestern Bell's managers have several concerns with the current pooling process. One of their major concerns is that few incentives exist for companies to control costs. IntraLATA toll service is a much larger portion of the total operations of many of the smaller LECs than of SWBT. Consequently, each dollar of additional cost incurred by the smaller companies results in approximately one dollar of additional settlements. On the other hand, Southwestern Bell's retained toll revenues (after settlement with other LECs) decrease by approximately $1 million for each one percent reduction in its costs. This situation is not conducive to the efficient provision of telephone service and therefore is not in the best interest of the public.

The company's managers also are concerned about the manner in which total expenses and investment related to intraLATA toll service are calculated. Each company's accountants computes these amounts using procedures developed by the Federal Communications Commission (FCC). The very complex procedures, referred to in the industry as "separations," allocate monthly journalized expense and investment amounts to various categories of telephone service based on factors developed from studies of call traffic patterns and studies showing how telephone plant resources are utilized. The separations process was developed to provide a means of dividing expenses and investment amounts between state and interstate jurisdictions to facilitate rate setting by regulatory agencies. It never was intended to represent an accurate allocation system.

The first step in separations is to divide expense and investment amounts into traffic-sensitive and non-traffic-sensitive (NTS) categories. Traffic-sensitive expenses are primarily variable and are relatively easy to trace to specific categories of service. NTS expenses are primarily fixed. These amounts (over half the total SWBT reports to the pool) are incurred to provide and service connections between customers' premises and company's central offices. The same investment is required whether a customer makes no calls, a few calls, or hundreds of calls, and also whether those calls are intrastate or interstate.

NTS amounts are separated into three categories: interstate, intrastate toll, and intrastate local. In 1982, the FCC froze at approximately 20% the portion of Southwestern Bell's NTS expenses and investment allocated to intrastate toll operations. Thus, the initial separation of NTS amounts does not represent the current usage of the telephone network's resources. However, the interLATA toll and intraLATA toll components of the 20% factor are determined monthly based on relative actual usage. Therefore, if interLATA toll usage is increasing at a faster rate than intraLATA toll usage, less will be allocated to the intraLATA toll category. IntraLATA toll expenses and related investment could be increasing, but due to the separations process fewer dollars would be assigned to the category and thus recoverable through the pooling process. SWBT's intraLATA toll NTS factor is approximately 8%, whereas the factors of several smaller telephone companies are in the 30% to 50% range.

A third concern of Southwestern Bell managers is that revenues from non-joint-provided toll calls are included in the pooling process. For example, consider that the largest intraLATA toll market in Texas is between Dallas and Ft. Worth. Most toll calls between the two cities use only SWBT facilities, but through the pooling process revenues from the calls are shared with the state's other LECs. Company officials believe both revenues and costs of single-company toll calls should be excluded from the pool, but currently there is no means to isolate those amounts.

A final concern relates to the telecommunications industry goal of providing adequate telephone service to all U. S. citizens at reasonable rates. All telephone companies as well as the entire nation have benefited from the subsidies that higher cost companies have received from lower-cost companies. If local telephone service, especially in rural areas, were priced to cover its costs, the number of residences with service would be substantially lower. The concern at Southwestern Bell is that subsidization of high-cost companies has exceeded its historical intent; publications of the Texas PUC show that many high-cost LECs are earning well over their authorized rates of return.

After reviewing the situation, Southwestern Bell's senior managers realized they had their work cut out for them. They know that the course of action they recommended would have to effectively address both the concerns of SWBT and the financial needs of the other companies.

REQUIRED:

1. Assuming toll revenue sharing will continue to be administered by the TECA, what is the most important modification that could be made to the pooling procedures to produce a more equitable distribution of revenues from the perspective of Southwestern Bell?

2. Should SWBT officials negotiate changes in the subsidization procedures directly with the other Texas LECs or take their concerns to the state Public Utilities Commission and seek mandated changes?

3. What strategy would you recommend to Southwestern Bell managers? How would your recommendation address the four concerns expressed in the case?

14-2. Mali Rice Growers

Rice is one of the staple foods in Mali, West Africa, and, happily for this country, most of what is consumed annually (between 72% and 85%) is grown on the rice paddies along the Niger River. However, a certain amount must be imported every year to make up for the deficit. About 90% of this importation is done legally by two or three major importers, one of whose operations is described in the following case.

Mali's role in the world rice market is small. The country imports only 4% of the total rice traded in the world; the average amount over the past five years has been about 60,000 tons. Still, for rice traders in Mali, an extra thousand or two tons in inventory can mean disaster for the trader's bottom line, and too little will mean lost revenues and serious shortages for the population. So making final decisions regarding the future marketability of rice is a difficult business, and Amadou Takoure, Chief Financial Officer at one of the largest rice trading companies in Mali, was currently facing this process.

It was 10am on June 15, 1993, when Takoure was already feeling that the day had stretched too long in this hottest season of the year. He needed to budget rice imports for the year. Currently prices stood at $610, about $30 above the variable costs of importing rice (half of these variable costs are transportation and customs charges). Prices usually rise and fall, but by how much depends on the rains and whether demand is rising.

Making the final decision about how much rice to import for arrival on August 15 in time for the fall market is an exercise in information gathering (calling large rice associations in Segou, Mopti, Baguineda, and Selingue to find out what their harvest may be), historical analysis (looking at the past for any evidence of trends), inventory taking (assessing the total amount of rice in stock currently in the country), psychology (anticipating what the other importers are going to do, as well as what the smugglers are going to smuggle), and star gazing (trying to anticipate rains and the resulting prices for the three months from now in a highly unstable economy with several unpredictable factors). Takoure was also concerned about overhead costs and the overall profitability of the business, and he was wondering about the profitability of the different product lines. He knew that the accurate prediction of rice demand would play a role in these issues. He called over his trusted assistant Dramane Couilbaly, to talk through the company's cost constraints and get some fresh ideas.

Takoure: Dramane, I need to get the right marketing mix among our main products—rice, refrigerators, air conditioners, and tiles—to cover our overhead and realize a profit. I have to say that I am thoroughly frustrated with our inability to bring down overhead costs, which continue to average $100,000 per month.

Coulibaly: Well, you know we have the electric company, which seems to enjoy it enormously when we turn on a bit of air conditioning. And at $10 per minute for the boss's overseas calls, no wonder our phone bill is so huge. Plus we have those huge interest payments on the financing of our imports. It won't help to complain—we just need to get the right product mix to cover it. And, as you know, part of covering the overhead is deciding on a reasonable allocation system. You know that we have been using your system for a few quarters, where we allocate based on relative sales dollars, but we never predict accurately what sales will be. We really need to be sure that we are at least trying to get prices adequate to cover all the costs.

Takoure: You're right. We need to determine an allocation base that reflects our biggest headache, which is getting our merchandise sold as quickly as possible. Our tiles languish in the warehouse for an average of six months, our air conditioners for as long as four months, and our refrigerators as much as three months. Currently our variable costs on tiles per ton are about $12,016; on air conditioners, per unit about $418; and on refrigerators per unit about $582.

Coulibaly: Did I tell you that interest rates have just gone up 50 basis points to 18%? You know this means that the longer our goods stay in those warehouses, the more we pay in interest, which is part of our overhead. We have very favorable arrangements at the bank, where principal is due 120 days after the merchandise lands. Still, since we are borrowing 100 percent of our variable costs, the faster we can sell, the faster we can pay the principal.

Takoure: By the way, what are we paying for our new warehouse?

Coulibaly: The warehouse for the durable goods costs $1,500 per month and can hold 30,000 cubic feet of merchandise. I asked our warehouse supervisor to tell me how much of each item we can fit into the place. He told me that the refrigerators take up about thirty cubic feet, the air conditioners require five, and each ton of tiles requires about fifty. Oh, and each ton of rice takes up one hundred cubic feet in a grain warehouse. And you may want to know the price of each of those 560,000 cubic foot grain warehouses, available as we need them, just doubled to one cent per cubic foot.

Takoure: OK. According to my market calculations, during this season we can import, store, and eventually sell 600 refrigerators, 1,000 air conditioners, and 15 tons of tiles. I estimate prices on these will be about $720, $600, and $18,000. Before I can make a decision on rice imports, I am going to have to do a little inventory study on current rice stocks in the country, and call around to the rice associations. Rains have begun to fall and though it is probably too early to tell, some of these farmers are pretty good at predicting the harvest for December anyway. We need to make a decision by this afternoon on the total we will import.

After calling the rice associations, Takoure determined that the harvest would probably increase from last year (rains have been good so far), and there would be at least 270,000 tons harvested in the 1993-4 season. (See T-A) If total consumption continued to rise, as it had over the past four years, to an average of 13.7% annually, then the consumption for 1994 would be 378,000 tons. If contraband imports returned to the 36,000 ton level (a conservative estimate), then the total deficit would be 68,000 tons.

His company traditionally had a large share of the rice import market, about 40%, so Takoure figured he could import at least 27,000 tons. Right now he could buy rice at $580 per ton, including the cost of transportation and customs duty, and it would arrive on August 15. He expected that prices would rise, even with a good harvest, because of rising demand. He wanted to sell the first sacks of rice by mid-September for about $635 per ton, and he hoped to raise prices by 1% for each of the months of October and November. Takoure expected that he would have to reduce prices to $630 in December during the harvest, and he hoped to have sold at least 26,000 tons by the New Year. He wondered whether fully absorbed costs would be covered by these prices.

REQUIRED:

1. What are the critical success factors for Takoure's business? What part does international trade play in these CSFs?

2. What are some possible allocation bases for the $1,200,000 overhead that Takoure might want to consider, given the information available? Choose the allocation method you prefer, explain why, and calculate the overhead allocation using this method. (AICPA)

Table A
Rice Stocks and Production (000s)

Fiscal Year: April 1-March 31	89-90	90-91	91-92	92-93	93-94*
Beginning Balance, National Stocks	34	55	23	22	24
+ Local rice production	158	186	155	245	270
- Imports of rice	40	8	118	70	68
+Legitimate resources available	232	249	296	337	362
+Contraband estimates	50	35	36	20	36
=Total Available for Consumption	282	284	332	357	398
-Ending balance, National stocks	55	23	22	24	20
=Total Consumption	227	261	310	333	378

*Projected based on available local agricultural data.

208

Reasonable Joint Cost Allocations in Nonprofits

Questions about the accuracy and reliability of nonprofits' financial statements have led to increased awareness of joint allocation.

By Dennis P. Tishlias

There is growing concern on the part of states' attorneys general that some charitable organizations have been "too liberal" in allocating costs to program expenses (instead of to administration or fundraising), particularly costs to educate the public. Without objective guidelines, auditors have difficulty determining the reasonableness of nonprofit organizations' joint cost allocations.

Joint cost allocations can have a serious impact on the evaluation of how responsibly a nonprofit social service organization is run. This gave rise to American Institute of CPAs Statement of Position no. 87-2, *Accounting for Joint Costs of Informational Materials and Activities of Not-for-Profit Organizations That Include a Fund-Raising Appeal*, which amended SOP no. 78-10, *Accounting Principles and Reporting Practices for Certain Nonprofit Organizations*, and the AICPA *Audits of Voluntary Health and Welfare Organizations*.

Questions about the accuracy and reliability of data in a nonprofit's financial statement led to increased awareness of joint cost allocation problems. In a notice to members the AICPA said auditors should "carefully review the requirements of SOP no. 87-2 and consider the sufficiency of evidence supporting any allocation of joint costs."

The article's purpose is to explore the bounds of reasonable allocations and offer some equitable solutions to achieve cost sharing within these boundaries.

ALLOCATION ISSUES

Current auditing and accounting standards fail to provide auditors with objectives for evaluating the reasonableness of joint cost allocations. For nonprofits, standards defining reasonableness are based on the relative amounts of money spent on programs versus fund-raising or administration. Reasonableness in cost allocations is crucial; it is directly linked to determining a nonprofit's use of voluntarily contributed funds.

SOP no. 87-2 offers guidance to auditors in deciding when joint cost allocations are appropriate. What is not specified is how allocations should be made. As SOP no. 87-2 says, there are many possible cost allocation methods. These techniques generally are based on the fundamental assumption joint costs should be allocated in a reasonable and fair manner, recognizing the cause-and-effect relationship between the cost incurred and where the cost is allocated. However, the very nature of jointness precludes such an allocation.

When a cause-and-effect allocation is difficult, impractical or impossible to determine, judgment is used to determine the cost assigned to each segment. The principles outlined in the following example help define a range of reasonable allocations.

EXAMPLE OF COST ALLOCATION

One reason nonprofit organizations incur joint costs is the expectation fund-raising, administration and programs can be served simultaneously for less cost than if these goals were pursued separately. The allocation problem arises from the premise that each segment benefiting from a joint action should share in its cost.

Consider an organization with two programs, P1 and P2, and one fund-raising function, FR. Exh. 1, provides data on these activities. The stand-alone cost of P1 is $40,000. The stand-alone costs of P2 and FR are $12,000 and $65,000, respectively, resulting in overall stand-alone costs of $117,000. If P1, P2 and FR act jointly, the total cost is $100,000, saving the organization $17,000.

While the organization as a whole benefits from incurring joint costs, the managements of the two programs and fund-raising must voluntarily collaborate

EXHIBIT 1
COST DATA FOR PROGRAM 1 (P1), PROGRAM 2 (P2) AND FUND-RAISING (FR)

Participants	Cost
P1	$40,000
P2	12,000
FR	65,000
P1,P2	44,200
P1,FR	88,200
P2,FR	75,000
P1,P2,FR	100,000

to obtain cost savings. If a segment's share of joint cost is expected to exceed its stand-alone cost, it has no incentive to act jointly. To motivate sharing or joint action, each segment's allocated share of joint cost must be no more than its stand-alone cost—the upper limit of joint cost a segment could reasonably be expected to absorb.

The lower limit should be no less than the incremental cost it adds to the total joint cost. As demonstrated in Exh. 1, the incremental cost of having P1 join P2 and FR is $25,000, the difference between the P1, P2, FR cost ($100,000) and the joint cost of P2, FR ($75,000). This is the least amount P1 should absorb. Anything less represents a subsidy from P2, FR to P1.

The range of reasonable cost allocation assignable to P1 is a minimum of $25,000 and a maximum of the stand-alone cost of $40,000, also shown in Exh. 1. For P2, the lower limit is $11,800, the $100,000 joint cost of P1, P2, FR minus the $88,200 joint cost of P1, FR. The upper limit is P2's stand-alone cost of $12,000. Likewise, the range for FR is $55,800 ($100,000 – $44,200) to FR's stand-alone cost of $65,000.

Finally, the total of joint costs allocated to all segments should not exceed the total joint cost to be allocated. Nor should any joint cost remain unallocated. In this example, the total of each segment's allocated cost must not be greater than or less than $100,000. While many possible allocation schemes can satisfy these constraints, only four are discussed below.

Method 1: Allocate on the basis of activity-based costs. An activity-based allocation is consistent with the cause-and-effect and the benefits-received criteria. It also provides a level of detail that can make the resulting allocations more defensible.

Activity-based accounting focuses on attaching costs to programs and fund-raising based on the activities performed to produce or support them. These costs are attached using cost drivers, which underlie actions or conditions that directly influence or create cost. For example, a joint mailing has at least four components (activities) of the joint cost—postage, printing, envelopes and handling. Each component can be allocated based on the cost driver for the particular activity.

An excellent basis for allocating postage is the incremental weight a program or fund-raising contributes to the mailing's weight. When the mailing's contents are particular to program and fund-raising, specific identification can be used to allocate printing costs. Since the mailing envelopes are shared, each segment is assigned one-third of their cost. Handling is allocated on the basis of the number of pieces put into each envelope.

Exh. 2, shows an example of this approach. Panel 1 shows the proportions of each activity assignable to the three segments. Panel 2 shows the total assumed cost of each activity. Multiplying the proportions in panel 1 by each activity's cost leads to the allocations shown.

EXECUTIVE SUMMARY

■THERE IS SOME CONCERN charitable organizations are too liberal in allocating costs to program expenses instead of to administration or fund-raising. Auditors have difficulty determining the reasonableness of these entities' joint cost allocation

■IDEALLY, A REASONABLE and fair joint cost allocation should recognize the cause-and-effect relationship between the cost incurred and where it is allocated. When such an allocation is not possible, judgment must be used.

■MOST ORGANIZATIONS INCUR joint costs with the expectation that cost savings will result. If one segment's share of joint costs exceeds the cost of acting alone, that segment has no incentive to act jointly.

■FOUR METHODS of allocating joint costs include activity-based allocations, equal sharing of costs, cost allocated relative to stand-alone cost and cost allocated in proportion to cost savings.

■JOINT COST ALLOCATIONS in nonprofit organizations influence perceptions about how well the organizations are run. As a result, auditors must carefully evaluate the chosen cost allocation methods.

P2's initial allocation of $14,250 exceeds its $12,000 stand-alone cost, violating the upper limit guideline. Assuming this difference is due to handling costs, one solution is to allocate P2's excess stand-alone cost to P1 and FR in a 2-to-1 ratio, the resulting proportions after eliminating P2. This is shown in panel 3.

This new allocation results in P1 and FR absorbing more handling costs than they would have if P2 had not been part of the joint mailing. However, their total costs are still within the reasonable range. In fact, after absorbing the additional handling cost, P1 saves $6,250 ($40,000 − $33,750) from its stand-alone cost; FR saves $10,750.

Method 2: Allocate equally. Many nonprofits do not have sufficiently sophisticated accounting systems to perform an activity-based allocation. Thus the resources required to gather the necessary data may not seem cost-effective. Under these conditions, management will tend to choose other allocation techniques.

One simple technique is to divide the total joint cost equally among the participants. Dividing the $100,000 total joint cost by three results in each segment receiving a $33,333 share. While P1 and FR's shares are less than their stand-alone costs, P2's share is more, exceeding its upper limit by $21,333. A solution is to charge P2 its $12,000 stand-alone cost and then allocate the $88,000 total cost balance equally to P1 and FR. The resulting allocation is $44,000 to P1, $12,000 to P2 and $44,000 to FR. Now P1's cost share exceeds its stand-alone cost by $4,000. This difference is assigned to FR. The final costs allocated are $40,000 to P1, $12,000 to P2 and $48,000 to FR.

The effect of this method is least costly segments benefit less, if at all, from participating in a joint effort than larger segments. This may be sufficient for cost measurement but could have at least two unintended effects. First, the method is based on an underlying assumption a segment's size is reflected in its cost and larger segments cause more cost savings than smaller segments. In voluntary nonprofits, cost may not reflect size since many inputs are contributed. Second, P1 and P2 are not motivated to participate with FR because no cost savings accrue to them.

EXHIBIT 2
METHOD 1: ACTIVITY-BASED COST ALLOCATIONS

Panel 1

Activity	Proportions			Total
	P1	P2	FR	
Weight	30.00%	15.00%	55.00%	100%
Specific identification	30.50	9.50	60.00	100
Quantity of envelopes	33.33	33.33	33.33	100
Number of pieces in envelope	50.00	25.00	25.00	100

Panel 2

Item	Assumed Total	Allocations		
		P1	P2	FR
Postage	$ 35,000	$10,500	$5,250	$19,250
Printing	50,000	15,250	4,750	30,000
Envelopes	6,000	2,000	2,000	2,000
Handling	9,000	4,500	2,250	2,250
Total	$100,000	$32,250	$14,250	$53,500

Panel 3

Item	Assumed Total	Allocations		
		P1	P2	FR
Postage	$ 35,000	$10,500	$5,250	$19,250
Printing	50,000	15,250	4,750	30,000
Envelopes	6,000	2,000	2,000	2,000
Handling	9,000	6,000	0	3,000
Total	$100,000	$33,750	$12,000	$54,250

EXHIBIT 3
METHOD 4: ALLOCATION IN PROPORTION TO COST SAVINGS

	P1	P2	FR	Total
Stand-alone cost	$40,000	$12,000	$65,000	$117,000
Incremental cost (a)	25,000	11,800	55,800	92,600
Benefits	$15,000	$ 200	$ 9,200	$ 24,400
Proportion	61.48%	0.82%	37.70%	100%
Allocation (b)	$ 4,550	$ 60	$ 2,790	$ 7,400
Total (a + b)	$29,550	$11,860	$58,590	$100,000

Method 3: Allocate on the basis of standalone cost. This method, which ensures all participants benefit, allocates a joint effort's cost in proportion to the amount of cost that would have been incurred separately. P1's stand-alone cost is 34,188% ($40,000 ÷ $117,000) of the total stand-alone cost. Applying this rate to the $100,000 joint cost results in P1 being assigned $34,188. P2's and FR's stand-alone costs are 10.256% and 55.556%, respectively, resulting in $10,256 being assigned to P2 and $55,256 to FR. As in method 2, implicit in this method is the assumption the segment with the largest cost causes the biggest savings and thus should receive the largest benefit. Unlike method 2, it provides an incentive for all three participants to act jointly.

Method 4: Allocate in proportion to cost savings. An allocation method that reflects benefits received from the group effort is one that allocates joint costs in direct proportion to segment's actual cost savings. Exh. 3, above, shows the proportionate savings (benefits from participating in the group effort) as the difference between a segment's stand-alone cost and its incremental cost of joining the group.

Exh. 1 shows the joint cost of P2 and FR acting together is $75,000. Adding P1 to P2, FR changes the total joint cost to $100,000, a $25,000 incremental increase. Comparing P1's incremental cost to its $40,000 stand-alone cost results in a $15,000 benefit to P1 if it joins P2, FR. Continuing with this logic, if P2 joins P1, FR, the difference between its stand-alone cost and its related incremental cost is $200. If FR joins P1, P2, its benefit is $9,200.

These benefits provide a basis for allocating the cost savings of acting together. That is, given the sum of the incremental costs, $92,600 for all participants, and a joint cost of $100,000, the benefit to be allocated is the difference, $7,400. Allocating this amount based on the proportion of benefit received results in P1 being assigned $4,550 (61.48% × $7,400). The 61.48% is found by dividing $15,000 by $24,400. P2 receives $60 (0.82% × $7,400) and FR

receives $2,790 (37.70% × $7,400). Each segment's allocation of benefits plus its incremental cost is the share of the joint cost assigned to it.

REASONABLE AND FAIR ALLOCATION

Joint cost allocations in nonprofit organizations can influence perceptions of organizational stewardship. Because of this, it is incumbent on auditors to evaluate carefully the application of SOP no. 87-2 and the cost-allocation methods chosen, ensuring these allocations are reasonable and fair.

While the above allocations do not cover all circumstances, they provide insight on the effects of different allocation assumptions on measurements of program and fund-raising costs and provide some guidance in evaluating a nonprofit's allocations. Perhaps this will suggest other ways of evaluating reasonableness in cost allocation.

To improve implementation of SOP no. 87-2, the AICPA accounting standards executive committee has authorized the not-for-profit organizations committee to undertake a project to draft guidance in the form of an SOP clarifying or perhaps revising certain aspects of SOP no. 87-2.

Chapter 15
The Flexible Budget and Standard Costing: Direct Materials and Direct Labor

Cases

15-1   Standard Cost Variance Analysis
15-2   Standard Costing and Revision of Standards
15-3   Standard Cost Variance Analysis

Readings

Carole B. Cheatham and Leo R. Cheatham: Redesigning Cost Systems: Is Standard Costing Obsolete?

The article shows some new ways to analyze standard costs data, going beyond the traditional emphasis of production costs variances which focus on price and efficiency. Variances for product quality are developed and explained, as well as sales variances based on sales orders received and orders actually shipped. There is also a discussion of how to incorporate activity-based costing, and continuous standard improvement, including benchmarking and target costing.

Discussion Questions:
1. What are the main criticisms of traditional standard cost systems?
2. What is meant by "push through" production? Is it preferred to "pull through" production, and why?
3. What are the best ways to make standard cost systems more dynamic?
4. Consider the suggestions made in this article in contrast to chapter 15's presentation of standard costing. Which ideas make the most sense to you, and why?

Cases

15-1. Standard Cost Variance Analysis

(Variance analysis and report; IMA case adapted) Henry Pacer is the general manager for the Ace Chemicals Division. Following is his division's Income Statement for the month just completed.

	Thousands of $'s	
	Actual	**Budget**
Sales	14,005	12,600
Cost of Goods Sold (COGS)	11,605	9,960
Gross Profit	2,400	2,640
Other Expense	705	640
Operating Income	1,695	2,000
Other Income	105	200
Pre-Tax Income	1,800	2,200
Income Taxes	900	1,100
Net Income	900	1,100

Henry knew before receiving the statement that sales were above budget for the month and that the effect of recent price increases on most products would be realized this month. As you would expect, he was very upset upon finding his income results were below budget, while his sales were more than 10% above budget. He has asked the accounting department for an immediate explanation. The accounting department has looked at its detailed budget and found the following data:

	Sales (in millions of pound)	Price Per Pound	Cost of Sales (per pound)	Profit (In $millions)
Product 1	2,000	.600	.600	0
Product 2	5,000	.800	.650	750
Product 3	7,000	.200	.120	560
Product 4	4,000	1.500	1.140	1,440
				2,750

Start-up and obsolescence charges were budgeted for $110M per month. Included in the budget for November were the following unfavorable volume variances:

	M$
Product 1	100
Product 2	—
Product 3	50
Product 4	100
Total loss	250

Following is a Gross Profit Report for the division for the month of November.

Product	Sales (M lbs)	Price ($/lb)	Sales (M$)	COGS (M$)	Gross Profit (M$)	% of Gross Profit
1	2,845	.735	2,091	1,692	399	19.1
2	3,280	.023	3,335	3,240	115	3.4
3	7,340	.195	1,431	991	440	30.7
4	4,320	.650	7,128	5,400	1,728	24.2
Start-up Product 2				257	(267)	—
Obsolescence Product 2			____	25	(25)	—
Total Division			14,005	11,605	2,400	17.1%

VARIANCES INCLUDED IN COGS WERE (M$) ( ) = Loss or Unfavorable

	Raw Mat'l/ utility prices	Performance	Volume	Total
Product 1	(225)	12	(20)	(233)
Product 2	(222)	82	(600)	(740)
Product 3	(146)	6	(50)	(190)
Product 4	(350)	(224)	(200)	(774)
	(943)	(124)	(870)	(1,937)

REQUIRED:

Provide Henry with the appropriate analysis of his business results (net income) for the month.

15-2. Standard Costing and Revision of Standards

(Changes of Standards; CMA adapted) NuLathe Co. produces a turbo engine component for jet aircraft manufacturers. A standard cost system has been used for years with good results.

Unfortunately, NuLathe has recently experienced production problems. The source for its direct materials went out of business. The new source produces similar but higher quality materials. The price per pound from the original source has averaged $7.00, while the price from the new source is $7.77. The use of the new materials does result in a reduction in scrap that lowers the actual consumption of direct materials from 1.25 to 1.00 pounds per unit. In addition, the direct labor is reduced from 24 to 22 minutes per unit because there is less scrap labor and machine setup time.

The direct materials problem was occurring at the same time that labor negotiations resulted in an increase of over 14 percent in hourly direct labor costs. The average rate rose from $12.60 per hour to $14.40 per hour. Production of the main product requires a high level of labor skill. Because of a continuing shortage in that skill area, an interim wage agreement had to be signed.

NuLathe started using the new direct materials on April 1 of this year, the same day the new labor agreement went into effect. The firm has been using standards that were set at the beginning of the calendar year. The direct materials and direct labor standards for the turbo engine are as follows.

Direct materials	1.2 lbs. @ $6.80/lb.	$ 8.16
Direct labor	120 min. @ $12.30 DLH	4.10
Standard prime cost per unit		$12.26

Howard Foster, Cost Accounting Supervisor, had been examining the performance report shown below that he had prepared at the close of business on April 30. Jane Keene, Assistant Controller, came into Foster's office, and Howard said, "Jane, look at this performance report. Direct materials price increased 11 percent and the labor rate increased over 14 percent during April. I expected greater variances, yet prime costs decreased over five percent from the $13.79 we experienced during the first quarter of this year. The proper message just isn't coming through."

"This has been an unusual period," said Jane. "With the unforeseen changes, perhaps we should revise our standards based on current conditions and start over."

Howard replied, "I think we can retain the current standards but expand the variance analysis. We could calculate variances for the specific changes that have occurred to direct materials and direct labor before we calculate the normal price and quantity variances. What I really think would be useful to management right now is to determine the impact the changes in direct labor had in reducing our prime costs per unit from $13.79 in the first quarter to $13.05 in April--a reduction of $.874."

NuLathe Co.
Analysis of Unit Prime Costs
Standrad Cost Variance Analysis for April

	Standard	Price Variance	Quantity/Variance	Actual
Direct materials	$6.8 x 1.2 = $8.16	($7.77 – $6.80) 1.0 = $.97U	(1- 1.2) x $6.8 = $1.36F	$7.77 x 1 = $7.77
Direct labor	$12.3 x 1/3 = $ 4.10 $12.26	($14.4 – $12.3) x 22/60 =$.77U	(22/60 – 20/60) x $12.30 = $ .41U	$14.4 x 22/60 = $5.28 $13.05

217

Comparison of Actual Costs

	First Quarter Costs	April Costs Increase (Decrease)	Percentage Costs
Direct materials	$ 8.75	$ 7.77	(11.2)%
Direct labor	5.04	5.28	4.8%
	$13.79	$13.05	(5.4)%

REQUIRED:

1. Discuss the advantages of:

    a. immediately revising the standards.

    b. retaining the current standards and expanding the analysis of variances.

2. Prepare an analysis that reflects the impact the new direct materials and new labor contract had on reducing NuLathe Co.'s prime costs per unit from $13.79 in the first quarter to $13.05 in April. The analysis should show the changes in prime costs per unit that are due to the:

    a. use of new direct materials.

    b. new labor contract.

    This analysis should be in sufficient detail to identify the changes due to:

    a. direct materials price.

    b. direct labor rate.

    c. the effect of direct materials quality on direct materials usage.

218

15-3. Standard Cost Variance Analysis

1. (CMA adapted) Allglow Company is a cosmetics manufacturer specializing in stage makeup. The company's best selling product is to protect the skin from frequent use of makeup. SkinKlear is packaged in three sizes—8 ounces, one pound, and three pounds—and regularly sells for $21.00 per pound. The standard cost per pound of SkinKlear, based on Allglow's normal monthly production of 8,000 pounds, is as follows:

Cost Item	Quantity	Unit Cost	Standard Total Cost
Cream base	9.0 oz.	.05/oz.	$ .45
Moisturizer	6.5 oz.	.10/oz.	.65
Fragrance	.5 oz.	1.00/oz	.50
			$ 1.60
Direct labor*			
Mixing	.5 hr	$4.00/hr.	$ 2.00
Compounding	1.0 hr.	5.00/hr.	5.00
			$ 7.00
Variable overhead**	1.5hr	$2.10/hr	$ 3.15
Total standard cost per pound			$11.75

*Direct labor dollars include employee benefits.
**Applied on the basis of direct labor hours.

Based on these standard costs, Allglow prepares monthly budgets. Presented below are the budgeted performance and actual performance for May 19x6 when the company produced and sold 9,000 pounds of SkinKlear.

Contribution Report for SkinKlear for the Month of May 19x6:

	Budget	Actual	Variance	
Units	8,000	9,000	1,000	F
Revenue	$168,000	$180,000	$12,000	F
Direct Materials	12,800	16,200	3,400	U
Direct labor	56,000	62,500	6,500	U
Variable overhead	25,200	30,900	5,700	U
Total variable costs	$ 94,000	$109,600	$15,600	U
Contribution margin	$ 74,000	$ 70,400	$ 3,600	U

Barbara Simmons, Allglow's President, was not pleased with these results; despite a sizeable increase in the sales of SkinKlear, there was a decrease in the product's contribution to the overall profitability of the firm. Barbara has asked Allglow's Cost Accountant, Brian Jackson, to prepare a report that identifies the reasons why the contribution margin for SkinKlear has decreased. Brian has gathered the information presented in the next column to help in the preparation of the report.

May 19x6 Usage Report for SkinKlear

Cost Item	Quantity	Actual Cost
Direct materials		
Cream base	84,000 oz.	$ 4,200
Moisturizer	60,000 oz.	7,200
Fragrance	4,800 oz.	4,800
Direct labor		
Mixing	4,500 hr.	18,000
Compounding-manual	5,300 hr.	26,500
Compounding-mechanized	2,700 hr.	13,500
Compounding-idle	900 hr.	4,500
Variable overhead		30,900
Total variable cost		$109,600

While doing his research, Brian discovered that the Manufacturing Department had mechanized one of the manual operations in the compounding process on an experimental basis. The mechanized operation replaced manual operations that represented 40 percent of the compounding process.

The workers' inexperience with the mechanized operation caused increased usage of both the cream base and the moisturizer; however, Brian believed these inefficiencies would be negligible if mechanization became a permanent part of the process and the workers' skills were improved. The idle time in compounding was traceable to the fact that fewer workers were required for the mechanized process. During this experimental period, the idle time was charged to direct labor rather than overhead. The excess workers could either be reassigned or laid off in the future. Brian also was able to determine that all the variable manufacturing overhead costs over standard could be traced directly to the mechanization process.

REQUIRED:

1. Prepare an explanation of the $3,600 unfavorable variance between the budgeted and actual contribution margin for SkinKlear during May 19x6 by calculating the following variances.

   1. Sales price variance.

   2. Materials price variance.

   3. Materials quantity variance.

   4. Labor efficiency variance.

   5. Variable overhead efficiency variance.

   6. Variable overhead spending variance.

   7. Contribution margin volume variance.

2. Allglow Company must decide whether or not the compounding operation in the SkinKlear manufacturing process that was mechanized on an experimental basis should continue to be mechanized. Calculate the variable cost savings that can be expected to arise in the future from the mechanization. Explain your answer.

Redesigning Cost Systems: Is Standard Costing Obsolete?

By Carole B. Cheatham and Leo B. Cheatham,
Professors at Northeast Louisana University.

***SYNOPSIS: Since the early 1980s standard cost
systems (SCSs) have been under attack as not
providing the information needed for advanced
manufacturers. In spite of its critics, SCSs are still
the system of choice in some 86 percent of U.S.
manufacturing firms.***

***This paper discusses the criticisms of SCSs that (1)
the variances are obsolete, (2) there is not provision
for continuous improvement, and (3) use of the
variances for responsibility accounting result in
internal conflict rather than cooperation. Updates
for SCSs in the form of redesigned variances,
suggestions for dynamic standards, and refocused
responsibility and reporting systems are presented.***

***The compatibility of SCSs and its main competitor
as a cost system, activity-based costing (ABC), is
examined. The authors discuss when it is
appropriate to use ABC or SCS or some combination
of the two.***

Since Eli Goldratt's (1983) charge that cost
accounting is the number one enemy of productivity
in the early 1980s, traditional cost systems have been
under attack. Although Goldratt subsequently
softened his stand to say that *cost* rather than
accounting was the culprit (Jayson 1987), others were
quick to jump on the bandwagon to condemn the cost
systems in use. New systems were proposed of which
the most popular was activity-based costing (ABC).

In spite of all the criticism, a 1988 survey shows
86 percent of U.S. manufacturers using standard cost
systems (Cornick et al. 1988). A survey by Schiff
(1993) indicates that 36 percent of companies use
activity-based costing, but only 25 percent of those
use it to replace their traditional cost system. It would
seem that only about 9 percent (25 percent of the 36
percent) of companies are using ABC as their main
system while the vast majority use a standard cost
system (SCS).

This is not to say that traditional SCSs could not
benefit from being updated. However, accountants in
industry (as well as academia) seem unaware that a
redesigned SCS can provide the information they
need, and that updating their present system is an
easier process than adopting a new system. The SCS
is one vehicle of articulation among managerial,
financial and operations accounting, and it is a *control*
system while the candidates for its replacement
typically are only cost *accumulation* systems.

In this article the major criticisms of SCSs are
examined along with ways that the weaknesses can be
remedied or ameliorated. The criticisms relate to the
use of specific variances, the lack of provision for
continuous improvement, and the fact that
administration of the system results in internal
competition rather than cooperation. The appropriate
use of ABC systems in conjunction with SCSs is also
discussed.

FIGURE 1
VARIANCES RELATING TO MATERIAL PURCHASING

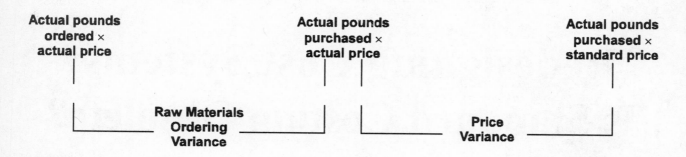

UPDATING THE VARIANCES IN AN SCS

Concerning the variables analyzed in an SCS, most criticisms center on the overemphasis on price and efficiency to the exclusion of quality. Other criticisms center on the use of the volume variance to measure utilization of capacity while ignoring overproduction and unnecessary buildups of inventory. In making such charges, critics fail to realize variance analysis is not "locked-in" to a particular set of variables. Standards are only benchmarks of what performance should be. The particular variables used can be changed as the need arises.

The following discussion focuses on concerns of the new manufacturing environment—raw material ordering and inventory levels, quality, production levels, finished goods inventory levels and completion of sales orders.

Variances Pertaining to Raw Materials

The set of variances in Fig. 1 centers on the function of raw material ordering and inventory levels (Harrell 1992). The Raw Material Ordering Variance gives information about the effectiveness of suppliers. It contrasts the raw materials ordered with the raw materials delivered (purchased). Any variation may be considered unfavorable because the goal is to have orders delivered as placed. Too much delivered will result in unnecessary buildups of raw material stocks. Too little delivered is unfavorable because production delays may result.

The Price Variance in Fig. 1 is the traditional price variance computed on materials purchased. This variance has been criticized on the grounds that overemphasis on price leads purchasing managers to ignore quality. However, price is a legitimate concern that should not be overlooked. This system also uses a Quality Variance (presented in a following section). If low quality materials are purchased in order to gain a low price, this will result in an unfavorable Quality Variance.

Variances Pertaining to Material Inventories and Efficient Use

The set of variances in Fig. 2 focuses on raw material inventory levels and quantity or efficiency of material use.

The Raw Materials Inventory Variance (Harrell 1992) shows either more material purchased than used (an inventory buildup) or more material used than purchased (an inventory decrease). With the JIT philosophy, purchasing more than used causes an unfavorable variance, while decreasing previous buildups causes a favorable variance.

The Efficiency Variance in Fig. 2 is based on the difference between the actual pounds of material used and the standard amount for *total* production. The traditional Efficiency or Quantity Variance is the difference between the actual pounds of material used and the standard amount for *good* production. The traditional variance is actually as combination of quality and efficiency factors. As can be seen in the next section, quality is better treated in a separate variance.

FIGURE 2
VARIANCES RELATED TO MATERIAL USAGE

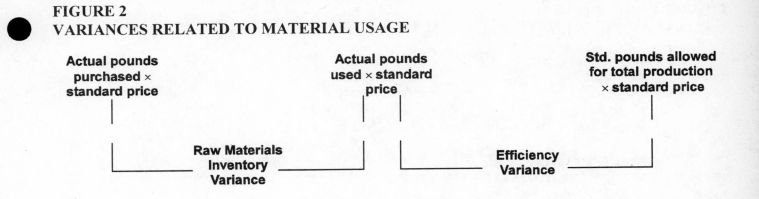

Variances Pertaining to Production Levels and Quality

The next set of variances (Fig. 3) turns from input analysis to output analysis and relates to production levels and quality. All cost factors are included in the "standard cost per unit" including labor and overhead.

The Quality Variance is the standard cost of units produced that did not meet specifications (the difference between total units produced and good units produced). In traditional variance analysis, this variance is buried in the efficiency variances of the various inputs.

Ignoring labor and overhead, suppose a company used two pounds of material per finished unit at a standard cost of $1.00 per pound. Further assume they used 4,900 pounds in the production of 2,500 total units, of which 100 were defective. Traditional variance analysis would show an unfavorable Efficiency Variance of $100 computed on the difference between the standard cost of the 4,800 pounds that should have been used to produce the 2,400 good units and the 4,900 pounds actually used.

A better breakdown of the traditional variance shows a favorable Efficiency Variance of $100 and an unfavorable Quality Variance of $200. The Production Department did use only 4,800 pounds to produce 2,500 units that should have taken 5,000 pounds. The fact that some of these units were defective should appear as a Quality Variance, as it does in this analysis. The Quality Variance is $200 unfavorable representing $2.00 per unit invested in 100 defective units.

This analysis also yields a Production Variance based on the difference between the standard cost of

FIGURE 3
VARIANCES RELATED TO QUALITY AND PRODUCTION LEVELS

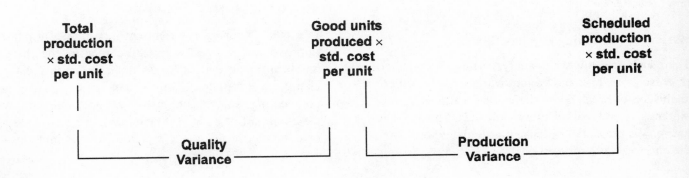

FIGURE 4
VARIANCES RELATED TO SALES

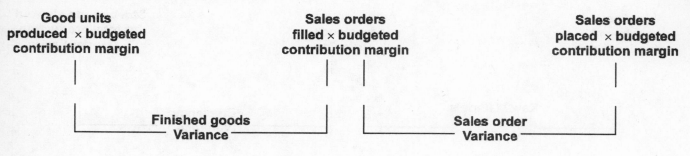

good units produced and the scheduled amount of production. The goal in advanced manufacturing environments is to produce exactly what is needed for sales orders (scheduled production). A variance from scheduled production either way is unfavorable because too much production results in unnecessary buildups of inventory while too little results in sales orders not filled. As is the case with the Raw Material Inventory variance, the critical factor is the cost of the capital invested in excess inventories. It is desirable to highlight this cost in responsibility reports by applying a cost of capital figure. to the excess (Cheatham 1989).

For simplicity's sake, the above illustrations of input analysis pertain to materials. Labor and volume-related variable overhead can be analyzed in a similar manner. Since there is no difference between labor purchased and labor used in production, the labor input variances would include the traditional Rate Variance and the updated Efficiency Variance. Other than showing a budget variance for the various elements of fixed overhead, there is no point in further analysis in terms of a Volume Variance. The updated Production Variance serves the same purpose in a far better fashion.

Variances Pertaining to Sales Analysis

There are various ways to analyze sales. One method is to use price, mix and volume variances. A further analysis is to break down the volume variance into market size and market share variances. The analysis in Fig. 4 is presented because it articulates well with the output analysis for production.

The sales variances indicate customer service as well as the cost of lost sales. The variances use budgeted contribution margin as a measure of opportunity cost. The Finished Goods Variance indicates the opportunity cost associated with orders completed but not shipped. A delay in shipment causes a loss because of subsequent delay in receiving payment. The Sales Order Variance represents the opportunity cost associated with sales orders that could not be filled during the time period for whatever reason—lack of capacity, scheduling problems, etc.

The above discussion presents a variety of variances that are not used in a traditional standard cost system. The variances can be used for control purposes alone or can be integrated into the financial accounting records (Cheatham and Cheatham 1993). The system is not intended to be a generic solution for any company's needs. It is intended to demonstrate that, with a little creativity, it is possible to redesign SCSs to measure variables that are important to a particular company in today's manufacturing environment.

UPDATING THE SCS FOR CONTINUOUS IMPROVEMENT

In a manufacturing environment in which continuous improvement is a goal of most companies, the charge has been made that SCSs do not encourage positive change. However, static standards based on engineering studies or historical data are not an essential part of an SCS. Standards can be adjusted to be dynamic, or changing, by any of several methods.

Using Prior Periods' Results as Standards

One way to have dynamic standards is to use last period's results as standards. This idea has been advocated in the past as a way for small business to have the benefits of standards without the expense of engineering studies (Lawler and Livingstone 1986; Cheatham 1987). The objection can be made that last period's results may not make very good standards if last period was unrepresentative for whatever reason. If this is the case, last period's results can be modified.

Another variation on using past performances as standards is the use of a base period. Comparisons can be made with the base period and all subsequent periods, if desired. Boer (1991, 40) describes a system of using a base year as a "pseudo flexible budget" from which unit costs are developed. He comments that the system "encourages continuous improvement and never implies that a level of performance is adequate. Instead, it encourages managers to improve continuously."

Still another variation on using prior periods' results as standards is the use of best performance-to-date (BP). BP is a rigorous standard for self-improvement because it motivates workers as well as managers to exceed all past performance.

Using Benchmarking

Although past performance costs may be used in a variety of ways to formulate dynamic standards, any such system has an inward focus. Benchmarking looks outside the firm to the performance of industry leaders or competitors. Benchmarking typically is applied to performance measures rather than standard costs. However, using the performance of industry leaders as a standard provides motivation to become world-class in much the same fashion.

The primary barrier to use of benchmarking standards is, of course, lack of information. Edward S. Finein (1990), former vice president and chief engineer of Xerox, lists the following sources of information when using benchmarking for performance measures: (1) external reports and trade publications; (2) professional associations; (3) market research and surveys; (4) industry experts; (5) consultants' studies; (6) company visits; and (7) competitive labs. In the absence of hard information, an approach may be taken to estimate the performance of industry leaders. Trying to meet the supposed standards of industry leaders (or other competitors) can have results that are useful as long as the company is striving toward beneficial goals.

Using Moving Costs Reductions

Still another way to have dynamic standards is through use of predetermined cost reductions. Horngren et al. (1994) describe a system of what they call a "continuous improvement standard cost" or a "moving cost reduction standard cost." This system reduces the standard cost by a predetermined percentage each time period, such as a one percent reduction in standard cost per month computed by setting the new standard at 99 percent of the previous month's standard.

The question that their system raises is how to determine the amount of the cost reduction. One possibility is the use of cost improvement curves. Cost improvement curves are a new variation of the old learning curve idea. Learning curves were based on reduction of direct labor costs due to learning by the workers. With a large percentage of product conversion being brought about by automated equipment rather than laborers, potential cost reductions relate to the experience factor for the organization as a whole which may be measured by cost improvement curves.

Pattison and Teplitz (1989) calculate the new rate of learning for an organization that replaces labor with automated equipment as:

$$Rate_{new} = Rate_{old} + (1 - Rate_{old}) * L * R$$

where $Rate_{old}$ is the rate of learning for the old system, L is the proportion of learning attributed solely to direct labor stated as a percentage, and R is the proportion of direct labor being replaced. The formula actually reduces the learning rate applicable to labor only, the assumption being that workers can learn but not machinery. An updated version of the formula is needed which encompasses factors such as managers', supervisors' and engineers' experience.

The Japanese stress the formula 2V=2/3C, or if volume is doubled, the cost should be two-thirds of what it was originally. This formula equates to a 67 percent learning curve which represents a high degree of learning. However, their attitude is that learning does not just happen—it should be made to happen.

Using Target Costs

Another idea borrowed from the Japanese is the use of target costs based on the market. Target costs are used in Japan primarily for new products that are still in the design stage. The idea is to set a cost that is low enough to permit a selling price that is viable on the market. The price is the starting point for calculating costs, and the various costs are backed out from the price. Typically, the target cost is very low. Hiromoto (1988) describes the use of target costs at the Daihatsu Motor company. First, a product development order is issued. Then an "allowable cost" per car is calculated by taking the difference between the target selling price and the profit margin. Then each department calculates an "accumulated

cost" based on the standard cost achievable with current technology. Finally, a target cost is set somewhere between the allowable and accumulated cost. All this takes place before the product is designed. The design stage typically takes three years. When the product is finally in production, the target cost is gradually tightened on a monthly basis. Later the actual cost of the previous period is used to drive costs down further.

Market-based target costs have a strong appeal on a basis for standard costs because they focus on the customer rather than on internal engineering capabilities. However, using target costs is easiest with new products because as much as 90 percent of product costs are set in the design stage (Berliner and Brimson 1988). The way a product is designed determines the way it has to be manufactured and sets the stage for further cost reductions.

Standard costs do not have to be static. Dynamic

FIGURE 5
WORK CELL A
VARIANCE TRADE-OFF REPORT FOR MONTH OF JULY 19X6

Raw Materials:

	Price	Quantity	Total
Material X	100 F	200 U	100 U
Material Y	50 F	100 U	50 U
Material Z	200 F	150 F	350 F
Total	350 F	150 U	200 F

Labor:

	Rate	Efficiency	Total
Type A	400 F	200 F	600 F
Type B	550 U	250 F	300 U
Total	150 U	450 F	300 F

Traceable Overhead Variances:

	Spending	Efficiency	Total
Power	150 F	50 U	100 F
Supplies	100 U	10 U	110 U
Other	50 F	10 F	60 F
Total	100 F	50 U	50 F

Quality Variance on Dept. A Contribution to Product Cost
100 Defective Units @ $7.00   700 U

Total   150 U

standards can be formulated using a variety of methods including past performance, industry leader's performance, or target costs based on predetermined reductions or the market. Market-based target costs have the most intuitive appeal because the focus is on the future and on the customer. However, they may work better for new products rather than for established products.

UPDATING MANAGEMENT RESPONSIBILITY AND REPORTING

Besides revamping the SCS to better reflect today's concerns in terms of variables to be measured and continuous improvement, there needs to be improved reporting of variances. Old reporting systems tended to foster internal competition and arguments about whose department was to blame for unfavorable variances. There needs to be an attitude of cooperation among workers, managers and departments.

Revised lines of responsibility used with new plant layouts are improving some of the competitive attitudes that once prevailed in manufacturing organizations. Plants that used to feature "push through" production with large masses of raw materials and semifinished product moving from one process to another are changing to work cells or similar arrangements. The work cell arrangement features equipment that can process a product from start to finish. Workers in the work cell typically can operate all or several types of machinery. This leaner "pull through" approach allows a sales order to be rapidly processed within the work cell which decreases cycle time and holds work in process and finished goods inventories to a minimum.

The work cell arrangement allows a team of workers to be responsible for the entire product and reduces the likelihood that defects will be passed along to the next department. Along with the work cell arrangement many companies are decentralizing functions such as engineering and making these personnel responsible for a particular work area or product line. With the decentralization, there is more focused responsibility. Decentralization and a team approach to production eliminates many conflicts that once existed.

In addition to the new attitudes about responsibility, there needs to be improved reporting. The variances outlined in this paper can be reported in two types of management reports. The report illustrated in Fig. 5 shows the trade-offs between price, efficiency and quality. This type of report can be done on a plant level or department level as well as a work cell level. The price variance for work cells or departments should be computed on material used rather than purchased because this gives a better picture of the trade-offs involved. Upper-level management reports should probably show both types of price variances if there are significant differences between purchases and use.

FIGURE 6
PROFITABLE MANUFACTURING COMPANY
EXCESS INVENTORY REPORT FOR MONTH OF JULY 19X6

	Cost	Cost of Capital
Raw Materials		
Excess from previous month	$5,000	$ 50
Current inventory variance	3,000 F	($ 30)
Total	$2,000	$ 20
Work in Process		
Cell A Production variance	$4,000 U	$ 40
Cell B Production variance	$1,000 U	$ 10
Total	$5,000 U	$ 50
Total Excess and Cost of Capital	$7,000 U	$ 70

Finished Goods:	Cost	Contribution
Finished goods variance	$ 5,000 F	$(1,500)
Sales order variance	3,000 U	2,400
Total	$ 3,000 U	$ 900
Total Cost of Capital and Lost Contribution Margins		$ 970

The report illustrated in Fig. 6 shows the effects of variances related to inventories. Raw material excesses at cost, related to both current and past purchases, are listed along with the related cost of capital. In this case it is assumed the excess was held the entire month and the cost of capital was one percent. Work in Process excesses are measured in terms of the Production Variance. This variance measures the difference between scheduled and actual production. Presumably if there were excesses from the previous month, there was an adjustment made in the scheduled production. Cost of capital figures show the effect of holding these excess inventories.

In the case of Finished Goods, the crucial factor is the opportunity cost of sales orders not filled measured by the lost contribution margins. Therefore, if orders are completed but not shipped or there is an inability to fill a sales order because of lack of capacity, this is indicated by the Finished Goods Variance or the Sales Order Variance. The illustration assumes a favorable Finished Goods Variance because more sales orders were filled than units

produced, indicating a decrease in previous finished goods stock.

Although a reporting system such as that illustrated in figures 5 and 6 may not eliminate all conflicts, it is certainly helpful to recognize that trade-offs occur. It is also beneficial for upper-level managers to see the cost of excesses or deficiencies in inventories measured in terms of lost contribution margins and cost of capital.

STANDARD COST SYSTEMS AND ABC

A final consideration in updating SCSs is how an SCS relates to ABC. Although ABC potentially has broader uses, it primarily has been used for manufacturing overhead.

When a company has a significant amount of indirect product cost, ABC results in better product costing because ABC is superior for allocating these costs among products. This permits company managers to more knowledgeably price products.

However, ABC is a cost *accumulation* system rather than a cost *control* system. When used with process value analysis (PVA) or activity based management (ABM), ABC can have a cost *management* feature, but there is no day-to-day monitoring system to assure that costs are within certain parameters.

Most companies can benefit from some combination of ABC and an SCS. One possibility is use of ABC for indirect costs and an updated SCS for direct costs. Another possibility is use of an SCS for financial records and ABC for analysis of indirect costs outside the main record-keeping system. A combination of the two systems retains the advantages of the superior control features of an SCS with the benefits of better overhead analysis from ABC.

CONCLUSION

SCSs are not really the dinosaurs of cost systems, but they may benefit from a little evolution. Updated variances along with dynamic standards will vastly improve the usefulness of most SCSs. ABC can coexist with an SCS and bring some order to the general area of indirect costs. Improvements in the reporting of variances can allow managers to assess trade-offs and inventory stocks and their impact on profits.

REFERENCES

Berliner, C., and J. Brimson, eds. 1988. Cost Management for Today's Advanced Manufacturing: The CAM-I Conceptual Design. Boston: Harvard Business School Press.

Boer, G.B. 1991. Making accounting a value-added activity. Management Accounting 73 (August): 36–41.

Cheatham, C. 1987. Profit and productivity analysis revisited. Journal of Accountancy 164 (July): 123–130.

_____. 1989. Reporting the effects of excess inventories. Journal of Accountancy 168 (November): 131–140.

_____, and L. Cheatham. 1993. Updating Standard Cost Systems. Westport, CT: Quorum Books.

Cornick, M., W. Cooper, and S. Wilson. 1988. How do companies analyze overhead? Management Accounting 69 (June): 41–43.

Finein, E.S. 1990. Benchmarking for superior quality and performance. Performance Measurement for Manufacturers Seminar, Institutes for International Research (October).

Goldratt, E.M. 1983. Cost accounting is enemy number one of productivity. International Conference Proceedings, American Production and Inventory Control Society (October).

Harrell, H. 1992. Materials variance analysis and JIT: A new approach. Management Accounting 73 (May): 33–38.

Hiromoto, T. 1988. Another hidden edge—Japanese management accounting. Harvard Business Review 69 (July-August): 22–26.

Horngren, C. et al. 1994. Cost Accounting: A Managerial Approach. 8th ed. Englewood Cliffs, NJ: Prentice Hall: 246.

Jayson, S. 1987. Goldratt & Fox: Revolutionizing the factory floor. Management Accounting 68 (May): 18–22.

Lawler, W., and J. Livingstone. 1986. Profit and productivity analysis for small business. Journal of Accountancy 163 (December): 190–196.

Noreen, E. 1991. Conditions under which activity-based cost systems provide relevant costs. Journal of Management Accounting Research 3 (Fall): 159–168.

Pattison, D., and C. Teplitz 1989. Are learning curves still relevant? Management Accounting 71 (February): 37–40.

Schiff, J. 1993. ABC on the rise. Cost Management Update Issue No. 24 (February). In Cost Accounting: A Managerial Emphasis, 1991, cited by C. Horngren, G. Foster, and S. Datar, 161. Englewood. Cliffs, NJ; Prentice Hall, Inc.

Chapter 16
Standard Costing: Factory Overhead

Cases
16-1   Standard Cost Variance Analysis

Readings

Jean C. Cooper and James D. Suver: Variance Analysis Refines Overhead Cost Control
This article takes the example of a healthcare organization that is attempting to analyze the full costs of selected medical procedures. A key feature of the analysis is how the overhead variances are handled, and in particular how to develop an understanding of the volume variance and how it affects profitability. Standard costs are determined for a hypothetical "Procedure 101" and there is an illustration of how variances can be obtained and interpreted, given example actual results for the procedure over a year's time. The analysis shows the effect of volume changes on overhead recovery and on profit contribution.

Discussion Questions:
1. What is the key driver of profitability based on the analysis in this article?
2. Explain how the two variances are developed and interpreted in Exhibit 3.
3. Consider the example in Exhibit 4. Why are expenses improperly matched and reported income overstated?

Robert E. Malcolm: Overhead Control Implications of Activity Costing
This articles points out some of the limitations of the traditional treatment of standard cost overhead variances. An example problem from the CMA exam is used as an illustration. The problem is solved both in a traditional format and also using activity-based cost drivers. Regression is used to identify the cost drivers, and a revised solution is derived.

Discussion Questions:
1. What are the limitations of standard cost overhead analysis?
2. How does the activity approach improve upon the standard cost analysis of overhead?

16-1. Standard Cost Variance Analysis

(**CMA, STRATEGY**) Paste Products manufactures paste for commercial customers that is marketed in ten-gallon metal containers. Always cost conscientious, the firm uses a standard cost system that is revised annually on November 1, the start of the company's fiscal year. Paste Products uses the standard costs to evaluate performance and prepares monthly variance reports for this purpose. The revised standard cost card that has been developed for commercial paste for the 20x6-7 fiscal year is shown below.

Standard Cost for Commercial Paste
One Ten-Gallon container

			Unit Cost	
Direct materials				
2 lbs monocloro		$ 6.00/lb	$12.00	
1 lb oxotone		.80/lb	.80	
4 gals distilled water		.30/gal	1.20	$14.00
Direct labor	2 hour	11.00/hr.	2.20	
Variable overhead				
.2 hours maintenance		15.00/hr.	$ 3.00	
.2 hours supplies		1.00/hr.	.20	
.2 hours indirect labor		18.00/hr.	3.60	6.80
Fixed overhead	.2 hours	2.00/hr.	.40	
Total standard cost			$23.40	

The composition of Paste Products' fixed factory overhead and the annual budget for the current fiscal year is as follows:

Factory supervision	$130,000
Contract maintenance	40,000
Utilities	120,000
Property taxes..	70,000
Factory depreciation..	550,000
Miscellaneous..	50,000
Total annual fixed factory overhead......................	$960,000

All direct materials and indirect supplies are purchased from outside vendors on a two-week production lead time basis. The variable maintenance cost is for maintenance performed by Paste Products' employees; contract maintenance is under annual contract with the manufacturers of specific equipment. Depreciation is calculated on the straight-line basis. Miscellaneous fixed overhead includes factory insurance and other sundry items.

Variable manufacturing overhead is considered to vary with direct labor hours. Therefore, Paste Products applies both variable and fixed overhead to production on the basis of direct labor hours. Manufacturing activities and the incurrence of production costs are expected to occur uniformly throughout the fiscal year.

In January 20x7, the company was forced to reduce its sales price from $79.95 per ten-gallon container to $49.95 due to aggressive foreign competition. Although the price reduction resulted in increased sales, the income statement for the first six months revealed dwindling profits. Management immediately mandated a product cost reduction program, and called upon Jill O'Connor, Cost Accountant, to prepare a report specifying target areas for such a program. O'Connor prepared the analysis of production costs shown on the next page to determine if any costs were above standard.

Paste Products
Analysis of Production Cost Variances
For the Six Months Ended April 30, 20x7
Actual production in units: 1,600,000

DirectMaterials	Standard Usage at Standard Rates	Actual Usage at Standard Rates	Actual Costs	Quantity (Efficiency) Variance	Price (Rate) Variance	Total Variance
Monocloro	$19,200,000	$19,323,096	$19,387,506	$123,096U	$ 64,410U	$187,506U
Oxotone	1,280,000	1,278,400	1,246,440	1,600F	31,960F	33,560F
Distilled Water	1,920,000	1,921,200	1,857,160	1,200U	64,040F	62,840F
Variable overhead						
Maintenance	4,800,000	4,860,000	4,310,050	60,000U	549,950F	489,950F
Supplies	320,000	324,000	335,400	4,000U	11,400U	15,400U
Indirect labor	5,760,000	5,832,000	5,978,000	72,000U	146,000U	218,000U
				$302,696U	$ 55,260U	$357,956U

	Applied Fixed Overhead	Budgeted Fixed Overhead	Actual Fixed Overhead	Fixed Variance	Spending Volume Variance	Budget
Fixed Overhead	$640,000	$480,000	$480,000	$160,000F	–0–	$160,000F
						$197,956U

After completing her analysis, O'Connor observed that the net production variances were unfavorable to budget; however, the fixed overhead volume variance partially offset the variable manufacturing variances. She also observed that the direct labor variances exceeded standard by almost 15 percent. Investigating further, she learned that the manufacturing plant had been working 10 hours per day, six days per week since late January. Workers are paid time-and-one-half for overtime. While she knew that the plant has scheduled overtime, she was not aware of the magnitude. A closer examination of production records revealed the following facts.

	Production	Production	Regular Total	Overtime
Direct labor hours		268,800	55,200	324,000
Direct labor cost	$3,091,200	$952,200	$4,043,400	
Units produced	1,350,000	250,000	1,600,000	

O'Connor plans to use her analysis of production variances as well as additional data she has accumulated as the basis for her recommendations.

Required:

1. In order to analyze the situation and advise management on the product cost reduction program, Jill O'Connor should determine the number of units Paste Products had planned to produce annually. Calculate the number of units Paster Products had planned to produce during its fiscal year beginning November 1, 20x6.

2. Jill O'Connor has decided to revise the variance analysis to reflect the impact that overtime had on direct labor production costs.

   a. Expand the direct labor variance analysis to reveal as much detail about the direct labor costs as possible from the information provided. This would entail a separate calculation of regular time and overtime variances.

   b. Based on your analysis in Requirement B.1., comment on the impact that overtime had on Paste Products direct labor production costs.

1. Jill O'Connor observed that the fixed overhead volume variance partially offset the variable production variances. She wondered if there would be an advantage to Paste Products of shifting variable costs to fixed costs.

   a. Explain the nature of the fixed overhead volume variance.

   b. Discuss the advantages and disadvantages of shifting variable costs to fixed costs.

1. Discuss the overall impact that Paste Products' recent change in pricing strategy has had on the company.

Variance Analysis Refines Overhead Cost Control

BY JEAN C. COOPER, PhD, CPA, AND
JAMES D. SUVER, FHFMA, DBA

ACCOUNTING

Many healthcare organizations may not fully realize the benefits of standard cost accounting techniques because they fail to routinely report volume variances in their internal reports. If overhead allocation is routinely reported on internal reports, managers can determine whether billing remains current or lost charges occur. Healthcare organizations' use of standard costing techniques can lead to more realistic performance measurements and information system improvements that alert management to losses from unrecovered overhead in time for corrective action.

Because of current cost reduction pressures from healthcare payers, healthcare decision makers need better cost information for performance measurement, pricing decisions, and management of activities. Like other service organizations, many healthcare facilities have adapted cost accounting systems and techniques developed for the manufacturing sector—such as standard costing and variance analysis—to generate necessary information. But healthcare managers may not realize all potential benefits from variance analysis.

Because of high fixed and indirect costs, estimated at 80 to 85 percent of total costs in most healthcare organizations, overhead control is challenging to healthcare managers.[a] Standard cost systems, such as overhead volume variance, can aid overhead cost control because they are based on predetermined measures of resource consumption. These measures help managers control operations and evaluate performance by giving them standards with which to compare actual results.[b]

PRICING DECISIONS

For effective management of pricing and budgeting decisions, full costs per unit must be determined in advance of providing a service. Determining a service's variable cost component is fairly straightforward because facilities use variable costs directly in the pricing process and can estimate them accordingly.

Most healthcare providers, however, have relatively few true variable costs—costs that vary directly with changes in volume of input or output. Although only fee-for-service and material-related costs such as food and inpatient supplies meet this definition, many healthcare providers treat nursing or other clinical labor costs as variable costs. But unless staff members are paid fee-for-service, their labor is not a true variable cost.

Since most caregivers are salaried, their pay does not change automatically with patient volume. Only their time allocation between patient and nonpatient activities will change as patient volume changes. To change total costs, administrators must decide to increase or decrease staff.

As a result, fixed costs present a more challenging pricing problem. A healthcare organization must estimate the total amount of fixed cost and the volume used as an allocation base. Because most organizations provide several products or services, using a common surrogate, such as labor hours, can be problematic. For example, when the amount of nursing time for a specific diagnosis related group (DRG) already is being recorded, it may be expedient to use nursing hours to allocate direct and indirect overhead costs. If more nursing hours are used than planned, more overhead would be allocated even if total overhead costs were not increased. This apparent change in overhead costs must be recognized in pricing and control decisions.

EXHIBIT 1
STANDARDS FOR ABDOMINAL SCAN PROCEDURE 101

Variable costs

Labor (1/2 hour at $12.00)	$ 6.00
Materials (7 scans at $3.00 per scan)	21.00

Fixed costs

Overhead A (direct and indirect)	100.00
Total cost per procedure	$127.00
Profit margin B (10% of total cost)	12.70
Charge for procedure 101 before deductions	$139.70
Deductions from revenue C	$24.65
Charge to be established	$164.35
Estimated number of procedures to be completed	50,000

a. The per-unit overhead costs are determined in the following manner:

Estimated total overhead costs	$5,000,000
Estimated number of labor hours for next accounting period (50,000 procedures x 0.5 hours)	25,000
Overhead rate per labor hour ($5,000,000/25,000 labor hours)	$200
Overhead rate for procedure 101 per labor hour (0.5 x $200)	$100

b. The profit margin in this organization is determined by a 10% markup on full cost.

Note: The flexible budget equation for procedure 101 would be:
$$\text{Total costs} = \$5,000,000 + (\$27.00 \times \text{quantity of procedures})$$

c. Deductions from revenue for uncompensated care are estimated at 15% of charges.

Estimated per-unit costs are unique, however, to the specific level of estimated fixed costs and the specific volume of estimated output. Whether fixed costs are direct fixed costs in a department or indirect fixed costs of general administration, both must be recovered through pricing.

Exh. 1 presents standard costs for a healthcare procedure. The per-unit costs ($127) and desired profit margin (10 percent or $12.70) could be used to evaluate offers discounted from the full charge of $164.35. Standard costs also can provide useful planning data for budgeting and control purposes.

A hospital department could develop an income statement to estimate the next month's profit for a certain procedure, assuming a forecast of 50,000 procedures. This income data also would determine the department's budget:

Gross revenues (50,000 × $164.35)	=	$8,217,500
Allowances for uncompensated care (50,000 × $24.65)	=	1,232,500

Net revenues (50,000 × $139.70)	=	6,985,000
Expenses: Standard cost of services (50,000 × $127.00)	=	6,350,000
Projected profit margin (10% of total cost)	=	
$ 635,000		

Projected profit of Procedure 101 for the next accounting period would be $635,000, assuming that:

50,000 procedures will be completed during the month and capacity in the department is sufficient to accomplish this level without additional costs (such as overtime) being incurred;

- All 50,000 procedures will be billed at the stated charge of $164.35 and allowances will equal 15 percent of charges;
- All cost figures (such as salary costs) occur as planned; and
- The organization achieves all productivity measures (0.5 labor hours per test).

If any assumption is incorrect, a variance from planned profit will occur. Administrators then must

EXHIBIT 2
ACTUAL RESULTS FOR PROCEDURE 101

Standards:

Procedures planned	50,000	
Planned profit (50,000 × $12.70)	$635,000	
Standard charge per procedure		$164.35
Standard costs per procedure		127.00
Standard profit per procedure		12.70
Standard discount from charges		24.65

Actuals:

Procedures completed	49,000	
Gross revenues (49,000 × $164.35)		$8,053,150
Discounts (49,000 × $24.65)		1,207,850
Net revenues (49,000 × $139.70)		6,845,300
Actual labor and material costs (49,000 × $27.00)		1,323,000
Actual overhead		5,000,000
Actual profit		$ 522,300

Variance between planned and actual profit for 49,000 procedures:

Expected profit (49,000 × $12.70)	$522,300
Actual profit	522,300
Variance	$100,000 under-recovery

---

determine whether variance was controllable and by whom.

PERFORMANCE MEASUREMENT

If the results for Procedure 101 were achieved as shown in Exh. 2, the 49,000 procedures actually performed would be expected to provide $622,300 in profits ($12.70×49,000). The actual profit ($522,300), however, is $100,000 less than the expected profit ($622,300) and $112,700 less than the projected profit in the original budget ($635,000).

To evaluate the actual results for Procedure 101, a variance analysis report (Exh. 3) could be constructed from the data in Exh. 1 and 2 to explain the difference in profits. A profit of $12,70 is lost on each of the 1,000 procedures not completed. In addition, the $5,000,000 in overhead is not fully allocated to the 49,000 procedures actually billed. Because the overhead rate of $100 assumes that 50,000 procedures will be performed ($5,000,000 / 50,000), completing only 49,000 procedures results in an under-recovery of $100,000 ($100 × 1000) in overhead never billed to clients.

Failure to achieve the planned volume used in developing the overhead allocation for pricing always will result in an under-recovery of overhead costs.

Each examination *not* completed results in a loss of $100 in fixed overhead recovery in addition to the loss of $12.70 in profit margin.

Because the planned and actual overhead totals were the same ($5,000,000), no overhead variance would show on the income statement. The charge for a procedure was established using the planned volume ($5,000,000 / 50,000 or $100), but the actual rate for 49,000 procedures would be $5,000,000 / 49,000 or $102. The difference results in an under-recovery of overhead. Unless a manager is aware of potential under-recovery of overhead, corrective action such as an increase in charges or a reduction in actual overhead expenses will not be taken in time to alleviate the shortfall in profit.

In this example, timely identification of the volume decrease of 1,000 could have led to a recovery of the $100,000 loss through overhead cost reductions or price increases. Managers can always estimate the amount of overhead that will be over- or under-recovered by multiplying the planned overhead rate by the forecasted difference between the planned volume used to establish the rate and the actual volume estimated to be billed.

Effective performance evaluation requires differentiation of costs controllable by managers from

239

EXHIBIT 3
VARIANCE ANALYSIS FOR PROCEDURE 101

	Projected budget (50,000 procedures)	(49,000 procedures)	Variances
Gross revenue	$8,217,500	$8,053,150	$164,350 Unfavorable
Discount	1,232,500	1,207,850	24,650 Favorable
Net Revenues	6,985,000	6,845,300	139,700 Unfavorable
Costs[A]	6,350,000	6,323,000	27,000 Favorable
Profit	$ 635,000	$ 522,300	$112,700 Unfavorable
Volume variance[B]		$ 100,000 Unfavorable	=$100,000 Unfavorable
Profit margin variance[C]			=$ 12,700 Unfavorable
Net variance			$112,700 Unfavorable

A. Based on flexible budget costs of $5,000,000 fixed costs + $27 variable costs per procedure.
B. 50,000 procedures were used to determine $100 overhead rate. 1,000 shortfall in procedures × $100 overhead rate per procedure = $100,000 of fixed overhead costs not recovered through billing process.
C. Profit margin lost due to reduced volume. 1,000 reduction in procedures × $12.70 profit per procedure = $12,700 reduction in profit.

those heavily influenced by external events. Most healthcare administrators and managers are not able to control volume of services or even prices set under prospective reimbursement agreements. Physicians admit patients and order services. Only when lost volume is due to capacity constraints can management be held responsible. Assigning responsibility and planning dollar implications *before* a contract is signed are the keys to successful contracting. Penalty clauses for not achieving volume and incentives for overachieving need to be negotiated with managed care organizations.

One way to prevent under-recovery of overhead is to stipulate contractually that HMOs will pay the fixed costs per day for each patient day not delivered and only the variable costs per day for each patient day in excess of the agreed on volume. Because variable costs per patient day are lower than fixed costs per patient day, HMOs have an economic incentive to deliver more than the negotiated total, limited, of course, by the provider's current capacity.

Focusing on the bottom line without fully understanding why variances occur can lead to dysfunctional decision making. A flexible budget, as shown in Exh. 3, separates the profit expected under the planned volume from the profit variance caused by under-recovery of fixed overhead. Due to their high fixed costs, healthcare providers are particularly vulnerable to overhead under-recovery.

MANAGEMENT CONTROL

Some managers eliminate overhead volume variances by treating overhead as a period expense and not allocating it to individual outputs as done above. Because direct expensing of overhead eliminates the potential for volume variances, it also eliminates two powerful management tools: identifying impacts of fixed overhead on per unit prices, and monitoring recovery of overhead expenses to determine if and when fixed expenses should be reduced.

A standard cost system that allocates fixed cost on a per unit basis provides information on the amount of fixed costs over- or under-recovered with volume changes. By monitoring changes between actual and planned (standard) volume, managers can make necessary changes in budgeted fixed costs as required. Volume shortfalls are also critical to other management decisions such as cashflow planning, hiring, and strategic planning. Effective management control requires understanding how volume changes help achieve planned levels of performance and profits.

EXHIBIT 4
STANDARDS FOR ROUTINE PHYSICAL EXAM

Standard charge per exam[A]	$ 80.00
Standard costs for the laboratories:	
Supplies per exam	$ 8.00
Labor per exam	6.00
Variable laboratory overhead	18.00
Fixed laboratory overhead per month[B]	10,000.00
Fixed general administrative expenses per month[C]	2,000.00
Planned volume of exams per month	500
Standard unit cost per exam:	
Supplies	$ 8.00
Labor	6.00
Variable overhead	18.00
Total variable cost per exam	32.00
Lab overhead costs [D]	20.00
Standard full cost per exam	$ 52.00

Standard profit per exam: $80–$52=$28

A. All patients pay charges for this exam. There are no uncompensated care accounts.
B. Fixed laboratory overhead is considered a product cost and allocated to individual products for control purposes.
C. Fixed administrative costs are treated as a period cost and not allocated to individual exams.
D. The per unit fixed overhead cost is determined in the following manner. $10,000 lab overhead cost divided by the 500 exams estimated to be completed for the month = $20 lab overhead per exam.

HIDDEN INVENTORY

Many healthcare organizations do not report work in process or finished goods inventories in their financial statements, implicitly assuming that all services provided by various cost centers have been entered in the billing system for accounting purposes. However, anecdotal evidence indicates that most clinical departments do not carry interim in-process charges, such as estimating inpatient charges for patients not yet discharged, on year-end financial statements.

The quantity of services provided by various cost centers can differ from the quantity reported in revenue accounts and recognized in accounting statements because of the normal time lag required to complete billing. For example, services (such as radiology, laboratory, and surgical procedures) provided to hospital inpatients usually are not billed until the entire procedure is finished.

Also, work completed at the end of a day typically is not forwarded to the accounting system immediately because patient care has highest priority, while billing comes later. (Time lag does not exist for expense accounts, which usually are recorded promptly.) Lost charges tend to increase when output and billing are not monitored.

Many overhead expenses are incurred as functions of time passing rather than patient volume. For example, most salaried employees insist on being paid without waiting for patient or client billing to be completed or cash received. If revenues and costs are to be monitored by departments, and if a matching of revenues and expenses is to occur, some type of cost system must be implemented to measure output that is in process or completed but not billed.

In manufacturing, unbilled activities are captured in work-in-process and finished goods inventories. As noted above, most healthcare providers do not maintain this type of formal inventory account. As a result, a "hidden inventory" of unbilled output can exist, distorting financial statements and information for management decisions.

For example, Exh. 4 presents data for a healthcare organization providing routine physical examinations including EKG and blood tests. Three hundred and ten examinations are billed on the income statement for the current period:

Revenues		
(310 exams × \$80)		\$24,800
Expenses: standard cost		
of service billed		
310 × \$52.00	\$16,120	
Volume variance	800	
Administrative expenses	\$2,000	18,920
Net profit		\$ 5,880

The 460 examinations completed in the reporting period are used in calculating the volume variance for the department. The shortfall of 40 exams (500 planned - 460 actual) times the overhead rate of \$20 equals the \$800 volume variance reported.

Management is concerned because the profit at 310 exams should be \$2,880 as determined below:

Revenues 310 × \$80		\$24,800
Expenses		
Variable 310 × \$32.00	\$9,920	
Fixed	\$12,000	
Total expenses		21,920
Expected profit		\$ 2,800

The \$800 unfavorable volume variance explains why the reported profit (\$5,800) is \$3,000 greater than planned (\$2,800).

While only 310 examinations were billed, the reported volume variance indicates that 460 were completed. Accordingly, 150 examinations (460 - 310) were *completed by the laboratory but not yet billed*.

Whether the paper work is still in the laboratory or has been lost (intentionally or unintentionally), revenues and expenses are improperly matched and reported income is overstated.

Performance evaluation is difficult to assess if only the bottom line is stressed and actual output measures are not available. A reconciliation can be determined in the following manner:

Expected net profit	\$2,880
Actual reported profit	5,880
Unbilled overhead (150 exams ×	\$3,000
\$20 fixed overhead)	
Actual net profit	\$2,880

The difference between examinations completed and examinations billed (460 - 310 = 150) times laboratory overhead costs per examination (\$20) equals the \$3,000 profit overstatement. If only 310 examinations had been completed, the volume variance would have been \$3,800 instead of \$800 and profit would have been as planned. Most managers like to report a higher level of productivity for their performance evaluation. Unless performance reports are matched with financial reports, unbilled charges will not be known.

In-process inventories exist in healthcare organizations whenever completed services are not billed. Standard cost accounting allows administrators to monitor both production and billing. Reporting unbilled services on internal financial statements or management reports draws attention to potential problems. Accounts similar to work-in-process and finished goods inventories for external reporting can be used to properly match revenues and expenses and provide more appropriate data for cost management and performance evaluation.

---

a Overhead costs in this article are defined as all general and administrative expenses. General expenses include indirect patient care costs and all direct patient care costs which are fixed in nature, such as equipment and personnel or salaries.

b Adapted from Fundamentals of Management Accounting by Anthony, Weber and Reece, 4th ed. (Richard D. Irwin, 1985), Problem 9–32, pp. 346–347.

Chapter 17
Marketing Effectiveness and Managing Productivity

Cases
17-1   Analysis of Sales Variance

Readings
Vijay Govindarajan and John K. Shank: **Profit Variance Analysis: A Strategic Focus**
This article uses a fictitious case to demonstrate how variance analysis can be tied explicitly to the strategies of the firm. It expands the Shank and Churchill framework for variance analysis to include explicitly the strategy and the competitive position of the firm in the analysis and interpretation of results.

Discussion questions:
1. Why is it inadequate and may even be misleading to rely only on the analysis reported in Table 3?
2. Does a favorable variance imply a favorable performance?
3. Table 4 shows a rather elaborate and detailed analysis of variances of operating results. The analysis provides us information on the effect of variations of relevant operating factors on the operating result. The analysis includes relevant and important operating factors such as total market size, market share of the firm, sales mix, selling price, and costs. The analysis considers almost all, if not all, the factors that are of interest and important to management. Why is the analysis incomplete?

Cases

17-1. Analysis of Sales Variance

(Comprehensive: CMA adopted) The financial results for the Continuing Education Department of BusEd Corporation for November 19x8 are presented at the top of the next page. Mary Ross, president of BusEd, is pleased with the final results but has observed that the revenue and most of the costs and expenses of this department exceeded the budgeted amounts. Barry Stein, vice president of the Continuing Education Department, has been requested to provide an explanation of any amount that exceeded the budget by 5 percent or more.

Stein has accumulated the following facts to assist in his analysis of the November results.

1. The budget for calendar year 19x8 was finalized in December 19x7, and at that time, a full program of continuing education courses was scheduled to be held in Chicago during the first week of November 19x8. The courses were scheduled so that eight courses would be run on each of the five days during the week. The budget assumed that there would be 425 participants in the program and 1,000 participant days for the week.

2. BusEd charges a flat fee of $150 per day of course instruction, i.e., the fee for a three-day course would be $450. BusEd grants a 10 percent discount to persons who subscribe to its publications. The 10 percent discount is also granted to second and subsequent registrants for the same course from the same organization. However, only one discount per registration is allowed. Historically, 70 percent of the participant day registrations are at the full fee of $150 per day and 30 percent of the participant day registrations receive the discounted fee of $135 per day. These percentages were used in developing the November 19x8 budgeted revenue.

3. The following estimates were used to develop the budgeted figures for course related expenses.

Food charges per participant day (lunch/coffee breaks	$ 27
Course materials per participant	8
Instructor fee per day	1,000

4. A total of 530 individuals participated in the Chicago courses in November 19x8, accounting for 1,280 participant days. This included 20 persons who took a new, two-day course on pension accounting that was not on the original schedule; thus, on two of the days, nine courses were offered, and an additional instructor was hired to cover the new course. The breakdown of the course registrations was as follows.

Full fee registrations	<u>704</u>
Discounted fees	
Current periodical subscribers	128
New periodical subscriber	128
Second registrations from the same organization	<u>320</u>
Total participant day registrations	<u>$1,280</u>

5. A combined promotional mailing was used to advertise the Chicago program and a program in Cincinnati that was scheduled for December 1988. The incremental costs of the combined promotional piece was $5,000, but none of the promotional expenses ($20,000) budgeted for the Cincinnati program in December will have to be incurred. This earlier than normal promotion for the Cincinnati program has resulted in early registration fees collected in November as follows (in terms of participant days).

Full fee registrations	140
Discounted registrations	60
Total participant day registrations	**200**

6. BusEd continually updates and adds new courses, and includes $2,000 in each monthly budget for this purpose. The additional amount spent on course development during November was for an unscheduled course that will be offered in February for the first time.

Barry Stein has prepared the quantitative analysis of the November 19x8 variances shown at the bottom of the next page.

REQUIRED:

After reviewing Barry Stein's quantitative analysis of the November variances, prepare a memorandum addressed to Mary Ross explaining the following.

1. The cause of the revenue mix variance.

2. The implication of the revenue mix variance.

3. The cause of the revenue timing difference.

4. The significance of the revenue timing difference.

5. The primary cause of the unfavorable total expense variance.

6. How the favorable food price variance was determined.

7. The impact of the promotion timing difference on future revenues and expenses.

8. Whether or not the course development variance has an unfavorable impact on the company.

BusEd Corporation
Statement of Operations Continuing Education Department
November 19x8

	Budget	Actual	Favorable/ (Unfavorable) in Dollars	Favorable/ (Unfavorable) in Percent
Revenue: Course fees	$145,500	$212,460	$66,960	46.0
Expenses:				
Food charges	$ 27,000	$ 32,000	$ (5,000)	(18.5)
Course materials	3,400	4,770	(1,370)	(40.3)
Instructor fees	40,000	42,000	(2,000)	(5.0)
Instructor travel	9,600	9,885	(285)	(3.0)
Staff salaries and benefits	12,000	12,250	(250)	(2.1)
Staff travel	2,500	2,400	100	4.0
Promotion	20,000	25,000	(5,000)	(25.0)
Course development	2,000	5,000	(3,000)	(150.0)
Total expenses	$116,500	$133,305	$(16,805)	(14.4)
Revenue over expenses	$ 29,000	$ 79,155	$ 50,155	172.9

BusEd Corporation
Analysis of November 19x8 Variances

Budgeted revenue		$145,500
Variances:		
Quantity variance {(1,280 - 1,000) x $145.50}	$40,740 F	
Mix variance {($143.25 - $145.50) x 1,280}	2,880 U	
Timing difference ($145.50 x 200)......................................	29,100 F	66,960F
Actual revenue		$212,460
Budgeted expenses		116,500
Quantity variances		
Food charges {(1,000 - 1,280) x $27}	$ 7,560 U	
Course materials {(425 - 530) x $8}	840 U	
Instructor fees (2 x $1,000)	2,000 U	10,400U
Price variances		
Food charges {($27.00-$25.00) x 1,280}	$ 2,560 F	
Course materials {($8.00-$9.00) x 530}	530 U	2,030F
Timing differences		
Promotion	$ 5,000 U	
Course development	3,000 U	8,000U
Variances not analyzed (5 percent or less)		
Instructor travel..	$ 285 U	
Staff salaries and benefits	250 U	
Staff travel	100 F	435U
Actual expenses		$133,305

Profit Variance Analysis: A Strategic Focus

ABSTRACT: This paper uses a disguised case to compare and contrast three different frame works in analyzing profit variances—two that are in common usage today and one that is not but, in our view, should be. The purpose of the paper is to demonstrate how variance analysis needs to be tied explicitly to the strategic context of the firm and its business units.

By Vijay Govindarajan and John K. Shank

Profit variance analysis is the process of summarizing what happened to profits during the period to highlight the salient managerial issues. Variance analysis is the formal step leading to determining what corrective actions are called for by management. Thus it is a key link in the management control process. We believe this element is underutilized in many companies because of the lack of a meaningful analytical framework. It is handled by accountants in a way that is too technical. This paper proposes a different profit variance framework as a "new idea" in management control.

Historically, variance analysis involved a simple methodology where actual results were compared with the budget on a line-by-line basis. We call this Phase I thinking. Phase II thinking was provided by Shank and Churchill [1977] who proposed a management-oriented approach to variance analysis. Their approach was based on the dual ideas of profit impact as a unifying theme and a multilevel analysis in which complexity was added gradually, one level at a time. We believe that the Shank and Churchill approach needs to be modified in important ways to take explicit account of strategic issues. Our framework, which we call Phase III thinking, argues that variance analysis becomes most meaningful when it is tied explicitly to strategic analysis.

John K. Shank is Noble Professor of Managerial Control and Vijay Govindarajan is Associate Professor of Accounting, both at the Amos Tuck School of Business Administration, Dartmouth College.

The authors wish to acknowledge helpful discussions with Ray Stephens.

This paper presents a short disguised case, United Instruments, Inc., to illustrate the three phases or generations of thinking about profit variance analysis. We believe it also demonstrates the superiority of integrating strategic planning and overall financial performance evaluation, which is the essence of Phase III thinking. The purpose of this paper is to emphasize how variance analysis can be, and should be, redirected to consider the strategic issues that have, during the past 15 years, become so widely accepted as a conceptual framework for decision making.[1]

UNITED INSTRUMENTS, INC.: AN INSTRUCTIONAL CASE[2]

Steve Park, president and principal stockholder of United Instruments, Inc., sat at his desk reflecting on the 1987 results (T-1). For the second year in succession, the company had exceeded the profit budget. Steve Park was obviously very happy with the 1987 results. All the same, he wanted to get a better feel for the relative contributions of the R&D, manufacturing, and marketing departments in this overall success. With this in mind, he called his assistant, a recent graduate of a well-known business school, into his office.

TABLE 1
UNITED INSTRUMENTS, INC.

		Budget (1,000s)		Actual (1,000s)
Sales		$16,872		$17,061
Cost of goods sold		9,668		9,865
Gross margin		$ 7,204		$ 7,196
Less: Other operating expenses				
Marketing	$1,856		$1,440	
R&D	1,480		932	
Administration	1,340	4,676	1,674	4,046
Profit before taxes		$ 2,528		$ 3,150

"Amy," he began, "as you can see from our recent financial results, we have exceeded our profit targets by $622,000. Can you prepare an analysis showing how much R&D, manufacturing, and marketing contributed to this overall favorable profit variance?"

Amy Shultz, with all the fervor of a recent convert to professional management, set to her task immediately. She collected the data in T-2 and was wondering what her next step should be.

United Instruments' products can be grouped into two main lines of business: electric meters (EM) and electronic instruments (EI). Both EM and EI are industrial measuring instruments and perform similar functions. However, these products differ in their manufacturing technology and their end-use characteristics. EM is based on mechanical and electrical technology, whereas EI is based on microchip technology. EM and EI are substitute products in the same sense that a mechanical watch and a digital watch are substitutes.

United Instruments uses a variable costing system for internal reporting purposes.

PHASE I THINKING: THE "ANNUAL REPORT APPROACH" TO VARIANCE ANALYSIS

A straightforward, simple-minded explanation of the difference between actual profit ($3,150) and the budgeted profit ($2,528) might proceed according to T-3. Incidently, this type of variance analysis is what one usually sees in published annual reports (where the comparison is typically between last year and this year). If we limit ourselves to this type of analysis, we will draw the following conclusions about United's performance:

1. Good sales performance (slightly above plan).

2. Good manufacturing cost control (margins as per plan).

3. Good control over marketing and R&D costs (costs down as percentage of sales).

4. Administration overspent a bit (slightly up as percentage of sales).

5. Overall Evaluation: Nothing of major significance; profit performance above plan.

How accurately does this summary reflect the actual performance of United? One objective of this paper is to demonstrate that the analysis is misleading. The plan for 1987 has embedded in it certain expectations about the state of the total industry and about United's market share, its selling prices, and its cost structure. Results from variance computations are more "actionable" if changes in actual results for 1987 are analyzed against each of these expectations. The Phase I analysis simply does not break down the overall favorable variance of $622,000 according to the key underlying causal factors.

TABLE 2
ADDITIONAL INFORMATION

	Electric Meters (EM)	Electronic Instruments (EI)
Selling prices per unit		
Average standard price	$40.00	$180.00
Average actual prices, 1987	30.00	206.00
Variable product costs per unit		
Average standard manufacturing cost	$20.00	$50.00
Average actual manufacturing cost	21.00	54.00
Volume information		
Units produced and sold–actual	141,770	62,172
Units produced and sold–planned	124,800	66,000
Total industry sales, 1987–actual	$44 million	$76 million
Total industry variable product costs, 1987–actual	$16 million	$32 million
United's share of the market (percent of physical units)		
Planned	10%	15%
Actual	16%	9%
	Planned	**Actual**
Firm-wide fixed expenses (1,000s)		
Fixed manufacturing expenses	$3,872	$3,530
Fixed marketing expenses	1,856	1,440
Fixed administrative expenses	1,340	1,674
Fixed R&D expenses		
(exclusively for electronic instruments)	1,480	932

PHASE II THINKING: A MANAGEMENT-ORIENTED APPROACH TO VARIANCE ANALYSIS

The analytical framework proposed by Shank and Churchill [1977] to conduct variance analysis incorporates the following key ideas:

1. Identify the key causal factors that affects profit.

2. Break down the overall profit variance by these key causal factors.

3. Focus always on the *profit* impact of variation in each causal factor.

4. Try to calculate the specific, separable impact of each causal factor by varying only that factor while holding all other factors constant ("spinning only one dial at a time").

5. Add complexity sequentially, one layer at a time, beginning at a very basic "common sense" level ("peel the onion").

6. Stop the process when the added complexity at a newly created level is not justified by added useful insights into the causal factors underlying the overall profit variance.

T-4 and 5 contain the explanation for the overall favorable profit variance of $622,000 using the above approach. In the interest of brevity, most of the calculational details are suppressed (detailed calculations are available from the authors).

What can we say about the performance of United if we now consider the variance analysis summarized in T-5? The following insights can be offered organized by functional area:

TABLE 3
THE "ANNUAL REPORT APPROACH" TO VARIANCE ANALYSIS

			Budget (1,000s)				Actual (1,000s)	
Sales			$16,872	(100%)			$17,061	(100%)
Cost of goods sold			9,668	(58%)			9,865	(58%)
Gross margin			$ 7,204	(42%)			$ 7,196	(42%)
Less: Other expenses								
Marketing	$1,856	(11%)			$1,440	(8%)		
R&D	1,480	(9%)			932	(6%)		
Administration	1,340	(8%)	4,676	(28%)	1,674	(10%)	4,046	(24%)
Profit before tax			$ 2,528	(14%)			$ 3,150	(18%)

Marketing

Comments:

Market Share (SOM) increase benefited the firm	$1,443 F
But, unfortunately, sales mix was managed toward the lower margin product	921 U
Control over marketing expenditure benefited the firm (especially in the face of an increase in SOM)	416 F
Net effect	$938 F
Uncontrollables: Unfortunately, the overall market declined and cost the firm	$680 U

Overall evaluation: Very good performance

Manufacturing

Comments:

Manufacturing cost control cost the firm	$ 48 U

Overall evaluation: Satisfactory performance

R&D

Comments:

Savings in R& D budget	$ 548 F

Overall evaluation: Good performance

Administration

Comments:

Administration budget overspent	$ 334 U

Overall evaluation: Poor performance

Thus, the overall evaluation of the general manager under Phase II thinking would probably be "good," though specific areas (such as manufacturing cost control or administrative cost control) need attention. The above summary is quite different—and clearly superior —to the one presented under Phase I thinking. But, can we do better? We believe that Shank and Churchill's framework needs to be modified in important ways to accommodate the following ideas.

Sales volume, share of market, and sales mix variances are calculated on the presumption that United is essentially competing in one industry (i.e., it is a single product firm with two different varieties of the product). That is to say, the target customers for EM and EI are the same and that they view the two products as substitutable. Is United a single product firm with two product offerings, or does the firm compete in two different markets? In other words, does United have a single strategy for EM and EI or does the firm have two different strategies for the two businesses? As we argue later, EM and EI have very different industry characteristics and compete in very different markets, thereby, requiring quite different strategies. It is, therefore, more useful to calculate market size and market share variances separately for EM and EI. Just introducing the concept of a *sales mix* variance implies that the average standard profit contribution across EM and EI together is meaningful.

TABLE 4
VARIANCE CALCULATIONS USING SHANK AND CHURCHILL'S MANAGEMENT-ORIENTED FRAMEWORK

Key Causal Factors:

Total Market	Expected	Actual	Actual	Actual	Actual
Market share	Expected	Expected	Actual	Actual	Actual
Sales mix	Expected	Expected	Expected	Actual	Actual
Selling price	Expected	Expected	Expected	Expected	Actual
Costs	Expected	Expected	Expected	Expected	Actual

Profit Calculation:

Sales	$16,872	$15,836	$18,034	$16,862	$17,060
Variable costs	5,769	5,440	6,195	5,944	6,334
Contribution	$11,076	$10,396	$11,839	$10,918	$10,726
Fixed costs	8,548	8,548	8,548	8,548	7,576
Profit	$ 2,528	$ 1,848	$ 3,291	$ 2,370	$ 3,150

Variance Analysis:

Level 1 — Overall variance = $622 F

Level 2 — Sales volume and mix = $158 U | Sales prices and costs = $780 F

Level 3 — Sales volume = $763 F | Sales mix = $921 U | Sales prices = $198 F | Costs = $582 F

Level 4 — Market Size = $680 U | Market Share = $1,443 F | EM $1,418 U | EI $1,616 | EI $1,616 | Variable costs of manufacturing EM $142 U | EI $248 U

Fixed costs
- Manufacturing $342 F
- Marketing $416 F
- Administration $334 U
- R&D $548 F

Note: F indicates a favorable variance and U indicates an unfavorable variance.

252

TABLE 5
VARIANCE SUMMARY FOR THE PHASE II APPROACH

Overall market decline	$ 680 U
Share of market increase	1,443 F
Sales mix change	921 U
Sales prices improved	198 F
EM $1,418 U	
EI $1,616 F	
Manufacturing cost control	48 U
Variable costs $390 U	
Fixed costs $342 F	
Other	
R&D	548 F
Administration	334 U
Marketing	416 F
Total	$ 622 F

For an ice cream manufacturer, for example, it is probably reasonable to assume that the firm operates in a single industry with multiple product offerings, all targeted at the same customer group. It would, therefore, be meaningful to calculate a sales mix variance because vanilla ice cream and strawberry ice cream, for instance, are substitutable and more sales of one implies less sales of the other for the firm (for an elaboration on these ideas, refer to the Midwest Ice Cream Company case [Shank, 1982, pp. 157–173]). On the other hand, for a firm such as General Electric, it is much less clear whether a sales mix variance across jet engines, steam turbines, and light bulbs really makes any sense. This is more nearly the case for United because one unit of EM (which sells for $30) is not really fully substitutable for one unit of EI (which sells for $206).

An important issue in the history of many industries is to determine when product differentiation has progressed sufficiently that what *was* a single business with two varieties *is now* two businesses. Some examples include the growth of the electronic cash register for NCR, the growth of the digital watch for Bulova, or the growth of the industrial robot for General Electric.

Following Phase II thinking, performance evaluation did not relate the variances to the differing strategic contexts facing EM and EI.

PHASE III THINKING: VARIANCE ANALYSIS USING A STRATEGIC FRAMEWORK

We argue that performance evaluation, which is a critical component of the management control process, needs to be tailored to the strategy being followed by a firm or its business units. We offer the following set of arguments in support of our position: (1) different strategies imply different tasks and require different behaviors for effective performance [Andrews, 1971; Gupta and Govindarajan, 1984a; and Govindarajan, 1986a]; (2) different control systems induce different behaviors [Govindarajan, 1986b; Gupta and Govindarajan, 1984b]; (3) thus, superior performance can best be achieved by tailoring control systems to the requirements of particular strategies [Govindarajan, 1988; Gupta and Govindarajan, 1986].[3]

TABLE 6
STRATEGIC CONTEXTS OF THE TWO BUSINESSES

	Electric Meters (EM)	Electronic Instruments (EI)
Overall market (units):		
Plan	1,248,000	440,000
Actual	886,080	690,800
	Declining Market	Growth Market
	(29% Decrease)	(57% Increase)
United's share:		
Plan	10%	15%
Actual	16%	9%
United's prices:		
Plan	$40	$180
Actual	30	206
	We apparntly cut price to build share	We apparently raised price to ration the high demand.
United's margin:		
Plan	$20	$130
Actual	9	152
Industry prices:		
Actual	$50	$110
	We are well below "market."	We are well above "market."
Industry costs:		
Actual	$18	$46
Procuct/market characteristics:	Mature	Evolving
	Lower technology	Higher technology
	Declining market	Growth market
	Lower margins	Higher margins
	Low unit price	High unit price
	Industry prices holding up	Industry prices falling rapidly
United's apparent strategic mission	"Build"	"Skim" or "Harvest"
United's apparent competitive strategy	The low price implies we are trying for low cost position	The high price implies we are trying for a differentiation position.
A more plausible strategy	"Harvest"	"Build"
Key success factors (arising from the plausible strategy)	Hold sales prices vis-à-vis competition. Do not focus on maintaining and improving SOM. Aggressive cost control Process R&D to reduce unit costs.	Competitively price to gain SOM. Product R&D top create differentiation Lower cost through experience curve effects

We will first define and briefly elaborate the concept of strategy before illustrating how to link strategic considerations with variances for management control and evaluation. Strategy has been conceptualized by Andrews [1971], Ansoff [1965], Chandler [1962], Govindarajan [1989], Hofer and Schendel [1978], Miles and Snow [1978], and others as the process by which managers, using a

TABLE 7
VARIANCE CALCULATIONS USING A STRATEGIC FRAMEWORK

Key Casual Factors:					
Total market	Expected	Actual	Actual	Actual	Actual
Market share	Expected	Expected	Actual	Actual	Actual
Selling price	Expected	Expected	Expected	Actual	Actual
Variable costs	Expected	Expected	Expected	Expected	Actual

Electric Meters (EM)					
Sales	$ 4,992	$ 3,544	$ 5,671	$ 4,253	$ 4,253
Variable costs	2,496	1,772	2,835	2,835	2,977
Contribution	$ 2,496	$ 1,772	$ 2,836	$ 1,418	$ 1,276

Market size = $724 U   Market share = $1,064 F   Sales price = $1,418 U   Manufacturing Cost = $142 U

Electronic Instruments (EI)					
Sales	$11,880	$18,652	$11,191	$12,807	$12,807
Variable costs	3,300	5,181	3,109	3,109	3,357
Contribution	$ 8,580	$13,471	$ 8,082	$ 9,698	$ 9,450

Market size = $4,891 F   Market share = $5,389 U   Sales price = $1,616 F   Manufacturing Cost = $248 U

Firmwide Fixed Costs (by responsibility centers)

	Budget	Actual	Variance
Manufacturing	$3,872	$3,530	$342 F
Marketing	1,856	1,440	416 F
Administration	1,340	1,674	334 U
R&D	1,480	932	548 F

three- to five-year time horizon, evaluate external environmental opportunities as well as internal strengths and resources in order to decide on *goals* as well as *a set of action plans* to accomplish these goals. Thus, a business unit's (or a firm's) strategy depends upon two interrelated aspects: (1) its strategic mission or goals, and (2) the way the business unit chooses to compete in its industry to accomplish its goals—the business unit's competitive strategy.

Turning first to strategic mission, consulting firms such as Boston Consulting Group [Henderson, 1979],

Arthur D. Little[Wright, 1975], and A. T. Kearney [Hofer and Davoust, 1977], as well as academic researchers such as Hofer and Schendel [1978], Buzzell and Wiersema [1981], and Govindarajan and Shank [1986], have proposed the following three strategic missions that a business unit can adopt:

BUILD:

This mission implies a goal of increased market share, even at the expense of short-term earnings and cash flow. A business unit following this mission is expected to be a net

TABLE 8
VARIANCE SUMMARY FOR THE PHASE III APPROACH

Electric Meters	
Market size	$ 724 U
Market share	1,064 F
Sales price	1,418 U
Variable manufacturing cost	142 U
Electronic Instruments	
Market size	4,891 F
Market share	5,389 U
Sales price	1,616 F
Variable manufacturing cost	248 U
R&D	548 F
Firmwide Fixed Costs	
Manufacturing	342 F
Marketing	416 F
Administration	334 U
TOTAL	$ 622

user of cash in that the cash throw-off from its current operations would usually be insufficient to meet its capital investment needs. Business units with "low market share" in "high growth industries" typically pursue a "build" mission (e.g., Apple Computer's MacIntosh business, Monsanto's Bioechnology business).

HOLD:

This strategic mission is geared to the protection of the business unit's market share and competitive position. The cash outflows for a business unit following this mission would usually be more or less equal to cash inflows. Businesses with "high market share" in "high growth industries" typically pursue a "hold" mission (e.g., IBM in mainframe computers).

HARVEST:

This mission implies a goal of maximizing short-term earnings and cash flow, even at the expense of market share. A business unit following such a mission would be a net supplier of cash. Businesses with "high market share" in "low growth industries" typically pursue a "harvest" mission (e.g., American Brands in tobacco products).

In terms of competitive strategy, Porter [1980] has proposed the following two generic ways in which businesses can develop sustainable competitive advantage:

LOW COST:

The primary focus of this strategy is to achieve low cost relative to competitors. Cost leadership can be achieved through approaches such as economies of scale in production, learning curve effects, tight cost control, and cost minimization in areas such as R&D, service, sales force, or advertising. Examples of firms following this strategy include: Texas Instruments in consumer electronics, Emerson Electric in electric motors, Chevrolet in automobiles, Briggs and Stratton in gasoline engines, Black and Decker in machine tools, and Commodore in business machines.

TABLE 9
PERFORMANCE EVALUATION SUMMARY FOR PHASE III APPROACH

	Electric Meters "Harvest" vs. "Build"	Electronic Instruments "Build" vs. "Skim"
Marketing Comments	If we held prices and share, decline in this mature business would have cost us $724 U But, we were further hurt by price cuts made in order to build our SOM (our prices was $30 vs. the industry price of $50). $1,418 U <u>1,064 F</u> Net effect <u>$1,078 U</u> This is a market that declined 29 percent. Why are we sacrificing margins to build market position in this mature, declining lower margin business? We underspent the marketing budget. $416 F But why are we cutting back here in the face of our major marketing problems?	We raised prices to maintain margins and to ration our scarce capacity (our price was $206 vs. The industry price of $110). In the process, we lost significant SOM which cost us (netted against $1,616 F from sales prices). $3,773 U This is a booming market that grew 57 percent during this period. Then why did we decide to improve margins at the expense of SOM in this fast growing, higher margin business? Fortunately, growth in the total market improved our profit picture. $4,891 F We underspent the marketing budget. $416 F But why are we cutting back here in the face of our major marketing problems?
Overall evaluation	Poor performance	Poor performance
Manufacturing Comments	Manufacturing cost control was lousy and cost the firm $142 U If we are trying to be a cost leader, where are the benefits of our cumulative experience or our scale economies? (industry unit costs of $18 vs. our costs of $21)	Variable Manufacturing costs showed an unfavorable variance of $248 U (industry costs of $46 vs. our costs of $54). Does the higher manufacturing cost result in a product perceived as better? Apparently not based on market share data.
Overall evaluation	Poor performance	Poor performance
R&D Comments	Not applicable	Why are we not spending sufficient dollars in product R&D? Could this explain our decline in SOM?
Overall evaluation		Poor performance
Administration Comments	Inadequate control over overhead costs, given the need to become the low cost producer ($334 U).	Administration budget overspent. $334 U How does this relate to cost control?
Overall evaluation	Poor performance	Not satisfactory

DIFFERENTIATION:

The primary focus of this strategy is to differentiate the product offering of the business unit, creating something that is perceived by customers as being unique. Approaches to a product differentiation include brand loyalty (Coca-Cola in soft drinks), superior customer service (IBM in computers), dealer network (Caterpillar Tractors in construction equipment), product design and product features (Hewlett-Packard in electronics), and/or product technology (Coleman in camping equipment).

The above framework allows us to consider explicitly the strategic positioning of the two product groups: electric meters and electronic instruments. Though they both are industrial measuring instruments, they face very different competitive conditions that very probably call for different strategies. T-6 summarizes the differing environments and the resulting strategic issues.

How well did electric meters and electronics instruments perform, given their stratetic contexts? The relevant variance calculations are given in Tables 7 and 8. These calculations differ from Phase II analysis (given in T-4) in one important respect. T-4 treated EM and EI as two varieties of one product, competing as substitutes, with a single strategy. Thus, a sales mix variance was comptued. Tables 7 and 8 treat EM and EI as different products with dissimilar strategies. Therefore, no attempt is made to calculate a sales mix variance. The basic idea is that even though a sales mix variance can always be calculated, the concept is meaningful only when a single business framework is applicable. For the same reason, Tables 7 and 8 report the market size and market share variances for EM and EI separately, and T-4 reported these two variances for the instruments business as a whole. Obviously, a high degree of subjectivity is involved in deciding whether United is in one business or two. The fact that the judgment is to a large extent subjective does not negate its importance. T-9 summarizes the managerial performance evaluation that would result if we were to evaluate EM and EI against their plausible strategies, using the variances reported in T-7 and 8.

The overall performance of United would probably be judged as "unsatisfactory." The firm has not taken appropriate decisions in its functional areas (marketing, manufacturing, R&D, and administration) either for its harvest business (EM) or for its build business (EI). The summary in T-9 indicates a dramatically different picture of United's performance than the one presented under Phase II thinking. This is to be expected because Phase II thinking did not tie variance analysis to strategic objectives. Neither Phase I nor Phase II analysis explicitly focused on ways to improve performance en route to accomplishing strategic goals. This would then imply that management compensation and rewards ought not to be tied to performance assessment undertaken using Phase I or Phase II frameworks.

CONCLUSIONS

Variance analysis represents a key link in the management control process. It involves two steps. First, one needs to break down the overall profit variance by key causal factors. Second, one needs to put the pieces back together most meaningfully with a view to evaluating managerial performance. Putting the bits and pieces together most meaningfully is just as crucial as computing the pieces. This is a managerial function, not a computational one.

Phase I, Phase II, and Phase III thinking yield different implications for this first step. That is, the detailed variance calculations do differ across the three approaches. Their implications differ even more for the second step. The computational aspects identify the variance as either favorable or unfavorable. However, a favorable variance does not necessarily imply favorable performance; similarly, an unfavorable variance does not necessarily imply unfavorable performance. We argue that the link between a favorable or unfavorable variance, on the one hand, and favorable or unfavorable performance, on the other, depends upon the strategic context of the business under evaluation.

No doubt, judgments about managerial performance can be dramatically different under Phase I, Phase II, and Phase III thinking (as the United Instruments case illustrates). In our view, moving toward Phase III thinking (i.e., analyzing profit variances in terms of the strategic issues involved) represents progress in adapting cost analysis to the rise of strategic analysis as a major element in business thinking [Shank and Govindarajan, 1988a, 1988b, and 1988c].

REFERENCES

Andrews, K.R., *The Concept of Corporate Strategy* (Homewood, IL: Dow-Jones Irwin, 1971).

Ansoff, H.I., *Corporate Strategy* (New York: McGraw-Hill, 1965).

Buzzell, R.D., B.T. Gale, and R.G.M. Sultan, "Market Share—A Key to Profitability," *Harvard Business Review* (January-February 1975), pp. 97–106.
_____, and F.D. Wiersema, "Modelling Changes in Market Share: A Cross-Sectional

Analysis," *Strategic Management Journal* (January-March 1981), pp. 27–42.

Chandler, A.D., *Strategy and Structure* (Cambridge, MA: The MIT Press, 1962).

Govindarajan, V., "Implementing Competitive Strategies at the Business Unit Level: Implications of Matching Managers to Strategies," *Strategic Management Journal* (May-June 1989), pp. 251–269.

_____, "Decentralization, Strategy, and Effectiveness of Strategic Business Units in Multi-Business Organizations," *Academy of Management Review* (October 1986a), pp. 844–856.

_____, "Impact of Participation in the Budgetary Process on Managerial Attitudes and Performance: Universalistic and Contingency Perspectives," *Decision Sciences* (1986b), pp. 496–516.

_____, "A Contingency Approach to Strategy Implementation at the Business Unit Level: Integrating Management Systems with Strategy," *Academy of Management Journal* (September 1988).

_____, and A.K. Gupta, "Linking Control Systems to Business Unit Strategy: Impact on Performance," *Accounting, Organizations and Society* (1985), pp. 51–66.

_____, and J.K. Shank, "Cash Sufficiency: The Missing Link in Strategic Planning," *The Journal of Business Strategy* (Summer 1986), pp. 88–95.

Gupta, A.K., and V. Govindarajan, "Business Unit Strategy, Managerial Characteristics, and Business Unit Effectiveness at Strategy Implementation," *Academy of Management Journal* (March 1984a), pp. 25–41.

_____, and _____, "Build, Hold, Harvest: Converting Strategic Intentions into Reality," *Journal of Business Strategy* (Winter 1984b), pp. 34–47.

_____, and _____, "Resource Sharing Among SBUs: Strategic Antecedents and Administrative Implications," *Academy of Management Journal* (December 1986), pp. 695–714.

Henderson, B.D., *Henderson on Corporate Strategy* (Cambridge, MA: Abt Books, 1979).

Hofer, C.W., and M.J. Davoust, *Successful Strategic Management* (Chicago, IL: A.T. Kearney, 1977).

_____, and D.E. Schendel, *Strategy Formulation: Analytical Concepts* (St. Paul, MN: West Publishing, 1978).

"Midwest Ice Cream Company," in J.K. Shank, Ed., *Contemporary Management Accounting: A Casebook* (Englewood Cliffs, NJ: Prentice-Hall, 1982), pp. 157–173.

Miles, R.E., and C.C. Snow, *Organizational Strategy, Structure and Process* (New York: McGraw Hill, 1978).

Porter, M.E., *Competitive Strategy: Techniques for Analyzing Industries and Competitors* (New York: The Free Press, 1980).

Shank, J.K., *Contemporary Management Accounting: A Casebook* (Englewood Cliffs, NJ: Prentice-Hall, 1982).

_____, and N.C. Churchill, "Variance Analysis: A Management-Oriented Approach," *The Accounting Review* (October 1977), pp. 950–957.

_____, and V. Govindarajan, "Making Strategy Explicit in Cost Analysis: A Case Study," *Sloan Management Review* (Spring 1988a), pp. 19–29.

_____, and _____, "Transaction-Based Costing for the Complex Product Line: A Field Study," *Journal of Cost Management* (Summer 1988b), pp. 31–38.

_____, and _____, "Strategic Cost Analysis—Differentiating Cost Analysis and Control According to the Strategy Being Followed," *Journal of Cost Management* (Fall 1988c).

Wright, R.V.L., *A System for Managing Diversity* (Cambridge, MA: Arthur D. Little, Inc., 1975).

---

[1] During the past 15 years, several books (e.g., Andews [1971], Henderson [1979], and Porter [1980]) as well as articles (e.g., Buzzell et al. [1975] and Govindarajan and Gupta [1985]) have been published in the field of strategic management. In addition, two new journals (*Strategic Management Journal* and *Journal of Business Strategy*) have been introduced in the strategy area during the past ten years. Also, traditional management journals such as *Administrative Science Quarterly, Academy of Management Journal,* and *Academy of Management Review* have, during the past decade, started to publish regularly articles on strategy formulation and implementation.

[2] This case is motivated by a similar case titled "Kinkead Equipment Ltd.," which appears in Shank [1982].

[3] Several studies have shown that when an individual's rewards are tied to performance along certain dimensions, his or her behavior would be guided by the desire to optimize performance with respect to those dimensions. Refer to Govindarajan and Gupta [1985] for a review of these studies.

Chapter 18
Management Control and Strategic Performance Measurement

Cases

Readings

***Frances L. Ayres:* Perceptions of Earnings Quality: What Managers Need to Know**

In using profit SBUs, it is important to understand the complexities of measuring earnings. This article explains the factors firms use in determining accounting earnings. These factors can be used by a firm to show earnings as relatively high ("low quality" earnings), given the results of operations. The factors include depreciation policy, inventory methods, the handling of accounting changes, among others. The author also makes the point that, based on research, firms which adopt a "high quality" approach to earnings benefit in relatively higher stock prices. That is, investors "see through" the attempts by some firms to influence market prices by increasing earnings through accounting methods (i.e., the "low quality" earnings approach).

Discussion Questions:
1. What is meant by the concept of earnings quality?
2. What are the factors involved in earnings management?
3. What approach to reporting earnings is the best strategy for the firm? For a divisional manager?

Cases

18-1. Analysis of the Accounting Function

For the past several years, a large U.S. based hotel/restaurant operator has been pursuing a strategy of disposing of its U.S. company-owned properties. Four years ago, the company owned and operated 106 properties. Today, that number is 40. The number of retained properties is expected to stabilize between 15 and 20 properties.

During this same period, there was a shift in control of property operations. Previously, headquarters operating personnel held control. Now, hotel operations is basically a decentralized organization, with primary responsibility for operating results resting with three regional vice presidents and each hotel's general manager. The three regional vice presidents report directly to the Executive Vice President of U.S. Hotel Operations, and each are responsible for between 10 and 15 properties. Each property's general manager is directly responsible to the regional vice president. Corporate headquarters provides staff support in operations policies, food and beverage, engineering and maintenance, and accounting.

Accounting support has stayed in a relatively unchanged centralized configuration. The staff of the U.S. hotel controller currently numbers approximately sixty-four. However, the ratio of accounting personnel to properties owned has increased. Previously, the ratio was approximately one headcount per property. Today, it is 1.6 headcount per property. T-A describes the department's major functions.

CENTRAL HOTEL ACCOUNTING

In his visits to the properties, the controller would often solicit comments concerning the accounting support being rendered by the headquarters' staff. An all-too-frequent response was that the properties would be better off without such support. The field operators felt that the accounting staff had no idea of the problems the properties had to deal with and demanded information and data without any consideration or knowledge of the situation at the property level.

The controller must now decide how to reduce his staff in order to get the headcount in line with property dispositions. In doing this he has several objectives:

1. To control and, where possible, immediately reduce costs related to accounting functions.

2. To make accounting functions more responsive to the needs of operators.

3. To foster greater familiarity and closer affiliation between accounting staff and field operators.

4. To improve productivity and increase morale among the accounting staff.

REQUIRED:

1. What organizational alternatives are available to the controller?

2. How can the accounting staff be reduced and still be responsive to the needs of operations?

3. Using this case as an example, comment on the effects of strategic initiatives on the proper scope and functioning of a firm's accounting department.

   (IMA, adapted)

TABLE A
Accounting Functions

Accounts Payable—Most vendors invoice the properties directly. Once approved, invoices are forwarded, at least weekly, to corporate headquarters for payment. Monthly volume over the last 15 months has averaged 21,300 invoices, ranging from 18,000 to 25,800 invoices.

Accounts Receivable—(a) Credit cards represent a significant portion of sales volume. Credit card vouchers are sent daily to corporate headquarters, where they are batched and forwarded to the various credit card companies for payment. In a typical month, 75,000 credit card vouchers will be processed. (b) Direct billing is done at the property. A customer must qualify in order to be billed in this manner. If the direct bill is outstanding for 60 days, it is forwarded to corporate headquarters for further action.

Data Entry—The data processing system requirements mandate three (3) different types of terminals, with three different types of screens, security, and operational procedures. This had led to a separate area of proficiency and dedicated skill.

Field Payroll—Payroll processing is initiated at the property with employees' daily use of time cards. The hours worked are summarized on payroll input sheets, which are sent to corporate headquarters bi-weekly. Payroll information is entered into an automated payroll system that generates paychecks, and maintains the appropriate payroll records. The paychecks are sent to the properties for distribution to employees. Monthly volume averages between 13,000 and 16,500 payroll checks (last year, 14,500 W-2's were prepared).

General Ledger—General ledger processing is by batching process. The general ledger contains about 450 accounts per property. Each property will have about 600 transactions per month. This includes direct feeds from various sub-systems (including accounts payable, payroll, and revenue reporting).

Management Contract Accounting—Management contract accounting makes use of accounts payable, payroll and general ledger functions to prepare daily cash reports and monthly profit and loss statements to be sent to the owners of managed properties.

18-2. Industrial Chemicals Company

In 19X5, events which were thought about and planned for the past several years in the Industrial Chemicals Company (ICC) culminated in the most significant change in the company's 80-plus year history. A major corporate restructuring was announced including the purchase of a large U.S. based pharmaceutical company, for $2.8 billion. ICC is a large multinational manufacturer of industrial chemicals. The parent company is located in Amsterdam, and manufacturing plants and customers are located worldwide.

In February of 19X6, the Chairman of the Board and Chief Executive Officer told a reporter of a major financial magazine: "We felt that if we were to build a strong technology base of biology and biotechnology that would simultaneously serve agriculture, animal nutrition, and health care, we could build a unique powerhouse backing it up in a way that companies in these individual businesses couldn't do; and we've built it." The changes initiated were thus not merely pruning and trimming, but changing the very direction of the company by getting out of commodity chemicals and into more innovative areas.

The magazine article made a key observation in its February 10, issue:

A major problem looms: Can ICC support the level of research needed to make a major impact in biotechnology? Earnings for the first three quarters of 19X5 dropped and the company expects to show a loss for the fourth quarter, even before write-offs on closed chemical plants.

The chairman of the board was well aware of this major concern. In fact, as 19X5 drew to a close, he commissioned a special subgroup of the Executive Management Committee (the EMC is the senior management group dealing with major strategic and operational issues) to review the company's overall R&D spending, its affordability and priorities, and bring back recommendations to the EMC in time for inclusion in the 19X6 budgeting process.

RESEARCH AND DEVELOPMENT

From a total corporate perspective, the R&D effort falls into three classifications:

Class I—Maintain existing businesses—

This effort is associated with managing existing business assets, maintaining competitiveness of products in existing businesses, and supplying technical service.

Class II—Expand existing businesses—

R&D associated with expanding existing business assets, expanding markets of existing products, or substantially lowering costs of existing processes.

Class III—Create new businesses—

R&D associated with creating new business assets.

Table A is a summary of total R&D costs from 19X0-19X4 within these three categories. Table B provides comparative data on overall R&D spending for the company and its new acquisition against competitors.

Organizationally, each of the operating units administers its own R&D efforts which cut across all three categories above. In very simple terms, the operating unit is relatively self-sufficient across all three categories where technology *already exists*. They "purchase" some support services from the corporate R&D group as described later. In terms of performance assessment for incentive compensation, the operating unit R&D groups are tied to the "bottom-line" results achieved by the respective units.

CORPORATE R&D

The corporate R&D group, in addition to providing support services to the operating unit's R&D efforts, is primarily responsible for required *new technology* in creating new businesses. At the point in time in the product invention time line when new-technology-based products reach a level of commercial viability, these programs are "handed-off" to an operating unit R&D group for eventual movement to commercialization. In the past several years, this corporate R&D group has been successful in "inventing" and "handing off" commercial leads despite some operating unit reluctance to fund the research costs. In these instances, funding sometimes remained with corporate R&D after the "hand-off."

A more detailed description of the corporate R&D group follows. The corporate research and development group is headed by a senior vice president reporting to the Chairman of the Board and CEO. The central research laboratory group consists of an information center (20 percent of its costs are charged to operating units on a fee for service basis), an MIS facility, bioprocess development and cell culture groups (which are essentially involved in devising production processes for biotechnology-based products),

---

SUMMARY OF CORPORATE RESEARCH AND DEVELOPMENT

Research Laboratory Group
    Information Center
    MIS Facility
    Bioprocess Development and Cell Culture
    Physical Sciences Center
    Analytical Chemistry Group
    Chemistry Group

Biological Sciences Group

Patent Group

---

a physical sciences center (a central analytical chemistry group providing very specialized and highly skilled support to many users across the company—65 percent of this group's costs are charged out directly on a fee-for-service basis), a group called controlled delivery which develops vehicles for the transfer of pharmaceutical and animal science products into the living systems within which they must act, and a chemistry group providing very specialized skills in both conventional and biotechnology process chemistry (about 25 percent of this group's costs are charged directly on a fee-for-service basis). In addition to the direct fee-for-service chargeouts described above, a portion of the costs of this central laboratory group (primarily the bioprocess development and cell culture groups) is assigned to the biological sciences segment. The remaining costs, along with overall corporate R&D administrative costs, are allocated as a part of corporate charges.

The biological sciences group has been the major focal point for new technology in the pharmaceutical and animal sciences area. It supports plant sciences for the agricultural unit as well. The costs for the biological sciences group are reported as being for new direction basic research. Also controlled within corporate R&D and reported in this segment are costs of key university relationships supporting basic and applied biomedical, crop chemicals, and animal sciences research efforts.

The patent group has always been decentralized with a patent counsel and staff assigned to each operating unit reporting on a "dotted line" basis to the operating unit and administratively to the general patent counsel. Thus, about 80 percent of patent cost is already directly borne by operating units with the remainder allocated as part of corporate charges.

REQUIRED:

As the controller reflected on the information obtained and the important issues being addressed by the EMC subcommittee, the following questions surfaced in his mind. Develop a response for each question.

1. What is the role of R&D in the firm's overall strategy?

2. Would operating unit control of our key R&D growth programs enhance or mitigate our chances of meeting our goals? That is, should R&D be organized as cost SBUs within each of the operating units? What amount and type of R&D, if any at all, should be done at the corporate level?

3. I know there'll be pressure to level off our R&D spending across the company, including corporate R&D. We've got to make sure we get more for our money in terms of prioritizing those efforts to go after the most promising commercial opportunities if we're going to achieve our goals in biotechnology! How can we be sure we're prioritizing these efforts toward increased commercial success? That is, how do we evaluate the effectiveness of both the R&D cost SBUs in the operating units and corporate-level R&D?

4. How does the fact that ICC operates in several different countries affect the decisions the controller is facing?

18-3. Absorption Versus Variable Costing and Ethical Issues

HeadGear, Inc is a small manufacturer of headphones for use in commercial and personal applications. The HeadGear headphones are known for their outstanding sound quality and light weight, which makes them highly desirable especially in the commercial market for telemarketing firms and similar communication applications, despite the relatively high price. Although demand has grown steadily, profits have grown much more slowly, and John Hurley, the CEO, suspects productivity is falling, and costs are rising out of hand. John is concerned that the decline in profit growth will affect the stock price of the company and inhibit the firm's efforts to raise new investment capital, which will be needed to continue the firm's growth. While the firm is now operating at 68% of available production capacity, John thinks the market growth will soon exceed available capacity.

To improve profitability, John has decided to bring in a new COO with the objective of improving profitability very quickly. The new COO understands that profits must be improved within the coming 10-18 months. A bonus of 10% of profit improvement is promised the new COO if this goal is achieved. The following is the income statement for HeadGear for 19X2, from the most recent annual report. Product costs for HeadGear include $25 per unit variable manufacturing costs and $2,000,000 per year fixed manufacturing overhead. Budgeted production was 125,000 units in 19X2. Selling and administrative costs include a variable portion of $15 per unit and a fixed portion of $2,400,0000 per year. The same units costs and production level are also applicable for 19X1.

HeadGear Inc. Income Statement for the Period Ended 12/31/19X2		
Sales (125,000 @$75)		$ 9,375,000
Cost of Sales:		
Beginning Inv: 5,000 @ $41	$ 205,000	
Cost of Production: 120,000 @ $41	4,920,000	
Goods Available: 130,000	$5,125,000	
Less Ending Inv: 0 @ $41	-0-	$5,125,000
Gross Margin		$4,250,000
Selling and Administrative		
Variable Costs: 125,000 @ $15	$ 1,875,000	
Fixed Costs	2,400,000	$4,275,000
Net Income (loss)		$ 25,000

The new COO is convinced that the problem is the need to aggressively market the product, and that the apparent decline in productivity is really due to underutilization of capacity. The COO increases variable selling costs to $16 per unit and fixed selling costs to $2,750,000 to help achieve this goal. Budgeted sales and production for 19X3 are set at 175,000 units.

Actual production was 175,000 as planned but sales for 19X3 turned out to be only 140,000 units, short of the target. The new COO claims that profits have increased considerably, is looking forward to the promised bonus.

REQUIRED:

1. Calculate the absorption cost net income for 19X3, assuming the new selling costs, and that manufacturing costs remain the same as 19X2.

2. Calculate the variable cost net income for 19X3 and explain why it is different from the absorption cost net income.

3. Is the new COO due a bonus? Comment on the effectiveness of Hurley's plan to improve profits by hiring the new COO and promising the bonus.

4. Identify and explain any important ethical issues you see in this case.

18-4. Strategic Performance Measurement

Johnson Supply Company is a large retailer of office supplies. It is organized into six regional divisions, five within the United States, and one international division. The firm is growing steadily, with the greatest growth in the international division. Johnson evaluates each division as a profit SBU. Revenues and direct costs of the divisions are traced to each division using a centralized accounting system. The various support departments, including human resources, information technology, accounting, and marketing, are treated as cost SBUs and the costs are allocated to the divisions on the basis of sales revenues. The international division has cash, receivables, payables, and other investments in foreign currencies. As a result, this division experiences occasional significant losses and gains due to fluctuations in the value of foreign currencies. Based on the idea that these effects are uncontrollable, the effects of currency changes on the international division is retained in a single home-office account and is not traced to the division. Similarly, taxes paid by this division to other countries is pooled in a home office account and is not traced to it.

Because of rapidly increasing costs in the information technology (IT) department, Johnson's top management is considering changing this department to a profit SBU. IT would set prices for its services, and the user divisions could choose to purchase these services from IT or from a vendor outside the firm. The manager of IT is upset at the idea, and has told top management that this move would eventually create chaotic and ineffective information services within the firm.

REQUIRED:

1. Should Johnson's six divisions be treated as profit SBUs or some other type of strategic performance measurement system? Explain.

2. Comment on the firm's decision not to trace currency gains and losses and foreign tax expense to the international division.

3. Comment on the firm's consideration of changing the IT department from a cost SBU to a profit SBU. What are the likely effects on the firm and on the IT department?

18-5. Strategic Performance Measurement Systems II

In its thirteen year of operations, Mount Drake Software is reviewing the methods it has used to evaluate its profit SBUs. Mount Drake has six product divisions, each of which is a profit SBU, and each markets specialized software products to specific customer groups. For example, one unit markets software systems to dental practices, and another provides software for real estate management firms. A critical factor in Mount Drake's success is the commitment and competence of its systems development and programming staff. While there is a relatively high turnover for these employees, Mount Drake has managed to retain the very best and to attract the very best. In recent months, as their business has grown, and as the software industry generally has grown significantly, it has become more and more difficult for Mount Drake to attract and to retain the best staff. Mount Drake is looking for ways to become more competitive in attracting and retaining these employees. One idea is to increase employee benefits by adding training opportunities, additional paid vacation, stock investment programs, and improved health insurance. The cost of some of these additional benefits could be traced directly to the divisions, while the cost of other benefits (such as improved group health coverage and company-wide training programs) could not be directly traced to the divisions.

REQUIRED:

How should Mount Drake handle employee benefits within its current performance measurement system? Should Mount Drake change the performance measurement system, and if so, how should it be changed?

Perceptions of Earnings Quality: What Managers Need to Know

Making the bottom line look better may have a negative result

By Frances L. Ayres, CPA

Certificate of Merit, 1992-93

Two firms, Topnotch and Lowdown, have developed new products through internal research. They both experience significant increases in earnings from sales of the products, which are expected to continue indefinitely into the future. The products are assumed to be manufacturable and salable using each company's existing capacity, and the products are of equal value for Topnotch and Lowdown. Will the earnings increases be perceived as equally valuable for the two companies?

The answer is probably not if Lowdown's earnings are perceived to be of lower quality because of certain patterns and behaviors that are thought to reduce the quality of earnings and hence the value of the signal associated with a change in earnings.

A firm that wants to provide a strong signal about future earnings performance should avoid giving the negative impression that earnings are low in quality. The capital market's perception of the quality of earnings may be as important as the underlying earnings number.

The term "earnings quality" has been defined in various ways. One view of earnings quality relates to the overall permanence of earnings. That is, high-quality earnings reflect earnings that can be sustained for a long period. Another view relates earnings and stock market performance. Under this view the stronger the relation between earnings and market returns the higher the earnings quality.

THE EARNINGS QUALITY CONCEPT

The concept of earnings quality is not new. It evolved from the fundamental analysis notion of searching for undervalued and overvalued securities, which developed in the 1930s. An under- or overvalued security was one priced at less or more than its "true" or intrinsic value. This true value could be ascertained by carefully analyzing a company's financial statements for information that would suggest a company should be trading for more or less than the present market value. Implicit in this concept is the idea that the market is not efficient and that a firm's stock price moves only gradually toward its true value.

The concept of earnings quality became better known in the late 1960s and early 1970s. One of the best known advocates of the earnings quality approach to financial analysis, Thornton L. O'Glove, published *Quality of Earnings*, an investor advisory report. O'Glove's approach involves detailed analysis of the components of earnings in order to assess the degree of permanence in reported earnings.[1]

PERCEPTIONS OF EARNINGS QUALITY

Being aware of a number of factors related to perceived earnings quality can be important to a manager faced with choices that affect the bottom line. These factors may affect investors' and creditors' perception of the quality of earnings. Managers need to consider the trade-off between improvement in reported earnings and a possible negative perception of earnings quality if the improvement in earnings is perceived to result in lower-quality earnings.

To illustrate this point, consider evidence provided by Beaver and Dukes that price/earnings (P/E) ratios differ systematically among firms as a function of the method of depreciation used. Firms using straight-line depreciation which tends to result in higher earnings, will have lower P/E ratios than firms using accelerated depreciation methods, other factors being equal.[2]

In our example at the beginning, the two firms, Topnotch and Lowdown, are the same except that Topnotch uses accelerated depreciation and has a P/E multiple of 15, while Lowdown uses straight-line depreciation and has a P/E multiple of 10. If Lowdown's use of straight-line depreciation is viewed as a signal to the market that the company is seeking to report higher earnings by slow asset writeoffs, its earnings will be perceived to be of lower quality than Topnotch's earnings. The market then may discount the future value of Lowdown's innovation. This perception can affect market participants' valuation of earnings increases even if the increase in earnings has no impact on reported depreciation. Essentially, Lowdown's use of straight-line depreciation can be viewed as a signal that the company can't afford to take the faster writeoffs associated with accelerated depreciation. In contrast, Topnotch, by using accelerated depreciation, signals its strong financial position.

Note that the P/E ratio example discussed above appears contrary to the popular wisdom that low P/E stocks are good buys while high P/E stocks may be overvalued. That is, the empirical results of Beaver and Dukes indicate that the market "sees through" the accounting method choice and capitalizes earnings at a rate unaffected by the method of accounting.

This reaction may be appropriate so long as earnings innovations result in proportionate increases in depreciation. However, if, as in the above example, the innovation results in increased earnings but no change in fixed charges, then capitalization of the earnings stream based on the pre-innovation P/E ratio would result in Topnotch's innovation being overvalued relative to Lowdown's. Lowdown's use of straight-line depreciation suggests to the market that Lowdown's earnings are lower quality because straight-line depreciation increases earnings relative to accelerated. As a result, the value of even permanent earnings increases not requiring additional depreciation charges may be reduced. The firm may convey the *impression* that earnings are lower quality than they really are by using accounting methods that tend to increase earnings.

FACTORS RELATED TO PERCEIVED EARNINGS QUALITY

Several factors can influence investors' perceptions of earnings quality. Managers should be aware of these factors and of the trade-offs in making accounting policy choices and in managing accruals.

One such factor is *impression management*, which suggests that perceptions can be as real as facts. Impression management refers to the conscious management of the image conveyed to others as a result of an individual's or organization's behavior. The area of impression management has been studied extensively by researchers in management. An excellent review of concepts and research in this area is provided in Giacalone and Rosenfeld.[3] The literature in the area of impression management suggests that the way a person is perceived can be as important to that person's success as his or her underlying qualifications. Similarly, perceived earnings quality may be as important to that person's success as his or her underlying qualifications. Similarly, perceived earnings quality may be as important as actual earnings quality in determining a firm's future market performance.

Two firms with the same basic financial situation can be perceived as being of different quality. This perception may be a self-fulfilling prophecy, but its potential costs can be avoided easily if managers and accountants consider carefully the implications of making choices that may solve short-run profitability problems but lead to longer-run difficulties. They must avoid choices that lead users of financial statements to conclude that one firm's earnings are of lower quality than other firms' earnings.

Income smoothing, a second factor (see Fig. 1), refers to an attempt to report a steady stream of earnings and/or growth in earnings. Various reasons have been suggested as to why managers might attempt to smooth earnings. They may believe that:

- Smooth earnings are more highly valued,
- Smooth earnings minimize the risk of possible debt and dividend covenant violations, and
- Income smoothing can maximize management bonuses.

Earnings management refers to an intentional structuring of reporting or production/investment decisions around the bottom line impact. It encompasses income smoothing behavior but also includes any attempt to alter reported income that would not occur unless management were concerned with the financial reporting implications.

Schipper defines earnings management as "...purposeful intervention in the external reporting process with the intent of obtaining some private gain" (p. 92).[4]

For example, if management chooses not to undertake an advertising campaign because it thinks the campaign will not be cost effective given the revenue projections, this decision would not be considered earnings management but sound decision making. In contrast, if a company has sufficient funds to undertake an advertising campaign and believes it is cost effective but decides not to conduct the campaign because of the "hit" to earnings, the decision is an example of earnings management.

In general, earnings that are smoothed or otherwise managed are thought to be less informative to investors, creditors, and other users and thus are lower quality. Although some forms of earnings management may not be visible to the reader of the financial statement (as in the advertising example), other forms are more visible. Certain factors have come to be associated with firms that appear to be trying to report earnings more favorable than the underlying cash flows would suggest. These factors are discussed next and are summarized in T-1.

FACTORS IN EARNINGS MANAGEMENT

Accrual management. Accrual management refers to changing estimates such as useful lives, collectability of receivables, and other year-end accruals to try to alter reported earnings in the direction of a desired target. While accrual management often is difficult to observe directly, analysis of patterns in accruals may reveal that the cash flow changes are moving in a different direction from accruals. Investors do not necessarily view increasing sales by a more generous collection period as good news. In so doing, a company may create the impression that it is in some degree of financial distress because financially distressed companies commonly act this way.

Adoption of mandatory accounting policies. A second form of earnings management involves the timing of adoption of mandatory accounting policies. Since its formation in 1973 the Financial Accounting Standards Board (FASB) has issued 117 accounting standards—an average of more than six new standards per year. Typically, the FASB standards are enacted with a two- to three-year transition period prior to mandatory adoption but with early adoption encouraged.

While not all firms are affected by each standard issued, the relative frequency of new standards combined with long adoption windows provides an opportunity for managers to select an adoption year most favorable to the firm's financial picture. For example, in previously published research the author examined characteristics of firms adopting Statement of Financial Accounting Standards 52 (SFAS 52), "Accounting for Foreign Currency Translation."[5] Adoption of SFAS 52 gave the early-adopting firms (in 1981) the opportunity to increase earnings an average of $.38 per share or about 11% of pre-change earnings.

In comparison to firms that adopted the standard later, the early-adopting firms were smaller, closer to debt and dividend constraints, and less profitable than later-adopting firms. Not including the increase in earnings provided by early adoption, the early-adopting firms had an average decrease in earnings of 10%, while firms deferring adoption for one or two years (until 1982 or 1983) had earnings increases of 11%. Early adoption of accounting standards that increase income may convey an impression that a company needs to find income from wherever possible. Early adoption can lower investors' perceptions of earnings quality.

Voluntary accounting changes. Another method of managing earnings is to switch from one generally accepted accounting method to another. While a firm cannot make the same type of accounting method changes too frequently, it is possible to make several different types of accounting changes either together or individually over several periods. Furthermore, some types of accounting changes do not preclude a later change. For example, firms often expand or reduce the use of one inventory method. The use of voluntary accounting changes to manage earnings results in a signal similar to that associated with early adoption of mandatory standards—the company is viewed as managing earnings.

WHY NOT SMOOTH?

At first glance, the favorable bottom-line earnings effect may appear to be a good reason to smooth or manage earnings. If judicious use of year-end accruals can even-out temporary fluctuations, then why not do it? The answer is that by acting to smooth earnings the manager may create a new problem—investors' impressions that earnings have been manipulated can lower their perception of the quality of earnings, leading to lower market values and potential future problems in capital markets.

In contrast, what happens if a firm seeks to use accounting methods that, in view of managers, most closely reflect underlying cash flows? If investors perceive that managers are seeking to report earnings fairly, then underlying values of the firm should reflect this perception. Temporary fluctuations in earnings will be viewed by the market as temporary, and new

	High	Low
Accruals	Consistent from year to year	Altered frequently as preaccrual income fluctuates
Accounting methods		
Depreciation method	Accelerated	Straight-line
Inventory method	Last in, first-out	First-in, first-out
Accounting changes	Decrease income	Increase income
	Occur seldom	Occur frequently
Income pattern	Reflects underlying cash flows	Appears "managed"
Disclosure level	High	Low or misleading

products and innovations will be valued at a level reflecting the underlying cash flows related to the innovation. This effect may be enhanced if the company conscientiously follows a pattern of full disclosure regarding good news and bad news. A company with a known pattern of reliable disclosure about bad news items is likely to be more credible when a good-news event occurs.

In summary, impressions do matter, and the conscientious financial manager and management accountant will take heed of some pitfalls, pointed out here, to avoid in financial reporting. A decision that provides a boost to short-run earnings can have some very real long-term costs.

---

[1] Thornton L. O'Glove, *Quality of Earnings*, Macmillan, Inc., New York, N.Y., 1987.

[2] W. Beaver and R. Dukes, "Interperiod Tax Allocation, Earnings Expectations and the Behavior of Security Prices," *Accounting Review*, April 1972, pp. 320-332.

[3] R.A. Giacalone and P. Rosenfeld, editors, Impression Management in the Organization, Lawence Erlbaum Associates, Hillsdale, N.J. 1989.

[4] K. Schipper, "Commentary on Earnings Management," *Accounting Horizons*, 3, 1989, pp. 91-102.

[5] Frances L. Ayres, "Characteristics of Firms Electing Early Adoption of SFAS 52," *Journal of Accounting and Economics*, 8, 1986, pp. 143-158.

Chapter 19
Strategic Investment Units and Transfer Pricing
Cases
19-1   Polymer Products Company (Strategic Performance Measurement)

Readings
Gerald Lander and Mohamed E. Bayou: Does ROI Apply to Robotic Factories?
This article provides a useful summary of the limitations of ROI performance evaluation of investment SBUs. Three criteria for appropriate ROI measures are proposed: (1) the ROI measure must include long-term performance, (2) the ROI measure must consider cash flows, and (3) the ROI measure must consider the time value of money. Also, the authors argue that the ROI measure should be consistent with the phases of the project life:
- First: acquisition of the new investment
- Second: use of the new investment
- Third: disposition of the investment

Four methods are developed and illustrated for a hypothetical investment in robotics. The four methods are: (1) annual book ROI, (2) average ROI (over the project's life), (3) discounted book ROI, and (4) discounted cash flow ROI. The authors explain how the different methods are to be used at the different phases of the project's life.

Discussion Questions:
1. Which ROI method(s) should be used at each of the phases of the project's life?
2. What is the profitability index and how is it used?
3. What are the limitations of ROI, and how does the authors' proposed approach deal with these limitations?

Note: This article makes extensive use of the concept of the time value of money, and thus can also be used in Chapter 11: Capital Budgeting.

Stephen Crow and Eugene Sauls: Setting the Right Transfer Price
This article uses a case study of a fictitious company, CrysCo, Inc, a manufacturer of crystals used in electronic audio and video equipment, to illustrate the role of international tax issues in transfer pricing. CrysCo has two foreign subsidiaries, one which sells the crystals manufactured in CrysCo's home country, and a second subsidiary which uses the crystals in the manufacture of a high-resolution amplifier. The subsidiaries are assumed to be independent for transfer pricing purposes. The article explains the four methods of setting a transfer price for management purposes: (1) cost-based, (2) market-based, (3) negotiated transfer price, and (4) dictated transfer price. Also, the six transfer pricing methods for tax purposes are explained for both tangible and intangible property. The concept of tangible and intangible property is important here because CrysCo can either transfer the crystals (tangible property) or the license to produce the crystals (an intangible). The tax requirements differ for the two approaches. Tax issues for Japan and for the People's Republic of China are discussed.

Discussion Questions:
1. What is an "advance pricing agreement," and what is its purpose?
2. What are the six tax methods for transfer pricing and how do they differ?
3. Should transfer prices be determined with management or tax purposes in mind?

Cases

19-1.   Investment SBUs; Strategy; International Issues

In 19X4, the Polymer Products Company was a multinational company engaged in the manufacture of a widely diverse line of products including chemical and agricultural products, man-made fibers, electronic materials, health care, process controls, fabricated products, and oil and gas. Sales in 19X4 were $6.7 billion with the following breakdown as to operating units and major markets:

Operating Unit	Percent	Major Markets	Percent
Agricultural products	18	Agriculture	20
		Construction and home	
Biological sciences	3	furnishings	19
Fibers & intermediates			
industrial chemicals	14	Capital equipment	13
		Pharmaceuticals &	
Polymer products	28	personal products	13
Electronic materials &			
fabricated products	8	Motor vehicles	9
Baker controls	8	Apparel	7
		Chemicals and	
Oil & gas	3	hydrocarbons	7
		Other markets	12

For the past five years the firm has been restructuring its core businesses (industrial chemicals, fibers and intermediates, and polymer products) by withdrawing from those product lines that do not fit with the firm's long-term strategy or which are not expected to produce adequate long-term results.

Polymer's management has carefully examined each of the various business units and is prepared to fully support those that have the potential to compete successfully in selected markets. Businesses which cannot produce returns that exceed the company's cost of capital have been, or will be, disposed of or shut down.

As 19X5 ended, the company realigned its financial reporting of operating unit segments to more closely align it with the restructuring and to better reflect the company's operations. These new operating unit segments are:

- Agricultural products
- Crop chemicals
- Animal sciences
- Chemicals
- Electronic materials
- Baker controls
- Pharmaceuticals
- Sweeteners
- Oil and gas (this business was sold during the 4th Quarter of 19X5.)

Fibers and intermediates, industrial chemicals, polymer products, and a portion of fabricated products have been combined to form a new segment—chemicals. Two new segments, pharmaceuticals and sweeteners, include the acquired operations of a pharmaceutical company. The electronics business has been made a separate segment and the separations business, previously part of fabricated products, has been transferred to and combined with Baker controls, serving similar process control equipment markets. The former biological sciences segment has been eliminated and their animal nutrition products are now part of animal sciences. The health care division was merged with the acquired company and is included in the pharmaceuticals segment.

Company Performance Measurement Philosophy

Up until the start of the decade, Polymer focused on a performance income measure of an operating unit's performance; assigning only the directly controllable elements of sales, cost of goods sold, marketing, administrative, technical expenses, inventory, and receivables to the operating units for internal reporting purposes. Non-directly controllable elements, such as corporate staff support groups, interest expense/interest income and foreign currency gains and losses were pooled corporately and various formulae were used to assign these corporate charges to operating units for determining a pro-forma net income, return on investment, and cash flow. Such overall indicators of performance were thus only directionally representative at the operating unit level.

As some of the company's core businesses matured and declined, an awareness began to emerge of the need to shift business strategies thus requiring tougher decisions as to divestment/investment/acquisition activities. Top management recognized the need for more accurate measurement and understanding of worldwide operating unit results.

For example, currency gains and losses were treated as a component of corporate charges. Thus, if a U.S. produced product were sold to a French customer on 180-day terms, the selling business unit reflected the full sales value at the then current exchange rate; leaving the company exposed to devaluation of the French franc. If devaluation occurred, performance of the operating unit was not affected but the company results were.

As another example, all operating units applied an average worldwide tax rate to compute a pro-forma net income, return on capital, and cash flow. When an operating unit had a choice to source the same product from Belgium or the U.K., a dilemma was created. Although costs were nominally higher in the U.K., lowering a unit's performance income, the company was in a non-tax position there which drastically improved real net income. However, by reporting results using an average worldwide tax rate, all product sourcing from the U.K. appeared disadvantageous. Also, the company was not taking advantage of an entity's tax loss carry-forward situation in various pricing and sourcing decisions.

Top management wanted a reporting and performance measurement system which brought operating unit management's' attention to *all* the financial impacts of a business decision. To accomplish this, it was decided in 19X2 that as many of the income statement and balance sheet items as was practicable would be identified with each operating unit and charged out accordingly. Each operating unit would then be measured by the achievement against goals established for return on investment and cash flow as defined below.

cash flow = net income + depreciation and obsolescence − capital expenditures
+/− (change in receivables, inventories, payables, net capitalized interest, deferred taxes, other assets, and other liabilities)

$$\text{return on investment} = \frac{\text{net income} + \text{after tax interest expense}}{\text{average capital employed *}}$$

(Where investment is defined as net long-lived investment, working capital, and deferred taxes)

The incentive compensation system employed for upper management positions is essentially based upon the relative success in achieving annual budgets established for the above measures. The total corporate annual incentive award is determined somewhat rigidly, based upon where earnings fall within a budget range determined at the beginning of each year. The award is apportioned to cascade down the organization. Thus a similar quantitative assessment of results is made to reward or penalize managers for their ultimate contribution to results. The incentive awards are then presented 2/3 in cash and 1/3 in restricted stock which is accessible only after 3 years and only if stock prices meet certain appreciation tests. This latter feature was recently employed to add a long-term dimension to the program in addition to near-term annual income/cash flow results.

Prior to the new reporting and measurement scheme (called asset management) the amount of corporately pooled costs allocated as a corporate charge was over 3 percent of worldwide sales. After the asset management program was instituted, along with selected decentralization of certain corporate staff groups, these corporately pooled costs were less than 2 percent of worldwide sales.

Required:

1. What type of performance measurement system did Polymer Products use prior to the recent change?
2. What type of performance measurement system is Polymer Products using now? Why did Polymer Products move to this new system? How does the change affect the firm's global competitiveness?
3. In the new performance measurement system, should managers be held responsible for foreign currency exchange gains and losses and income taxes. (IMA, adapted)

Setting the Right Transfer Price

International managers must consider tax regulations as part of their decision criteria.

By Stephen Crow, CPA, and Eugene Sauls, CPA

When multinational companies transfer products between business segments, the prices they impose on those transfers affect many areas of decision making. An appropriate transfer price satisfies corporate management and strategy requirements and promotes congruency among corporate goals.

The cost of determining an appropriate transfer price depends on the level of harmony inherent among company goals and between those goals and the economic and regulatory environment in which the company operates. Factors affecting harmony include the company's organizational form, its corporate definition (contracts), its information systems, and the diversity of the economic and regulatory climate in which it operates.

When a company's operations are domestic, that is, conducted within a single tax jurisdiction, decision criteria reflect these conditions. When a company goes international, the cost of crossing tax borders increases proportionally with the diversity of the company's operations and the tax environment. Using a fictional company, we'll take you through transfer pricing issues for managers of multinational firms and demonstrate the magnitude of the potential impact of these rules in selected countries of the Asia/Pacific Rim Community (APRC).

CASE STUDY

CrysCo, Inc., is the parent company of a fictitious multinational corporate group that includes two subsidiaries—ManCo, Inc. (ManCo) and SalCo, Inc. (SalCo). CrysCo is domiciled in the United States, and ManCo and SalCo are its foreign subsidiaries. CrysCo produces crystals used in electronic video and audio components and is not the market's sole producer. ManCo buys a custom version of the crystal from

CrysCo and uses it in a patented high-resolution amplifier that it sells as a packaged unit. SalCo sells the basic crystal produced by CrysCo to foreign audio and video manufacturers.

If CrysCo sets an inappropriate transfer price, problems could occur on several levels. For example, if the transfer price of the custom CrysCo unit is too high. ManCo may buy from outside the organization even though buying from CrysCo may be better for the organization as a whole. Conversely, if CrysCo sets the transfer price too low, it may not provide the product to ManCo because it could get more money elsewhere. In either case the firm loses because the optimal quantity will not be exchanged.

The multinational corporate group also could be exposed to tax deficiencies, penalties, and audit costs. CrysCo may decide not to comply with foreign tax rule if the U.S. tax rate is lower than the tax rate in ManCo's foreign domicile. Profits can be shifted to CrysCo by setting a high transfer price, but if the transfer price doesn't comply with the tax rules of ManCo's domicile, the benefits gained by the income shift may be lost to tax sanctions including tax assessments and penalties. Less obvious, but just as serious, are the potential costs of double taxation or underutilized tax credits stemming from transfer price revisions based on tax audit findings.

Revenue flight is a problem for national treasuries, stimulating tax legislation and enforcement activity. It has been estimated that as much as $30 billion per year is lost to the United States from transfer pricing problems. This issue will become more significant as countries grow increasingly competitive for the international tax dollar, bringing more pressure on managers and higher costs to firms to maintain appropriate income allocations.

When the transfer price does not satisfy both the corporate management and strategy and tax requirements, the company can resolve the problem in one of three ways. First, it can take no action and accept the status quo, which may be costly and illegal. Second, the firm can redefine its contractual

TABLE 1
TRANSFER PRICING METHODS FOR TAX PURPOSES: TANGIBLE PROPERTY

Method Description	Comparable Uncontrolled Price	Resale Price	Cost Plus	Comparable Profits	Profits Split	Other
Comparables	Comparable sales between unrelated parties	Price to unrelated party less related gross profit; nonmanufacturing.	Production costs plus gross profit on unrelated sales.	Priced to yield gross profits comparable to those for other firms.	Split of combined operating profits of controlled parties.	Gross profit reasonable for "facts and circumstances."
Comparability and Reliability Standards	Similarity of property; underlying circumstance.	Comparable gross profit relative to comparable unrelated transfer.	Gross profit from same type of goods in unrelated resale.	Gross profit within range of profits for broadly similar product line.	Allocation of combined profits of controlled parties.	As appropriate.
Measures of Comparability	Functional diversity; product category; terms in financing and sales; discounts; and the like.	Functional diversity; product category; terms in financing and sales, intangibles, and the like.	Functional diversity; accounting principles; direct vs. indirect costing, and the like.	Business segment; functional diversity; different product categories acceptable if in same industry	Profits split by unrelated parties or splits from transfers to unrelated parties.	Fair allocation of profits relative to "unrelated" party sales.
Same Geographic Market	Required	Required	Required	Required	Required, but some flexibility.	Required, but some flexibility.
Comments	Deemed the best method for all firms, minor accounting adjustments allowed to quality as "substantially" the same."	The best method for distribution operations, only used where little or no value added and no significant processing.	Internal gross profit ratio is acceptable if there are both purchases from and sales to unrelated parties; if not, GPR based upon comparable firms.	Not if seller has unique technologies or intangibles, because resale price is fixed, adjust the transfer price from seller.	Controlled transaction allocations compared to profits split in uncontrolled transactions.	Least reliable; uncertainty and costs of being wrong are severe.

relationships, which may be so expensive as to be impractical and, in some cases, may not be an option—such as debt covenants. Third, the company can revise its information systems to support multiple transfer price methods. This approach provides the most practical and generally most economical (but not at zero cost) solution and will be the choice of most companies.

TRANSFER PRICE METHODS FOR MANAGEMENT PURPOSES

Four general types of transfer prices are acceptable for management purposes: cost-based, market-based, negotiated, and dictated.

Cost-based implies a cost-plus model, using full or variable cost. Two major advantages of this method

INTANGIBLE PROPERTY TRANSFER PRICING TAX RULES

Transfer pricing methods for management control and reporting purposes are substantially the same for both intangible and tangible property, but the tax rules are different. The basic "arm's-length" and "best method" tests are common to transfer pricing tax rules for both tangible and intangible property. The specifics of the methods prescribed for each are significantly different.

In Table 2, the methods are compared on four features. "Comparables" are elements that make up the acceptable transfer price, "Comparability and Reliability Standards" are the relative components of a transfer subject to comparison for each method. "Measures of Comparability" are features upon which comparability of the transfer components are assessed. "Same Geographic Market" means comparables must be taken from the same geographic market. This test is necessary but not sufficient.

If CrysCo transfers licenses to ManCo to produce and sell the crystal products rather than produce and transfer the products itself, how would these rules affect the pricing structure of the licensing arrangements between CrysCo and ManCo?

Comparable Uncontrolled Transaction—This method is preferred for pricing intangible property transfers for tax purposes. The method uses comparable transactions between unrelated parties, including contractual terms and economic conditions (such as net present value of potential profit). The rules also state that the intangibles must be used for similar products or similar industries. This method is similar to the comparable uncontrolled price method, but it focuses on the comparability of the whole transaction, not just the product being sold.

Under comparable uncontrolled transactions, the transfer is viewed as a royalty for licenses between CrysCo and ManCo. The amount of the royalty is set by reference to uncontrolled transfers of comparable intangible property under comparable circumstances. This method is preferred when the intangibles compared are the same, but it also is acceptable when they are only similar. In its review of the rules, however, even Congress admitted that it is unlikely that a company such as CrysCo can find uncontrolled companies engaged in similar activities with similar intangibles.

Although the comparable uncontrolled transaction is the preferred method, the comparability and documentation requirements make it extremely difficult, at best, for companies to comply with the criteria.

Comparable Profits Method—Under this method CrysCo sets ManCo's profit ratio at a number that is within a range of the profit ratios of comparable but unrelated competitors. The method is similar to the comparable price for tangible property because the premise is that similarly situated companies should realize similar returns. In the case of intangibles, however, the new tax rules require that the benchmark companies own similar intangibles. Similarity is based on the similarity of the product and process in which the intangible is used, the industry, contractual terms, and geographic market. Under these compliance and documentation constraints, there is little chance that comparable price can be used to determine a transfer price between CrysCo and ManCo.

Profits Split Method—CrysCo and ManCo also can consider the profits-split method. It is an acceptable method for the transfer of intangible as well as tangible property, but there is a major difference. In addition to the combined profits-split method that CrysCo could use for tangible property transfers, the company can use a residual profits-split approach. Due to the nature of intangible property, the tests of comparability and data reliability are more onerous than with tangible property transfers and seem to preclude the combined approach. In the residual profits-split method, the portion of combined profits attributable to routine business activities may be allocated between CrysCo and ManCo using some other appropriate tax method. The residual profits are attributable to the intangibles and would be allocated between CrysCo and ManCo according to an estimate of the relative value of each entity's contributions of such property. One suggested measure of such relative value is capitalized intangible development expenses.

The practical difficulties inherent in the residual profits-split method include the burden of segregating routine activities, identifying income allocation methods for each, and extracting information for comparable but uncontrolled transfers. If CrysCo and ManCo cannot accomplish these tasks, they cannot use the profits-split method.

"Other" Methods—The final option is some other method that is reasonable under the facts and circumstances. As with the tangible property transfers, there are virtually no objective guidelines under this option, there is little certainty, and there is a very high risk of challenge by tax agencies such as the IRS that could result in high costs of noncompliance

As with tangible property transfer rules, the intangible rules are fraught with comparability and reliability criteria that hamper compliance, which may encourage managers to take conservative positions for tax purposes. It also may encourage taxpayers to seek ex ante agreements with tax agencies for prospective pricing arrangements.

compatibility with market pricing policies. A major disadvantage is the lack of incentive to control costs because costs are passed on to the buying division.

A *market-based* transfer price is set as a percentage of the market value of the product or service. The transfer price should reflect the cost savings from internal transactions, for example, reduced sales force or credit department, and allocate these cost savings between the purchasing and selling divisions on some acceptable basis. If the transfer price is set at full market value, the purchasing division may transact more business with outsiders than with other divisions. A major advantage of a market-based transfer price is that it is objective—in the sense that it is set by forces outside the organization—but the market price information may not be readily available.

A negotiated transfer price is set by the managements of the buying and selling divisions meeting and agreeing on a price. A major advantage of a negotiated transfer price is that both parties presumably are satisfied with it. A major disadvantage is that divisional profits may be determined more by the negotiating ability of the managers than by their management skills. Further, a great deal of time and effort may be expended in the negotiations.

A *dictated transfer price* is set by top management. If top management has good information concerning the costs and demand characteristics, it could set a price that would optimize profits for the organization as a whole. A disadvantage of a dictated transfer price is that division managers concerned with divisional performance may be suspicious of—and unfavorably disposed toward—the dictated transfer price.

In our case study, CrysCo should choose a cost-based method for pricing its transfers to ManCo because the special production applications it performs are not duplicated in the marketplace. The transfer price to ManCo would be based on CrysCo's cost plus a specified profit margin. CrysCo will price the transfers to SalCo using a market-based transfer price method. CrysCo is not the only crystal producer, so CrysCo can obtain the necessary unrelated sales or market price information from other suppliers.

TRANSFER PRICING FOR TAX PURPOSES

T-1 describes the six transfer pricing methods that are acceptable for tax purposes. They are compared based on four features. "Comparables" are the elements of a transfer that are examined in the comparability test under each method. "Comparability and Reliability Standards" are the components of the "Comparables" subject to comparison under each method. "Measures of comparability" are the characteristics of the "Comparables" components that are assessed as measures of that comparability. The final characteristic, "Same Geographic Market," means comparables must be taken from the same geographic market. This last item is necessary for acceptability but is not sufficient.

How do these rules affect CrysCo and the other members of the multinational corporate group? (See sidebar, "The Advance Pricing Agreement Program (APA).")

Comparable Uncontrolled Price—For all companies, comparable uncontrolled price using comparable sales transactions between unrelated parties is the preferred method of pricing for tax purposes and market-based corporate management and strategy. CrysCo will find that it cannot use this method for either the ManCo or SalCo transfers. The ManCo crystal is a custom-order product, and there are no sales by CrysCo to unrelated parties, nor are there any purchases by ManCo from unrelated parties.

The SalCo transfers have a related but different problem. While CrysCo has sales to unrelated parties that otherwise would qualify, they are not sales to parties in the same geographic area as ManCo. This problem is common to most multinational corporate groups because the parent generally won't compete with its subsidiary in the subsidiary's own backyard.

Resale Price Method—This method is the best for distribution or market based organizations where little or no value is added and no significant assembly or manufacturing activity takes place. This pricing method is the preferred alternative for SalCo. The transfer price set under this method is the amount received by SalCo on reselling the crystal units to an uncontrolled outsider, reduced for an appropriate markup. CrysCo cannot show sales to unrelated parties in the "same geographic area." Therefore, the markup or gross profit ratio used must be established by reference to information on the profit ratios of unrelated companies distributing products in the "same broad product categories." The companies CrysCo uses as comparable sources also must meet the "same geographic market" requirement. Usually documentation of information on competitors is not readily available or economical to obtain.

The Cost-Plus Method—The cost-plus price is the preferred method of the manufacturing company, ManCo. Under this method CrysCo's cost of production is adjusted for an appropriate gross profit ratio (GPR). CrysCo has no unrelated party sales for comparison, so the appropriate gross profit ratio must be established from information on the profit ratios of, "comparable companies" that manufacture products "within the same broad product category" or are "within the same industry." Even though CrysCo performs custom-order work for ManCo, the same broad product category criteria should gibe the multinational corporate group sufficient flexibility to find a suitable product line in the same geographic market.

Comparable Profits Method—Failing to meet the requirements for the preferred methods, CrysCo should use the comparable profits method, which is a profit markup method using a markup percentage established by reference to a range of industry averages. The profit ratio should be based on some internal profit indicator, such as rate of return. If the product or process involved is unique in the market, there is little chance that this method can be used for determining a transfer price. It will not be a problem in transfers to SalCo but likely will preclude the use of the comparable profits method for transfers to ManCo because of the custom job order manufacturing services.

Profits-Split Method—The profits-split method re-

lies on an allocation of the combined profits of the controlled entities as calculated after the transfer to customers outside the group. This method can be used by either ManCo or SalCo in its transfers from CrysCo. It requires that the CrysCo group determine combined operating profit on intercompany transfers. The profit for each member involved in the transfer, hence the transfer price, is comparable to unit profits where uncontrolled entities are engaged in similar activities with comparable products.

The difficulty inherent in this method is isolating reliable detailed data for similar activities and comparable products. While aggregate profit data often are available for product line, the data do not have enough detail to provide for the required analysis and comparison. Therefore, the reliability of this method as the best measure of comparable transfers is compromised.

"Other" Methods— Where none of the five specific

TABLE 2
TRANSFER PRICING METHODS FOR TAX PURPOSES: INTANGIBLE PROPERTY

Method Description	Comparable Uncontrolled Transaction	Comparable Profits	Profits Split	Other
Comparables	Comparable transactions between unrelated parties	Priced to yield gross profits comparable to those for other firms.	Combined operating profits of controlled parties.	Gross profit reasonable for "facts and circumstances."
Comparability and Reliability Standards	Similarity of intangible property; underlying circumstance.	Gross profit within range of profits for similar intangibles.	Allocation of combined profits of controlled parties to emulate that of unrelated parties	As appropriate.
Measures of Comparability	Product and process category; terms in financing and sales; discounts; and the like.	Terms of intangible transfer; same industry; terms of contract.	Profits split by unrelated parties or splits from transfers to unrelated parties. Separate out intangible property profits and allocate by relative values added by each division	Fair allocation of profits relative to "unrelated" party sales.
Same Geographic Market	Required	Required	Required, but some flexibility.	Required, but some flexibility.
Comments	Deemed the best method for all firms, minor accounting adjustments allowed to find similarity and comparables.	Not if seller has unique technologies or unique intangibles.	Controlled transaction allocations compared to profit split in uncontrolled transactions.	Least reliable; uncertainty and costs of being wrong are severe.

methods can "reasonably be applied" to a transfer, the taxpayer may use another method (read as an "other" method) that is reasonable under the facts and circumstances. A major problem with this particular approach is that the method selected is vulnerable to challenge by a tax agency, so the company risks the costs of noncompliance. More onerous is that the burden of proving why a method was chosen lies with the taxpayer.

TAX METHODS IN JAPAN AND THE PEOPLE'S REPUBLIC OF CHINA

Multinational operations add a dimension to the transfer price decision matrix. For example, assume that ManCo or SalCo is domiciled in either Japan or China. Japanese methods generally are consistent with acceptable tax methods because they were adopted from an agreement of the Organization for Economic Cooperation and Development (OECD), which was modeled after U.S. rules and is the basis for most international transfer price rules. The Japanese version of the comparability standards, however, is different from the standards adopted in the U.S. rules, implying additional substantiation and documentation costs for ManCo or SalCo. Japan is now among the most aggressive countries in the world in enforcing compliance with transfer price rules, which implies a greater likelihood of audit and litigation costs, even in the absence of actual tax adjustments.

The People's Republic of China takes a very different approach. The Chinese income allocation rules do not dictate specific transfer pricing methods. Their approach is to adjust prices to market when they deem the transfer price artificially low or high. Further complicating the problems of CrysCo's managers, China is on the verge of adopting a new tax base, a value-added tax (VAT). It is not clear that any of the methods discussed earlier is acceptable for VAT purposes.

THE ADVANCE PRICING AGREEMENT PROGRAM (APA)

In March 1991, the IRS set into place the Advance Pricing Agreement Program (APA) in Revenue Procedure 91-22 (soon to be updated) as an alternative to resolving transfer pricing disputes. The following information is taken from a document prepared by the Office of the Associate Chief Counsel (International).

Designed as an alternative dispute resolution process, the APA program supplements the traditional administrative, judicial and treaty mechanisms for resolving intercompany pricing issues.

The APA process depends on coordination, cooperation, and assistance among the various IRS functions and treaty partners involved with the taxpayer. That way, transfer pricing disputes can be resolved in an effective and less labor-intensive manner for all parties. Under this approach, taxpayers can submit a timely filed return to the IRS that is in compliance with the arm's-length standard and section 482 of the Internal Revenue Code.

The general objectives of the APA process are:

- To enable taxpayers to arrive at an understanding with the IRS on three basic issues: the factual nature of the intercompany transactions to which the APA applies; an appropriate transfer pricing method (TPM) applicable to those transactions; And the expected range of results from applying the TPM to the transactions. (A range of results is not a mandatory element of an APA. The IRS will, in appropriate cases, consider APAs that set forth a TPM without the specification of any range.)
- To do so in an environment that encourages common understanding and cooperation between the taxpayer and the IRS and that harmonizes and incorporates the opinions and views of all the IRS functions involved with the taxpayer.
- To come to an agreement in an expedited fashion, as compared to the traditional method, which entails separate and distinct dealings with the Examination, Appeals, and Competent Authority functions and/or possible subsequent litigation.
- To come to an agreement in a cost effective fashion for both the taxpayer and the IRS.

The IRS team is a multifunctional partnership of personnel from District Office Examination, Appeals, Assistant Commissioner (International), and Associate Chief Counsel (International). Meeting with the IRS team is an important benefit of the program because the taxpayer does not have to deal separately with the various functions of the IRS involved with transfer pricing.

For more information on the advance Pricing Agreement Program, contact: Cindra Rehman, Prefiling Coordinator, APA Program, IRS Reporter's Building, RM 606, 300 7th St. S.W., Washington, D.C. 20024. Phone (202) 260-9825, fax (202) 260-9850.

ECONOMIC AND ORGANIZATIONAL IMPLICATIONS

A diverse transfer price environment poses several problems for a company like CrysCo in its efforts to maintain goal congruency and mitigate related cost increases. First, traditional management transfer price methods involve quantitative analysis techniques, such as linear programming, and economic analysis based on marginal revenue and marginal cost. A review of the criteria set forth by tax rules in the United States and most other countries shows that these techniques will satisfy neither the substantiation nor documentation criteria. If CrysCo is intent on using quantitative or economic analysis to set or verify its transfer price based on corporate management strategy, that alone will not satisfy the documentation and verification rules for tax purposes.

Second, there is evidence that managerial performance evaluation autonomy, optimal production decisions, and segment efficiency are the dominant organizational objectives managers use in selecting a transfer price method. They are not tax criteria, and it is not clear from the descriptions that tax and financial criteria are compatible. It is unlikely that CrysCo's transfer price method using tax criteria will meet the corporate management and strategy criteria also.

Third, tax rules require that transfer price methods meet comparability and unrelated or uncontrolled party standards. The implication for CrysCo or any other multinational corporate group is increased information costs incurred to satisfy the more rigorous information and documentation criteria of the tax code. In the international setting, the potential for diversity among countries' tax rules, the range of alternative transfer price methods, and the diversity of compliance requirements exacerbate the problem.

Last, failure to act—that is, accept a status quo—could prove the most economically disadvantageous action of all. The penalties for noncompliance with U.S. rules were changed in January 1993. Japan and a number of other Asia/Pacific and European countries have threatened to make similar changes in their penalty provisions. If, on audit, noncompliance is found, CrysCo could face penalties of up to 40% of the tax deficiency assessed plus $10,000 per month for every month in which CrysCo and the group fail to meet the compliance requirements.

As you can see, an inappropriate transfer price manifests as strategy and control inefficiencies, tax costs, or contracting and information systems costs. A manager must analyze carefully all the potential economic consequences of setting a transfer price to ensure that it is in compliance with corporate management strategy and tax requirements, that it mitigates incremental costs of information and contracting system adjustments, and that it promotes goal congruency throughout the company.

Does ROI Apply to Robotic Factories

By Gerald H. Lander and Mohamed E. Bayou

Return on investment (ROI) has been the most popular method of performance evaluation in most companies for the past 50 to 70 years. Many companies adopted a decentralized management philosophy along with the RO technique. Even though the decentralized structures in large corporations were very complex, the easily understandable ROI ratio offered top management a handy tool for comparing performances of numerous divisions. But ROI has come under increasing criticism, raising the question: Does the growing trend toward automation alter the validity of this criticism? In other words, is the traditional ROI still valid for managerial performance evaluation in the new robotic manufacturing environment?

MAJOR ATTACKS ON ROI

We evaluate various measures of ROI in the context of the three phases of the decision cycle: acquisition, utilization, and disposition of robotic equipment. Then we present an ROI measure that satisfies the other criteria of acceptance.

Several critics have questioned the validity of the ROI method of performance evaluation. Elements targeted by this criticism appear in the ROI model commonly known as the DuPont formula, shown in T-1. Typically, the variables of earnings, sales, and investments in this formula are all measured annually. Cash flows, time-value of money, and analysis beyond one year are excluded from the ROI measurement. As machinery replaces labor, with the consequent shift to more fixed costs and fewer variable costs, this criticism becomes more cogent. For example, Dearden contends that while ROI is a valid measure of past performance, it is not valid for setting future objectives because the historical costs of assets used in the formula are meaningless in planning future actions.[1]

Another criticism is that ROI creates dysfunctional intercompany goals. For example, an investment project with an ROI higher than the firm's cost of capital may be acceptable, yet the divisional manager may reject it unless it exceeds the currently attained ROI rate. Acceptance would dilute the manager's current ROI level, so many acceptable projects probably never get proposed to top management.

Another dysfunctional type of behavior arises when the investment in the denominator of the ROI formula is evaluated at net book value. Thus, as assets get older, stable earnings augment ROI, which in turn, may lead to management reluctance to replace the old assets with new advanced technology. This criticism of ROI is especially to the point in a robotic factory—robot obsolescence is more significant than obsolescence gnificant than obsolescence in a labor-intensive factory.

Send argues that the use of ROI motivates management to operate near full capacity in order to maximize ROI,[2] Even worse, divisional management may manipulate short-term income, and the asset base to the point of long-term detriment to the earning power of the company.[3] Consider this scenario: An insecure manager would be unlikely to accept projects that generate negative ROI results during the earlier years and large positive ones during later periods. Recognizing this problem, the corporation may be obliged to centralize several strategic discretionary programs such as R&D in order to minimize these ROI manipulations. Such interference by corporate headquarters does not harmonize with the decentralization philosophy.

In spite of these criticisms, ROI still enjoys internal popularity in evaluating managerial performance, for several reasons:

- As a ratio, ROI is simpler to understand than other evaluation methods such as residual income.
- It is a single measure that combines the effects of three critical performance variables—sales, earnings, and investment.
- ROI is popular with financial analysts, investors, creditors, and other external information users, a fact that encourages corporate top management to tie divisional performance to the way the public views the corporation.[4]

So strong are these reasons that ROI gained popularity as attacks on it increased during the '70s.[5]

Because the use of ROI as an evaluation method undoubtedly will continue in practice, managers and other business people need to understand the mechanics and limitations of ROI.

CRITERIA FOR AN ACCEPTABLE ROI MEASURE

Given the serious criticisms of ROI and the nature of machine-intensive environments, the following criteria become necessary for an acceptable ROI measure:

- An ROI measure must consider long-term performance. This criterion is particularly relevant to the robotic factory; automation decreases variable labor and variable overhead costs and increases fixed costs over several years.
- An ROI measure must consider cash flows, a corollary of the first criterion. In the long run, cash flows are more relevant than accrual income because most accrued revenues and expenses will be settled in cash. In addition, the use of cash flows instead of accrual income avoids the distortions caused by the latter, namely, discouragement of growth by the use of net book value in ROI computations[6] and the meaningless use of historical costs of assets for planning future actions.[7]
- An ROI measure must consider the time-value of money, a corollary of the first two criteria. Because the ROI measure incorporates cash flows in long-run planning, discounting these flows in the ROI computations becomes natural.

To apply these criteria properly, managers need to understand the role of ROI in the various decision processes for acquisition, utilization, and disposition of robotic assets.

THE DECISION CYCLE FOR ROBOTIC ASSETS

The life cycle of a robotic asset as an investment generally goes through three different phases. First, it is acquired, then used in operations, and finally disposed of by replacement, sale, or discarding. Each phase requires different decisions and information. Furthermore, each phase has a different impact on the goals of the manager making the investment decision and on the goals of the division as an economic entity.

For fairness and accuracy in performance measurement, the three phases have to be analyzed from the manager's viewpoint separately from that of the division. Dearden argues that the current performance evaluation system fail to distinguish between the fi-

TABLE 1
THE DUPONT FORMULA

$$ROI = \frac{Earnings}{Sales} \times \frac{Sales}{Investment} = \frac{Earnings}{Investment}$$
$$= Margin \times Turnover$$

nancial performance of the manager and that of the organizational unit being managed.[8] The distinction is important because the manager's potential for success and failure often differs from the division's. Moreover, the extent of the manager's controllability of revenues and expenses is irrelevant to measuring a division's performance because the division's performance incorporates both controllable and uncontrollable income determinants.

Fig. 1 shows how ROI and capital budgeting techniques generally are applied in practice to the three phases of the decision cycle.

The acquisition phase includes all activities necessary for the purchase, installation, and preparation for use of a new robotic asset. Capital budgeting models such as the net present value, internal rate of return, profitability index, and payback period commonly are applied in practice for this phase (Box 1 in Fig. 1). ROI usually is not applied in the evaluation of the division's performance during this phase (Box IV in Fig. 1).

The utilization phase involves the actual use of the asset in operations, which normally affects the manager's performance. Hence, ROI is applied frequently (Box V in Fig. 1), and capital budgeting models rarely are applied (Box V in Fig. 1), and capital budgeting models rarely are applied (Box II). This phase has two problems. First, with robotic assets, the manager's controllability decreases because of the large value of the assets, with costs that become sunk as soon as the assets are acquired. In addition, in some companies top management evaluates major investments in robots, reducing the divisional manager's influence over the investment base and decreasing the applicability of ROI as a means to

FIGURE 1
ROI AND CAPITAL BUDGETING MODELS APPLIED TO THE THREE PHASES OF THE DECISION CYCLE

	Acquisition	Utilization	Disposition Replacement
Capital Budgeting	I Applied	II N/A	III Applied
ROI	IV N/A	V Applied	VI Applied

TABLE 2
ROI ANALYSIS IN THE SHORT AND LONG RUN

		Year 1	Year 2	Year 3	Year 4	Year 5
Cost of robot and accessories	(a)	90,000	90,000	90,000	90,000	90,000
Installation	(b)	10,000	10,000	10,000	10,000	10,000
Total (a + b)	(c)	100,000	100,000	100,000	100,000	100,000
Annual Costs:						
Depreciation	(d)	20,000	20,000	20,000	20,000	20,000
Maintenance	(e)	1,000	2,000	3,000	4,000	5,000
Operating & program	(f)	3,000	3,000	3,000	3,000	3,000
Insurance	(g)	3,000	3,000	3,000	3,000	3,000
Total (d + e + f + g)	(h)	27,000	28,000	29,000	30,000	31,000
Annual Benefits:						
Quality effect:						
On sales & rework	(i)	20,000	20,000	20,000	20,000	20,000
Materials savings	(j)	12,000	12,000	12,000	12,000	12,000
Labor savings:						
$10/hour	(k_1)	20,000	20,000	20,000	20,000	20,000
$20/hour	(k_2)	30,000	30,000	30,000	30,000	30,000
$30/hour	(k_3)	40,000	40,000	40,000	40,000	40,000
Overhead savings (30% of labor cost):						
$3/hour	(l_1)	6,000	6,000	6,000	6,000	6,000
$6/hour	(l_2)	9,000	9,000	9,000	9,000	9,000
$9/hour	(l_3)	12,000	12,000	12,000	12,000	12,000
Annual Net Benefits $= (l + j + k_l + l_l) - h = m_l$						
Labor = $10/hour	(m_1)	31,000	30,000	29,000	28,000	27,000
Labor = $20/hour	(m_2)	44,000	43,000	42,000	41,000	40,000
Labor = $30/hour	(m_3)	57,000	56,000	55,000	54,000	53,000

1. Annual Book ROI $= \dfrac{\text{Net Annual Benefits}}{\text{Initial Investment}} = \dfrac{m_i}{c}$

The term "net benefits" indicates the use of accrual income rather than cash flows in the computations.

Annual Book ROI:

	Year 1	Year 2	Year 3	Year 4	Year 5
at $10/hour	31%	30%	29%	28%	27%
at $20/hour	44%	43%	42%	41%	40%
at $30/hour	57%	56%	55%	54%	53%

2. Average ROI $= \dfrac{\text{Average Net Benefits Over 5 Years}}{\text{Initial Investment}} = \dfrac{\sum m/5}{c}$

This ROI also is known as the accounting rate of return

Average ROI when labor is $10/hour = 29%
Average ROI when labor is $20/hour = 42%
Average ROI when labor is $30/hour = 55%

3. Discounted Book ROI $= \dfrac{\text{Present Value of Net Benefits}}{\text{Initial Investment}}$

(The discount rate, i.e., cost of capital used = 10%)

Discounted ROI when labor is $10/hour = 111%
Discounted ROI when labor is $20/hour = 160%
Discounted ROI when labor is $30/hour = 209%

4. Discounted-Cash-Flow ROI (DCF ROI) $= \dfrac{\text{Present Value of Net Cash Inflows}}{\text{Initial Investment}}$

Because depreciation expense (d) is not a cash item it is added back:

Net Cash Inflows $= m_i + d - c = n_i$ for year 1
$= m_i + d = n_i$ for each of years 2-5

		Year 1	Year 2	Year 3	Year 4	Year 5
$10/hour	(n_1)	(49,000)	50,000	49,000	48,000	47,000
$20/hour	(n_2)	(36,000)	63,000	62,000	61,000	60,000
$30/hour	(n_3)	(23,000)	76,000	75,000	74,000	73,000

The discount rate, i.e., cost of capital used = 10%: DCF ROI:
When labor is $10/hour = 0.86
When labor is $20/hour = 1.36
When labor is $30/hour = 1.85

evaluate the manager's performance. Yet these limitations do not affect ROI's usefulness in evaluating the investment center's performance. Second, the apparent inconsistency of applying capital budgeting models for the acquisition phase (Box 1) and ROI for the utilization phase (Box V) creates confusion and unfair reporting if only one performance report is issued for evaluation.

The disposition phase is, in effect, an acquisition phase if it leads to replacing the old asset with a new one. Thus, capital budgeting models usually are applied (Box III) but only as a secondary justification. That is, a manager rationally would apply ROI first to determine if the replacement improves the currently attained ROI level (Box VI). If it improves the ROI, the manager models to justify the replacement decision to senior management. On the other hand, if the replacement decision negatively affects the current ROI, the replacement issue may be suppressed and never be made known to superiors even if it is acceptable to the corporation.

SCREENING DIFFERENT ROI MODELS

To avoid these conflicts, a modified ROI model should be used in all of the six boxes of Fig. 1. T-2 illustrates how to accomplish this consistency. A flexible robotic system with an economic life of five years is considered as a replacement for an older labor-intensive system. Flexible manufacturing systems are the new trend in manufacturing. They integrate machines and systems to produce a particular product or a major component from start to finish. A flexible manufacturing system can take different forms. It can be a series of interlocked electronic machining centers, controlled by a computerized robot, which performs a set of prescribed operations or it can be one machine performing a complex series of mechanical tasks. These systems normally provide several benefits: reduced material handling and work-in-process and increased quality, flexibility, and throughput.[9] The example in T-2 is designed to capture most of these features. In reality, precisely predicting benefits and costs beyond one year is difficult. Probability distributions can be applied to incorporate these uncertainties, but to simplify the analysis, T-2 does not include probability assessments.

T-2 shows four different measures of ROI:

1. The Annual Book ROI. This traditional ROI measure, which involves no discounting or averaging and ignores cash flows and the time-value of money, concentrates on a single year of performance. Notice in T-2 that the ROI ratio increases as automation replaces labor costs. This measure is simple to understand.

2. The Average ROI. This method also is known as the accounting rate of return. The method improves upon the traditional annual ROI because it considers the entire life of the asset. (A moving average ROI may be employed. For example, when the first year of the planning period expires, the sixth year would be added at the end of the period. Thus, a new average for ROI will be calculated every year, giving the manager a continuous five-year planning horizon.) The average ROI method, however, ignores cash flows and the time-value of money.

3. Discounted-Book ROI. This method considers the time-value of money and the long-run performance. Nevertheless, it includes accrual income (which we call net benefits) rather than cash flows in the computations. Accordingly, depreciation expense on line "d" in T-2, which is not a cash item, is incorporated into the computation. Can the discounted-book ROI be used to evaluate a manager's performance? A manager's performance should be measured over a period longer than one year, a requirement for applying this method, using budgeted and actual data. Therefore, a good performance results when the actual discounted-book ROI ratio equals at least the budgeted ratio.

TABLE 3 THE CAPITAL BUDGETING MODEL OF PROFITABILITY INDEX			
Profitability Index	=	$\dfrac{\text{Present Value of Total Cash Inflows}}{\text{Initial Investment}}$	
Since Net Cash Inflows	=	Total Cash Inflows − Initial Investment	
Profitability Index	=	$\dfrac{\text{P.V. of Net Cash Inflows} + \text{Initial Investment}}{\text{Initial Investment}}$	
	=	$\dfrac{\text{P.V. of Net Cash Inflows}}{\text{Initial Investment}} +$	$\dfrac{\text{Initial Investment}}{\text{Initial Investment}}$
	=	DCF +	1.00
Thus...DCF ROI	=	Profitability Index −	1.00

4. Discounted-Cash-Flows ROI (DCF ROI). This method satisfies all three criteria for acceptance, and it considers the time-value of cash flows over the life of the robotic asset. The mathematical format of this model is shown in the first line of section 4, T-2. The DCF ROI measure relates to the capital budgeting model of the profitability index. This index is defined in the literatures of accounting and finance as shown in T-3.

T-2 shows DCF ROI ratios of .86, 1.36, and 1.85 when hourly labor wage rates are $10, $20, and $30, respectively. Thus, larger savings in labor costs increase the DCF ROI ratio. Generally, interpretation of DCF ROI ratios parallels that of the profitability index. For instance, if a project has a DCF ROI ratio of zero, it indicates that the project's internal rate of return (IRR) equals the interest rate (or cost of capital) used in the discounting process. Similarly, a positive DCF ROI ratio indicates an IRR greater than the cost of capital, and a negative DCF ROI means an IRR lower than the cost of capital. In general, the larger the DCF ROI ratio, the more profitable the project. Greater cost of capital used in discontinuing the cash flows also lowers the DCF ROI ratio.

The application of this DCF ROI model to the six cells of the decision cycle depicted in Fig. 1 eliminates the inconsistency problems caused by applying capital budgeting and the traditional ROI models to the decision cycle as discussed above. The DCF ROI model satisfies the three acceptance criteria of: (1) the emphasis on long-run performance, (2) cash flows, and (3) time-value of money. Finally, the DCF ROI can be used in conjunction with the traditional ROI. Probability distributions can be incorporated into the analysis to account for uncertainties of future cash flows. These computations can be made easily by using available software packages on present value applications.

[1] J. Dearden, "The Case Against ROI," *Harvard Business Review*, May-June 1969, pp. 124-135; his arguments on the subject are still valid today.

[2] A. H. Seed, III, "Cost Accounting in the Age of Robotics," MANAGEMENT ACCOUNTING®, October 1984, pp. 39-41.

[3] L. B. Hoshower and R. P. Crum, "Straightening the Tortuous—and Treacherous—ROI Path," MANAGEMENT ACCOUNTING®, December 1986, pp. 41-44.

[4] J. S. Reece and W. R. Cool, "Measuring Investment Center Performance," *Harvard Business Review*, May-June 1978, pp. 28-176.

[5] Ibid.

[6] J. J. Mauriel and R. N. Anthony, "Misevaluation of Investment Center Performance," *Harvard Business Review*, March-April 1966, pp. 98-105.

[7] J. Dearden, "Measuring Profit Center Managers," *Harvard Business Review*, September-October 1987, pp. 84-88.

[8] Ibid.

[9] R. A. Howell and S. R. Soucy, "The New Manufacturing Environment: Major Trends for Management Accounting," MANAGEMENT ACCOUNTING®, July 1987, pp. 21-27.

Beyond the Numbers

To help financial managers in this endeavor, we developed a Business Assessment Model, that should improve the quality of management decisions that depend on financial analyses. The model, which resembles a pyramid, frames financial decisions in the context of the entire business (see Fig. 1). It is segmented horizontally into three subsets that increase in importance from the pyramid's base to its peak. The foundation includes the core business, market, and competition, which gauge a company's ability to *generate revenue*. The second tier contains the operations and performance elements, which measure a company's ability to *create value* for customers and stockholders, respectively. Finally, the pyramid's peak is the management element, which evaluates a company's *leadership quality*.

It is the interrelationships of the elements that strongly influence a business's overall prospects and particularly its resilience during turbulent periods. The model emphasizes the assessment of revenue because it is the least controllable item that an analyst evaluates. Hence, the reasons why the Business Assessment Model improves decision making become clear:

- First, management accountants and financial analysts often are closer to the data source than executive management, so they usually know which information is reliable and which is not.

- Second, it is common for analysts to rely on someone else's work, which, if flawed, can taint the financial analysis that is used for management decisions.

- Third, there is a difference between precision and accuracy, which can be shaded by the robust data and sophisticated quantitative methods that are at the analyst's disposal. An analyst can be quite precise in method yet very wrong in outcome.

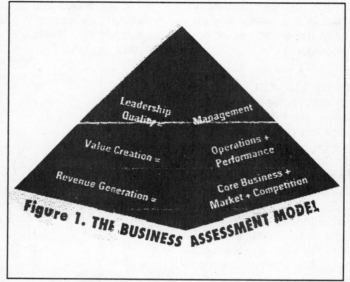

Figure 1. THE BUSINESS ASSESSMENT MODEL

The Business Assessment Model intentionally de-emphasizes quantitative methods because most analysts, who already are steeped in data and formulas, need a framework for sifting and sorting through information not another algorithm. Moreover, given that financial statements simply translate decisions and actions into accounting language, analysts must avoid the common pitfall of failing to see beyond the numbers. The Business Assessment Model should enhance the ability of the management accountant or financial analyst to interpret the results of a business assessment accurately.

UNDERSTANDING THE PROCESS

The analyst can gather the data required for the six elements by posing the questions found in T-1 about a business that is under review.

CORE BUSINESS; "What is their business?" The answer to this question conveys the essence of a company. Indeed, a company that exhibits such clarity of purpose, which is part of a strong mission statement, tends to consistently outperform its competitors because its resources are concentrated on a relatively narrow area for maximum effect.[1]

An often-used illustration involves a company whose business could be defined as either railroads or transportation. Although both are correct, the term transportation conveys what the company actually does, which is moving certain types of cargo from one place to another via steel rails for a particular type of customer. The company's expertise, therefore, is transportation. But this fact does not imply that it should diversify into building cargo ships, which is a different business altogether, nor does it suggest that the company limit itself to steel rails because innovation, like interstate highways and airplanes, eventually will erode too narrow a focus. The nuance here is

TABLE 1	
INPUT FOR BUSINESS ASSESSMENT MODEL	
Key Elements	**Input Requirements**
Core Business	"What is their business?"
Market	"Who is the customer?"
	"What customer needs do they satisfy"
	"What are the macro drivers of demand?"
Competition	"What are the key opportunities and risks?
Operations	"How do they make money?"
Performance	"What is the revenue growth rate?"
	"What is the contribution margin?"
	"What is the return on capital?"
Management	"Are they up to the task at hand?"

subtle, but it communicates the focal point of management's attention.

MARKET: "Who is the customer?" "What customer needs do they satisfy?" "What are the macro drivers of demand?" These questions help the analyst understand how a business generates revenue and from whom. Without this knowledge, any budgeting, financing, or strategic analysis will be of limited value because the analyst cannot be confident that sales will meet expectations. "Who is the customer?" addresses three issues.

1. Who, exactly, is purchasing a company's products or services? The answer to this question should be as specific as possible. Moreover, the analyst should differentiate between actual customers—those who are buying the products or services—and potential customers the company is targeting; they may not be one in the same.

2. What causes the customer to make a purchase? Typical variables to be considered include impulse purchases vs. those that are planned; luxury items vs. necessities; and whether or not the product or service is a complement to another that has a significant influence on demand. An analyst also should consider how price changes influence revenue (price elasticity of demand). Simply knowing that revenue is generated via direct sales, telemarketing, or advertising is insufficient.

3. Are there multiple customer levels to account for in a purchase decision? In other words, who really makes the purchase decision for a given product or service? Consider the average hospital, which has at least three "customers" who are parties to each transaction: the patient who receives the services, the physician who admits the patient and provides the medical care, and the HMO or insur-

ance company that pays the bill. In order to generate revenue, hospitals must market themselves to everyone who participates in the decision to purchase hospital services.

Asking *"What customer needs do they satisfy?"* is the analyst's attempt to specify the core benefit the product or service provides. The answer to this question gives the solution to the fundamental need that must be satisfied to create demand; as such, it must be broad enough to convey the essence of customers' needs. The management accountant or financial analyst must understand this issue because even subtle changes in customers' needs will affect revenue.

To illustrate the foregoing, we could say that automobile manufacturers do not really sell cars but rather freedom and mobility. To test the validity of this benefit, consider what you don't have when your car's engine won't start. You don't have either freedom or mobility (assuming, of course, that adequate substitutes are unavailable). Therefore, you could conclude that future revenues for the automobile industry are contingent upon satisfying the need for freedom and mobility by producing reliable cars.

Finally, *"What are the macro demand drivers?"* focuses on external forces that could have a material effect on revenue. Examples of such demand drivers include:

*   Government regulations,
*   Interest rates and raw material prices,
*   Weather conditions,
*   Demographics, and
*   General economic conditions.

In looking at these variables, the analyst considers the external factors that create uncertainty in the revenue line as well as how the company can hedge against these risks, if at all.

COMPETITION: "What are the key opportunities and risks?" The model also allows the analyst to expose the strengths and vulnerabilities of a company and its competitors. It is not enough to rank competing firms by sales dollars, market share, geographic coverage, or some other measure. So the model integrates the opportunities and risks of a given competitive environment into a matrix that presents the company vis-à-vis its major competitors in terms of the factors that influence purchase decisions. By identifying the nature of each factor for each company and then arranging the information in the matrix, the analyst can evaluate each one individually and in relation to its peer group.

TABLE 2
COMPETITOR MATRIX: AUTOMOBILE MANUFACTURERS

	Competitor A	Competitor B	Competitor C	ACME
PRODUCT (Reliability; 10 is highest)	10	6	3	7
PRICE (% of mean)	85%	100%	125%	100%
PLACE (Dealerships/1mm population)	35	15	50	20
PROMOTION (Television advertising budget)	$60 million	$85 million	$150 million	$90 million
5-Year Growth Rate – Unit Sales	20%	5%	2%	7%

In the process of completing the matrix, the analyst should gain two critical insights. First, the company's vulnerabilities become quite obvious (and are, incidentally, synonymous with advantages for the competition). Second, each competitor's weaknesses also become evident, which provides opportunities for the company under review to exploit as competitive advantages. The following hypothetical example illustrates this point.

An automobile manufacturer, ACME Motors, is considering building a new plant that would be funded by cash reserves and the issuance of 30-year bonds. The capital investment analysis indicates that it should proceed, but how confident would you be in the revenue forecast? Demand for automobiles probably will continue, but it is uncertain from whom they will be purchased. To address this problem, measure ACME's prospects in relation to those of its three primary competitors. Assume that all companies produce only one model.

The answer is shown in T-2, a competitor matrix that highlights ACME's areas of opportunity and risk. Variables that drive consumer decisions in automobile purchases are shown in column 1 and are based on a marketing mix[2] that isolates them. The information in the matrix suggests several things about ACME's revenue prospects. First, market research indicates that the decision to buy a new car is influenced strongly by four factors: reliability, relative price, access to dealerships, and advertising on network television. Second, of ACME's three competitors:

- Competitor A is experiencing the fastest growth because of excellent product reliability, value pricing, broad distribution, and adequate advertising.
- Competitor B resembles ACME Motors most closely, at least from the consumer's perspective. Only marginal differences exist in product reliabil-

ity, dealership access, ad spending, and unit sales growth.
- Competitor C appears to be surviving because of huge advertising spending and a reputation that once deserved premium pricing, but the stagnant growth rate and horrible product reliability clearly indicate a weakened competitor.

To be confident that the revenue and cash flows will materialize to sustain the new plant, ACME needs to verify that it can attain and sustain sufficient market share. Initiatives that offer such confidence include commitments from management to improve product reliability, maintain or reduce prices, increase the number of dealerships, and maintain media spending on network TV advertising.

If management doesn't commit to these initiatives, the long-term revenue forecast, from which net present value and internal rate of return analyses are derived to justify the new plant, should be reconsidered.

OPERATIONS: "How do they make money?" With this question, the analyst is identifying where in the company's operating cycle value is actually created by delivering to the customer a core benefit or solution to a fundamental need. In this context, value is defined from the customer's perspective. In addition, the analyst can understand any business operation as a system in which resources, such as cash, raw material, information and other assets, are converted and transformed from inputs to outputs.[3] The operations element of the model is important for two reasons:

1. Knowing exactly where value is created (what the customer really pays for) is like knowing which goose, among all others, lays the golden eggs. With this information, it becomes possible to set priorities regarding the allocation of capital and other scarce resources.

TABLE 3
VALUE-ADDED OPERATIONS ANALYSIS—ADVERTISING AGENCY

Time	t	t + 1	t + 2	t + 3	t + 4	t + 5	t + 6
Steps in the operating cycle (benefits for clients)	Agency wins competition for a new account	Advertising plan is developed	Market re-search is planned and conducted	Advertising ideas are created	Ad is filmed and edited	Media time purchased from TV networks for $10,000,000	Submit and collect invoice (15% of media time purchased)
Responsible department*	Account team	Account team	Research department	Creative directors	Production team	Media department	Accounting department
Value created for clients (0 to 5)	0	3	2	5	3	1	0

*For simplicity, the cells in the "Responsible Department" now are limited to one department in each step. But in any company, most of the steps in an operating cycle require input from other departments as well, so the analyst should differentiate between departments having primary or secondary responsibility for each step.

2. The vibrancy of the value-creating area indicates a company's future prospects. For example, a high rework rate in a manufacturer or a high turn-over rate of creative personnel in an advertising agency may indicate major problems for those companies in the near future.

But classifying each part of a business as either "value added" or "support" does not suggest that sup-port functions (or the people in them) are superfluous. To the contrary, they permit the value-added functions to operate smoothly and efficiently.

Here's one approach to determining where in its operating cycle a company creates value:

- Specify the "...customer needs...they satisfy..." and the benefits they deliver as prescribed in the market assessment.

- Identify the major steps involved in the operation.

- Document the critical resources required for each step in the process, such as labor, raw material, and information. Then,

- Assign numerical values to each step to signify the "value added" created for the customer.

Let's use an advertising agency, the classic ex-ample of a service firm that relies on "intellectual capital" to create value for its clients, as an illustration. After determining the customer needs that the agency satisfies (defined here as enhancing demand for the client's products or services), we could assemble the information in T-3.

From this analysis, it is clear that the greatest value added for the client is in developing advertising ideas, such as writing a memorable phase or devel-

oping a powerful visual image. Among all of the agency functions, it is what the client pays for. This fact also is reflected in the remuneration paid to senior creative directors, who usually are the best-paid em-ployees in an advertising agency. Therefore, an agency's greatest source of value is in this depart-ment.

PERFORMANCE: "What is the revenue growth rate? "What is the contribution (or gross) mar-gin?" "What is the return on capital?" When ad-dressing these questions, the analyst finally has a need to sharpen his or her pencil. But this element of the model is limited to three measures: growth in sales, contribution (or gross) margin, and return on capital. I'm not denying the importance of other ratios and financial measures, especially cash flow analysis, but I'm emphasizing three measures that:

- Are appropriate for assessing any business re-gardless of its industry or maturity.

- Focus on the economic essence of a company and reveal either fundamental problems or earning power that otherwise may not be obvious; and

- Are not overly complex or time-consuming to cal-culate.

A caveat: All financial ratios have limitations, es-pecially the ease of manipulation and the reliability of the financial statements on which they are based.

Sales growth: The sales growth ratio is the clear-est measure of the demand for a company's products or services especially over a period of years and in comparison to competing firms. Sales growth is cal-culated as:

Sales Growth

$$\frac{S_t - S_{t-1}}{S_{t-1}}$$

Where: S = Sales
t = Current Period
T − 1 = Previous Period

Adjustments the analyst will find useful include comparing the growth of unit sales to that of dollar sales and factoring out the effects of acquisitions and divestitures on sales. Red flags that warrant closer inspection include:

- Stagnant or falling sales, especially when competitors report growing or stable sales, respectively;

- Divergence in the trend lines of unit sales and dollar sales; and

- Sales growth attributable to acquisitions, especially if the revenue of the base business or acquired companies is actually contracting.

Contribution or gross margin: The contribution or gross margin indicates the franchise power, or brand equity, of a given enterprise. A margin in excess of 50% often suggests the presence of proprietary advantages (such as valuable patents, trademarks, or an extraordinary consumer preference for the goods or services the firm sells). Such advantages usually can support a premium pricing strategy. The formulas for these ratios are:

Contribution or Gross Margin

Contribution Margin: $\dfrac{S - VC}{S}$

Gross Margin: $\dfrac{S - CGS}{S}$

Where:
S = Sales
VC = Variable Costs
CGS = Cost of Goods Sold

Margins that either remain constant or increase (especially when compared in relation to a competitor's) are favorable signs. Moreover, the safety, high contribution or gross margins also can be a quantifiable competitive advantage.

Of these two measures, preference should be given to the contribution margin because it highlights the company's ability to cover fixed charges, which becomes particularly important in turnarounds, start-ups, and highly-leveraged firms. When variable cost

information is not readily available, however, or when a company has few variable costs (as is often the case in information technology enterprises), the gross margin ratio is an excellent substitute.

Red flags indicating a need for further analysis include:

- Income that increases at a slower rate than sales or that decreases at a faster rate than sales:

- Margins that vary more than 5% (+/−) each year over three or more years; and

- Margins that, while at least satisfactory, are the result of relatively few products or services in a company's portfolio (concentration risk). But concentration risk can be mitigated by proprietary advantages such as intellectual property or franchise power.

Return on capital: Return on capital (ROC) conveys a company's overall financial well-being by indicating how efficiently the company uses all of the capital with which management is entrusted to generate a profit, regardless of whether the capital is obtained from stockholders or lenders. Furthermore, as stated in the seminal book, *Graham & Dodd's Security Analysis*, "The most comprehensive gauge of success of an enterprise is the percentage earned on invested capital."[4] It becomes clear that a company must earn an acceptable return on capital, or its prospects will dim quickly. The formula for this ratio is:

Return on Capital

$$\frac{EBIT}{Capital}$$

Where
EBIT = Earnings Before Interest and Taxes ("operating profit")
Capital = (Equity + LTD + Deferred Taxes)
Equity = (Preferred Stock + Common Stock + Retained Earnings − Treasury Stock)
LTD = (Long-Term Debt + Current Maturities of Long-Term Debt)

Note: Short-term debt, such as commercial paper, should be included in LTD if used to finance long-term assets; any mezzanine securities should also be included in LTD.

Generally speaking, a high ROC minimizes a company's dependence on external capital sources, giving it more financial flexibility. It is essential, however, to compare a company's ROC with that of its competitors in the industry, as well as the industry average ROC with that of other industries, to assess performance fully. The maturity of both the company and its industry, as well as the capital-intensive nature of the industry, are relevant. Of greatest importance for our purposes, however, is that the ROC ratio permits the analyst to determine the real return on capital, or whether or not the company is creating or destroying corporate value. By comparing the firm's ROC with the weighted average cost of capital (WACC), which includes the cost of equity as well as the interest costs of debt, the universal goal of creating shareholder value can be measured unequivocally. This relationship is expressed as:

If ROC > WACC, then value is created.
If ROC < WACC, then value is destroyed.

To quantify the amount of value a company creates or destroys in a given year in dollar terms, consider the financial information about a hypothetical company shown in T-4. If the ROC had been 4.6% lower than the WACC, then $4,600,000 of value would have been destroyed. A company that consistently earns less than its cost of capital is on a slippery slope

that only becomes more so with the passage of time because it cannot sustain such an imbalance indefinitely. At some point, the capital markets, both public and private, will become less than enthusiastic about investing additional funds. Also, customers will gravitate toward competitors and if the company is publicly owned, hostile suitors will emerge. If not rejuvenated soon, the company is likely to complete its slide into insolvency.

MANAGEMENT: "Are they up to the task at hand?"
Evaluating management is the least precise and most difficult element of any business assessment, yet it is the most critical Professional investors, particularly those who focus on illiquid, high-risk venture capital and leveraged buyout transactions, often agree that management quality is the best predictor of business success or failure. The quality of management and leadership is important because business is fraught with risk. Markets change direction quickly, and these changes often are fueled by new technology and fierce foreign and domestic competition. As such, a company's prospects often are dependent on management's ability to navigate through turbulent and tumultuous times.

To the extent that individual businesses are

TABLE 4
REAL RETURN ON CAPITAL

If:	EBIT	= $15,000,000 and
	Capital	= ($40,000,000$_{Equity}$ + $60,000,000$_{Debt}$) = $100,000,000 and
	WACC*	= 10.4%

And:	ROC	= EBIT/Capital
		= $15,000,000/$100,000,000
		= 15%
		= Return on Capital

Then:	ROC – WACC	= 15.0% – 10.4%
		4.6%
		Real Return on Capital

Therefore:	Value Created	= Real Return X Capital
		= 4.6% × $100,000,000
		= $4,600,000
		= Value Created

*In this example, the WACC is calculated as follows:

	Capital	Weight	Cost	WACC
Equity (market value)	$ 40,000,000	0.4	18.0%	7.2%
Debt (after-tax cost)	$ 60,000,000	0.6	5.4%	3.2%
Total	$100,000,000	1.0		10.4%

unique in terms of industry, scale, maturity, historical performance, and specific challenges and opportunities, so, too, are managerial requirements. The skills, abilities, and personalities of the management team must complement the business. True excellence in leadership often can be found in the corporate culture, especially in the manner in which young talent is selected and developed and in the ways management's successors are groomed.

Here are four areas that should be stressed, given the importance of evaluating management.

- "Can the managers demonstrate long-term success during both favorable and unfavorable market conditions?"
- "Do they have the capacity, by means of formal education, intelligence, business acumen, and both physical and emotional well-being, to grow with the business as it grows? If not, do they recruit and empower talented and capable lieutenants?"
- "Are they truly hardworking and appropriately motivated to lead?"
- "Is there any indication that they are less than completely honest and ethical?"

A deficiency in even one of these areas, however minor it may seem, must be considered serious. Although no one is perfect, analysts who discount these particular issues do so at their company's peril. In making these judgments, the analyst must rely on less formal sources of information, especially casual interviews and observations. Above all, he or she should listen carefully to his or her intuition, for often therein lies the answer.

DEVELOPING STRATEGY

Management accountants and financial analysts can use the Business Assessment Model to enhance the value of their work, particularly when they are involved in business combinations, debt or equity funding, capital investments, and new corporate ventures. The model synthesizes data on the core business, the market, competition, operations, historical performance, and management to provide a holistic assessment of a business, regardless of its type industry, or economic sector. Although analysts' contributions traditionally have been limited to accounting and financial issues, it is imprudent to use financial information in a vacuum, particularly in an increasingly competitive business environment. Understanding the elements that drive financial information is crucial. Further, as accounting and finance managers increasingly are called upon to develop and execute corporate strategy, they must go beyond accounting and

finance to ensure that strategic business decisions are optimized.

[1] James B. Hobbs, *Corporate Staying Power*, D. C. Heath & Co., 1987, p. 22.
[2] Robert D. Hisrich and Michael P. Peters, *Marketing Decisions for New and Mature Products: Planning Development, and Control*, Charles E. Merrill Publishing Co, 1984, p. 77.
[3] Roger G. Schroeder, *Operations Management: Decision Making in the Operations Function*, third edition, McGraw-Hill, Inc., 1989, p. 195.
[4] Sydney Cottle, Roger F. Murray, and Frank E. Block, Graham & Dodd's Security Analysis, fifth edition, McGraw-Hill, Inc., 1988, p. 351.

Chapter 20
Management Compensation and the
Evaluation of the Firm

Cases
20-1   Midwest Petro-Chemical Company (Evaluating a Firm)
20-2   Evaluating a Firm
20-3   OutSource, Inc. (Economic Value Added)

Readings
Nick Fera: Using Shareholder Value to Evaluate Strategic Choices
The basic principle of the article is that performance evaluation based on accounting measures alone is not sufficient. The evaluation of a business unit or of the unit's manager must also consider the business unit's performance in creating shareholder value. Based on ideas from Alfred Rappaport's book, Creating Shareholder Value, the article develops the measures of cash flow and market risk. An illustration for a hypothetical firm is provided.

Discussion Questions
1. Explain the differences between the two measurement methodologies presented in the article.
2. Why is it important for firms and managers to consider shareholder value?
3. What are the key factors in determining shareholder value?

Cases

20-1. Midwest Petro-Chemical Company (Evaluating a Firm)

Midwest Petro-Chemical, an industrial chemical distributor, was formed in 1960 by James Fletcher, a chemical engineer who had spent 10 years with the petrochemical division of a major oil company. His oil company experience which included a variety of technical, sales, and management positions, provided valuable business training. His final oil company position was regional marketing manager. He felt hindered by the slow-moving oil company bureaucracy, so he left a corporate career to begin Midwest Petro-Chemical.

The company began operation in Chicago in a rented warehouse with Fletcher as the only full-time employee. First-year sales totaled $113,000 and the company reported a loss of $6,200. Although first-year sales were less than planned and most of his initial capital was lost, Fletcher remained optimistic. Unable to obtain debt capital, he sought equity investors. He approached his college fraternity brothers and oil company colleagues to invest in the new venture. Six accepted, with each providing between $10,000 and $20,000 of much needed capital.

Sales exceeded $300,000 the second year of operations, but the company still reported a small loss of $4,000. The company reported its first profit of $14,000 in year three. Its first bulk distribution facility, capable of handling truck, rail, and barge transportation, was leased the next year.

Over the next 35 years, the company expanded operations beyond Chicago. New offices and plants were opened in five metropolitan cities: St. Louis, Kansas City, Louisville, Cincinnati, and Memphis. Plants were built in industrial areas on sites ranging from two to four acres. Each facility included a warehouse and tank farm with multiple-size tanks with capacities ranging from 1.5 million gallons (barge shipments) to 10,000 gallons (truck shipments). Chemical manufacturers and oil companies were the major supplier of chemicals. Midwest would purchase in bulk (barge, rail, or truck), blend chemicals as necessary, repackage, and ship product in smaller quantities (less than truckload, tote tanks, 55-gallon drums, and other smaller package sizes) to a variety of users.

Current Situation

The company prospered and remains a privately held corporation. Annual sales exceeded $95 million in 1995, and a profit of $2,315 million was reported. Fletcher, now in his late 60s, is still CEO and the largest shareholder, owning 314,260 shares or 41.8% of the total shares outstanding. Three of the original investors (Stan Davis, Tom Williams, and Don Stewart) own another 326,216 shares (43.4%), and the company's pension fund owns 78,000 shares. Ron Allen, the company's chief financial officer, is the pension trustee and votes the shares. The remaining 32,524 shares are owned by 37 current or former employees.

There is not an active market for Midwest's stock. Sales or transfers of the stock occur infrequently between a buyer and seller, and Midwest does not participate in the exchange transaction. The sale price of stock is negotiated at arm's length between the buyer and seller. During 1995, approximately 18,000 shares were exchanged in 27 transactions at prices ranging from $21 to $24 per share.

Fletcher, the three remaining original investors (Davis, Williams, and Stewart) and Midwest's local counsel, Frank Armstrong, compose the Board of Directors. Despite Midwest's consistent growth and profitability, recent Board meetings have resulted in heated discussions concerning three issues.

1. **Succession plan**. Despite his age, Fletcher remains a more capable leader and has no desire to retire or even plan for retirement. The Board is concerned that no succession plan exists.
2. **Stock value and liquidity**. Stan Davis (age 72) wants to sell his Midwest stock (126,415 shares) but feels the stock is substantially undervalued at its recent trading range of $21 to $24. Like Fletcher, Davis has started his own business—Western Solvents, Inc., a chemical distribution company on the West Coast. With the aid of an investment banking firm, he recently sold Western Solvents at a price that was 16 times earnings. He has been pressuring Fletcher to purchase his Midwest shares.
3. **Offer to purchase the company**. Davis's interest in selling has been heightened due to an unsolicited purchase inquiry from Georgia Chemical, a chemical distributor in Atlanta. The inquiry was made via letter to Fletcher asking if there were any interest in selling Midwest. It is Fletcher's position that Midwest is not for sale, and he does not want to talk about the offer.

At the most recent Board meeting, Fletcher stated he was going to send a letter to Georgia Chemical indicating Midwest is not for sale. Davis objected and argued that it is their fiduciary responsibility as directors to consider all serious offers. Fletcher responded by saying, "Georgia Chemical's inquiry didn't even include a price, so how could it be considered an offer to buy?" Fletcher, Davis, and Allen offered their opinions as to what the stock was worth, but all agreed that their value estimates were not based on systematic or quantifiable processes. They also felt the current stock trading range was low. Stewart felt that without an established valuation of the stock, it would be very difficult, if not impossible, to evaluate objectively any offer to buy the firm. Frank Armstrong agreed with Stewart.

Before a response can be given to the Atlanta inquiry, a reasonable price must be determined. Don Stewart suggested an independent study be undertaken to determine the fair market value of Midwest's common stock. Stan Davis agreed and recommended using the investment banking firm of Warner and David, which recently valued his company. Ron Allen had worked with Warner and David with his previous employer and also thought highly of that firm's ability. Allen also commented that one of the hot new services offered by public accounting firms is business valuation. In fact, a partner in Midwest's auditing firm had mentioned this service in a recent meeting.

Despite his many years in business, Fletcher is unfamiliar with the procedures used to value a business. He is unwilling to bring in any outsider at this point. As a compromise, Tom Williams, a retired banker, suggested that Allen perform an in-house valuation by comparing Midwest's performance with industry norms. Analyses of ratios such as profit margin, return on assets, and return on equity were effective profit measures. Benchmarking Midwest's performance with industry data should be an indication of strength or weakness, which relates to value. Williams also mentioned the price-to-earnings ratio and the price-to-book-value ratio as other possible value indicators. He said that as a banker, he began evaluation all loan requests with a detailed historic performance analysis using ratios. Sources such as Value Line Investment Survey and Robert Morris Associates Annual Statement Studies provide industry data. Allen agreed that financial analysis was beneficial but was skeptical about it yielding a usable value. Another approach Williams suggested was to perform a valuation using the market values of the firm's assets (appraisals were performed on all properties over the last two years for insurance purposes).

Allen thought a valuation process based on projected future cash flows might be a more accurate measure of the firm's value. Fletcher agreed with Allen because he feels the company is poised for considerable future growth. Davis suggested Allen use the sale of Western Solvents as a reference because the businesses were almost identical except for geographic location.

As the Board members began discussing the various proposals and the advantages and disadvantages of each, Frank Armstrong proposed yet another course of action: giving Ron Allen and his staff the assignment to (1) investigate valuation alternatives, (2) perform an in-house valuation, and (3) prepare a report for review at the next Board meeting (one month away). All Board members agreed, and Allen was given the assignment.

THE ASSIGNMENT

The next day, Ron Allen met with Linda Warren, Midwest's controller, to discuss the task. Warren mentioned that her previous employer used yet another valuation method—capitalization of earnings—to determine its worth. Allen said he planned to use all the methods suggested by the board members plus any other appropriate methods.

Together they reviewed each valuation method and prepared a description of each. They also listed information needed for each technique.

1. *Financial Ratio Analysis*: Allen directed Warren to obtain industry comparative data and suggested starting with Value Line Investment Survey. Other sources of industry comparative data are Robert Morris Associates Annual Statement Studies and Standard and Poor's Industry Surveys.

2. *Asset-Based or Market Value Method*: Although Tom Williams didn't refer specifically to this valuation method, Ron Allen thought he was describing it when he suggested using "market value of the assets." Linda Warren was to gather the most recent appraisals based on replacement values (see T-1).

3. *Market Comparison Method*: This approach suggested by Stan Davis is based on the assumptions that value of a privately held company can be estimated by comparing it to a similar company whose market values are known. As Davis's company recently sold at 16 times earnings, it can be used as the known market value.

4. *Discounted Cash Flow*: Ron Allen and James Fletcher favor this approach based on expected future cash flows. Linda Warren pointed out that this technique requires forecasting future cash flows. Allen agreed and thought forecasting for five years would be appropriate. In preparing the forecasts, Allen suggested they project revenues to grow at 3.5% per year and forecast operating expenses (including depreciation) as a percentage of sales using an average of actual 1995 and 1994 percentages. As annual depreciation expense has been about $1.4 million the past two years, and no major acquisitions are expected, it was decided to use $800,000 for annual net cash from depreciation (assume $600,000 is reinvestment in existing operations). To keep it simple, Warren suggested forecasting interest expense of $900,000 in 1996 and reducing the amount by $50,000 each subsequent year. She also suggested projecting income tax expense at 30% of income before income taxes. Allen recognized this was an oversimplification, but agreed.

Warren asked how she should handle working capital changes, dividends, and residual values. Allen commented that because the current relationship between revenues, current assets, and current liabilities was close to optimum, they should assume it is maintained. Dividends per share of $.35 should be projected for 1996 with a $.05 per share increase each year thereafter. Book value should be used for residual values.

The rate of return that investors require on equity capital depends on the riskiness of the cash flow stream. The risk premium on equity frequently is regarded at 3% higher than debt capital. Further, the risk and liquidity premium on private small companies without a liquid market indicated an additional premium in the range of 20%.

5. *Capitalization of Earnings*: The capitalization of earnings approach embodies the concept that an investor in a going business has in mind a desired or "target" return on capital. Warren thought it would be another good technique but that they should perform two calculations, one based on past earnings and another using projected earnings. Allen agreed. The target return is expressed as a percentage of after-tax earnings to invested capital or equity and is referred to as return on equity (ROE). Warren thought they should use a capitalization rate based on an average ROE for 1995 and 1994. Allen concurred but told her to use beginning-year equity to calculate ROE.

Required:

Assume the roles of Ron Allen, Midwest Petro-Chemical's chief financial officer, and Linda Warren, controller, and prepare the required report for the Board. The report should address the following:

1. What is Midwest's strategic competitive advantage, and what type of compensation plan is most consistent with this strategy?

2. Analyze company performance using financial ratio analysis and industry norms as a bench mark. What are the strengths and weaknesses of this evaluation process?

3. Why did financial ratio analysis serve as an effective tool for Tom Williams?

4. Discuss each valuation method. What are the strengths and weaknesses of each? What difficulties are encountered when applying each method?

    a. Asset-based or market value

    b. Market comparison

    c. Discounted cash flow

    d. Capitalization of earnings

        1. Historic earnings

        2. Projected earnings

5. Develop values for Midwest Petro-Chemical's stock using the methods discussed in part 3.

6. Based on your previous answers, develop a fair-market value for Midwest's common stock. Support your value.

7. Recommend a negotiating strategy for dealing with the inquiry from the Atlanta company.

8. Once a price is agreed upon by a buyer and seller, sale terms must be structured.

   a. Will the price be paid in cash at closing? As an initial cash payment plus future payments? As stock or some combination of the aforementioned?

   b. Will stock or assets be sold? Will the sale terms affect price? If so, how? Explain your answer.

   (IMA adapted)

table 2

	Acquisition Date	Land	Plant Prop.& Equip	Accumulated Depreciation	Net Book Value
Chicago	1963	$ 634	$ 4,415	$ 3,012	$ 2,037
St. Louis	1967	960	4,602	3,118	2,444
Louisville	1970	1,100	5,809	4,019	2,890
Cincinnati	1980	2,600	6,222	3,216	5,606
Memphis	1982	2,466	7,214	3,037	6,643
		$7,760	$28,262	$16,402	$19,620

	Appraisal Date	Land	Plant. Prop. & Equip	Total
Chicago	1994	$2,010	$2,050	$ 4,060
St. Louis	1991	1,580	1,738	3,318
Louisville	1992	1,720	1,612	3,332
Memphis	1989	2,910	3,702	6,612
Cincinnati	1990	2,700	4,313	7,013
				$24,335

		Shares	%
James Retcher	CEO/Director	314,260	41.8
Stan David	Director	126,415	16.8
Tom Williams	Director	105,060	14.0
Don Stewart	Director	94,741	12.6
Pension fund*		78,000	10.4
Other		32,524	4.4
	Total	751,000	100.4

*Shares voted by trustee Ron Allen

FINANCIAL STATEMENTS
MIDWEST PETRO-CHEMICAL, INC.
Statement of Income (000s)
For the Years Ending December 31

	1995	1994	1993	1992
Net Sales	$95,652	$92,333	$90,114	$86,414
Costs of Sales and Selling cost				
Cost of sales	77,719	74,882	74,374	70,859
Selling	13,712	13,388	13,049	12,703
Total costs	91,431	88,270	87,423	83,562
Operating income	4,221	4,063	2,691	2,852
Interest expense	914	1,214	1,612	1,728
Income before income	3,307	2,849	1,079	1,124
Income tax expense	992	854	270	259
Net Income	2,315	1,995	809	865
Earnings per share	$3.08	$2.66	$1.08	$1.15
Dividends per share	.30	.25	.22	.20

Statement of Cash Flows (000s)
For the Year Ending December 31, 1995

Operating activities	
Net income	$2,315
Additions (sources of cash)	
Depreciation	1,407
Decrease in inventory	1,153
Increase in accounts payable	2,320
Increase in accrued expense	500
Subtractions	
Increase in accounts receivable	(1,109)
Increase in prepaid assets	(332)
Net Cash provided by operating activities	6,254
Long-term investing activities	
Cash used to acquire fixed assets	(1,030)
Financing activities	
Decrease on long-term debt	(4,701)
Payment of dividends	(225)
Net cash provided by financing activities	(4,926)
Net increase in cash	298
Cash at beginning of year	212
Cash at end of year	$ 510

Balance Sheets (000s).
December 31

	1995	1994		1995	1994
Current assets			**Current liabilities**		
Cash	$ 510	$ 212	Accounts payable	$11,264	$8,944
Receivables	13,925	12,815	Accrued expenses	2,245	1,745
Inventories	9,310	10,463	Total current liabilities.	13,509	10,689
Prepaid expenses	745	413			
Total current assets	$24,490	$23,904	Long-term obligations	10,899	15,600
			Total liabilities	24,408	26,289
Property and equipment at cost			**Shareholders' equity**		
Land	7,760	7,760	Common stock $1 par value		
Plant, property and equipment	28,262	27,232	2,000,000 shares authorized		
Less accumulated depreciation	(16,402)	(14,995)	751,000 shares outstanding	751	751
Total plant and property	19,620	19,997	Paid in capital	2,253	2,253
			Retained in earnings	16,198	14,608
			Total shareholders' equity	19,702	17,612
Total assets	$44,110	$43,901	Total liabilities and equity	$44,110	$43,901

20-2. Evaluating a Firm

Required:

Consider the financial data below for the Example Company, and assess the value of the Company. Explain your choice(s) of valuation method(s).

Account Description	19X8	19X9	19X0	19X1	19X2	19X3
Example Company						
Selected Financial Data						
Cash	25,141	25,639	32,977	34,009	49,851	30,943
Accounts Receivable	272,450	312,776	368,267	419,731	477,324	542,751
Prepaids	3,982	4,402	5,037	5,246	5,378	6,648
Inventories	183,722	208,623	222,128	260,492	298,696	399,533
Property & Equipment (net)	47,578	49,931	55,311	61,832	77,173	91,420
Other Assets	18,734	20,738	23,075	26,318	36,248	39,403
Total Assets	551,607	622,109	706,795	807,628	944,670	1,110,698
Accounts Payable	49,831	64,321	70,853	80,861	94,677	78,789
Accrued Expenses	86,087	102,650	113,732	131,899	143,159	164,243
Notes Payable	99,539	118,305	182,132	246,420	237,741	390,034
Long-term Debt	62,622	43,251	35,407	32,301	128,432	126,672
Deferred Taxes Payable	7,551	7,941	8,286	8,518	9,664	11,926
Other Liabilities	5,279	5,521	5,697	5,593	5,252	4,695
Total Liabilities	310,909	341,989	416,107	505,592	618,925	776,359
Capital Stock	73,253	87,851	79,009	71,601	81,238	73,186
Retained Earnings	167,445	192,539	211,679	230,435	244,507	261,153
Total Stockholders Equity	240,698	280,120	290,688	302,036	325,745	334,339
Total Liabilities & Equity	551,607	662,109	706,795	807,628	944,670	1,110,698
Net Sales	982,244	1,095,083	1,214,666	1,259,116	1,378,251	1,648,500
Cost of Goods Sold	669,560	739,459	817,671	843,192	931,237	1,125,261
Depreciation Expense	8,303	8,380	8,972	9,619	10,577	12,004
Interest Expense	11,248	13,146	14,919	18,874	16,562	21,128
Income Tax Expense	26,650	34,000	38,000	32,800	26,500	25,750
Dividends Paid	13,805	17,160	19,280	20,426	20,794	20,807
Net Income	32,563	37,895	41,809	39,577	35,212	37,787
Number of common shares outstanding at year-end	12,817	13,714	13,728	13,684	14,023	13,993
Market price per share	38	43	55	65	43	31

20-3.   Economic Value Added; Review of Chapter 19; Strategy

I've been hearing a lot lately about something "called EVA, which stands for Economic Value Added, and I was curious whether it is something we can use at OSI," Keith Martin said as he finished his lunch. Keith is president and CEO of OutSource, Inc. His guest for lunch that day was a computer industry analyst from a local brokerage firm. Keith had invited him to lunch so he could get more information on EVA and its uses.

"Yes," the analyst replied, "I've heard a great deal about EVA. It's a residual income approach in which a firm's net operating profit after taxes--called NOPAT—is reduced by a minimum level of return a firm must earn on the total amount of capital placed at its disposal.

"Have you seen the recent articles on EVA? The after-tax operating profit, NOPAT as you called it, and the amount used for capital don't come directly off the financial statements. You have to analyze the footnotes to determine the adjustments that have to be made to come up with those amounts."

"The article sounds like interesting reading for me, especially at this point," Keith said. "Can you send me a copy?"

"Sure," said the analyst. "But tell me, what is it about EVA that piqued your interest in trying it at OSI?"

"In tracking our industry," Keith replied, "I see the stock prices of some of our key competitors, like Equifax, increasing. Yet, when I compare OSI's recent growth in sales and earnings, our return on equity and earnings per share compare well to those firms, but our stock price doesn't achieve nearly the same rate of increase, and I don't understand why."

The analyst suggested, "Some of those firms might be benefiting from using EVA already, and the market value of their stock probably reflects the results of their efforts. It has been shown that a higher level of correlation exists between EVA and a stock's market value than has been found with the traditional accounting performance measures like ROE or EPS."

"But will EVA work in a small service firm like OSI?"

But I've read about EVA being used at smaller firms," said the analyst. "I'm not an expert on EVA, but I don't see any reason why it wouldn't work at OSI."

"I'd like to find out more about EVA and how we can use it at OSI. For example, we've talked about a new incentive plan-will EVA work in that area? And, if so, will it help us in deciding how we should organize and manage our operations as we expand and grow? What can you do to get more information on these things to me?"

COMPANY INFORMATION

OutSource, Inc. (OSI) is a computer service bureau that provides basic data processing and general business support services to a number of business firms, including several large firms in the immediate local area. Its offices are in a large city in the mid-Atlantic region, and it serves client firms in several Mid-Atlantic States. OSI's revenues have grown rapidly in recent years as businesses have downsized and outsourced many of their basic support services.

The CorpInfo Data Service (CIDS) classifies OSI as an Information Services firm (SIC 7374). This group is composed, in large part, of smaller, independent entrepreneurs that provide a variety of often disparate services to both corporate and government clients. Market analysts feel a continuously healthy economy translates into strong potential for higher earnings by members of this group. A factor sustaining an extended period of growth is the increased attention of firms to control costs and to outsource their non-core functions, such as personnel placement, payroll, human resources, insurance, and data processing. This trend is expected to continue, probably at an increasing rate. Several firms in this industry have capitalized on their growth and geographic expansion to win lucrative contracts with large clients that previously had been awarded on a market-by-market basis.

Although OSI operates out of its own facilities, which include some computing equipment and furniture, the bulk of its computer processing power is obtained from excess computer capacity in the local area, primarily rented time during third-shift operations at a large local bank. To be successful in the long term, however, OSI management knows it must expand its business considerably, and, to ensure it has full control over its operations, it must set up its own large-scale computing facility in-house. These items are included in OSI's strategic plan.

As OSI's reputation for accurate, reliable, and quick response service has spread, the firm has found new business coming its way in a variety of data processing and support services. The issue has been deciding which services to take on or to stay out of in light of the current limitations on OSI's computing resources and assurance it can continue to provide high-quality service to its customers. Things definitely are looking up for OSI, and industry market analysts recently have begun to look more favorably on its stock.

In 19X3, OSI's board decided to pursue additional opportunities in payroll processing and tax filing services, and OSI purchased a medium-sized firm that had an established market providing payroll calculations, processing, and reporting services for several Fortune 500 firms on the East Coast. Now OSI is in the midst of developing a new payroll processing system, called PayNet, to replace the outmoded system that was originally created by the firm it acquired.

Once PayNet is developed, it will give users an integrated payroll solution with a simpler, more familiar graphic user interface. From an administrative perspective, it will allow OSI to reduce its manual data entry hiring, to speed data compilation and analysis, and to simplify administrative tasks and the updating of customer files for adds, moves, and changes. PayNet will serve as the backbone for OSI's service bureau payroll processing operations in the future, but developmental and programming costs have been higher than expected and will delay the roll out of the final version of the new payroll program. Beta testing of the production version of PayNet is being delayed from the second to the third quarter of 19X6.

ADDITIONAL ACCOUNTING INFORMATION

OSI's financial statements for 19X5 appear in T-1. The following list of information is pertinent to calculating a firm's EVA extracted from the footnotes to OSI's annual report for 19X5.

A. Inventories are stated principally at cost (last-in, first-out), which is not in excess of market. Replacement cost would be $2,796 greater than the 19X4 inventory balance and $3,613 greater than the 19X5 inventory balance.

B. On July 1, 19X3, the company acquired CompuPay, a payroll processing and reporting service firm. The acquisition was accounted for as a purchase, and the excess cost over the fair value of net assets acquired was $109,200, which is being amortized on a straight-line basis over 13 years. One-half year of goodwill amortization was re-corded in 19X3.

C. Research and development costs related to software development are expensed as incurred. Software development costs are capitalized from the point in time when the technological feasibility of a piece of software has been determined until it is ready to be put on line to process customer data. The cost of purchased software, which is ready for service, is capitalized on acquisition. Software development costs and pur-chased software costs are amortized using the straight-line method over periods ranging from three to seven years. A history of the accounting treatment of software development costs and purchased software costs follow:

	Expensed	Capitalized	Amortized
19X3	$166,430	$ 9,585	0
19X4	211,852	5,362	$ 4,511
19X5	89,089	18,813	5,111
	$467,371	$33,760	$ 9,622

ADDITIONAL FINANCIAL INFORMATION

OSI's common stock is currently trading at $2 per share. A preferred dividend of $11 per share was paid in 19X5, and the current price of preferred stock is approximately at its par value. Other information pertaining to OSI's debt and stock follows:

Short-term debt	$ 8,889	8.0%
Long-term debt:		
Current portion	$ 18,411	10.0%
Long-term portion	$ 98,744	10.0%
Total long-term debt	$117,155	

Stock market risk-free rate	=	
(90-day T-bills)	=	5.0%
Expected return on the market	=	12.5%
Expected growth rate of dividends	=	8.0%
Income tax rate	=	35.0%

REQUIRED:

1. The management of OutSource, Inc. has asked you to prepare a report explaining EVA (Economic Value Added), how it is calculated, and how it compares to tradi-tional measures of a firm's financial performance. As part of your answer, calculate EVA from OSI's financial report.

2. What are the advantages and disadvantages of using EVA to evaluate OSI's perform-ance on an on-going basis, as well as in assessing the performance of individual man-agers throughout its organization? How might EVA help OSI attain its strategic goals?

3. OSI management wants to know if EVA can be used as part of an incentive program for its employees, and if so, how it should be implemented. (IMA, adapted)

Using Shareholder Value to Evaluate Strategic Choices

Financial metrics is a realistic way for companies to measure value.

By Nick Fera

Creating shareholder wealth or value has become the mantra for most corporate boards, especially in the United States. Yet as recently as the mid-1980s, the idea of "shareholder value" or "shareholder wealth" was not an overwhelmingly accepted principle. But as academics began to teach the principle in business schools around the world, such noted authorities as Professor Alfred Rappaport of Northwestern University's J. L. Kellogg Graduate School of Management, author of *Creating Shareholder Value*,[1] began to apply it to corporate mergers and acquisitions in the 1980s. Shareholder value, or free cash flow analysis, became the measurement standard for the 1980s and into the 1990s. Given today's increased demand for international capital returns, as well as the proliferation of private baby boomer pension funds in the United States, investors have imposed new stringency in their vigil against corporate wealth destruction. Even the brightest stars are not immune to the pressure of pension funds or Wall Street. Witness the pressure that CALPERS (the state of California's teachers' retirement funds) placed on Michael Eisner at Walt Disney Co. despite Eisner's laudable success in increasing Disney's market value from $5 billion to more than $42 billion during his first 10 years in office. During a 10-year period from January 1986 to December 1996, Disney's stock price grew at a cumulative annual growth rate of more than 21%, while the S&P 500 index has returned approximately 15%. Historical performances are not always enough; investors continue to ask for more.

Measuring performance no longer can be left to the traditional accounting department's calculations of earnings per share (EPS) or return on equity (ROE), as these accrual-based accounting measures aren't always useful indicators of future growth or performance. Thus, it is necessary to understand and adopt measurement techniques that will help make decisions while driving increasing profitability. One of the economic measurement techniques that can be used is free cash flow analysis or Shareholder Value Analysis (SVA).

SHAREHOLDER VALUE ANALYSIS

Because managers began to realize that businesses needed a more realistic means of assessing their value than accrual-based accounting standards offered, such respected academics as Professor Rappaport sought to develop sophisticated economic models for strategic evaluations. As a result, shareholder value analysis was conceived. SVA works by explicitly measuring the economic impact of each strategy on the value of a business. Any strategic decision, regardless of whether it involves internal or external investment, should be evaluated. Examples of such strategic decision-making situations include mergers and acquisitions, joint ventures, divestitures, new product development (R&D), and capital expenditures (major plant and equipment investments).

The actual measurement of shareholder value combines three main factors: 1) cash flow, 2) cash as measured over a given period of time (value growth duration), and 3) risk, otherwise known as the cost of capital. (See Fig. 1.) With a basic understanding of these three components, you are well on your way to valuing a business or entity. Next, let's discuss the difference between corporate value and shareholder value.

CREATING VALUE

Corporate value is equal to the net present value of all future cash flows to all investor types, including both debt and equity holders. Shareholder value is the corporate value minus all future claims to cash flow (debt) before equity holders are paid. Future claims typically include both short-and long-term debt, capital lease obligations, underfunded pensions, and other

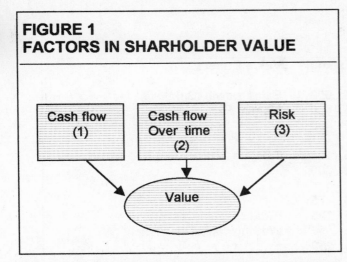

FIGURE 1
FACTORS IN SHARHOLDER VALUE

Cash flow (1) · Cash flow Over time (2) · Risk (3) → Value

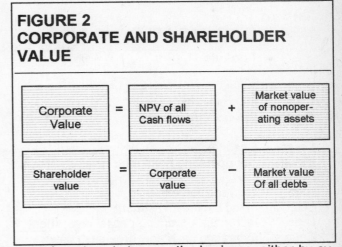

FIGURE 2
CORPORATE AND SHAREHOLDER VALUE

Corporate Value = NPV of all Cash flows + Market value of nonoperating assets

Shareholder value = Corporate value − Market value Of all debts

claims such as contingent liabilities—lawsuits brought against the company. (See Fig. 2.) Another way to define shareholder value is to say that it is equal to the net funds a company generates that shareholders could receive in the form of a cash distribution, such as a dividend.

Be careful not to confuse this figure with the actual dividend a company pays. A company's dividend policy has little or nothing t do with the actual cash the company generates. Look at the high growth of businesses such as computer software or biotechnology. Few pay dividends because they have strategic opportunities to reinvest cash flows and earn the higher returns investors desire.

Generally, it's easy to determine the market value of future obligations or debt. In most cases, it's the accumulation of several debt instruments. To obtain the market value of these financial instruments, use the yield to maturity to calculate the *market value* of each debt instrument. Avoid adding the face value of each debt or bond issue. The question to ask is, "If this obligation were to be paid in full today, how much would the lender need to retire it?"

MEASURING CASH FLOW

After determining corporate and shareholder value, the next step is to measure cash flow. The most tangible measurement of cash flow (also referred to as operating cash flow or free cash flow) can be calculated as shown in Table 1.

Notice that the calculation focuses on the relationship between operating cash income and expenses, specifically by using operating cash taxes rather than the provision for income taxes. It accounts for the in

vestments made on the balance sheet. Many companies measure cash flow by looking at net operating profit after taxes (NOPAT), but it tells only part of the

story. Investments to grow the business, either by expansion of the plant and facilities or with working capital policies such as extending the receivable period from net 30 to net 60 days, have a significant impact on the capital employed. Remember: Shareholders are looking for returns on their capital invested in business growth, which requires well-planned capital expenditures. Failure to account for the investment makes for a crucial mistake in the evaluation of strategic alternatives.

CALCULATING CASH FLOWS

The calculation of cash flow illustrates a high level of performance in an organization and produces a result that approximates the net cash of a company. In effect, these funds are a potential dividend to shareholders because they reflect optimal use of shareholder monies for ongoing growth. That is why dividend policy and free cash flow are not synonymous. Few companies base their dividend payout on net cash flow, while others are justified in generating free cash flow, without paying dividends.

To forecast cash flow, most companies require a more detailed formula, as presented in Table 1. In most cases, sales growth tells very little about actual sales activity, so companies use metrics such as price, volume, GNP, and other micro or macroeconomic factors to forecast revenues and costs more realistically. This calculation usually is conducted at a strategic business unit level and then consolidated for corporate purposes. The key is to plan accurately at the appropriate level of business activity (business unit, value chain, or some other distinction).

Sales or market growth estimations can be achieved many different ways. Predicting price and volume, for instance, provides for a more manageable metric that can be evaluated readily and used later for compensation purposes. In other words, sales growth is a "*value driver*." But what *drives* the value drivers?

TABLE 1
MEASURING CASH FLOW

	Formula	Example	Value Drivers
	Sales	$1,000	Sales growth (Sg)
Less	Operating expenses	–$ 600	Margin (P)
Equals	Pre-tax profit	$ 400	
Less	Cash taxes	–$ 100	Tax rate (T)
Equals	Net operating profit after taxes (NOPAT)	$ 300	
Add	Depreciation expense	$ 75	
Less	Fixed capital investment	–$ 125	Fixed capital investment (F)
Less	Incremental working capital investment	–$ 50	Working capital investment (W)
Equals	Operating cash flow (free cash flow)	$ 250	

Herein typically lies the metric operational professionals can get their hands on. Planning and forecasting can become a real *operating activity rather than a boardroom exercise.*

CASH FLOW OVER TIME

Once cash flow has been defined, the next step is to determine the length of the forecast period. The definition of cash flow over time or value growth duration is the length of time expected for a company to invest in opportunities that will yield internal rates of return (IRR) above their weighted average cost of capital (WACC). This premise is the core of value creation—performing above expectations for a sustainable period of time.

Management usually plans for cycles of three to five years. If this is the case and if the cash flows are discounted over a period of time, the valuation probably will be inaccurate as it does not allow for fluctuations in cash flow throughout the requisite growth period. To determine the appropriate length of the forecast period (or the value growth duration), consider several factors.

One is Michael Porter's work on the competitive structure and five forces of industries (see Fig. 3). Porter says that management's responsibility is to map the company and its competition according to several factors. Some areas to consider are distribution channels, established brand names, and research and development. Take the pharmaceutical industry, for instance. It has a relatively long value growth duration because of patented products, proven processes, and research and development investment that raise the barriers of entry.

Also, read Alfred Rappaport's discussion of the use of public information to assess the market's expectation for a company's value growth duration.[2] He suggests gathering forecasting information on a particular company as well as identifying competitors. He also advises managers to employ the researched information and forecast the cash flows, as discussed previously. But rather than changing any value driver assumptions, change only the length of the forecast until the present value of the cash flows less debt equals the market value of your company. Surprisingly, most companies in a given industry tend to fall within a certain range; thus, the market is suggesting an implied value growth duration. These "market signals" are helpful for starting an internal analysis and discussion.

RESIDUAL VALUE

Once you have determined the value growth duration, you must address the value of the cash flows beyond the current period. This determination is called the terminal or residual value. Assume that, after the forecast period, new investments (fixed and working capital) will yield returns equal to the cost of capital. In other words, the internal rate of return is equal to the weighted average cost of capital. Therefore, the net present value of cash flows from new or incremental investments beyond the value growth duration will be equal to zero. The only cash flow left to value in the residual period is the preinvestment cash flow, or NOPAT (see Table 1). Note that depreciation is *not* included because it is viewed as a proxy for reinvestment. Given that the cash flows are valued infinitely, the business probably would not continue to generate the same level of cash flow if the plant, equipment, or other physical assets were allowed to deteriorate fully. In fact, some companies recognize a higher level of "maintenance" spending and will adjust the cash flow in the residual period to reflect higher replacement costs.

TERMINAL VALUE

At this point, it is necessary to discuss some assumptions of terminal value. The net present value of the residual cash flows is equal to an infinite stream of cash flow (as measured by NOPAT) discounted back at the WACC. Mathematically, this is NOPAT at the end of the value growth duration divided by the WACC. Once this calculation is complete, it is necessary to discount the value back to the current period. The formula is presented in Table 2 (assuming a five-year value growth duration and 12% WACC).

DEFINING RISK

The last component of determining the value of an entity is deciding on the overall risk. The risk of a company usually is measured with WACC. The approach assumes there is some mixture of debt and equity that is financing the company. The cost of debt is measured as the after-tax cost, that is, the cost accounting for the tax deductibility of interest payments. The marginal cost of debt is not necessarily the average coupon rate on various debt instruments. Instead, it is the rate for which banks will lend the company an incremental dollar.

The cost of equity is somewhat more complex. If companies use the Capital Asset Pricing Model approach developed by economists Sharpe, Lintner, and Treynor in the mid-1960s, the cost of equity has two basic components: a risk-free return required by investors and a premium for investing in equities that are of higher risk. The risk-free rate is the treasury rate on 30-year U.S. government bonds. This standard generally is used because these bonds typically are seen as delivering the most risk-free, long-term returns investors can earn. The second component is the premium for investing in something that is of higher risk than the U.S. government. This element is called the market risk premium (MRP itself and a multiplier, called beta, for investments that are more or less risky than the market portfolio.

MARKET RISK PREMIUM

The market risk premium is calculated and published by sources such as Ibbotson Associates in its annual SBBI (Stocks, Bonds, Bills, and Inflation). Historically, the premium for holding a portfolio of equities, as opposed to investing in a risk-free instrument, is between 6% and 7%, depending on whether you use the arithmetic or geometric average.

Beta is a measure of the relative riskiness of an individual company or portfolio as compared with the market. Thus a beta of 1.0 correlates exactly

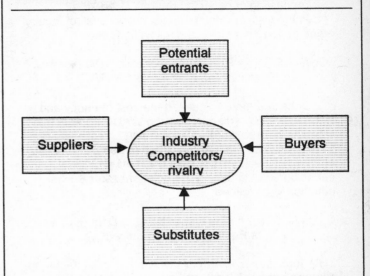

FIGURE 3
FORCES DRIVING INDUSTRY COMPETITION

with market returns. Beta is measured by comparing the returns of an individual security or portfolio with those of the market. Sources of beta estimates include Merrill Lynch, ValueLine, and Alcar.

There is another way to measure the MRP that is consistent with a forecasting approach. This tack uses estimates of the expected return on the market for the next year. Each month Merrill Lynch publishes a 12-month expected return on the market (S&P 500). Using this forecast, you can determine the expected MRP by subtracting the current risk-free rate, as measured by 30-year treasuries, from the current forecast of market returns. As of October 1, 1997, Merrill Lynch's forecast of market returns was 10.9%, while the risk-free rate is currently 6.38%. As a result,

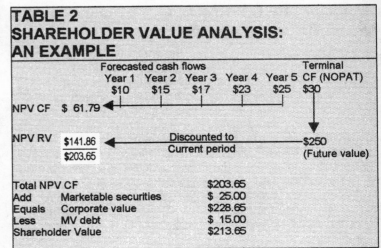

TABLE 2
SHAREHOLDER VALUE ANALYSIS: AN EXAMPLE

		Forecasted cash flows					Terminal
		Year 1	Year 2	Year 3	Year 4	Year 5	CF (NOPAT)
		$10	$15	$17	$23	$25	$30
NPV CF	$ 61.79						
NPV RV	$141.86		Discounted to				$250
	$203.65		Current period				(Future value)

Total NPV CF		$203.65
Add	Marketable securities	$ 25.00
Equals	Corporate value	$228.65
Less	MV debt	$ 15.00
Shareholder Value		$213.65

317

the expected market risk premium is 4.52%. Some companies prefer to use the ex-ante approach because it matches the *forecasting* of cash flows with the *forecasting* of expected returns.

Putting all the components of the cost of equity equation together yields the following formula:

$$\text{Cost of Equity} = \text{Risk-free rate} + \text{Beta} * (\text{Market Risk Premium}) \text{ or, } K_e = R_f + ß * (\text{MRP})$$

Once you have calculated the cost of equity and the cost of debt, you may use the WACC approach to combine both costs (debt and equity). In calculating the WACC, use the market values of debts and equity, not the book values, because the market costs of each source of financing are being measured. The equation is as follows:

$$\text{WACC } (K_c) = \% \text{ of Debt} * [\text{Cost of Debt } (K_d)] + \% \text{ of Equity} * [\text{Cost of Equity } (K_e)]$$

Let's look at an example involving a manufacturing company using risk estimation:

A U.S. manufacturing company is publicly traded and has a market capitalization of $550 million. Its outstanding debt totals $250 million at a marginal borrowing rate of 8.5% (assume this is the market value of debt and includes all obligations of the company). The current risk-free rate is 7%, the expected return on the market is 12%, the beta of this company has been published as .90, and its marginal tax rate is 28%. What is the weighted average cost of capital (WACC)?

MRP	$= 12 - 7$	$= 5\%$
K_e	$= .07 + .9(.05)$	$= 11.5\%$
K_d	$= .085 * (1 - 28)$	$= 6.12\%$ (after tax)
WACC	$= (250/800) * .0612 + (550/800) * .115 = 9.8\%$	

FROM THE BOARDROOM TO THE SHOP FLOOR

Once you have established the methodology, take it out of the boardroom (as a planning exercise), and implement it at all levels, including the shop floor (or any manufacturing or operating activity). The importance of moving the analysis out of the boardroom and into regular practice is that managers and shareholders will have the same economic interests. If managers are compensated on accrual-based accounting measures, they may optimize their own interest when there is a conflict between cash flow and accrual accounting. But if you align the interest and performance measurement of all managers to be the same, both are optimized.

Measurement Methodologies:
1. Economic Principles
   <u>Shareholder Value Analysis (SVA)</u>—also known as Discounted Cash Flow analysis (DCF) or Net Present Value (NPV)

   - Evaluates cash inflows to cash outflows on a risk-adjusted basis

   - Most widely accepted approach to business evaluation

   <u>Economic Value Analysis (EVA)</u>

   - Primarily used as a performance measurement tool to calculate period-by-period performance

   - Helps an organization to focus on value creation or increased cash flow

   - Measuring the change in EVA also may be an effective financial measurement tool

   <u>Cash Flow Return on Investment (CFROI)</u>

   - Derived from market data to determine cash flow growth and the overall discount rate

   - Helps an organization to focus on value creation or increased cash flow

   - Seen as a complex financial measurement device

2. Accounting Principles
   Return on Capital (ROC)
   Return on Invested Capital (ROIC)
   Return on Equity (ROE)
   Earnings per Share (EPS)

Moving the methodology to the shop floor may pose a challenge. Not only is it more difficult to identify key value drivers on the shop floor (such as production yield, waste, inventory management), but there also is an important educational component. Not all managers have been introduced to the concepts and methodologies of financial metrics. Many still are entrenched with the simpler accrual-based accounting measures. Yet once key drivers are identified and their relative impact on value is measured, managers relate to the results.

ONGOING MAINTENANCE AND PER-FORMANCE MEASUREMENT

Once the methodology is in place, the final challenge is to put it into practice every year. What adds to the complexity of the implementation is the ability to monitor performance in a timely manner due to the multitude of manual and multiple systems currently in place to do the job. Many companies implement and attempt to monitor their performance with the use of disconnected spreadsheet technology. Beyond all the difficulties of performing rigorous economic analysis in a spreadsheet (with factual integrity and documentation leading the pack), the use of spreadsheets can create pockets of information that are disjointed from the rest of the organization. These pockets of information make it difficult to monitor performance, test new scenarios regularly, and make new, informed decisions on a timely basis.

Fortunately, the recent development of new technologies that interface seemlessly with each other is making it easier to gather data quickly and spend the majority of analytical time on planning, testing, and choosing new strategic alternatives. Thus, the planning process is changing from an annual event generally found on the bookshelf to a regularly used strategic exercise that becomes a living document, enabling companies to manage their business by making value-based strategic choices in our ever-evolving environment.

---

[1] Alfred Rappaport, *Creating Shareholder Value: The New Standard for Business Performance*, New York: The Free Press, 1986.

[2] Alfred Rappaport, "Stock Market Signals to Managers." Harvard Business Review, November-December 1987, pp. 57-62.